2 SAMUEL

BERIT OLAM
Studies in Hebrew Narrative & Poetry

2 Samuel

Craig E. Morrison, OCarm

Jerome T. Walsh
Editor

A Michael Glazier Book

LITURGICAL PRESS
Collegeville, Minnesota

www.litpress.org

A Michael Glazier Book published by Liturgical Press

Cover design by Ann Blattner.

1   2   3   4   5   6   7   8   9

Library of Congress Cataloging-in-Publication Data

Morrison, Craig E., 1958–
    2 Samuel / Craig Morrison, OCarm ; Jerome Walsh, editor.
        pages   cm. — (BERIT OLAM: studies in Hebrew narrative & poetry)
    A Michael Glazier book.
    Includes bibliographical references and index.
    ISBN 978-0-8146-5043-1
    1. Bible. Samuel, 2nd—Criticism, interpretation, etc.   I. Walsh, Jerome T., 1942–   II. Title.   III. Title: Second Samuel.

    BS1325.52.M67 2013
    222'.4407—dc23   2013028485

For Bella and Henry Tovey, from whom I learned to distinguish an aleph *from a* beth *and much, much more.*

CONTENTS

And I made a rural pen,
And I stain'd the water clear

Songs of Innocence, *Introduction*
William Blake

PREFACE

As I embarked on this commentary on 2 Samuel, I assumed that my task was to interpret, or "exegete," the life of King David for my readers. But the more I tried to interpret him, the more elusive, complex, and distant he became. A king, a father, a warrior, a diplomat, a murderer, a manipulator, a tyrant, a beguiler who is often beguiled, David, as baffling as he is ambiguous, interprets and exposes the fictions of those who meet him. Over the past several years, I have spoken to many people about David, and their ideas are buried in these pages. Rev. Stephen Pisano, SJ, an Old Testament professor here at the Pontifical Biblical Institute, critiqued my shifting deliberations and then took the time to read my final draft and offer suggestions. Rev. Quinn Conners, OCarm, PhD, a clinical psychologist at St. Luke's Institute in Silver Spring, Maryland, offered insights into my interpretation of 2 Samuel 13: the rape of Tamar. Sharmila Andrews, Rita Mary Cote, and Adrienne Corti also helped me with this section of the commentary. Joan E. Cook, SC, president of the Sisters of Charity of Cincinnati and Old Testament Book Review Editor for *The Catholic Biblical Quarterly*, saved me from a couple of inopportune remarks regarding Tamar. Larry and Rita Novakowski read the entire manuscript and made critical observations. Conversations with Federico Giuntoli, an Old Testament professor here at the Pontifical Biblical Institute, have enhanced the final result. I am especially grateful to my sister, Laurie Morrison, a librarian at Brock University in St. Catharines, Canada, to whom I often turned for help in tracking down resources. I also want to thank Richard and Kerry Demers and my own Carmelite brothers, especially the Carmelite communities in Rome; Washington, DC; and Niagara Falls, Canada, for their support and encouragement. Thanks also to Rev. David Cotter who asked me to take on this project several years ago. This commentary also reflects reactions from the students here at the Pontifical Biblical Institute upon whom I first tried out my ideas. Finally, Jerome Walsh, the current editor of this series, has been an immense support. Insights from his book, *Style and Structure in Biblical Hebrew Narrative* (Collegeville, MN: Liturgical Press, 2001), are embedded throughout this volume. He pointed out to me details in the biblical text that I had overlooked and regularly sharpened my prose. I am grateful that he delayed his own retirement to assist me in bringing this volume to publication.

This book is lovingly dedicated to Bella and Henry Tovey. When I began learning Hebrew from Bella some twenty-five years ago at her dining room table, I soon grasped that she and her husband had much to teach me beyond the Hebrew alphabet. I am most grateful to them. As for the foibles in this volume, I claim them as my own, hoping that David, the first real person to be depicted by the written word, and you the reader will excuse them.

ABBREVIATIONS

ABD	*The Anchor Bible Dictionary*
BASOR	*Bulletin of the American Schools of Oriental Research*
BHS	*Biblia Hebraica Stuttgartensia*
Bib	*Biblica*
CBQ	*The Catholic Biblical Quarterly*
JBL	*Journal of Biblical Literature*
JSOT	*Journal for the Study of the Old Testament*
JSOTSup	Journal for the Study of the Old Testament: Supplement Series
KHAT	Kurzer Handkommentar zum Alten Testament
MT	Masoretic Text
NAB	New American Bible
NIV	New International Version
NJB	New Jerusalem Bible
NJPS	New Jewish Publication Society Version
NRSV	New Revised Standard Version
REB	Revised English Bible
TLOT	*Theological Lexicon of the Old Testament.* Edited by E. Jenni with assistance from C. Westermann. Translated by M. E. Biddle. 3 vols. Peabody, MA: Hendrickson, 1997.
ThWAT	*Theologisches Wörterbuch zum Alten Testament.* Edited by G. J. Botterweck and H. Ringgren. Stuttgart: W. Kohlhammer, 1970–.
VT	*Vetus Testamentum*

The English text of the Bible is taken from the NRSV unless otherwise noted. In instances where a Hebrew word is cited and the Masoretic Text and NRSV have different verse numbers, the NRSV's versification is given, then the Masoretic number is noted in parentheses. For other ancient texts, if no source is given for the English translation, then the translation is mine. All citations from the works of William Shakespeare are taken from *The Norton Shakespeare* (edited by Stephen Greenblatt; New York and London: Norton, 1997). Citations of 2 Samuel are sometimes given without noting the biblical book, whereas citations from other biblical books always include the book reference.

Chapter 1

INTRODUCTION

For 'tis your thoughts that now must deck our kings,
Carry them here and there, jumping o'er times,
Turning the accomplishment of many years
Into an hour-glass: for the which supply,
Admit me Chorus to this history;
Who prologue-like your humble patience pray,
Gently to hear, kindly to judge, our play.

King Henry V, *Prologue*

Shakespeare greeted the audience awaiting his *King Henry V* with a chorus that reminded them of their role in the events about to unfold on stage. They should deck the kings of England and France with their thoughts and compress a king's reign into an hour-glass so that history might "jump o'er times." The biblical narrator could have introduced the history of King David to his audience with a similar prologue. This ancient history, appearing not on a stage but on the printed page, makes demands on our imagination beyond that of *King Henry V*. We must bedeck our hero David with his sling and five smooth stones as he approaches the Philistine champion, Goliath. We must ascend with him onto the palace terrace in the late afternoon as he peers at the wife of Uriah and trail after him as he climbs the city gate wailing for his dead son. Just as King Henry V's reign, in the bard's hands, is compressed into an hour-glass, so King David's reign, in the narrator's hands, is compressed into forty-two biblical chapters. We hold the narrator's art in our hands, *gently to read, kindly to judge* his tale.

The Second Book of Samuel, by its very title, suggests that it is a sequel. But unlike a modern sequel, 2 Samuel was not separated from 1 Samuel for literary reasons. David's history spills over the borders of

2 Samuel to include his anointing and flight from King Saul in 1 Samuel 16–31 and his withdrawal from public life and eventual death in 1 Kings 1–2. While Saul's death at the end of 1 Samuel seems like a logical break, even this event spans the two books, illustrating just how entwined 1 and 2 Samuel are. Similarly, even though 2 Samuel 23:1 announces David's final words, his final discourses continue into 1 Kings 2:1-10, thus joining the closing episodes in 2 Samuel to the opening scenes in 1 Kings. This commentary on 2 Samuel, notwithstanding its literary focus, observes the ancient, unliterary divisions of these biblical books. It is the nature of historical writing to resist literary divisions, a problem that Shakespeare confronted in his history plays. Both *King Henry V* and 2 Samuel begin and end *in medias res*. Our narrator references events that preceded David's reign[1] and foreshadows events that follow it, including the eventual destruction of Jerusalem in 2 Kings 25.[2] Though this catastrophic ending is attenuated by King Jehoiachin's transfer from prison to the Babylonian king's table (2 Kgs 25:27-30), our narrator's story ends with Israel's fortunes lying in the rubble of David's city. Within this arc of Israelite history the narrator tells the story of David.

1.1 A Portrait of David and His Reign

Historical narrative, because it shapes and organizes time, offers only a selection of events that have occurred in real time. Since David's life-story takes little more than a few hours to read, we can assume that it captures only a small portion of his exploits during his forty-year reign. It is not a royal chronicle of the Davidic court but rather a carefully crafted story, a series of episodes woven together to create a novelized portrait of David and his reign. Seemingly insignificant details are included in this portrait, such as in the buildup to Tamar's rape. We watch her take dough, knead it, bake cakes, and set them before her brother Amnon (2 Sam 13:8-9). Later, we listen to a lengthy conversation between a bogus widow and a beguiled king (14:4-20) that lays the groundwork for Absalom's return to court. Why are such minutiae included? A chronicler would have reported the rape of Tamar or Absalom's rehabilitation with a stroke of the pen, eliminating these ostensibly insignificant particulars.

---

[1] When Nathan (his oracle in 2 Sam 7:6) and David (his prayer in 7:23) reprise Israelite history, they begin with the Exodus from Egypt. When Joab sends news of Uriah's death to David, he references the death of Abimelech (11:21) from the book of Judges (Judg 9:53).

[2] See 2 Samuel 24.

But our task is to discover how they contribute to the portrait of David because our narrator does not write with the broad strokes of a chronicler. He recounts his episodes in miniature. He creates a masterpiece.

The classics of historical literature are more than just chronicles. Shakespeare's *King Henry IV, Part 1* shifts between the political debates at court to the shenanigans at a tavern in Eastcheap. Geopolitical affairs fade into the shadows when King Henry bids his court to depart so that he might converse with the Prince of Wales alone. King Henry, now more father than king, expresses his disappointment with his son's behavior ("yet let me wonder, Harry, / At thy affections" [act 3, sc. 2, lines 29–30]), and we are allowed a glimpse into the heart of a king. King David must crush a son's rebellion and retake his capital city. But his final orders to his generals come from a father, not a king (18:5: "Deal gently for my sake with the young man Absalom"), and we gain a glimpse into David's heart. And at the end of his life, King Henry orders his courtiers from his deathbed so that he might converse with "Harry" for the last time (*King Henry IV, Part 2*, act 4, sc. 5). The father very nearly accuses the son of usurping the throne, but when he perceives his son's grief, he calls him to his bedside for his "very latest counsel." (Did Shakespeare have the biblical David in mind when he created this scene?) David from his sickbed contends with a usurping son (1 Kgs 1:5-53) and then, just before he dies, he too bestows on his successor, Solomon, his "very latest counsel." As in *King Henry IV, Part 1* and *Part 2*, so in 2 Samuel, the father-son relationship that pervades these "histories" reminds us that there is more at stake in these marvels of historical literature than the chronicling of the geopolitical events of the day.

1.2 The Narrative Approach and Source Criticism

Biblical interpretation includes a symphony of approaches and methods, such as textual criticism and the historical-critical method, and this commentary appeals to each of them in order to understand the David Narrative (1 Sam 16 to 1 Kgs 2), but particular attention is given to the narrative approach. A narrative reading observes how a particular biblical story, such as the Abraham Cycle or, in this case, the David Narrative, can be read as a coherent unity. Source criticism and redaction criticism identify the various sources and strata behind the final form of a particular biblical text along with the various levels of redaction (such as, for example, the Deuteronomistic redactions). These approaches uncover the seams (the hands of various authors and editors) in the narrative by observing repetitions and contradictions in the storyline. At first glance, the two methods seem to be at odds with one another. But, in fact, the narrative approach complements the efforts of source critics. For example, from a source-critical point of view, there seem to be two accounts of David sparing Saul's life (1 Sam 24 and 26). Source critics do well to distinguish the earlier account from the later one, though scholarly opinions are divided on the question: some believe that 1 Samuel 24 is older, while others argue for 1 Samuel 26. But most agree that the same event is recounted twice and that a comparison of the two accounts offers insight into the development of the biblical text. The narrative approach observes how these two accounts can be fruitfully read as elements of a unified narrative. What is the effect of preserving both? Perhaps the second account, repetitive as it is, serves to convince us of David's loyalty to Saul. Since David spares Saul's life on *two* occasions, he is no usurper and should not be accused of complicity in Saul's eventual demise, despite what Shimei son of Gera says later in 2 Samuel 16:5-13. The narrative approach observes how the narrator's art has given thematic cohesion to disparate elements of the story.

Sometimes information given in one part of the narrative is incompatible with a later account. In 7:1 we learn that God has given David rest from his enemies. But in 1 Kings 5:3 Solomon tells King Hiram that David could not build the Temple because God had not yet put his enemies under his feet. The apparent contradiction between these two verses suggests different sources. But from a narrative perspective, 1 Kings 5:3 acknowledges that even if in 2 Samuel 7:1 David enjoyed God-given "rest from all his enemies" after he transferred the ark to Jerusalem (6:1-23), that "rest" was temporary since he returns to the battlefield in the very next chapter (8:1). Such inconsistencies are not unique to the Bible. The narrator in *Pride and Prejudice* (Jane Austen, 1813) allows Mrs. Reynolds, the housekeeper at Pemberley, to describe Mr. Darcy as "the sweetest-tempered, most generous-hearted boy in the world." But near the end of the novel Mr. Darcy's recollection of his childhood to Lizzy contradicts Mrs. Reynolds' memory: "I was spoilt by my parents, who . . . allowed, encouraged, almost taught me to be selfish and overbearing; to care for none beyond my own family circle; to think meanly of all the rest of the world." The reader expects some comment from Lizzy or the narrator on these two irreconcilable descriptions but both are silent. Two thousand years from now, will critics suppose that there are two sources behind Austen's masterpiece? Or can these contradictory recollections be shown to serve the narrator's purpose?

The seams that source critics identify in the David Narrative do not so overwhelm the storyline that it decomposes into a mere collection of isolated episodes (see the discussion of the theme below). Even its subplots help to bind the narrative into an organic whole. Mephibosheth, Jonathan's son, is mentioned in an aside in 4:4: learning of Abner's murder, his nurse picked him up to flee, but he fell and was left crippled. He reappears in 9:1-13 when David asks if there are any of Saul's descendants to whom he can express his loyalty "for Jonathan's sake" (9:1). David's question reaches back to the beginning of the David Narrative, to the agreement between Jonathan and David (1 Sam 18:3) that developed into an oath that David would protect Jonathan's descendants (1 Sam 20:15, 42). Mephibosheth comes back on stage during Absalom's rebellion to reaffirm his loyalty to David (2 Sam 19:24-30). He is mentioned for the final time near the end of the narrative when David spares his life and the narrator reminds us of David's oath to Jonathan (21:7). That interjection reaches back to the covenant between David and Jonathan at the beginning of David's public life. Thus, the Mephibosheth subplot, running almost the entire length of the David Narrative, contributes to the cohesion of the story.

Admittedly, some "seams" in the story are more difficult for the narrator to compel us to cross. Saul contacts David's father, Jesse, to ensure that David remains at court (1 Sam 16:22), but, when David defeats Goliath, Saul asks his chief general who David's father is (1 Sam 17:55). How could Saul not know the answer to his question? And who killed Goliath? Was it David (1 Sam 17:51) or Elhanan (2 Sam 21:19)? While such inconsistencies witness to the various sources behind the David Narrative, our narrator does not seem concerned that they mar his reasonably coherent portrait of David's reign.[3]

1.3 The Theme of the David Narrative (1 Sam 16–1 Kgs 2)

Many scholars have argued that the David Narrative was composed from various sources such as the "History of David's Rise" (1 Sam 16–2 Sam 5), the "Succession Narrative" (2 Sam 9–20 and 1 Kgs 1–2), an "Appendix" (2 Sam 21–24), and other isolated pieces, though they disagree as to the exact parameters of each of these hypothetical sources. How has the narrator brought these once-separate documents together into a coherent story? Evidence of his art lies in two of David's speeches that introduce and reprise the central theme of the David Narrative. The first speech comes when David, standing before an incredulous Saul, claims that God will rescue him from Goliath (1 Sam 17:34-37a). The

---

[3] There are also inconsistencies within the chapters that critics argue come from the same source. In the so-called succession narrative, Absalom dies without a son to carry on his name (18:18) despite the notice in 14:27 that Absalom had three sons.

second speech comes near the end of his public life (2 Sam 22) in which he praises God who always rescued him. These two speeches function as a literary inclusion to David's public life and lend cohesion to the episodes that lie in between.

1.3.1 David's Opening Speech (1 Sam 17:34-37a)

In 1 Samuel 16:1-13 David is introduced into the narrative of Israelite history and is immediately anointed king. But in this scene the new king never utters a word. Summoned from his father's flocks to stand before Samuel, how did David react to the chrism-bearing Samuel? The narrator offers no comment and does not allow David to speak. In the subsequent machinations that result in his transfer to Saul's court, our hero is still voiceless. This delay builds our anticipation for David's opening speech, which occurs when he presents himself to Saul:[4]

> But David answered Saul, "Your servant was a shepherd for his father's flocks. Whenever a lion or bear would come and carry off a lamb from the flock, I would go out after it, strike it and deliver [*nṣl*] the lamb from its mouth. If it rose against me, I would grab it by the beard, strike it down and kill it.
>
> *Conclusion*
> "Your servant struck both lions and bears. So this Philistine, this uncircumcised, will be like one of them because he has reproached the ranks of the living God."
>
> *Second Conclusion*
> Then David said, "The LORD who delivered [*nṣl*] me from the power of the lion and from the power of the bear will deliver [*nṣl*] me from the power of this Philistine." (1 Sam 17:34-37a; translation mine)

The youthful David needs to convince King Saul of his skills as a warrior. He sets out his premise: he rescued sheep from pilfering lions and bears. Therefore he can vanquish Goliath. This argument would seem to be sufficient. But then he adjoins a second conclusion that develops the significance of the verb "to deliver" (*nṣl*) in his premise. When David delivered the sheep from the lion and bear, *it was God who delivered David!* These are David's opening lines on stage. Hamlet's first line, "A little more than kin and less than kind" (act 1, sc. 2, line 65), is written with a

---

[4] David's first utterances come when he asks about the reward for dispatching the Philistine (1 Sam 17:26) and in response to his older brother's accusation (1 Sam 17:29).

polyvalent pithiness that sums up the tragedy that follows. David's opening speech, in particular the second conclusion, has the same function: what follows is a story about divine deliverance, or more specifically, the story of how God delivered David.

1.3.2 David's Speech in 2 Samuel 22

As his public life is drawing to a close, David sings a song that reprises this theme of deliverance. The verb "to deliver" (*nṣl*), which appeared three times in David's opening speech before Saul, appears the same number of times in 2 Samuel 22. The incipit, or superscription in 2 Samuel 22:1, offers a rereading of this song into the context of the David Narrative:

> David spoke to the LORD the words of this song on the day when the LORD delivered [*nṣl*] him from the hand of all his enemies, and from the hand of Saul.

This superscription conditions our interpretation of the song that follows: it is about God rescuing David, and so we spontaneously apply the song's deliverance motifs to events in David's life (for a more detailed study of these motifs, see the discussion of 2 Sam 22 below, pp. 289–96), while we recall his opening speech before Saul. At the beginning of his public life David announced that God would deliver him. Now as his public life draws to a close, David sings that God has done just that.

The programmatic verb in these two speeches, "to deliver" (*nṣl*), appears several times in the David Narrative. David, having safely absconded with Saul's spear, addresses Saul and prays that God might protect him (1 Sam 26:24): "May he [the LORD] rescue [*nṣl*] me from all tribulation." After Nathan beguiles David with the parable of the poor man's lamb, he reminds David of what God has done for him (2 Sam 12:7): "Then Nathan said to David, 'You are the man! Thus says the LORD, the God of Israel. I anointed you king over Israel and I rescued [*nṣl*] you from the hand of Saul.'" Nathan's oracle focuses our attention on two aspects of God's role in David's life: God anointed and rescued him. Nathan reminds David (and us) that his opening speech before Saul is gradually being realized. The last time the verb "to deliver" (*nṣl*) appears in the narrative is in David's Song when at last we grasp the full significance of David's opening lines.

But it is not only the explicit use of the verb "to deliver" that illustrates the centrality of this theme in the narrative. Between David's opening speech and his song in 2 Samuel 22 the reader observes a series of divine rescues that characterize the David Narrative. Early in the story, the narrator comments that God guarantees David's victories (1 Sam 18:14 and 30:8). Through God's advice David defeats the Philistines (1 Sam 23:1-5) and eludes Saul's clutches (1 Sam 23:10-11). After David takes Jerusalem, there is a series of battles with the Philistines in which God even charts David's battle strategy (2 Sam 5:17-21, 22-25). David renames the battlefield where he defeated the Philistines Baal-perazim, explaining, "The LORD has burst forth against my enemies before me" (5:20). And if we forget God's role, the narrator's interjections remind us of it (8:6, 14): "The LORD gave victory to David everywhere he went." When Rechab and Baanah think that they have saved David from the threat of Ishbaal (4:8), the king, as he pronounces their death sentence, informs them that it is God who saves him (4:9).

At a critical moment in the narrative, divine rescue comes to David without which he would have lost his life. While fleeing from his son Absalom, he learns that a key member of his court, Ahithophel, has betrayed him. In this, his darkest hour, he implores God for help (15:31): "O LORD, I pray you, turn the counsel of Ahithophel into foolishness." Two chapters later, God, in his first appearance since the Bathsheba affair, effects David's prayer:

> Absalom and all the men of Israel said, "The counsel of Hushai the Archite is better than the counsel of Ahithophel." For the LORD had ordained to defeat the good counsel of Ahithophel, so that the LORD might bring ruin on Absalom. (17:14)

The narrator observes that Ahithophel's advice was better than Hushai's. Thus, had Absalom followed it he would have been victorious and reigned in his father's place. But God intervenes, and David is rescued from Absalom's designs.

Complementing this theme of divine rescue is the fact that David's own missteps contribute to this crisis in his reign. David is, as Leonard Cohen sings, "a baffled king composing hallelujah."[5] He is "the first human being in world literature": "He grows, he learns, he travails, he triumphs, and he suffers immeasurable tragedy and loss."[6] To this characterization of David I would add shrewd and gullible. On one hand, David is often a shrewd leader: he dodges Saul's murderous designs (1 Sam 20) and evades Achish's interrogatives (1 Sam 27:10-11). On the other hand, he allows Amnon access to Tamar (2 Sam 13:6-7) and then fails to punish

---

[5] Leonard Cohen, *Hallelujah.*

[6] Baruch Halpern, *David's Secret Demons: Messiah, Murderer, Traitor, King* (Grand Rapids, MI: Eerdmans, 2001), 6.

him (13:21). He believes Absalom's request that Amnon attend his phony sheep-shearing party (13:26) and is duped by the pretending Tekoite widow (14:1-20), who even succeeds in making him swear an oath—a scene that verges on comic relief. But his most egregious misjudgment comes when he accepts the legitimacy of Absalom's request to journey to Hebron to sacrifice (15:9). That calamitous decision allows his rebel son to muster the forces of insurrection. But for God's rescue, the divine thwarting of Ahithophel's advice, David would not have survived. Thus, David's opening speech before an incredulous Saul foreshadows the story that lies ahead: God will rescue him from Goliath and much more, and before he exits the public stage, he will sing about how God rescued him his life long. This theme of divine deliverance binds these episodes from David's life into a coherent narrative.

1.4 A Narrative Approach to Reading the Bible

1.4.1 The Art of Hebrew Narrative

Hebrew narrative, like English narrative, distinguishes events in the foreground from those in the background. My purpose here is not to present a grammar of Hebrew narrative but to focus briefly on how Hebrew signals background information. In general, foregrounded information is presented in clauses that begin with the Hebrew verb form *wayyiqtol*. Background information (flashbacks or the report of events concurrent to the action in the foreground) is introduced by interrupting this series of *wayyiqtol* clauses with verbless clauses (including clauses such as *wĕqātēl* or *wĕ X qātēl*, where "X" represents the subject) or finite verb clauses, such as *wĕ X qātal*. For readers of Hebrew, such a shift in the clause structure alerts them to background information. For English readers this shift can go unnoticed and so the background information that is often critical for interpreting events in the foreground is overlooked. For example, as the foreground action moves toward Joab's murder of Abner, the Hebrew text at the end of 3:26 interrupts the series of *wayyiqtol* clauses with a *wĕ X qātēl*, clause: "but David did not know about it [Joab's plot]." The narrator intrudes into the foreground action with a background comment that guides our interpretation of this event: David was completely unaware of Joab's scheme to eliminate Abner. Though David might benefit from Abner's murder (see the commentary), this background clause informs us that he had nothing to do with it. Examples of this feature of Hebrew narrative abound and will be brought to the attention of the reader.

1.4.2 The Narrator

When we read the Bible we can imagine that the "author" is speaking directly to us through his or her composition. But it is the narrator who relates the story. The biblical narrator is a sort of external consciousness, "a second self,"[7] created by the author and endowed with superhuman powers. Thus, when David walks alone on the roof and spies the beautiful Bathsheba, the narrator is with him (and therefore so are we). The biblical narrator can tell us if someone is lying (1 Kgs 13:18), give reports from opposing camps in a battle (2 Sam 2:24-32), and even relate God's state of mind (11:27). The distance between author and narrator is more easily observed in a work such as Emily Brontë's *Wuthering Heights* in which Brontë creates the narrator Mr. Lockwood who then cedes his narrator role to Nelly Dean. But Emily Brontë is neither Mr. Lockwood nor Nelly Dean. They are her creations. Mr. Lockwood is similar to our biblical narrator in that he knows the entire story before he begins to tell it. But because he is dramatized in the story, he is quite different. He is also not very perceptive, describing Heathcliff as "a capital fellow" after their first encounter and for this reason literary critics consider him an "unreliable narrator." Unlike Mr. Lockwood, our biblical narrator gives us no reason to consider him less than reliable.

But labels like "reliable" or "omniscient" fail to capture the complexity of the biblical narrator's art. He knows all but does not tell all, doling out information as he sees fit so as to keep us on edge. For example, after Joab kills Abner, David declares himself innocent of Abner's blood (3:28-29). But we have to wait until the deathbed scene (1 Kgs 2:5) to learn that, in David's judgment, Joab's crime had to do with avenging wartime blood in peacetime. That information would have been helpful in 2 Samuel 3. Moreover, by announcing twice (3:27, 30) that Joab killed Abner to revenge the death of Asahel his brother, the narrator appears obtuse, failing to recognize that Joab may also have wanted Abner (and later Amasa) dead in order to preserve his position as David's chief military officer.[8]

The narrator can also remain silent on questions that seem critical to the outcome of the story, leaving us baffled. Ishbaal accuses Abner of having sex with Saul's concubine Rizpah (3:7). Did Abner do it? Was

---

[7] Wayne C. Booth, *The Rhetoric of Fiction* (Chicago: The University of Chicago Press, 1983), 71.

[8] See the discussion of the "obtuse narrator" in David M. Bevington, "The Obtuse Narrator in Chaucer's House of Fame," *Speculum* 36 (1961): 288–98. Bevington describes how the narrator in Chaucer's poem has only a weak grasp or a superficial understanding of the event he recounts.

Abner planning to usurp Ishbaal's succession to his father's throne? The question is hardly inconsequential. But we never find out. As David flees Jerusalem, Ziba tells David that Mephibosheth has betrayed him (16:3). But as David returns to Jerusalem, Mephibosheth declares his innocence (19:26-27). Was Mephibosheth a traitor? We would like to know for sure, but the narrator does not pronounce on the question. Throughout *Wuthering Heights* the reader cannot help but wonder what in the world led Mr. Earnshaw to introduce Heathcliff into his family. But neither Mr. Lockwood nor Nelly Dean speculates on an answer to what seems to me a most baffling question. Both ancient and modern narrators can leave their readers bewildered.

On other occasions the biblical narrator refers to information that was never provided. Because of the deceased Nahash's loyalty, David sends emissaries to his son Hanun at the time of his succession and his father's death (10:2). But the narrator offers no background information on the political alliance between Nahash and David. Similarly, when Adonijah declares himself David's rightful successor, Bathsheba comes to David complaining, "My lord, you swore to your servant by the LORD your God, saying: Your son Solomon shall succeed me as king" (1 Kgs 1:17). When did David make such a promise? When neither David nor the narrator objects, we infer (perhaps mistakenly) that Bathsheba's reminder is accurate. As Erich Auerbach famously noted, the biblical narration "remains mysterious and 'fraught with background.' "[9]

The narrative approach attends not only to what the narrator says but also to how he says it—the drama of the telling. This requires an acute eye on the text itself to observe its structure and to detect the narrator's strategies.[10] What is the speed at which the narrator tells the story (real time versus narrative time)? He can report David's battles with lightning speed (2 Sam 8:1-8), but he brings Tamar into Amnon's web ever so slowly (13:8-11). The narrator controls our point of view as well. As we watch David leading the ark into Jerusalem, suddenly the narrator has us look up at Michal gazing out the window at her dancing husband (6:16). The narrator can also guide our judgment of events. In 2 Kings 17, after reporting the fall of Samaria in two verses (2 Kgs 17:5-6), the narrator shapes our interpretation of this defeat for the next seventeen verses (2 Kgs 17:7-23: "This occurred because").

[9] Erich Auerbach, *Mimesis: The Representation of Reality in Western Literature*, trans. Willard R. Trask (Princeton, NJ: Princeton University Press, 1974), 12.

[10] According to Vladimir Vladimirovich Nabokov, "Style and structure are the essence of a book; great ideas are hogwash" (John Updike, introduction to *Vladimir Nabokov: Lectures on Literature* [San Diego/New York/London: Harcourt, 1980], xxiii).

Finally, readers can raise issues that are outside the narrator's horizon. Saul is sent to exterminate the Amalekites, including women and children (1 Sam 15:3). The order is horrific and modern readers do well to question this and other violent acts in the Bible. But this question is not within the narrator's purview. The narrator does not explain why God condemns to death the son born to David and Bathsheba after their adulterous affair (2 Sam 12:14), casting the punishment for their sin on the next generation, and he remains silent when seven of Saul's descendants are impaled to atone for Saul's sins (21:9). When Absalom has sexual relations with David's concubines (16:22), the narrator says nothing about what a modern reader might consider rape. Absalom's counsel to Tamar to remain silent about her rape is scandalous to modern ears (13:20) and rightly so. Some might even wonder whether David should not have developed his autocratic rule into a constitutional monarchy in order to favor the growth of democracy in ancient Israel. These sorts of questions arise when we read literature from another age and culture. In the *Odyssey*, the bard has no problem with the fact that Penelope is expected to be faithful to her long-absent husband while Odysseus is not held to the same standard. Margaret Atwood's *The Penelopiad* (Knopf, 2005) does well to probe that inconsistency for today's audience. When the ancient narrator ignores our questions we sense the distance between our world and the world of the narrator.

1.4.3 The Characters in the David Narrative

Commenting on the characters in Shakespeare's *Henry IV, Part 1*, Harold Bloom writes, "Falstaff is a person, while Hal and Hotspur are fictions."[11] This provocative observation turns the historical Prince Hal and Sir Henry Percy into fictions while Falstaff, mostly an invention of the bard, becomes a real person. But the invented Falstaff is real because he unmasks the fictions through which the historical figures in the play, such as Hal, Hotspur, and even King Henry, live. Bloom's statement reminds us that historical personages, whether they appear in *Henry IV, Part 1* or in the David Narrative, are in the narrator's (or the bard's) hands. Was Bathsheba a real person? Of course she was. But in 2 Samuel the narrator denies us access to a complex view of her. Did she love Uriah? Did she know that David had him killed? Did she desire the advantages of a royal liaison? Because the narrator is not interested in

---

[11] Harold Bloom, *Shakespeare: The Invention of the Human Mind* (New York: Riverhead Books, 1998), 282.

presenting her as a complex character, we do not learn the answers to these pressing questions, and thus in 2 Samuel 11–12 Bathsheba remains largely undeveloped.

DAVID

While all the characters in the David Narrative were multifaceted people in real life, the narrator grants that status to David alone. David is a complex, unfolding, and inconclusive character who, on occasion, steps outside his expected role and acts unpredictably. He is a bold experiment in the exploration of the human person despite the limits and frustrations of the narrator's only medium, the written word. In the midst of the official rites of mourning for King Saul and his son Jonathan, the narrator allows us to observe David as he abandons his official function as chief mourner to express his personal affection for Jonathan (1:26). For an instant we are granted a privileged entry into David's inner experience as we gaze into the depths of his grief over the loss of his friend and ally. He steps outside his role as king when, with a father's broken heart, he wails for his rebel son (18:33). This brief, intimately personal moment is abruptly interrupted by David's commander, Joab (19:5-8), who orders him back into his role as king ("So go out at once and speak kindly to your servants" [19:7]). The father obeys and becomes a king again, but it's too late. We know too much. The narrator's art has made visible his divided heart, his inner conflict: a king who should celebrate the execution of a rebel is really a father mourning his dead son.

The narrator investigates the nature of the human person through contradictions and questions that emerge from David's character. Each of David's notable qualities immediately conjures evidence to the contrary. David trusts in God's fidelity (1 Sam 17:37) yet plots the murder of his mistress's husband (2 Sam 11:14-15). This politically shrewd leader, who ensures that his alliance with the remnants of Saul's government survives the murders of Abner, Saul's general (3:27), and Ishbaal, Saul's son (4:9-12), is easily duped by a Tekoite widow (14:1-17) and beguiled by his son's request to travel to Hebron (15:7). He acknowledges Joab's power (3:39) and would like to get rid of him (his one attempt in 19:13 fails), but he also uses him to eliminate Uriah. Is David faithful to his covenant with Jonathan when he brings Mephibosheth to court (9:1-13) or is he placing a claimant to the throne under house arrest, or both? David's inconsistencies, contradictions, and moments of shameless transparency allow us, modern readers, to reclaim our own experience. We meet our own half truths, duplicities, fictions, and moral ambiguities in David more than in any other character in the David Narrative and perhaps in the entire Hebrew Bible.

We might be tempted to decode the interrogative that David's complex character poses, but Hamlet's angry counsel to his false friends Rosencrantz and Guildenstern bids us beware:

> You would play upon me; you would seem to know
> my stops; you would pluck out the heart of my
> mystery; you would sound me from my lowest note to
> the top of my compass: and there is much music,
> excellent voice, in this little organ; yet cannot
> you make it speak. 'Sblood, do you think I am
> easier to be played on than a pipe? Call me what
> instrument you will, though you can fret me, yet you
> cannot play upon me. (act 3, sc. 2, lines 335–41)

David, like Hamlet, will not be "played." Why did he send Tamar to Amnon? Why did he allow Absalom back at court? And why did he not get rid of Joab during his reign? To demand precise answers to all these questions would be to pluck out David's mystery and play him like a pipe, even if those few glimpses we receive into the king's heart tempt us to do so.

Joab

Joab, David's chief military officer, is the only other major character in the narrative, though he does not rise to the level of David's complexity or transparency. Predictably cruel, calculating, and ready to eliminate any threat to his power, he is neither unfolding nor mysterious. We are not surprised when he murders the defenseless Absalom despite the king's direct order (18:5). This act of defiance reveals the tense balance of power between king and general in the world of the David Narrative. Today's democratic governments in which civil leaders command the military are not a helpful paradigm for understanding the relationship between David and his general Joab.

Abner, Saul's general, seats Ishbaal, Saul's son, on the throne (2:9). The general is the kingmaker! So when Ishbaal accuses Abner of treason,[12] the general pushes the king off the throne (3:9). Like Abner, Joab can order David about and can reject royal decisions. After Joab interrupts his attack on Rabbah at the king's bidding, in order to eliminate Uriah (11:17), he commands the king to the battlefield, threatening treason

---

[12] Ishbaal thinks that Abner has had sexual relations with Rizpah, Saul's concubine (3:7).

(12:27-28) if the king does not obey. When David establishes an alliance with Abner (3:13), Joab enters the court and demands an explanation from the king (3:24)—not what we might expect from a general. Later on Joab defies David when he murders Amasa (20:10), whom David had appointed as Joab's replacement (19:13). By giving Amasa, the rebel general, a place in his court, David signaled to Absalom's rebels that they would be included in his government, a clever political maneuver. But Joab flouts David's strategy and contributes to the further instability of David's rule at a very precarious time. When Joab returns to David's court, the king is unable to confront his general regarding this willful act of insubordination. Thus, David's earlier claim that he is powerless before Joab (3:39) has merit. Joab is not a kingmaker like Abner, but his power at court is considerable.

Joab's ruthlessness is revealed in an exchange he has with one of his soldiers who has seen Absalom trapped in a tree. When Joab asks why he did not kill Absalom, the soldier retorts, "Had I killed Absalom, you would have let me take the fall for it alone" (a free translation of 18:13). He openly accuses his superior officer of duplicity. When the rebel Sheba son of Bichri takes refuge in Abel of Beth-maacah, Joab besieges the town until one of its wise citizens challenges his violent conduct: "why will you swallow up the heritage of the LORD?" (20:19). That wise woman, not King David, is the first person in the David Narrative to confront Joab's brutality. Finally, Joab is an opportunist and so, near the end of his life, when he sides with Adonijah and his cohorts (1 Kgs 1:7), we assume that he considered Adonijah's chances of succeeding to David's throne to be optimal. At one point Joab surprises us when he impedes the king's order for a census, taking the high ground and piously pleading with David to reconsider ("May the LORD your God" [2 Sam 24:3]). But apart from this moment, David's general is usually predictable.

The literary term "foil" derives from the "thin sheet of bright metal placed under a jewel to enhance its brilliance."[13] David's leadership, despite his errors in judgment, shines more like a jewel when Joab, the other major character in this story, is seen as his foil. David is a leader whose personal affections can cloud his decision making, as when he orders Joab, Abishai, and Ittai to deal gently with his rebellious son Absalom (18:5). His ill-advised hope for Absalom contrasts with Joab's swift execution of the usurper (18:14). Joab's execution-style justice makes David's missteps seem less egregious. We may want to laugh at David for the attention he pays to the pretending Tekoite widow (14:4-17),

---

[13] M. H. Abrams, *A Glossary of Literary Terms* (Boston, MA: Thomson, Wadsworth, 2005), 234.

but we have the impression that no widow would receive a hearing from Joab unless it served his interests. While Abner delayed killing Asahel, Joab's brother, and tried to convince him to give up his pursuit, Joab exacts his revenge on Abner (3:27) without uttering a word to him. Even the troops that Joab commands recognize that their general is self-serving, underhanded, and ruthless (18:13). His leadership, cruel and conniving, can attenuate a harsh judgment of David, whose flaws nearly lead to his ruin. David himself draws out the contrast between himself and Joab when he declares that the "sons of Zeruiah" (Joab is a son of Zeruiah) are too violent for him (3:39). We can imagine that Joab, upon hearing the king's exclamation, would have thought to himself, "This king is too gentle for me." Joab's ruthlessness and his violence are the metal foil placed behind David's character that encourages us to prefer the jewel of David's leadership, with all its failings, to the cruelty that we meet in Joab.

Other Characters

A specific quality attributed to a minor character usually serves the outcome of the scene (direct character description is rare). Asahel may be as swift as a gazelle (2:18), but that swiftness leads to his own death. Absalom's hair-cutting schedule (14:26) will eventually leave him suspended between heaven and earth, awaiting Joab's spear (18:9-15). The beauty attributed to Tamar quickly captures Amnon's attention (13:1). Ahithophel, described as a good advisor (16:23), offers wise advice to Absalom (17:14). The only quality the narrator provides for Mephibosheth is his disability (4:4, he is lame), which sustains Mephibosheth's claim (if we believe him) that he remained faithful to David (16:1-4 and 19:24-30). Other qualities of minor characters, such as Absalom's rebellious spirit and Tamar's strength of character (she refuses Amnon), emerge only as the plot unfolds. But many of their actions, such as Ahithophel's suicide, cannot be anticipated because of their scanty character development.

Except for David and Joab, the characters in 2 Samuel are episodic, and essential questions about them are left unanswered. What were Absalom's thoughts about killing his father (16:11 and 17:2)? Why did Ahithophel join the rebels? How did Tamar manage in Absalom's house (the narrator sums up the remainder of her life in one line: "So Tamar remained, a desolate woman, in her brother Absalom's house" [13:20]). Did Michal love Paltiel (3:15-16)? Did Bathsheba feel raped by a powerful king? The narrator does not invest in these characters, and we struggle to identify with them because we have so little information about their plight. Whether we want to call them flat characters or agents,[14] one thing is certain: their presence in the story serves the portrait of David and his reign. The narrator's interests lie there.

1.4.4 The Plot: A Story in Six Acts

During Saul's reign, Samuel informed the king (and us) that God had already chosen his replacement, one who would be better than he (1 Sam 15:28) and who is like God's own heart (1 Sam 13:14). Thus, before Act 1 of the David Narrative begins, we are already anticipating the introduction of a new character. The story of Saul's reign comes to a tragic end when the narrator announces that the relationship between Saul and Samuel has been irreparably broken (1 Sam 15:35): they would never meet again in life.[15] Beginning in 1 Samuel 16, David becomes the dominant character for the next forty-two chapters of the Bible until his death in 1 Kings 2:10. This narrative can be divided into six acts:

• *Act 1: David's anointing and his flight from King Saul (1 Sam 16–31)*
   The beginning of David's public life is characterized by conflict with Saul. Immediately after his anointing he is brought to Saul's court but soon has to flee the king's spear. For much of 1 Samuel 16–31 David manages to escape Saul's deadly pursuit, thus underscoring the theme of the David Narrative: God rescues David. When David's own men reject his (and God's) plan to attack the Philistines and defend Keilah, God assures David of victory (1 Sam 23:1-5). Saul's son Jonathan aligns himself with David (1 Sam 18:1-4) and they make a pact in which David swears to remain loyal to Jonathan and his descendants (1 Sam 20:14-17). The effects of that oath continue into 2 Samuel (see 2 Sam 9:1 and 21:7), long after Jonathan's death. Though David demonstrates his loyalty to Saul, sparing his life on two occasions (1 Sam 24 and 26), he never again risks being in Saul's presence. Fleeing to Philistine territory, he lives under the protection of King Achish of Gath and settles in Ziklag (1 Sam 27:6). With Saul's death, David's life on the run comes to an end.

---

[14] In *Aspects of the Novel* (New York: Penguin Books, 1990), E. M. Forster describes a flat character: "In their purest form, they are constructed round a single idea or quality; when there is more than one factor in them, we get the beginning of the curve towards the round" (p. 73).

[15] Saul converses with the dead Samuel in 1 Samuel 28:15-19.

- *Act 2: David rules in Hebron (2 Sam 1:1–5:5)*

After mourning the deaths of King Saul and his son Jonathan, David moves back to Judah and establishes his rule in Hebron. The fugitive is now king (2:4), though his reign is by no means secure. Attempts to assert his authority over Saul's dominion are rebuffed and war ensues between the "house of Saul and the house of David" (3:1). A protracted war is avoided when Abner, Saul's chief commander, betrays Ishbaal, Saul's son and successor. David's pact with Abner to absorb Saul's territory under his rule is not thwarted by the murders of Abner and Ishbaal, and these episodes draw to a close when Saul's subjects acclaim David as their king (5:1-3). The narrator signals a caesura with a notice of David's regnal years that anticipates his rule in Jerusalem.

- *Act 3: David establishes his reign in Jerusalem (5:6–8:18)*

With the relocation of David's capital to Jerusalem, a new era of Davidic rule begins. David quickly moves to secure his city, defending it from Philistine aggressors (5:17-25). The relocation of the ark of the covenant to Jerusalem further solidifies his kingship and establishes Jerusalem as his royal city (6:1-23). To bolster his capital, he decides to build a Temple, but God rejects his plan (7:1-29). David then extends his dominion by defeating various enemies (8:1-14), and the Philistines, his main enemy, do not attack again until very late in David's reign (21:15). The strife that lies ahead will be internal to the house of David. The narrator concludes this act by introducing the members of David's court (8:15-18). David, having secured his city, establishes his government.

- *Act 4: Divine rescue for a beguiled king (9:1–20:26)*

The opening episodes in this act tell of a shrewd king who continues to consolidate his rule. Mephibosheth (Jonathan's son), a potential threat to the throne, is brought into David's orbit (9:1-13). Then David settles a score with the Ammonites and their Aramean mercenaries (10:1-19). But these two victories are followed by a series of imprudent decisions that put his life and kingdom at risk. His liaison with Bathsheba and the subsequent murder of Uriah are condemned by the prophet Nathan (11:1–12:31). When Amnon, playing sick, wants David to send Tamar to him, David complies (13:1-22). These two missteps do not directly threaten the security of his reign: God forgives David's sin against Uriah and we cannot expect David to have known of Amnon's plan to rape Tamar. But then come more serious lapses in judgment. David fails to hold Amnon accountable for the rape (13:21) and so Absalom takes matters into his own hands. When David falls for Absalom's scam, Amnon is murdered (13:23-39). The chaos in David's family is increasing. Then the king is taken in by a phony widow and concedes to Joab's proposal to reinstate the future rebel Absalom to his court (14:1-33). But these errors reach their apex when David allows Absalom out of his sight and then must flee Absalom's insurrection (15:1–20:3). Second Samuel 9–20 comes to a climax when God intervenes to rescue David (the main theme of the David Narrative) from what would have been certain defeat. As the story of Absalom's rebellion draws to a close, David is confronted with another short-lived revolt by Sheba the son of Bichri (20:4-22). Once it is quashed, the narrator intervenes with a conclusion similar to that of the previous act: he names the members of David's court (20:23-26). David's reign, which nearly collapsed due to his errors, is once again secure and so he can reestablish his government.

- *Act 5: David's public life draws to a close (21:1–24:25)*

After providing Saul and his sons with proper burial (21:10-14), David grows weary in combat and is ordered off the battlefield for good (21:15-22). This begins his withdrawal from public life. He sings a song that summarizes his life story and outlines how he wants to be remembered (22:1-51). The narrator then signals that David's final words have begun (23:1), a process that will continue until 1 Kings 2:9. And finally, just before our hero exits public life, he builds the first altar in Jerusalem (24:1-25).

- *Act 6: The kingdom is transferred to Solomon and David dies (1 Kgs 1:1–2:12)*

Time has passed. David is now so old and weak that he cannot even keep warm (1 Kgs 1:1). But his physical decline does not prevent him from orchestrating the suppression of another family-based rebellion and seating Solomon on his throne. After he delivers a final discourse to his son, he dies. The narrator concludes with a traditional summary of the king's regnal years (1 Kgs 2:11), and Solomon's reign begins.

This commentary, because it is limited to 2 Samuel, begins with Act 2 of the David Narrative and ends with Act 5. Each act is divided into episodes and each episode is divided into scenes.

1.5 The Reader

We stand before an enormously compelling story. The David Narrative, a literary masterpiece, swiftly humbles its interpreters, anyone who would dare to make it "jump o'er times" with ease. Since it presents a world so different from our own, it pleads for a slow and attentive reading. In our information age, the rapid reading of various texts has become a necessity for survival. We swim in a flood of e-mails and text messages. The David Narrative cannot be consumed as simply another text floating in this sea of words. The Bible (a rather short book in view of its impact on human history and culture) wants its every word to be carefully observed: Why this turn of phrase? Why this detail? Why this episode? Why this point of view? Why this digression now? Why these characters now? Why "Second Samuel" at all? The Bible invites us to recline at its table, not for a drive-through meal, but for what medieval monks called the *lectio divina*, a sacred reading that savors each morsel. Attending to this narrative with its rich detail challenges our view of ourselves and of the world we inhabit.

This commentary is more a "paraphrase" than an "analysis" of the narrative, a distinction I have borrowed from E. M. Forster's *Aspects of the Novel*. A paraphrase describes a masterpiece like an art lover (not art critic) who, gazing upon Rembrandt's *David and Jonathan*, is moved by David's intense despair (1 Sam 20:41). I hope to attend to our narrator's canvas in all its vibrant detail, pointing out its interesting brush strokes. But a definitive grasp of the David Narrative lies beyond the scope of this commentary. Here I am guided by the insights of Ephrem the Syrian, a fourth-century writer who wrote a commentary on a gospel harmony known as the *Diatessaron*.[16] As he reflects on the encounter between Zechariah and the angel Gabriel (Luke 1:8-20), he pauses to meditate on the nature of biblical interpretation:

> Who is capable of comprehending the extent of what is to be discovered in a single utterance of Yours? For we leave behind in it far more than we take from it, like thirsty people drinking from a fountain. . . . Anyone who encounters Scripture should not suppose that the single one of its riches that he has found is the only one to exist; rather, he should realize that he himself is only capable of discovering that one out of the many riches which exist in it. Nor, because Scripture has enriched him should the reader impoverish it. Rather, if the reader is incapable of finding more, let him acknowledge Scripture's magnitude. Rejoice because you have found satisfaction, and do not be grieved that there has been something left over by you. A thirsty person rejoices because he has drunk: he is not grieved because he proved incapable of drinking the fountain dry. Let the fountain vanquish your thirst, your thirst should not vanquish the fountain! If your thirst comes to an end while the fountain has not been diminished, then you can drink again whenever you are thirsty; whereas if the fountain had been drained dry once you had had your fill, your victory over it would have proved to your own harm. Give thanks for what

---

[16] Usually associated with Tatian, the *Diatessaron* was written probably in Syriac around 170 CE.

you have taken away, and do not complain about the superfluity that is
left over. What you have taken off with you is your portion, what has been
left behind can still be your inheritance.[17]

Reading the Bible is like drinking from a fountain whose waters satiate
the thirsty just as the Bible satiates its readers. But, Ephrem reminds
us, we leave far more water behind than we can consume. He cautions
us not to impoverish the Bible by pretending to limit its meaning with
definitive interpretations. Such interpretations suggest that the biblical fountain has been vanquished—its waters have dried up. Rejoice
at what we receive and do not be discouraged that we leave so much
behind. An inheritance of meaning awaits us. This image of the thirsty
person at the fountain impels us to yet another task: the Bible requires
many trips to the fountain. It wants to be read again to secure the many
details that escape an initial reading. Who is capable of registering the
significance of Madame Defarge's knitting on a first reading of Dickens' *A Tale of Two Cities*? But that detail leaps off the page on a second
reading! In the same way, the significance of David's opening speech
before Saul (1 Sam 17:34-37a) is only fully comprehended when he
sings his song at the end of his life (2 Sam 22). The David Narrative,
like all classics, begs to be revisited: "you can drink again whenever
you are thirsty."

1.6 A Final Word

This commentary is not intended to substitute for your personal
reading of the portrait of David and his reign. Nothing in these pages
wants to replace that unique experience. Since the biblical text is not
presented in this commentary, you will need to have the Bible at hand
(the NRSV is the version cited unless otherwise indicated). My hope
is that the ink that stains these pages renders the biblical page more
cogent for you, though the opus we are about to read dwarfs its commentators as poet J. V. Cunningham acknowledges in his poem "To
the Reader":[18]

---

[17] *Commentary on the Diatessaron*, 1:18–19. This translation is taken from Sebastian
Brock's *The Luminous Eye: The Spiritual World Vision of Saint Ephrem the Syrian* (Ka-
lamazoo, MI: Cistercian Publications, 1992), 50–51.

[18] Timothy Steele, ed., *The Poems of J. V. Cunningham* (Athens: Swallow Press/Ohio
University Press, 1997), 38.

To the Reader

> Time will assuage.
> Time's verses bury
> Margin and page
> In commentary,
> For gloss demands
> A gloss annexed
> Till busy hands
> Blot out the text,
> And all's coherent.
> Search in this gloss
> No text inherent:
> The text was loss.
> The gain is gloss.

I pray that my busy hands have not rendered the David Narrative so coherent as to have blotted out the mysteries and enigmas that lie within it. Such gain would be mere gloss.

Chapter 2
ACT 2: DAVID RULES IN HEBRON
2 SAMUEL 1:1–5:5

2.1 Introduction

Secretly anointed king in 1 Samuel 16, David passed the first years of his mandate fleeing Saul's murderous designs (act 1; see section 1.4.4 above). With Saul's death on the last page of 1 Samuel, God's design for David, announced some sixteen chapters earlier, moves toward its realization. As 2 Samuel begins, David is still in the Philistine city of Ziklag, where he fled for safety. The reader already knows that his fugitive status is over. His assailant is dead. But the news has not yet reached David. Second Samuel opens with the report of Saul's death by an Amalekite messenger who presents David with the dead king's crown (1:2-16). After the proper mourning rites (1:17-27), David abandons Philistine territory for Judah (2:1-3) and is publicly anointed king (2:4). He immediately sends missives to Saul's subjects (2:5), but his overtures are apparently rebuffed (2:8-11) and war breaks out between David and Ishbaal, Saul's successor (2:12-32). When Abner, Ishbaal's chief military commander, comes over to David's side (3:9-10), the tribes of Israel that were once loyal to Saul agree to accept Davidic rule and they too anoint David as their king (5:3). The politically savvy David ensures that the intervening murders of Abner (3:27) and Ishbaal (4:5-7) do not derail his coronation. As the curtain drops on act 2 of the David Narrative, Saul's crown sits on David's head.

STRUCTURE

A. Looking back to the final scenes of 1 Samuel (1:1)
   B. David receives Saul's crown (1:2-12)
      C. David executes Saul's killer (1:13-16)
         D. David's lament for Saul and Jonathan (1:17-27)
            E. Two kings in the land (2:1–3:6)
            E'. One king in the land: Abner switches sides
               (3:7-27)
         D'. David's lament for Abner (3:28-39)
      C'. David executes Ishbaal's killers (4:1-12)
   B'. David wears Saul's crown (5:1-3)
A'. Looking forward to David's reign in Jerusalem (5:4-5)

Act 2 of the David Narrative is framed by an opening verse that looks backward to the final chapters of act 1 (Saul's death and David's refuge in Ziklag) and closing verses that look forward to Davidic rule in Jerusalem in act 3 (A/A' sections). The action begins when David receives Saul's crown and concludes when he is finally able to wear that crown (B/B' sections). David executes the Amalekite who claims to have assisted Saul with his suicide and those who murdered Ishbaal (C/C' sections). He sings two laments: one for Saul and Jonathan and another, much shorter lament, for Abner (D/D' sections). At the center are the two key episodes that determine the outcome of act 2. Two kings cannot continue to rule the land if David is to succeed Saul in accordance with God's design set out at the beginning of the David Narrative (1 Sam 16:1-13). But Joab's forces cannot conquer Saul's territory on the battlefield (E section). When Ishbaal foolishly challenges Abner's loyalty, Abner switches sides (E' section). That unforeseen event at the center of act 2 will eventually bring Saul's dominion under Davidic rule.

2.2 Looking Back to the Final Scenes of 1 Samuel (1:1)

A pithy summary of the closing events of 1 Samuel opens 2 Samuel. Saul is dead and David has defeated the Amalekites. The conflict that occupied the David Narrative to this point, Saul's deadly pursuit of David, is now resolved, and David is about to learn that his pursuer is no longer a threat. The mention of David's victory over the Amalekites in the same verse as Saul's death is bitterly ironic: it was precisely Saul's infelicitous campaign against the Amalekites that led to his downfall—a kingdom ripped from his hands just as he ripped the hem of Samuel's cloak (1 Sam 15:27). As recently as 1 Samuel 28 we were reminded of the reason for the collapse of Saul's rule by an irritated Samuel, disturbed by the necromancer at Endor (1 Sam 28:17-19: "The LORD has done to you[1] just as he spoke . . . and tomorrow you and your sons shall be with me"). Though Saul strove against this divine injunction, his death fulfills the ill-fated words spoken by his young companion before he had ever met Samuel: "Whatever he [Samuel] says always comes true" (1 Sam 9:6). Indeed, Samuel's words have come to pass: Saul is dead and David is about to receive his predecessor's crown. In the episodes that follow, the narrator will exploit every opportunity to contrast Saul's disobedience with David's fidelity to God. The narrator is on David's side, and God's plan, begun with David's anointing in 1 Samuel 16, marches onward. Saul could not stop it. Finally, the mention of David's residence in Ziklag reminds us of his recent campaign: he recaptured the spoils of Ziklag from the marauding Amalekites, liberating his two wives, Ahinoam of Jezreel and Abigail of Carmel (1 Sam 30:18). Now a messenger comes on stage.

2.3 David Receives Saul's Crown (1:2-16)

A warrior offers a rendition of the final moments of Saul's life that departs significantly from the narrator's account in 1 Samuel 31:1-7. As David learns that the one who sought his life is dead, we watch for his reaction. Will the fugitive king be relieved, delighted, distressed . . . ?

STRUCTURE

A. The messenger falls down before David (1:2)
  B. David questions the messenger (1:3-5)
    C. The messenger describes Saul's death (1:6-10)
    C'. David's reaction to the news that Saul and Jonathan are dead (1:11-12)
  B'. David questions the messenger (1:13-14)
A'. The messenger is struck down and dies before David (1:15-16)

When the "man from Saul's camp" *falls down* before David at the beginning of the scene, he prefigures (ironically) his final fall at the end of the scene. The center of the scene reports Saul's death and the sym-

---

[1] Reading with the LXX.

bols of his kingship are transferred to David, who begins to mourn. The confirmation of David's kingship by the people governed by that crown still lies in the future. But the crown has arrived.

COMMENTARY

On the third day of David's stay in Ziklag, a battle-worn messenger arrives from Saul's camp. His mournful appearance (torn clothes and dirt on his head) witnesses to Israel's defeat and anticipates David's reaction to the news (he too will tear his own clothes, 1:11). For the moment, the narrator withholds the messenger's ethnic affiliation, telling us only that "a man came." Later we learn he is an Amalekite, a member of the clan whose extermination was ordered by God in 1 Samuel 15.[2] More recently, the Amalekites had led a retaliatory attack against David in Ziklag (1 Sam 30:1-2), the town that King Achish had transferred to him (1 Sam 27:6). Because of this attack, David's own people wanted to stone him (1 Sam 30:6). With the help of an Egyptian slave, David located the Amalekite raiders and routed them, though four hundred managed to escape on camels (was this Amalekite messenger among those escapees?). The phrase "the third day" echoes David's return to Ziklag *on the third day* (1 Sam 30:1) after the city had been raided by the Amalekites. On that third day he discovered his defeat by the Amalekites. On this third day he executes one.

Given this recent history between David and the Amalekites, one has to wonder what this Amalekite was thinking when he presented himself to David. He is wise to deliver his news and plunder before revealing his race. David's first question—"Where have you come from?"—allows the response, "I escaped from the camp of Israel." What was this Amalekite doing in Saul's camp? Was he a prisoner of war who escaped Israelite custody? Was he fighting on the side of the Israelites? The narrator ignores our questions. The Amalekite (still unidentified as such) announces the defeat of Israel and the deaths of Saul and Jonathan. This much we knew. When David questions further, the Amalekite begins spinning his tale—in the narrator's account of Saul's suicide (1 Sam 31:4) there was no Amalekite!

The Amalekite is embellishing the events (just as he "bowed down" to David upon his arrival) to gain the king's favor. He reports that he was nearby when Saul called out to him. The Hebrew expression, a finite verb modified by an infinitive absolute (2 Sam 1:6; *niqrōʾ niqrêtî*, "I just happened to be" [translation mine]), underscores how much the Amalekite

---

[2] The Amalekites incurred a divine vendetta for opposing the Israelites' passage through the Sinai (Exod 17:8-15).

wants to present his arrival on the scene as pure happenstance. He was not trying to kill Saul, even if we would have expected him to be allied with the Philistine war machine and thus in pursuit of Saul. He reports that Saul was leaning on his spear, dying and at risk of being captured. So when Saul begged for help in his final hour, the Amalekite obliged him. Since this story is at variance with the account in 1 Samuel 31 and there is no reason to doubt the narrator's presentation of Saul's death, we suspect that the Amalekite has invented his report, though the narrator teases us by refusing to pronounce him a liar. We alone know the narrator's account of Saul's death; David has no source other than the Amalekite and will never know the truth about how Saul died.

What might be the true story, given that the Amalekite bears Saul's crown and armlet? Accepting the narrator's version of events, it seems that this Amalekite came upon the dead king and removed his royal trappings before the Philistines reached his body the day after the battle (1 Sam 31:8). When the Philistines stripped Saul's body of his armor no mention was made of the symbols of kingship that would have undoubtedly caught their attention (1 Sam 31:9). The Amalekite got to the body first. Now it seems he wishes to win favor with the new strong man in the area by presenting Saul's crown to him. The irony in this scene is poignant: an Amalekite, a member of the very people by which Saul lost his kingdom, now presents the dead king's crown to his rival. Had Saul accomplished the divine edict against the Amalekites (1 Sam 15:3), God would have heard his plea when the Philistines attacked (1 Sam 28:5-6), and he would still be alive and an Amalekite would not be in possession of his crown.

David rips his clothes in mourning, and the narrator, by focusing on David's display of anguish (2 Sam 1:11), develops a theme central to the David Narrative: David remained loyal to Saul and thus was not complicit in his death (despite what Shimei will say in 16:5-8). This loyalty endures long after Saul's passing: one of David's final public acts will be to ensure that Saul's remains receive proper burial. For now, they rest under a tamarisk tree in Jabesh (1 Sam 31:13), and there they will stay for much of David's reign. But near the end of David's public life, he will transfer those remains to the tomb of Saul's father, Kish (2 Sam 21:13-14). Thus, even though David benefits from the elimination of his longtime pursuer, the narrator ensures we understand that David had nothing to do with his predecessor's death. And by means of his public mourning and other gestures and decrees still to come, David will do his best to gain the loyalty of the remnants of the Saulide court. He mourns not only for Saul and Jonathan but also for all those fallen in the battle from "the house of Israel." The presentation of David's commemoration of Saul is so important to the narrator that he flashes forward to later that same day (after the death of the Amalekite messenger still to come) to inform us of David's all-day fast so that we can appreciate the genuineness of his grief. Then the narrator returns us to the dialogue with the Amalekite.

David's order that the Amalekite messenger be executed may seem overly harsh to modern readers. But within the narrative several issues are at stake. First, David, by killing the Amalekite, fulfills the divine order that Saul failed to accomplish in 1 Samuel 15. Second, the Amalekite's response to Saul's dying request contrasts with that of Saul's armor-bearer (1 Sam 31:4). That foot soldier, implicitly recognizing Saul as the anointed of God, avoids complicity in his death and, in contrast to the Amalekite, joins his master's fate. Third, up to this point in the scene, Saul's name has been mentioned without its title. But once the Amalekite finishes his fabrication, David asks the loaded question: "Were you not afraid to raise your hand against the LORD's anointed?" "What anointed?" the Amalekite might have responded. But, for the reader, this title on David's lips hearkens back to two accounts in 1 Samuel in which David, invoking that very title, spared Saul's life. In the second account, when he prevents Abishai from killing Saul, he asks a rhetorical question: "Who can raise his hand against the LORD's anointed, and be guiltless?" (1 Sam 26:9). Certainly not this Amalekite! Thus, the keen reader is duly prepared for the penalty about to be exacted from this messenger. David's final words to the dead Amalekite, "your own mouth has testified against you, saying, 'I have killed the LORD's anointed'" (2 Sam 1:16), echo 1 Samuel 26:9, even though the Amalekite never articulated his actions in such terms.

Finally, David is concerned about the "bloodguilt" incurred by murdering the messenger. He declares that the guilt for shedding the Amalekite's blood falls on the Amalekite's own head (see section 2.7 below for a discussion of "bloodguilt") because David acted only to avenge Saul's death. The Amalekite who fell before David in obeisance now falls before him dead and the audience should be convinced that David was not in league with Saul's murderer. But not everyone is convinced. Shimei, a member of Saul's clan, will interpret David's flight from Absalom as a sign that God has brought the "blood of the house of Saul" on David's head (16:5-8). While he does not specifically mention Saul's death, his accusations, which come much later in the David Narrative, reveal that lingering questions about David's succession to Saul's throne remained.

2.4 David's Lament for Saul and Jonathan (1:17-27)

With Saul's crown in hand, David's first public act is to honor the memory of the dead king and his son. This public mourning ceremony should quash any speculation of David's involvement in his predecessor's demise. His particular attention to Jonathan (1:26) recalls the covenant between them and how Jonathan saved David's life.

STRUCTURE

Introduction to the poem (1:17-18)
A. Refrain: "How the mighty have fallen" (1:19)
  B. Let not the daughters of the Philistines rejoice (1:20)
    C. Direct address to the mountains—why they should mourn (1:21)
      D. Elegy for Jonathan and Saul (1:22-23)
        a. Blood and fat (1:22a)
          b. Jonathan and Saul (1:22b)
          b'. Saul and Jonathan (1:23a)
        a'. Eagles and lions (1:23b)
  B'. Let the daughters of Israel mourn (1:24)
A'. Refrain: "How the mighty have fallen" (1:25)
(Aside: direct address to Jonathan [1:26])
A''. Refrain: "How the mighty have fallen" (1:27)

The concentric elements of this poem include the refrain, the contrast between the gleeful Philistine daughters and the grief-stricken Israelite daughters, and the names of Saul and Jonathan at the center. The C element (with no counterpart) and David's personal aside to Jonathan knock the poem off balance, drawing our attention to them.

COMMENTARY

The narrator categorizes the poem that follows as a lament for Saul and for Jonathan his son. This lament, a *qînâ* in Hebrew, is quite different from the laments we read in the Psalter,[3] which normally include an address to God, a complaint, a plea, an expression of trust, and a vow to praise God. Because David's lament has only one of these elements, the complaint, it is closer in form to a modern funerary lament, namely, an elegy for the deceased, than to a lament psalm. David decrees that the people are to be taught this elegy, titled "The Bow," in commemoration of Saul and Jonathan and that it is to be chronicled in the Book of Jashar (this book, mentioned also in Josh 10:13, is lost).[4] The Hebrew reader hears the

---

[3] Laments in the Psalter are not referred to as *qînôt*.

[4] References to other royal chronicles often appear in the death notices of later kings, as in 1 Kings 14:19: "Now the rest of the acts of Jeroboam . . . are written in the Book of the Annals of the Kings of Israel."

import of the title Jashar, which means "upright" in English: the names of Saul and Jonathan are to be inscribed in the Book of the Upright. The action pauses so that we might attend to the words of David's lament (the narrator could have opted for just a brief summary of the scene).

The poem opens with an acknowledgment of the defeat by the Philistines: the bodies of slain warriors, the glory of Israel, lie on the high places. Further along in the lament, David will link the "glory of Israel" to Jonathan (2 Sam 1:25): "Jonathan lies slain upon your high places." This opening delays the word the Hebrew audience is listening for, namely, the traditional word that signals a funerary lament in Hebrew: *ʾêk*, which is the first word in the book of Lamentations (*ʾêkâ*). This primordial cry temporarily abandons language, which is so inadequate in such moments. Often translated "how" (as in "how could this have happened!"), *ʾêk* draws our attention to the events that have provoked David's lament—Israel's defeat and the loss of Saul and Jonathan.

The reference to "high places" in the first line of the poem looks back to 1 Samuel 31:1, 8: the Israelites, along with Saul and Jonathan, died on Mount Gilboa. But the phrase "high place" was not used in 1 Samuel 31 to refer to this mountain. This terminology recalls the opening scene of Saul's public life (1 Sam 9) in which Saul is sent to recover his father's lost donkeys. When he reaches the land of Zuph, the youth traveling with him suggests they consult a "man of God" (Samuel). Upon entering the town, they meet Samuel on his way to the "high place" (translated with "shrine" in the NRSV [1 Sam 9:14], but it is the same Hebrew word as in 2 Sam 1:19). Samuel abruptly summons Saul to join him at the "high place" where they will share a meal. After the meal, they descend from the high place to the town and the next morning Samuel anoints Saul king. Saul's kingship, inaugurated on a high place, comes to an end on a high place.

Having announced the occasion for this lament, David turns to the assembly: they should not speak of this victory in Philistine cities where the Philistine daughters will celebrate Israel's undoing. David knows how victorious warriors are welcomed home. When he returned from slaying Goliath, the daughters of Israel came out to meet him (and Saul) with singing and dancing (1 Sam 18:7). Now, in his grief, he imagines the Philistine daughters doing the same as their warriors return victorious to Gath and Ashkelon. He bids God to express divine displeasure at Israel's defeat: let no rain fall on the mountains of Gilboa where Saul died (1 Sam 31:8).[5] They too should be in mourning.[6] David has us visualize

---

[5] God can punish the land by withholding rain (see 2 Sam 21:1).

[6] The prophet Isaiah visualizes the land of Israel in mourning without rain:
   The land mourns and languishes;
     Lebanon is confounded and withers away;

Saul's shield lying on the ground, never to be oiled again. (The leather covering of a warrior's shield was kept supple with oil.[7])

At the center of the elegy comes the tribute to Saul and Jonathan. David celebrates their lives as warriors and recalls their military accomplishments (1 Sam 11–15). Immediately after his anointing by Samuel, Saul successfully defended the people of Jabesh-gilead against a threat from the Ammonites (1 Sam 11:11). He defeated the Amalekites as well (1 Sam 15:7), even though he failed to follow God's command to the letter. David memorializes Saul's mighty sword that now lies still. Jonathan too proved himself a fearless warrior when almost singlehandedly he defeated the Philistines (1 Sam 14:1-23a). He was agile with his bow, which he gave to David (1 Sam 18:4) when their alliance first began.

David commemorates these two fierce warriors with hyperbolic language: they were swifter than the swiftest raptors, more ferocious than ravenous lions. In life and in death they were not divided. Indeed, they died on the same mountain. But were they undivided in life? The fact is that Jonathan was allied with David and Saul knew it. When David failed to appear at Saul's table for the new moon festival, Jonathan promptly intervened to explain his absence. But his father rejected this phony alibi, reminding his son that, as long as David lived, his own succession to the throne was threatened. When Jonathan questioned further, his father flung his spear at him (1 Sam 20:30-34). Now both lie dead on the same mountaintop and David exploits this image to suggest that as they died so they lived, undivided. But David knows (and we know) that *he* was the source of their division. The audience listening to the elegy does not know of David's alliance with Jonathan and it would hardly serve David's interests to reveal this now, as such information could raise questions about his role in Saul's death. David bids the daughters of Israel, who should be dashing out to greet the victorious Saul (1 Sam 18:7), to weep for their fallen leader as they look upon their crimson garments with gold ornaments that commemorate the prosperity of Saul's reign.[8] The lament seems to conclude in 2 Samuel 1:25 with the repetition of the opening line: "How the mighty have fallen."

Sharon is like a desert;
   and Bashan and Carmel shake off their leaves. (Isa 33:9)

[7] The prophet Isaiah, ordering Judah to prepare for battle, bids them to "oil the shield" (Isa 21:5).

[8] The ritual vestments for the priest Aaron are made from linen with gold and crimson thread (Exod 28:5), and a crimson cloth covers the table of the bread of the Presence (Num 4:8). Those who dwell in the house of the wise woman are clothed in scarlet and linen (Prov 31:21).

But the lament is not over. David steps out of his role as the chief public mourner for a king and a crown prince to speak in the first person. This is the point in a modern eulogy when the speaker shifts from speaking about the deceased to speaking directly to the deceased, and the audience, in hushed silence, eavesdrops on the final words between the mourner and the beloved departed. David, now more friend than king, arrests our attention with his intimate thoughts on the passing of Jonathan. He confesses his emotional distress, calls Jonathan his brother (Saul is not mentioned), and grieves over how "beloved" (*n'm* is also used in reference to Saul in 1:23) he was to him. David declares that the love of Jonathan meant more to him than the love of a woman.[9] This exclamation continues the hyperbolic language (eagles, lions, undivided, and so forth) of this funerary lament as David compares his love for Jonathan with the superlative experiences of love in his life (with two, soon to be three, wives and numerous concubines). When Shakespeare compares his beloved "to a summer's day" (Sonnet 18, line 1), he too chooses a superlative image of beauty for the comparison and then claims that his beloved is "more lovely." Had David declared that he loved Jonathan more than a toothache, or had Shakespeare compared his beloved to an ordinary day, we would question the intensity of their affection. But David's extravagant comparison, consonant with the exaggerated language of this elegy, exposes the heights of his love and the depths of his grief. David's focus on Jonathan comes as no surprise. Had Jonathan not intervened to save his life, David would be dead and Jonathan would be singing a private lament for his fallen friend and ally.

After this brief personal aside David reenters his role as king and president of the public mourning ceremony and sings the refrain again. But this personal aside, which interrupted the structure of the poem, has allowed us a glimpse into David's heart. Another glimpse will come later when David cries out for his dead son Absalom (18:33 and 19:4). It is because of these unexpected moments of self-revelation and untainted honesty that David's character towers over everyone else in the story.

2.5 Two Kings in the Land (2:1–3:6)

Saul is dead and David possesses his crown, but will Saul's territory now accept David's kingship? No. David will return to his homeland but Abner, Saul's general, will ensure that Saul's son, Ishbaal, succeeds his

[9] The Hebrew poetry here is ambiguous. It can be interpreted as Jonathan's love for David or David's love for Jonathan.

father. The war that ensues between these two kings ends in a stalemate. David cannot defeat the remnants of the Saulide regime on the battlefield.

2.5.1 Two Kings (2:1-11)

2.5.1.1 DAVID MOVES BACK TO JUDAH (2:1-3)

With Saul dead, David prepares to abandon Ziklag, the Philistine city that King Achish gave him (1 Sam 27:5-6), and return to Judah. In this brief command-fulfillment scene, David inquires, God gives an order, and David executes that order faithfully.

STRUCTURE

Inquiry/response (2 Sam 2:1a)
Inquiry/response (2:1b)
Execution of the divine order (2:2-3)

COMMENTARY

The narrator signals a break in the story by means of the Hebrew expression *wayĕhî ʾaḥărê kēn*, translated weakly in the NRSV with "After this" but better in the NJPS with "Sometime afterward." David spent a year and four months in Ziklag (1 Sam 27:7), and this Hebrew expression marks the break between that period and what follows. Moreover, his status as a fugitive is over; he can now return to his homeland. But before relocating, he consults the Lord on whether he should return and then to which town he should go. The Hebrew root *ʿlh*, "to go up" or *hiphil*, "to bring up," repeated five times (perhaps tiresome to modern readers), discloses the narrator's interest: David consulted God and then obeyed the divine imperative to the letter. This brief scene also replays the contrast between the obedient David and the disobedient Saul (1 Sam 15:13-14). The last time Saul consulted God (1 Sam 28:6), no response was forthcoming. But when David consults God, the response is immediate. And David faithfully executes a divine order, unlike the disobedient Saul, whose failure to do so (1 Sam 15:26) lost him the crown that David now possesses.

God locates the seat of David's first government in Hebron, a city just over thirty kilometers (twenty miles) south of Jerusalem. The actual name is delayed since God's affirmative response to the first question leads to the second (the narrator could have simply reported that God

told David to go to Hebron). The delay raises the tension as we wait for
God to name the city where David will inaugurate his reign. Special mention is given to David's wives, Ahinoam and Abigail. Abigail, the wife of
the unfortunate Nabal, prevented David from shedding innocent blood
(1 Sam 25). He married her and Ahinoam of Jezreel at the same time
(1 Sam 25:42-43).[10] David had recently rescued them from the clutches
of the Amalekite raiders and had brought them safely back to Ziklag
(1 Sam 30:18). Noticeably absent from this list is David's first wife, Michal
(last mentioned in 1 Sam 25:44, just after the announcement of David's
marriage to Abigail and Ahinoam). At present she is married to Palti
son of Laish, but soon she will be back with David (2 Sam 3:14-16). So
David, obedient to the Lord, settles his family and his forces in Hebron,
a city about twenty kilometers (fourteen miles) south of Bethlehem, his
birthplace. He has returned to his homeland.

2.5.1.2 Two Kings but Only One Anointed (2:4-11)

David, fresh from his anointing as king by the people of Judah, is
informed that the inhabitants of Jabesh-gilead buried Saul. He immediately attempts to exert his authority over Saul's subjects, but as he does
so, Abner puts Ishbaal, Saul's son, on his father's throne. Now there are
two kings in the land.

STRUCTURE

1. The newly anointed King David seeks to extend his reign
    over Saul's dominion (2:4-7)
    A. David is anointed king over the house of Judah (2:4a)
        B. Saul is dead and buried (2:4b)
            C. The people of Jabesh-gilead were loyal to Saul (2:5)
                D. May God be loyal to them (2:6a)
            C'. David will be good to them (2:6b)
        B'. Saul is dead (2:7a)
    A'. David has been anointed king over the house of Judah (2:7b)

---

[10] Are Ahinoam of Jezreel and Ahinoam (known as the daughter of Ahimaaz),
Saul's wife (1 Sam 14:50), the same person? When Nathan confronts David after
Uriah's death, he reminds David that God transferred Saul's wives to him (2 Sam
12:8). If Ahinoam of Jezreel mentioned here is also Ahinoam daughter of Ahimaaz,
then David appropriated one of Saul's wives before the king died, as Levenson and
Halpern have argued. See Jon D. Levenson, "1 Samuel 25 as Literature and History,"
CBQ 40 (1978): 11–28; and Jon D. Levenson and Baruch Halpern, "The Political Import
of David's Marriages," *JBL* 99 (1980): 507–18.

2. Background information: The people of Jabesh-gilead already
   have a king (2:8-9)

3. A summary of the regnal years (2:10-11)
   A. Ishbaal reigned over Israel two years (2:10ab)
      B. But the house of Judah went after David (2:10c)
   A'. David reigned over Judah seven years and six months (2:11)

This episode is divided into three sections. In the first section, the
concentric structure places David's good wishes for the people of Jabesh-
gilead at the center (D element) and the inclusion (A/A' elements) repeats that David is king in Judah. The second section provides critical
background information that explains why the people of Jabesh-gilead
did not respond to David's overtures. The third section chronicles the
regnal years of David and Ishbaal.

COMMENTARY

*2.5.1.2.1 The Newly Anointed King David Seeks to Extend His Reign over
Saul's Dominion (2:4-7)*

The scene of David's anointing is reported so swiftly that its significance can be overlooked. Its language recalls David's first anointing—the
verb "anoint" in reference to a person has not been used since that scene.[11]
Then it was God who chose David and it was Samuel who poured the oil
(1 Sam 16:12-13). Until now, David's private anointing has received no
public acclamation. But that moment has arrived as the people of Judah
gather at Hebron and anoint him king. The divine plan that began in
1 Samuel 16 moves closer toward its realization.

David's first royal act is to receive messengers who provide him
with information that we already know: the inhabitants of Jabesh-gilead
provided Saul with proper burial (1 Sam 31:11-13). The Philistines had
fastened Saul's body to the walls of Beth-shan in an act of public igno-
miny. But *all* the valiant men of Jabesh-gilead traveled *all night* to retrieve
his body (and the bodies of his sons). After the burial, they fasted seven
days, a further expression of fidelity to their fallen king. Saul had rescued
them from Nahash the Ammonite (1 Sam 11), who had threatened to
gouge out the right eye of each inhabitant. While David is unaware of
the extent of their public grief (but we know about it), he must realize

---

[11] This verb appears in 2 Samuel 1:21 where it refers to Saul "anointing" his shield.

that their reverence for Saul's remains means that they could look for his successor among Saul's surviving sons. Without delay he sends envoys, hoping to extend his reign over Saul's subjects who, David thinks, are bereft of a leader. But Abner, Saul's commander, has taken matters into his own hands.

When the heralds reach the residents of Jabesh-gilead, they announce that David has invoked a blessing upon them: may God recompense the people of Jabesh-gilead for their fidelity to Saul who was their "lord." (Is he avoiding the more obvious title, *king*, for Saul?[12]) Then the messengers submit two conclusions on the basis of these good wishes. First, they beg that God might be loyal (Hebrew *ḥesed* is translated with "steadfast love" in the NRSV when it refers to God's *ḥesed*) to the people of Jabesh-gilead and, second, that they might be valiant warriors even though their leader is dead. The second half of both conclusions is introduced with the Hebrew expression *wĕgam*, a particle that underscores the first-person pronoun that follows it.

> Now then may the LORD be faithful and true with you, *and I too* will do what is good with you because you have done this.
> Let your hands be strong and be warriors, for your lord Saul is dead, *but [wĕgam] me* the House of Judah has anointed as king over them. (2 Sam 2:6-7; translation mine)

The Hebrew text focuses the attention of the addressees, the people of Jabesh-gilead, on the sender, David. The new king, promising to be "good" to them because of their fidelity to Saul, wants to gain legitimacy in their eyes as Saul's rightful successor. But, just in case they fail to grasp his point, he includes a veiled threat: he reminds them that they are without a leader and that he enjoys Judah's backing. They should accept him as their king. For the moment, the narrator passes over their response (they must have had some reaction to these messengers). Were they ready to negotiate with David? Later, when Abner seeks to convince the elders of Israel to accept David's kingship, he reminds them that "for some time" they had wanted David as their king (3:17). His affirmation suggests that the inhabitants of Jabesh-gilead would have accepted David's proposal. But they were not able to because Abner had already seated Ishbaal on Saul's throne (the next scene).

---

[12] When all the people of Israel come to anoint David as their king, they refer to Saul as their previous king (2 Sam 5:2).

2.5.1.2.2 Background Information: The People of Jabesh-gilead Already Have a King (2:8-9)

We await a response from the people of Jabesh-gilead to David's overtures. Instead, the scene shifts abruptly by exploiting one of the most powerful devices in the grammar of Hebrew narrative. As discussed in the introduction (see "The Art of Hebrew Narrative," section 1.4.1), in Hebrew, the progression of events in a story is signaled by the verb in the initial position of the sentence (the *wayyiqtol* form) whereas a noun in the initial position, as in 2 Samuel 2:8, signals a break in the progression of events (captured by the NRSV with: "But Abner son of Ner, commander of Saul's army, had taken"). By means of this pause, the narrator intervenes to provide us with critical background information: the coronation of Saul's son Ishbaal occurred sometime before David's messengers arrived. David's "good wishes" were, in fact, a waste of time. For the reader, this development suffices as a response (David does not know yet about Ishbaal's ascension) since it answers the real reason for David's missives to the people of Jabesh-gilead: David's intention to extend his dominion over Saul's territory. For the moment, his plans will have to be put on hold.

This is Abner's first appearance since David confronted him for his failure to protect King Saul (1 Sam 26:13-16). The narrator reintroduces him with his full title "son of Ner, commander of Saul's army." Mentioned for the first time in 1 Samuel 14:50, Abner, a cousin to Saul, sat beside the king at festival meals (1 Sam 20:25) and slept beside him during military campaigns (1 Sam 26:5). Given the vulnerability of a sleeping king, we recognize that Saul trusted Abner with his life. It is hardly surprising that Abner, a leading member of Saul's court, would have little interest in David's kingship. Thus, he takes one of Saul's sons, Ishbaal,[13] and declares him king. The narrator subtly contrasts the two coronations: Abner *took* Ishbaal and *made* him king (2 Sam 2:9), whereas the people of Judah *anointed* David king (2:4 and 2:7). David is acclaimed by the people, Ishbaal by Abner. King Ishbaal is a mere pawn that Abner takes and uses to preserve his power in Saul's realm. When King Ishbaal attempts to exercise his authority, the general will remind him that he

---

[13] Ishbaal's name in the Hebrew text is Ishboshet (meaning "shameful person"), which reflects the preference of some Hebrew copyists, who preferred to avoid the mention of the god Baal in the name Ishbaal. The name Ishbaal, which appears in one Greek (Lucianic) ms, is thought to be the original reading (see P. Kyle McCarter, *II Samuel*, Anchor Bible 9 [Garden City, NY: Doubleday, 1984], 82) and therefore it is adopted in most English translations. Esh-baal is mentioned as one of Saul's sons in 1 Chronicles 8:33, though he has not been mentioned as one of Saul's sons up to this point in 1 and 2 Samuel.

keeps him on the throne (3:8). David too will have to contend with the power of his own general, Joab, during his reign.

The place names in this passage do not require a lengthy geography lesson. David's territory, Judah, is the region south of Jerusalem, while Abner and his king, Ishbaal, control the areas north of Jerusalem. Mahanaim is about seventy kilometers (forty-four miles) northeast of Jerusalem, on the other side of the Jordan River. Ephraim and Benjamin are territories northeast of Jerusalem while Jezreel is about ninety kilometers (fifty-six miles) to the north. The narrator summarizes the list of Ishbaal's territories with the notice that he ruled over "all Israel," a reference to Saul's dominion north of Jerusalem. This territory will eventually come under David's sway when the elders of Israel anoint him as king over Israel (5:3).

2.5.1.2.3 A Summary of the Regnal Years (2:10-11)

For the next two years there will be rival kings in the land. The narrator introduces a formulaic summary of the regnal years for both Ishbaal and David. In 1 and 2 Kings such summaries normally appear at the beginning of a king's reign (as here), and they can include the king's age at the time of his ascension, his territory, and the duration of his reign (see, for example, 1 Kgs 14:21 or 2 Kgs 15:1-2). Other information, such as the king's mother's name, can be reported as well. After the summary of Ishbaal's regnal years, the narrator offers a qualification that reveals his partiality to David: "but the house of Judah went after David." The summary of David's reign is limited to his time in Hebron as the narrator quietly anticipates Davidic rule in Jerusalem. After David is anointed king over "all Israel" (2 Sam 5:3), a second summary of his regnal years will include his Jerusalem reign (5:5). The last formulaic summary of David's reign appears in 1 Kings 2:11, after his death. These formulas divide his rule into three periods: 1 Samuel 16–2 Samuel 2:11, from his anointing by Samuel to his becoming king over Judah; 2 Samuel 2:12–5:5, his reign in Hebron; and 2 Samuel 5:6–1 Kings 2:11, his reign in Jerusalem.

2.5.2 Rival Kings at War (2:12-32)

This episode, comprising three battle scenes, reveals that the armies of Joab and Abner are evenly matched. And even though between the first and second scenes our overly enthusiastic narrator reports that Abner's men were defeated by David's men (2:17), it is Asahel, one of David's key military commanders, who dies in the second scene. After the final battle, despite the higher casualty count on Abner's side (2:30-31), neither side has attained a decisive victory, and Ishbaal remains on his father's throne. If David is to win over Saul's territory, it will not be on the battlefield. The three battles take place over a twenty-four-hour period. The first battle begins when the combatants set out, Abner from Mahanaim (2:12) and Joab, presumably, from Hebron (2:13). The third battle concludes when Abner returns to Mahanaim (2:29) and Joab reaches Hebron (2:32) at dawn the next morning.

STRUCTURE

A. The first engagement: no decisive victory (2:12-16)
  B. The second engagement: Abner kills Asahel (2:17-23)
A'. The third engagement: no decisive victory (2:24-32)

2.5.2.1 THE FIRST ENGAGEMENT (2:12-16)

STRUCTURE

A. Abner comes (2:12)
  B. Joab comes (2:13a)
    C. Both together (2:13b)
A'. Abner speaks (2:14a)
  B'. Joab speaks (2:14b)
    C'. Both together (2:15a)
A". Benjamin (2:15b)
  B". Judah (2:15c)
    C". Both together (2:16a)
Epilogue (2:16b)

The structure of the passage reflects its content: both armies are perfectly balanced in strength.

COMMENTARY

The narrator focuses our attention on the simultaneity of the troop movements (*wayyiqtol* + *wĕ X qātal*). The parity of the two forces is complemented by their military positions. Facing each other across the pool of Gibeon (about eight kilometers [five miles] northwest of Jerusalem), neither side has a strategic advantage. Abner and Joab negotiate for a limited number of troops to engage in combat, a procedure similar to how David engaged the champion Goliath, who challenged the Israelite army to produce a soldier who could oppose him (1 Sam 17:8-9). When David routed the Philistines' prize fighter, the rest of the Philistine army ran away. Thus, when Joab accepts Abner's challenge, we can assume that both leaders will choose their twelve best fighters in the hope that this limited contest will determine the outcome. But when it is over, twenty-four corpses lie on the battlefield. To describe the result as a draw would be an understatement. Both sides are perfectly matched and, with no apparent victor in this first round, the battle continues.

In this scene Joab makes his first appearance in 2 Samuel. He was mentioned in passing in 1 Samuel 26:6, probably in anticipation of his future role in the David Narrative. He is the son of Zeruiah, who, on the basis of 1 Chronicles 2:16, is David's sister. Joab, together with his two brothers Abishai and Asahel, form the core of David's military company. Though the narrator gives him no introduction, he will have a critical role to play in David's court. (See the discussion of Joab's character in section 1.4.3 above.)

The narrator pauses the action at the end of the scene to interject that, because of this battle, the place acquired the name Helkath-hazzurim. This formulaic notation occurs elsewhere in the Bible. Sometimes a character provides the name: Abraham names the place where he bound Isaac "The LORD will provide" (in Hebrew *YHWH yirʾeh*, Gen 22:14), and Jacob, after he wrestles with God, names that place Peniel (Gen 32:30), which means "face of God." In other instances, the narrator introduces the name. When the wandering Israelites spy out the land of Canaan, they return with a single cluster of grapes between two poles. The narrator then interjects that the name of the place was Wadi Eshcol (Num 13:24), which means the "Wadi of the Cluster of Grapes." Such interjections hint at the historicity of the event, as if the narrator implies that the reader can visit the site where that first cluster of grapes was picked. In the case of Wadi Eshcol, the meaning of the place name is related to the events that the narrator has just recounted. But in 2 Samuel 2:16 the precise meaning of *hazzurim* is obscure (the first word, *Helkath*, is clear: "field of"), and the ancient versions and modern scholars offer numerous solutions: "Field of Flints," referring to the flint tipped weapons in the hands of the combatants; "Field of the Enemies" (reading *haṣṣārîm*); and "Field of the Sides" (each combatant killed his opponent by thrusting the sword into his side).[14] All three solutions want to relate the place name to the battle scene.[15]

---

[14] See Samuel R. Driver, *Notes on the Hebrew Text and the Topography of the Books of Samuel* (Oxford: Clarendon, 1913), 242–43; McCarter, *II Samuel*, 96; Hans W. Hertzberg, *I and II Samuel*, trans. J. S. Bowden (Philadelphia: Westminster Press, 1960), 251–52; and Henry P. Smith, *A Critical and Exegetical Commentary on the Books of Samuel*, The International Critical Commentary (Edinburgh: T & T Clark, 1899), 271.

[15] See P. J. van Dyk, "The Function of So-Called Etiological Elements in Narrative," *ZAW* 102 (1990): 19–33.

2.5.2.2 War Update: Abner Is Losing to David's Forces (2:17)

The narrator reports that the battle was terribly fierce, something to be expected when two armies are evenly matched. But now David's men gain the upper hand. The NRSV translation leaves the impression that the battle is over ("Abner and the men of Israel were beaten [*ngp*] by the servants of David"). Is the narrator so partial to David that he anticipates his victory? Probably not, since the third scene (2:24-32) ends not in a victory but in a truce, though Abner's forces suffer more casualties. Perhaps the verb *ngp* [the NRSV's "were beaten"] in this context does not mean that Abner was defeated but that, as the battle progressed, Abner and his men were losing. This would explain why, as the next scene opens, Abner is on the run with Asahel in close pursuit. But at the end of that scene, David's men have lost their advantage as Abner has killed Asahel, one of their best warriors.

2.5.2.3 The Second Engagement: The Death of Asahel (2:18-23)

STRUCTURE

   A. Introduction: Asahel is swift (2:18)
      B. Asahel pursues Abner (2:19)
         C. A private dialogue between Abner and Asahel
            a. Abner questions (2:20a)
               b. Asahel answers (2:20b)
            a'. Abner warns (2:21a)
               b'. Asahel ignores (2:21b)
            a". Abner warns again (2:22)
               b". Asahel ignores again (2:23a)
      B'. Abner kills Asahel (2:23b)
   A'. Conclusion: All stood still (2:23c)

The scene opens with a remark from the narrator that Asahel is an able runner. When it ends, not only does the speedy Asahel lie still, but all the troops who come upon his corpse stand still too. At the center of this passage is a private dialogue between Asahel and Abner in which we learn that Abner tried to avoid killing Asahel.

COMMENTARY

The three sons of Zeruiah are named as combatants. We have already met Joab (see 2:13). Abishai joined David in a clandestine visit to Saul's camp and would have killed Saul but for David's injunction (1 Sam

26:8-9). The third son, Asahel, is introduced for the first time, and the narrator focuses on a particular trait of this new character that serves the plot: Asahel is as fast as a gazelle. Thus, as the action begins, we are certain that Asahel will soon overtake Abner. His tenacity in pursuing Abner is underscored by the Hebrew expression that he turned "neither to the right nor to the left." In Deuteronomy this phrase denotes Israel's determination to obey God's commandments (Deut 5:32; 17:29; and 28:14). So Asahel, fast as a gazelle, is fiercely determined to catch Abner.

Most of the scene is taken up with dialogue, which Abner initiates when he asks the identity of his pursuer. His question ("Is this you, Asahel?") suggests that he knows Asahel, a fact that is confirmed by the ensuing exchange. He begs him to give up his pursuit, borrowing the narrator's words in 2 Samuel 2:19: "Turn to your right or to your left." Abner recognizes that Asahel's determination and his gazelle-like speed mean that hand-to-hand combat is inevitable. Still, wanting to avoid a final showdown, he encourages Asahel to fight someone else ("take his spoil"). In a second exchange, Abner complements his previous order ("turn aside") with two more reasons: "Why should I kill you?" and "How could I raise my face to Joab, your brother?" The first reason suggests that while Abner knows he cannot outrun Asahel, he is certain of a victory in combat. The phrase "to strike to the ground" (meaning "to kill"; see 18:11) leaves no doubt as to what Abner fears he will have to do to Asahel. But Abner's threat has no effect. At the end of the first exchange, the narrator reports that Asahel was unwilling to break off his pursuit. But at the end of the second exchange, the narrator underscores Asahel's obstinacy with the Hebrew verb *mʾn*: "he refused."

Since the narrator could have limited the scene to Asahel's death at Abner's hands, what is the function of this lengthy dialogue at the center of this scene? Not once but twice Abner tries to convince Asahel to give up his pursuit. He even expresses his anguish at the thought of seeing Joab (his enemy) after he has killed Asahel. His words increase our empathy for him: we alone know he killed Asahel only as a last resort. Thus, when Joab murders Abner and the narrator recalls that he did so to avenge the death of his brother Asahel (3:27), we remember the extenuating circumstances around Asahel's death, that, in fact, it was Asahel's obstinacy that cost him his life (David and Joab are ignorant of these details). Abner's last question to Asahel—"How can I face Joab your brother?"—foreshadows his own death. When Abner faces Joab in a gateway at Hebron, that hour is his last (3:27). Asahel refuses to give up his pursuit. Just as Absalom's famous hair becomes the instrument of his defeat (14:26 and 18:9), so Asahel's speed leads to his downfall. The description of his death leaves the impression that Abner just stopped running and the tenacious Asahel ran into the butt of Abner's spear. He was traveling at such speed that the blunt end of the spear came out his back! This detail also implies that Abner's intention was not to kill Asahel, otherwise he would have used the sharp edge of the spear. Abner just wanted to knock the wind out of him. But even the blunt end was deadly for the swift-footed Asahel. Had Asahel heeded Abner's advice, he would still be alive.

When Asahel's fellow combatants reach his corpse they stand still. That detail brings the irony of the scene to the surface: the "swift gazelle" is now still, and those that see his corpse are as well. This gesture of halting at a leader's corpse will occur again when Joab kills Amasa and the troops "stand still" at his corpse until it is removed from the road and covered (20:12-13). The narrator assumes his audience understands the significance of this custom (is it out of respect for the fallen leader, shock at his defeat, or fear that the battle is lost?) and makes no comment. But Joab and Abishai, Asahel's brothers, do not observe it for the moment. They will return to bury their brother later (2:32). For now they pursue Abner, whom they consider Asahel's murderer, though it is not that simple.

2.5.2.4 THE THIRD ENGAGEMENT (2:24-32)

STRUCTURE

A. Inclusion (2:24a)
    a. The brothers continue the pursuit (Asahel's body is without burial)
    b. The sun sets
  B. Troops align for battle (2:24b-25)
    C. Abner calls to Joab and asks three questions (2:26)
    C'. Joab responds and sounds the trumpet (2:27-28)
  B'. Battle lines are withdrawn and battle losses are enumerated (2:29-31)
A'. Inclusion (2:32)
    a'. Joab buries Asahel's remains
    b'. The sun rises

As Joab and Abishai continue their pursuit of Abner, the sun is setting. When they arrive back in Hebron, "dawn breaks upon them." This inclusion situates the entire scene within the nocturnal arc. As the scene begins Asahel's corpse lies exposed to the elements. When it ends, that corpse has received proper burial. The dialogue, which stands at the center (as in the previous scene), results in a truce and an end to the conflict.

COMMENTARY

This scene is closely linked to the preceding one since Asahel's corpse lies unburied until after the final confrontation between the two warring sides. The thought of a dead body abandoned to the elements cannot be far from the minds of the audience, whether ancient or modern. Goliath's ultimate threat to David is that his body will be left as food for the birds of the air and the beasts of the field (1 Sam 17:44). The people of Jabesh-gilead go to great lengths to retrieve the unburied bodies of Saul and his sons from the walls of Beth-shan (1 Sam 31:11-13). William Faulkner captures the efforts that contemporary society extends to human remains in his *As I Lay Dying*, and, while Asahel's corpse does not receive the attention of Addie Bundren's, his corpse cannot be left out in the elements. Thus, as we head off with Joab and Abishai in pursuit of Abner, we await a final word on the disposition of Asahel's remains.

Our narrator shifts between camps to report each side's troop movements and their final casualty count. Abner enjoys the full support of the Benjaminites, the tribe to which he belongs (the tribe to which Saul also belonged). The wilderness of Gibeon locates the military campaign in the region just north of Jerusalem in what should be Ishbaal's territory. The locations of Ammah and Giah, mentioned only here in the Bible, are unknown. What is important is that Abner and his troops are on "the top of a hill" (2 Sam 2:25). Though he is fleeing, he now holds the higher ground. If Joab and Abishai are to continue their pursuit, they will have to scale that hill. Abner once again seizes the opportunity for diplomacy.

Abner shouts three questions down to Joab. The first two are rhetorical questions (a style of persuasion that seems to appeal to Abner), while the third, a real question, wants an answer. By means of the first two questions, Abner hopes to condition Joab's response to the third one. The first, exaggerated question—"Is the sword to keep devouring forever?"—requires a negative answer (at least we hope so). The second rhetorical question—"Do you not know that the end will be bitter?"—expects an affirmative response. But this question is a bit ambiguous: for whom will the end be bitter? Presumably, Abner is trying to persuade Joab that the conclusion of this conflict will be bitter for him, given what just happened to Asahel, his brother. The two questions constitute a preamble to the real question: "How long will it be before you order your people to turn from the pursuit of their kinsmen?" This is the issue at stake for Abner. Joab provides a somewhat complex response to this question. He starts out with an oath formula, "by the living God," followed by a past contrary-to-fact condition: "if you had not spoken, the people would have continued to pursue their kinsmen, not stopping until morning." Abner's rhetoric has met with success (would that he could have convinced Asahel so easily in the previous scene). Joab sounds the trumpet and the pursuit is called off. The narrator betrays his knowledge of events in the next chapter by adding that Joab's troops no longer pursued or went into battle with Abner's forces (2:28). A military solution is now off the table.

This scene, like the previous one, presents Abner in a positive light since his diplomacy resolves the conflict. But how did his rhetorical questions convince Joab to call off the battle? The truce leaves Ishbaal on his father's throne; Joab's aggression into Ishbaal's territory has failed. The key to Abner's persuasive rhetoric lies in "their kinsmen," the last words of his third question—literally, "How long before you say to the army to return from after *their kinsmen?*" These words occupy the same place in Joab's response—literally, "If you had not spoken, until morning the army would have pursued after *their kinsmen.*" This is the first time that the warring factions acknowledge each other as "kinsmen," and Abner's introduction of this term to describe David's troops convinces Joab that this combat between *kinsmen* should be suspended. (Abner acknowledged to us his kinship with Joab when he forecasted his regret over Asahel's death: "How then could I show my face to your brother Joab?" [2:22].) Soon Abner will unite his kinsmen with Joab's under Davidic rule (3:10).

We follow the adversaries' movements back to their respective capitals. Abner journeys through the night to Mahanaim where he once made Ishbaal king (2:8-9), and, at the same time, Joab backtracks to Asahel's corpse and then on to Bethlehem for its burial. As the curtain drops on this nocturnal scene Joab and his troops reach Hebron and are greeted by the morning light.

2.5.3 David's Offspring Born in Hebron (3:1-6)

A. War update: David's house becomes more powerful as Saul's house declines (3:1)
   B. David's offspring (3:2-5)
A'. War update: Abner is becoming more powerful (as Ishbaal declines) (3:6)

The report of David's offspring is framed by two updates on the war between the two rival kingdoms. The previous update (2:17) reported that Abner was losing. The battle that followed that update ended in a truce. Since we know from the previous scene that the two armies are not engaging each other for the moment (2:28), the term "war" in the

NRSV must refer to the tense standoff that continued between the house of Saul and the house of David. According to the update in this verse, David now has the upper hand over Saul's house. Still, his advantage is not so great that he orders Joab back onto the battlefield. If he is to extend his rule over Saul's territory, it will not be through military means.

The chronicle of David's reign normally distinguishes between his years in Hebron and his years in Jerusalem (see 5:5 and 1 Kgs 2:11), and the list of his offspring reflects this division (the list of his Jerusalem-born offspring appears in 2 Sam 5:14-16). The Hebron list, because the mothers are included (there is no mention of the mothers in the Jerusalem list), functions as a sort of hinge in the narrative. It looks backward to David's marriages to Abigail, the widow of Nabal (1 Sam 25), and to Ahinoam, and it looks forward as the narrator names the major players who will appear on stage: the rapist Amnon, the usurper Absalom, and Adonijah, who will claim his right to succeed his father. The narrator, who can add a proleptic remark at the birth of a child,[16] is silent as these three critically important characters are named. We learn why Absalom, after he murders his brother Amnon, will flee to Talmai, king of Geshur (2 Sam 13:37). Talmai is his grandfather. The other sons, Chileab, Shephatiah, and Ithream, are not mentioned again in the David Narrative.

The stalemate continues with a new detail: Abner is becoming ever more powerful in the Saulide court, and, by implication from the parallel with 3:1, Ishbaal's power is declining. But this observation is so understated as to be almost comical. Abner had put Ishbaal on his father's throne (2:8-9)! How much more power could he accrue in Ishbaal's court? Abner is about to exercise that power.

2.6 Abner Delivers Saul's Kingdom to David (3:7-27)

Abner, already recognized as a mediator in conflict resolution (2:26), now becomes an ambassador to the Davidic kingdom. Angered by Ishbaal's accusation that he had sexual relations with Saul's concubine, he convinces Saul's subjects to accept Davidic rule. David then hosts a state dinner for Abner and his delegation to announce their anticipated agreement. But before David can be crowned king over Saul's dominion, Joab murders David's new ally, potentially ruining the proposed treaty while leaving us worried that the war between the rival kingdoms will reignite.

---

[16] When Solomon is born, the narrator tells us that "the LORD loved him" (2 Sam 12:24).

STRUCTURE

A. Abner, the general, confronts King Ishbaal (3:7-11)
>   B. Abner sends messengers to David: Abner seeks a treaty
>   with David (3:12-16)
>   C. All Israel will come under Davidic rule (3:17-21)
A'. Joab, the general, confronts King David (3:22-26a)
>   B'. Joab sends messengers to Abner: Joab ruptures the treaty
>   (3:26b-27)

The center of this scene announces a dramatic turn of events: the people once ruled by Saul intend to accept David as their king. This center is framed by parallel scenes. In the A/A' scenes generals confront kings and then take charge of the situation. Both generals send messengers (B/B'): Abner sends messengers to David to initiate the process of Davidic rule over Saul's territory, and Joab sends messengers to Abner in order to kill him, disrupting that process. A parallel to the C section is delayed until 2 Samuel 5:3 when the elders of Israel come to anoint David as their king (see section 2.9.1 below). For now we wait to learn what will become of this new treaty, which is so critical for David's future kingdom.

2.6.1 Abner, the General, Confronts King Ishbaal (3:7-11)

Ishbaal tries to be king over Abner as the lights come up on this scene. But when the stage darkens, Abner has pushed the king off his throne.

STRUCTURE

A. Ishbaal demands an answer from Abner (3:7)
>   B. What Abner has done for Saul's house (3:8)
>   Judah
>   House of Saul
>   David
>   B'. What Abner is about to do for David (3:9-10)
>   David
>   House of Saul
>   Judah and Israel
A'. Ishbaal is powerless to answer Abner (3:11)

At the center of the scene Abner announces that his once-faithful service to the house of Saul is now transferred to David. He will accomplish what Joab could not do on the battlefield: Saul's kingdom is about to come under Davidic rule.

COMMENTARY

Ishbaal's pathetic attempt to exert his authority over Abner (had he forgotten who put him on the throne?) proves disastrous. The narrator told us that Abner was working to increase his power at court (3:6). If Ishbaal's accusation against Abner is true (sexual relations with Saul's concubine), now we know one of the ways he was increasing his power. Rizpah is named for the first time (see her role in 21:10); the Saul Cycle (1 Sam 9–31) does not mention any royal concubines.

The narrator brings us into the room just as Ishbaal launches his accusation: Abner has had sexual relations with Rizpah, his father's concubine. The charge is treason. When Adonijah, David's son and Solomon's older brother, solicits the queen mother, Bathsheba, to seek King Solomon's permission to take Abishag, his dead father's concubine (1 Kgs 1:1-4), as his wife, Solomon detects treason ("ask the kingdom for him") and orders Adonijah executed (1 Kgs 2:22-24).[17] Ishbaal perceives a similar threat in Abner's activities with Rizpah: he has tried to sire an heir through Saul's concubine that would replace Ishbaal's line with his own on the throne of Israel. Treason!

Abner's response leaves us in the dark as to exactly what happened between himself and the dead king's concubine. He does not deny the charge outright. Instead, Abner, an expert at rhetorical questions (see 2 Sam 2:24-32), responds, "Am I a dog's head belonging to Judah?" The phrase "dog's head" does not occur elsewhere in the Bible. The "dog" metaphor normally is used to express self-deprecation. When Goliath spies the young David he asks, "Am I a dog, that you come to me with sticks?" (1 Sam 17:43). When Elisha speaks to King Hazael about the anguish the future king of Aram will bring upon Israel, Hazael denies it: "What is your servant, who is a mere dog, that he should do this great thing?" (2 Kgs 8:13). In both of these cases, the self-deprecating dog image appears in a rhetorical question, similar to Abner's question in this scene.[18] Thus, a liberal translation of Abner's question would be: "Do you think I am some kind of cur who has been collaborating with Judah?" To this rhetorical question Ishbaal is expected to respond no. But Abner's clever retort does not answer the accusation.

---

[17] When Absalom usurps his father's throne, he makes a public display of his sexual relations with his father's concubines (2 Sam 16:21-22).

[18] When David meets Shimei, who accuses him of usurping Saul's throne, Abishai, one of David's military commanders, ridicules Shimei as a "dead dog" (2 Sam 16:9).

Ishbaal, by charging Abner with treason, probably hoped to eliminate the one who set him on the throne, thus freeing himself from Abner's sway and securing his own lineage. But Abner quickly quashes that prospect by reminding Ishbaal that he has always been in charge and could have betrayed him at any time. He protests his loyalty to the house of Saul as he deflects the charge of treason by asking how Ishbaal dares make such an accusation. This too is not an answer to the king's charge. Did Abner try to sire a successor to Ishbaal's throne through Saul's concubine? We might suppose that Abner, having put Ishbaal on Saul's throne, would have been interested in naming his own son as Ishbaal's successor (or usurper). But the narrator, who could resolve the question in a word, remains silent.

When Abner abruptly switches sides, Ishbaal's strategy to eliminate Abner through a charge of treason backfires. Abner, recognizing the mortal threat of Ishbaal's accusation, shifts his allegiance to David. And to ratify his newfound loyalty, he brings an imprecation on himself (2 Sam 3:9). In some English renderings of this ancient formula, Abner's self-cursing is less than clear. The NRSV's literal translation, "So may God do to Abner and so may he add to it!" doesn't sound much like a curse to modern ears. The NJB paraphrase seems more appropriate: "May God bring unnameable ills on Abner, and worse ones, too." That's a curse! When Ishbaal hears Abner cursing himself before God, he has to recognize his general's determination: Abner is ready to put his life on the line for David.

In his brief speech, Abner refers to what God *swore* to David: "to transfer the kingdom from the house of Saul, and set up the throne of David over Israel and over Judah, from Dan to Beer-sheba" (3:10).[19] He is developing the theme begun in 1 Samuel 16. God chose David (1 Sam 16:12) as king and later even Saul recognized this divine decision: "Now I know that you shall surely be king, and that the kingdom of Israel shall be established in your hand" (1 Sam 24:20). Abigail of Carmel blocked David from harming her husband Nabal by reminding David of God's promise to him: "When the LORD has done to my lord according to all the good that he has spoken concerning you, and has appointed you prince over Israel" (1 Sam 25:30). Abner now announces that God *swore* to David that he would rule over Judah and Israel. He even charts the borders of David's future realm: from Dan to Beer-sheba. Later, the Israelites, who were once loyal to Ishbaal and Abner, will also acknowledge this divine promise to David (2 Sam 5:2).

---

[19] That God swore an oath to David, which in the David Narrative is mentioned explicitly only here, also appears in Psalms 89:49 and 132:11, though the content of God's oath in Psalm 132:11 is different from the oath that Abner knows.

Abner's speech provides Ishbaal with proof of treason beyond those innuendos about sex with Saul's concubine Rizpah. We could expect the king to order the traitor's immediate execution. Instead, poor Ishbaal, paralyzed by fear, is silent. Without Abner, not only has he no authority but his life may be at risk as well. Can there be two kings in the land? That question will be resolved in 2 Samuel 4. The puppet king walked into this scene hoping to extend his power over Abner. As he exits, he is about to lose his crown.

2.6.2 *Abner Sends Messengers to David: Abner Seeks a Treaty with David (3:12-16)*

STRUCTURE

A. Abner sends messengers to David to request an alliance (3:12)
   B. David responds and demands Michal (3:13)
A'. David sends messengers to Ishbaal and demands Michal (3:14)
   B'. Ishbaal sends the order, but Abner executes it (3:15-16)

COMMENTARY

Abner acts independently of the now-irrelevant Ishbaal. (Did Ishbaal ever have any authority in Saul's court?) He orders his messengers to David's court, who, relating Abner's words, begin, as expected, with a rhetorical question: "To whom does the land belong?" The unexpressed answer is "to David." With that question settled, Abner's appeal, "Make your covenant with me," indicates that he is seeking terms for an alliance in which he will become a vassal to David. And for his part, he guarantees that "all Israel" will come over to David.

David accepts the proposal immediately. "Good!" he declares, but he appends a restriction: he wants Michal, his first wife, restored to him. We may have forgotten about her, but David has not. Saul had used his daughters to try to eliminate David. He betrothed his eldest, Merab, to him as a prize for fighting the Philistines but then reneged and Merab was married off to Adriel the Meholathite (1 Sam 18:17-19). Michal, his younger daughter, loved David (1 Sam 18:20), and when Saul learned of it, he tried again to rid himself of David through a contest with the Philistines. But David returned victorious and so Michal became his wife. Later she helped David escape from her father's murderous designs and was accused of treason for it (1 Sam 19:11-17). That scene ended abruptly with her quick-thinking deception: "He [David] said to me, 'Let me go; why should I kill you?'" She is not mentioned again until, in a passing comment after David's marriage to Abigail, the narrator informs us that Michal had been given to Palti as his wife (1 Sam 25:44; in 2 Sam 3:15 Michal's husband's name is spelled Paltiel). Thus, a second time Saul reneged on his marriage agreements with David. Back then, David the fugitive could hardly have demanded his wife. But now he has the power to settle that old score and, given that Abner seeks a treaty, he does so.

David expresses no affection for Michal. She is the wife that he acquired "at a price," as the NRSV aptly puts it, and she is rightfully his as part of a deal that Saul breached. Later when David will transfer the ark of the Lord to Jerusalem, Michal, "daughter of Saul," will spy her husband dancing (2 Sam 6:16) and despise him (by then her affections for him have diminished). She probably realizes that her restitution to David in this scene expresses the new king's political eclipse of Saul, her father, which the transfer of the ark of the Lord to David's city later solidifies. Her return to court also strengthens David's legitimacy as Saul's successor. Thus, we should not expect the narrator to present on stage the tender reunion of husband and wife after years of separation. David's demand for Michal's swift return was driven not by his affection for her but by his desire to signal to his court that he has supplanted her father's house. And she knows it.

The scene then shifts abruptly to David's messengers at Ishbaal's court. David reminds Ishbaal of the agreement he had with Saul: he acquired Michal for one hundred Philistine foreskins. Ishbaal is powerless to do anything but execute David's request. He orders that Michal be taken from her present husband. Does Ishbaal know that, by providing Michal, he is helping Abner gain an audience with David? If he does, he has to recognize that his kingship is over.

Paltiel, Michal's current husband, follows behind his wife weeping. His affection for Michal contrasts with David's dispassionate demand for the restoration of his asset. Paltiel seems to have really loved her. We can only speculate on whether Michal returned Paltiel's affection (she is not said to be weeping). The scene closes with a surprise appearance by Abner. Whether or not Ishbaal sent Abner to fetch Michal is not explicit in the text (3:15). But it is clear that Abner went to secure his ticket into David's court. When they reach Bahurim, Abner orders the weeping husband back home. Bahurim is a Benjaminite village (19:16) north of the Mount of Olives and, given its proximity to Jerusalem, the last thing Abner needs is a weepy husband trailing after him as he crosses into David's territory. With Michal in hand, Abner is ready to negotiate with his new liege.

2.6.3 All Israel Will Come under Davidic Rule (3:17-21)

STRUCTURE

A. Abner persuades Israel and Benjamin to accept David as their
   king (3:17)
   B. The covenant with David: God will save Israel through
      David (3:18)
      C. Abner informs David in Hebron that all (*kol*) Israel and
         all (*kol*) Benjamin are with him (3:19)
      C'. Abner comes to David in Hebron, who ratifies their
          agreement with a banquet (3:20)
   B'. Abner will muster his people to enter into a covenant
       with David (3:21a)
A'. Abner tells David that all (*kol*) Israel will accept David as *king*
    (3:21b)

COMMENTARY

In preparation for his audience with David, Abner moves to secure
the support of the leaders of the region once governed by Saul (areas
north of Jerusalem). King Ishbaal is entirely sidelined. Abner addresses
the elders of Israel, reminding them of their aspirations: "For some time
past you have been seeking David as king over you." But when did the
remnants of Saul's house express their desire to have David as their
king? Abner's premise suggests that, immediately after Saul's death,
the people of Jabesh-gilead would have responded favorably to David's
envoys and accepted him as their king (2:5-7). But their response was
obviated when Abner seated Ishbaal on Saul's throne (2:8).

Abner, quoting God, introduces a key tenet of Davidic theology—
David is God's servant[20]—and he summarizes God's design for David:
God has promised *to save the people of Israel* from the Philistines and all
their enemies through David. (The narrator does not disclose whence
Abner acquired this Davidic theology.) The reader is already acquainted
with David's victories over the Philistines. Soon after his private anointing as king, he killed Goliath and put the Philistines to flight (1 Sam 17).
When he inquired about retaking Keilah (1 Sam 23:2), a town of Judah
about thirteen kilometers (eight miles) northwest of Hebron, he asked
God, "Shall I go and attack these Philistines?" God answered, "Go and
attack the Philistines and *save* Keilah." So with God's help, David *saved*

---

[20] This title for David will appear regularly in 2 Samuel and 1–2 Kings (see 2 Sam
7:5, 8; 1 Kgs 11:32, 34, 36, 38; 14:8; 2 Kgs 19:34; and 20:6; see also Ps 89:3, 20).

the people of Judah who lived in Keilah from the Philistines. (The same Hebrew verb, *yšʿ*, appears in 1 Sam 23:2 and in 2 Sam 3:18.) Now Abner encourages the elders of Israel to accept David as their king because it is God's plan to save them from their enemies, especially the Philistines, through him.

The Benjaminites, Saul's tribe (1 Sam 9:1-2), were probably most interested in seeing the Saulide line continue. So Abner, a Benjaminite himself and Saul's cousin (1 Sam 14:50-51), gives them an exclusive colloquy. Will they continue to support Ishbaal? Abner had depended on their support in the battle with Joab and Abishai (2 Sam 2:25). The narrator omits the Benjaminites' response to Abner, leaving the impression that they (like the elders of Israel) accepted David with no debate. But this seems unlikely. Later Absalom will garner support for his rebellion from among the tribes of Israel (15:1-12) and Shimei, a Benjaminite, will charge David with murdering members of Saul's clan (16:5-13). Moreover, the union between Israel and Judah will be short-lived, collapsing after the death of Solomon (1 Kgs 12:16), and traces of their enmity will persist under Davidic rule (see the discussion on the unification of Israel and Judah in section 2.9 below). But for the moment the strongman Abner is able to bring Israel into David's camp.

The scene shifts to David's court. Abner arrives in Hebron with a delegation of twenty people and David hosts a banquet to ratify the new alliance. When the meal is over, Abner informs David that he is prepared to keep his side of the bargain (Michal's return happens off stage). King David is now Abner's sovereign and when he dismisses his new subject in peace, he signals to his court that all hostilities have ceased. Everything is in place for David to assume the governance of Saul's territory. We expect that the next scene will present David's coronation by the elders of Israel and the Benjaminites. But those festivities are about to be delayed. Enter Joab.

2.6.4 Joab, the General, Confronts King David (3:22-26a)

STRUCTURE

A. Joab arrives (3:22a)
   B. Abner has left in peace (3:22b)
      C. Joab is informed that Abner has left in peace (3:23)
   B'. Joab questions David as to why he let Abner leave
      (3:24-25)
A'. Joab leaves (3:26a)

This scene, framed by Joab's arrival and departure, has at its center the message that David dismissed Abner "in peace." This information moves Joab to kill Abner.

COMMENTARY

By means of the Hebrew expression *wĕhinnēh* (3:22), appropriately translated in the NRSV with "just then" (the KJV employs the traditional phrase "and behold"), the narrator brings Joab on stage just as Abner exits. Had the two met in David's presence, it seems likely that the king would have intervened to save his new ally from Joab's sword. I am reminded of Balthasar's haste that brought the news of Juliet's supposed death to Romeo before the arrival of Friar Lawrence's missive, an unforeseen mischance summed up by the friar's cry: "Ah, what an unkind hour is guilty of this lamentable chance" (act 5, sc. 3, lines 145–46). And so Romeo and Juliet die. In the same way, *wĕhinnēh*, "just then," underscores this unkind hour in which Abner just misses Joab's arrival. And so Abner dies.

Joab enters carrying the bountiful plunder of his successful raids—he is a gifted warrior. Informed that Abner visited David and was dismissed *in peace*, he realizes that an alliance has been formed between the king and Saul's chief military officer. Given that Joab's last contact with Abner was in combat, he must be surprised by this development. His enemy and his king have entered into a pact in which he had no voice. What will be his rank in this new configuration of David's court? Will he be under Abner's command? When he confronts David, he puts a different spin on Abner's departure (translated literally):

The narrator: David sent Abner away and he went *in peace*. (3:22)
The messengers: The king sent Abner away and he went *in peace*. (3:23)
Joab: Why did you [David] dismiss him and he *went off*? (3:24)

The messenger's report agrees with that of the narrator: Abner left in peace. But Joab sees Abner's departure as an escape from justice (thus, the NRSV translation, "so that he got away"). According to Joab, the real purpose of Abner's expedition was espionage. The king is beguiled! And Joab knows how easy it is to con David. Later on he will employ a phony widow who will successfully dupe the king (14:2). But we know Abner's mind—his motives are sincere. So why didn't David explain to Joab the advantages of the alliance with Abner? It seems that Joab would not wait for an answer, and David did not have the power to order him to stay and listen.

David's relationship with his general, Joab, resembles Ishbaal's relationship with Abner. When Joab demands an explanation from the king—"What have you done?" (3:24)—we can be sure that they are not in a traditional vassal-liege relationship. Joab has a power base (perhaps in that army that accompanies him [3:23]), and, as we shall see, he can thwart the king's direct order (see 18:5, 14). David, at the end of this episode (3:39), acknowledges he is powerless before Joab (though perhaps he is exaggerating Joab's power to guard his own innocence in Abner's death). Before David dies, he warns Solomon about the threat Joab poses (1 Kgs 2:5-6), and he encourages his son to get rid of him. But why didn't David do this himself instead of handing it off to his son on his deathbed? Events in this episode suggest that he might have if he had had the power. Joab, who looks after his own best interests, may be beyond David's reach. We should be worried about Joab's next move.

2.6.5 Joab Sends Messengers to Abner: Joab Ruptures the Treaty (3:26b-27)

STRUCTURE

A. Joab sends messengers after Abner (3:26b)
  B. Abner is "brought back" (*šwb*) (3:26c)
    C. David knows nothing of this event (3:26d)
  B'. Abner's return (*šwb*) (3:27a)
A'. Joab pretends to deliver a message to Abner (3:27bc)
The narrator's aside (3:27d): Abner died for shedding the blood of Asahel, Joab's brother.

The scene opens as Joab departs the king's presence ready to act against Abner and closes when he accomplishes his plan. At the center of this scene the narrator provides critical background information: David was ignorant of Joab's plans. The center is framed by the repetition of the Hebrew root *šwb* (the first time in *hiphil*, "to bring back," and the second time in *qal*, "to return").

COMMENTARY

When Abner pleaded with his pursuer, Asahel, to desist, he asked rhetorically, "How then could I show my face to your brother Joab?" (2:22). The moment for Abner to show his face to Asahel's brother has now arrived. Abner, who had pleaded with Asahel to give up the chase, becomes the victim of Joab's vengeance. Had there been a short exchange between them (as there was between Abner and Asahel), Joab might have learned that his brother's death at Abner's hands came only as a last resort. Joab's swift assault on Abner contrasts with Abner's hesitation in killing Asahel. Our sympathies are with Abner.

Joab sends messengers to fetch Abner, who must have presumed that David had notified his general of their new alliance and so he returned of his own accord (Joab did not have to apprehend him). Pretending to impart a confidential communiqué, Joab maneuvers Abner away from the protection of his company and into the close confines of a gateway where he will have less chance of escape.[21] He stabs him in the stomach, the same place that the blunt end of Abner's spear pierced Asahel (2:23). The narrator concludes with a notation on Joab's motivation: his intention was to avenge his brother's blood (Num 35:19). But can this be the only reason that Joab wanted Abner dead?[22]

At the center of this otherwise fast-moving scene the narrator stops the action to insist that we grasp that David was ignorant of Joab's murderous intentions.[23] David gains nothing from the murder of Abner, who was on his way to rally Israel into the Davidic kingdom. Joab's interference could have derailed this fragile alliance and led to a resumption of hostilities with the remnants of Saul's house. It is Joab, not David, who benefits from Abner's elimination, since Abner threatens his position in David's court. Much later in the David Narrative, after David defeats Absalom (with Joab's help), he replaces Joab with Amasa, Absalom's commander (19:13). The appointment of the rebel general as his own commander is a shrewd political move designed to bring the insurgents back under Davidic governance. But Joab quickly murders his replacement (20:10) and returns to his position as commander in David's court (20:23). He defies the king with impunity. The appointment of Abner to

---

[21] For a description of an ancient gate (but a gate younger than the one in which Joab killed Abner), see James Fleming, "The Undiscovered Gate Beneath Jerusalem's Golden Gate," *BAR* 9, no. 1 (January/February 1983): 24–37. See also William G. Dever, "Monumental Architecture in Ancient Israel in the Period of the United Monarchy," in *Studies in the Period of David and Solomon and Other Essays*, ed. T. Ishida, 269–306 (Winona Lake, IN: Eisenbrauns, 1982).

[22] See the discussion of the "obtuse narrator" in section 1.4.2.

[23] When Solomon pronounces Joab's death sentence he reiterates that David knew nothing of Joab's plans against Abner (and Amasa): "The LORD will bring back his bloody deeds on his own head, because, without the knowledge of my father David, he attacked and killed with the sword two men more righteous and better than himself, Abner son of Ner, commander of the army of Israel, and Amasa son of Jether, commander of the army of Judah" (1 Kgs 2:32).

replace Joab would have had similar political advantages (solidifying David's authority over Saul's territory for David's nascent kingdom), but Joab denies David those benefits in a gateway at Hebron. Thus, even if David had intuited Joab's plot, he had no reason to want Abner out of the way at this particular moment, but, as he confesses at the end of this episode (3:39), he could not have stopped Joab either, just as he will be powerless to stop him from murdering Amasa (20:10).[24]

In his final discourse to Solomon, David collapses the murders of Abner and Amasa into a single charge against Joab:

> Moreover you know also what Joab son of Zeruiah did to me, how he dealt with the two commanders of the armies of Israel, Abner son of Ner, and Amasa son of Jether, whom he murdered, retaliating in time of peace for blood that had been shed in war, and putting the blood of war on the belt around his waist, and on the sandals on his feet. (1 Kgs 2:5)

While he accuses Joab of revenging in peacetime the blood shed on the battlefield, the fact is that Joab thwarted David's political maneuvers to secure his reign in times of acute instability. He assures his son Solomon that Joab is not protected by the laws of bloodguilt (discussed in the next section) and that he should go ahead and execute him (1 Kgs 2:31-33).

Will Ishbaal, who tried to eliminate Abner through a capital charge of treason (2 Sam 3:7), work Abner's murder by David's general to his advantage? Will he consult with the elders of Israel, appoint another general and reignite the war with David's kingdom? The future of David's reign hangs in the balance.

2.7 David Laments for Abner (3:28-39)

David needs to convince his new allies that he had nothing to do with Abner's murder, and all the elements in this scene serve that function.

STRUCTURE

A. David proclaims his innocence and curses Joab (3:28-30)
   B. David orders public mourning as he himself mourns (3:31-32)
      C. David's lament (3:33-34)

---

[24] For a different interpretation of David's role, see James C. VanderKam, "Davidic Complicity in the Deaths of Abner and Eshbaal: A Historical and Redactional Study," *JBL* 99 (1980): 521–39.

C'. The king refuses to eat (3:35)
B'. All the people recognize the authenticity of David's
    mourning (3:36-37)
A'. David reaffirms his innocence and reprises his curse against
    Joab (3:38-39)

The scene opens and closes with David affirming his innocence and bidding God to punish Joab. He orders his people to mourn and everyone, including "Israel," is convinced by his gestures (B/B' sections). The heart of the scene focuses on David's own public display of mourning: his lament and his refusal to eat.

COMMENTARY

We shift from the gateway in Hebron, where Abner lies dead, to David's formal announcement that he and his kingdom are innocent of Abner's blood. Only later do we learn that David is addressing Joab and "all the people" (3:31), including Israel (3:37). The king focuses on the bloodguilt (both individual and collective) that arises from this murder: who is responsible for Abner's death and, more important, who has the right to avenge that death? From Joab's point of view, Abner was murdered to avenge his brother Asahel's blood. David, with a solemn declaration, proclaims that he and his kingdom are innocent of Abner's blood, and he casts the guilt squarely on Joab and his house.[25] He wants to annul any claim that a blood avenger could have against him and his people, a tradition later codified in the book of Deuteronomy:

> But if someone at enmity with another lies in wait and attacks and takes the life of that person, and flees into one of these cities, then the elders of the killer's city shall send to have the culprit taken from there and handed over to the avenger of blood to be put to death. Show no pity; you shall purge the guilt of innocent blood from Israel, so that it may go well with you. (Deut 19:11-13)

But do the norms concerning bloodguilt apply to Joab? He was at enmity with Abner and lay in wait for him. But he does not flee because, in his mind, he did nothing wrong. Should David hand Joab over to the elders

---

[25] The responsibility for bloodguilt was an important question in the minds of the ancient audience. Thus, after the execution of the Amalekite, David declares himself innocent of his blood: "Your blood be on your head" (1:16), and Solomon declares himself innocent of Joab's blood and rejects any idea that Joab was protected by the bloodguilt laws when he murdered Abner (1 Kgs 2:33).

of Israel for punishment according to the rule of bloodguilt? Only at the end of this scene do we learn the answer to that question.[26]

For the moment, David's primary interest is to ensure that his alliance with Abner will continue to hold when the elders of Israel learn that their commander was murdered by David's general. He not only declares Joab guilty but also adjoins *five* curses on Joab's family: may Joab's house never be without

1. one who has a discharge
2. or who is leprous
3. or who holds a spindle
4. or who falls by the sword
5. or who lacks food

This quintuple malediction should convince his new allies that he was not in league with Joab. The introductory formula—literally, "may there not be cut off from"—appears in Joshua's curse against the Hivites: "Now then, you are cursed and may it not be cut off from you slaves, wood hewers, and water drawers" (Josh 9:23, translated literally). Joshua would doom the Hivites to the menial tasks of slaves. David's curse is far more severe. The first two elements, that those in Joab's house might have a discharge or be leprous, refer to states of disease that leave a person weak, ritually unclean, and unable to contribute to the welfare or warfare of the tribe. The third element, one "who holds a spindle," wishes that Joab's descendants not be sword-bearing soldiers but spindle-bearing weavers. A populace armed with spindles would be no threat to the crown.[27] The fourth curse wishes him defeat on the battlefield, and the fifth one augurs him starvation in his house. There will not be much left of Joab's house if David's curses befall it. Will this exaggerated imprecation keep the elders of Israel in David's camp?

The narrator interjects again his understanding that Joab *and Abishai* (who was not mentioned at the murder scene) murdered Abner for killing Asahel their brother in the battle at Gibeon. The different Hebrew verbs that characterize these deaths are reflected in the NRSV translation: Joab "murdered" (*hrg*) Abner whereas Abner "killed" (*mwt, hiphil*) Asahel. The verb *hrg* is used when Cain murders Abel (Gen 4:8), and, though it does not always refer to an unwarranted killing (see Lev 20:16), the narrator

---

[26] If the bloodguilt is not resolved, then God may intervene to exact vengeance as in 2 Samuel 21:1 when God brings a drought on David's kingdom for the blood of the Gibeonites that Saul shed.

[27] Steven W. Holloway, "Distaff, Crutch, or Chain Gang: The Curse of the House of Joab in 2 Sam iii 29," *VT* 37 (1987): 370–75.

here may be trying to persuade us that Abner's murder was without warrant. David, by cursing Joab, also rejects Joab's right to vengeance. But for the moment David does not need to engage in a debate over Joab's right to vengeance. He must distance himself from this murder in order to preserve his tenuous rule over Saul's territory. How will the elders of Israel and the Benjaminites, whom Abner convinced to support David (2 Sam 3:17-19), react?

David orders all the people, and *Joab* in particular, to mourn Abner's death (hardly what a blood avenger should do), a further indication that David rejects the blood vengeance justification for Abner's murder. Tearing clothes and putting on sackcloth suggest not only mourning but also penance: the king becomes chief mourner and penitent as he follows the bier and weeps at the grave.[28] Instead of returning Abner's remains to his native soil, Saul's territory, David has him buried in his capital city, Hebron. The king honors Abner and the alliance he made with him, hoping that the elders of Israel will keep their part of the bargain.

While the NRSV properly reports that the king "lamented" for Abner (3:33: *wayqōnēn*), what David sings is closer to an elegy than a biblical lament, similar to what he sang for Saul and Jonathan, though shorter (see the discussion of 1:17-18 in section 2.4 above). He begins with a rhetorical question (translated literally): "Like the death of a fool should Abner die?" The question recalls *how* Abner died. He returned to Hebron and went with Joab into the restricted space of the gateway without coercion (3:34: his hands and feet were not bound or fettered). Was he a fool to trust Joab in such a space? No, David insists; his assailant was wicked, a further condemnation of Joab. David fasts until sunset just as he fasted when he received the news of the deaths of Saul and Jonathan (1:12). When "all the people" urge David to break off his fast (they did not intervene when he fasted for Saul and Jonathan), the king refuses and swears an oath. In the opening scene of this episode, Abner swore an oath that David would rule "over Israel and over Judah, from Dan to Beer-sheba" (3:10). Just as Abner's oath is about to be realized, David pays his respects to the deceased Abner with an oath: he will not eat until after sunset.

The king's torn clothes, his sackcloth, his lament, his fasting, his trailing behind Abner's coffin, and his oath win the people's approval: the king was not complicit in Abner's murder. The narrator, who enthusiastically supports David, interjects that *everything* David did "was good in the opinion of all the people." Moreover, *all Israel*, namely, those Israelite

[28] When Ahab learns of the divine judgment against him for expropriating Naboth's vineyard, he expresses his repentance by tearing his clothes, putting on sackcloth, and fasting (1 Kgs 21:27).

elders whom Abner convinced to come under Davidic rule, exonerates David. David has saved his alliance with Abner!

The scene closes with David praising Abner's memory with another rhetorical question: "Do you not know that a prince and a great man has fallen this day in Israel?" Similarly, he will praise Ishbaal's memory before his murderers in the next scene: "wicked men have killed a righteous man" (4:11). Then David turns to his relationship with Joab. As the scene opened, David ordered Joab to mourn; as it closes, David distances himself further from Joab and his brother Abishai, confessing that he is powerless before their violence. Is this a final hyperbole offered to the elders of Israel as further evidence of his innocence in Abner's death? Unlikely, since they have already acquitted him (3:37). Instead, David's final statement explains to the audience why he failed to deliver Joab into the hands of those who could avenge Abner's blood. David does not hand Joab over because he cannot. He exacted vengeance for Saul's death from an Amalekite messenger (1:15-16) and will avenge Ishbaal's death as well (4:12). But he is powerless to exact vengeance for Abner's death from Joab. Joab may have obeyed the king's command to mourn for Abner, but that is as far as it goes. David will be dead before Joab pays for this crime (1 Kgs 2:28-35).

2.8 David Executes Ishbaal's Killers (4:1-12)

The narrator, shifting from David's court and the mourning ceremony for Abner to Ishbaal's court, presents an episode that can be divided into four sections:

1. The setting (4:1)
2. Background information on Saul's sons (4:2-4)
3. Ishbaal's murder (4:5-7)
4. The bloodguilt for Ishbaal's death (4:8-12)

2.8.1 The Setting (4:1)

As we learn about Israel's reaction to Abner's murder, our concern that Ishbaal might launch further hostilities is put to rest. As the last scene closed, "all Israel" was pleased with David's display of grief for Abner. Now, as "all Israel" considers the future of Ishbaal's court in light of Abner's death, they are, according to the NRSV, "dismayed." This Hebrew verb (*bhl*) was used to describe the terror that overwhelmed Saul after he spoke with Samuel's ghost at Endor: he lay prone and refused to eat (1 Sam 28:21). The Israelites in Ishbaal's court may, in fact, be more alarmed than the English word "dismayed" conveys. The Hebrew text reports that King Ishbaal's hands go limp (the NRSV has the more idiomatic "his courage failed"); the king, who once tried to rule Abner (2 Sam 3:7), is now without his mighty warrior. "Limp hands" is hardly the expected royal reaction to this underhanded murder. The king's hands should be raised for war! When Hanun, the Ammonite, humiliates David's envoys, David sends out the army (2 Sam 10). But poor Ishbaal is helpless. Does he realize he will soon share Abner's fate?

2.8.2 Background Information on Saul's Sons (4:2-4)

The narrator halts the progression of events to provide background information necessary for the upcoming episodes. Baanah and Rechab, Ishbaal's murderers, are introduced as members of Ishbaal's court who, like Joab (3:22), lead raiding bands. As Benjaminites, they are from the same tribe as Saul and Ishbaal. The narrator speaks directly to the reader regarding the current status of the people of Beeroth.[29] The debate over the precise location of Beeroth does not impede our understanding of this episode; the narrator informs us that Beeroth was under Benjaminite governance, though at the time the narrator recounts these events, the people of Beeroth have fled to Gittaim. This information anticipates one of the consequences of Ishbaal's murder: after Baanah and Rechab, Beerothites, kill Ishbaal and are executed by David, the rest of the Beerothites, perhaps fearing repercussions, will abandon the Saulide, now Davidic, realm for Gittaim. While the location of Gittaim is disputed, we imagine that they were living outside David's sway, perhaps near Gath (Philistine territory).[30] The expression "to this day," appearing here for the first time (see also 6:8 and 18:18), lends vividness to the story: the historical events recounted in this verse have vestiges that persist

[29] Their town was taken by Joshua after the Hivites, to whom the city of Beeroth belonged (Josh 9:17), duped him into thinking that they were not residents of the land (Josh 9:3-21) in order to escape extermination.

[30] For more on the debate over the location of Gittaim, see Benjamin Maisler, "Gath and Gittaim," *Israel Exploration Journal* 4, no. 3–4 (1954): 227–35; Hanna E. Kassis, "Gath and the Structure of the 'Philistine' Society," *JBL* 84 (1965): 259–71; and Israel Finkelstein, "The Philistines in the Bible: A Late-Monarchic Perspective," *JSOT* 27 (2002): 131–67.

down to the original audience's own time and confirm the veracity of the narrator's version of events.

The narrator also introduces us to Mephibosheth. But before hearing his name, we learn that he is Jonathan's son and that he is disabled. As a member of the Saulide line, he is a claimant to his grandfather's throne. The day that his father and grandfather died, when he was five years old, Mephibosheth's nurse, recognizing that the young heir's life could be at risk, rescued him, but as they fled, the boy fell and was permanently maimed. Mephibosheth's infirmity follows him like a refrain through the David Narrative (9:3; 9:13; and 19:26), and he will appeal to it to explain why he did not accompany David in his flight from the usurping Absalom (19:26). Mephibosheth's history introduces the theme of David's fidelity to his pledge to protect Jonathan's descendants (1 Sam 20:13c-15; see further discussion in section 4.2 below). David will make Jonathan's son a dependent of his court, fulfilling his oath (2 Sam 9:10). When Mephibosheth is accused of treason (16:3), David will accept his alibi instead of ordering his immediate execution (19:29). And when the Gibeonites demand the lives of seven of Saul's descendants, David will spare Mephibosheth because of his promise to Jonathan (21:7). The Mephibosheth subplot in the David Narrative underscores David's fidelity to his covenant with Jonathan. For the moment, David does not know of the existence of this descendant of Jonathan.

2.8.3 Ishbaal's Murder (4:5-7)

STRUCTURE

  A. Rechab and Baanah travel to the king's palace at noontime (4:5)
     B. The accounts of Ishbaal's murder (4:6-7ab)
  A'. Rechab and Baanah depart the king's palace and travel all night (4:7c)

COMMENTARY

With the background information finished, the action resumes. Rechab and Baanah set out in the heat of the day, a rather unpleasant time for travel, but an opportune moment for the task at hand—the murder of a king. The two accounts of Ishbaal's murder (4:6-7) treat two different questions. The first account, though a bit confusing, wants to explain how Rechab and Baanah attained such unfettered access to the sleeping king. The narrator may be preoccupied with the credibility of his account: can anyone just walk into the king's bedchamber? One interpretation of the Hebrew—that Rechab and Baanah entered the palace on the pretext of fetching wheat (NJPS and NRSV)—was rejected by Samuel Driver over a century ago.[31] Most translations (NAB, REB, and NJB) read with the LXX, which reports that Rechab and Baanah gained access to the palace because the portress had fallen asleep. (I suppose we are not meant to ask how a king could be left with only a portress for protection.) Sleeping kings are easy targets. King Hamlet's ghost laments that his brother, King Claudius, dispatched him as he slept: "Sleeping within mine orchard, / My custom always in the afternoon" (*Hamlet*, act 1, sc. 5, lines 59–60). Because Baanah and Rechab are the king's chief raiders, their unhindered access to the undefended Ishbaal is not inconceivable. When Joab returns from his raids, he enjoys immediate access to King David (3:22-24), though David was not asleep in his bedchamber. The second account focuses on Ishbaal's beheading since his head is the main prop in the next scene. After the murder, they set out straightaway (during the night!) for David's palace with Ishbaal's head in their hands. David should be pleased to learn that Saul's kingdom is again without a king. Rechab and Baanah are already counting their reward.

2.8.4 The Bloodguilt for Ishbaal's Death (4:8-12)

STRUCTURE

A. David receives Ishbaal's head from Rechab and Baanah at Hebron (4:8a)

   B. Rechab and Baanah: Ishbaal sought (*bqš*) David's life (4:8b)

      C. David's oath, part 1: What God did for David (4:9)

         D. The messenger thought he announced good news (*bśr*) (4:10a)

            E. David killed him (4:10b)

         D'. The reward for his good news (*bśr*) (4:10c)

      C'. David's oath, part 2: What David will do (4:11a)

   B'. David will seek (*bqš*) the lives of Rechab and Baanah (4:11b)

A'. David executes Rechab and Baanah and buries Ishbaal's head at Hebron (4:12)

---

[31] Driver, *Notes*, 196.

As the scene begins, Rechab and Baanah present Ishbaal's head to David. As it ends, that disgraced head has received a solemn burial and the dead bodies of Rechab and Baanah hang in public disgrace (A / A' sections). They announce that they have executed Ishbaal who "sought" (*bqš*) David's life. David then borrows their own word (*bqš*) to inform them that he "seeks" their lives. Near the center of the scene David swears an oath: in the first part he announces that God has saved him (C section), and in the second part he declares Ishbaal righteous and his killers wicked (C' section). At the turning point of the scene (D and E sections), as David recounts what happened to the Amalekite messenger who thought he was bringing David the good news of Saul's death (1:15), Rechab and Baanah learn that they will share the Amalekite's fate.

COMMENTARY

Rechab and Baanah present David with the dead king's head and announce that the Lord has avenged David against the one who *sought* (*biqqēš*) his life. Ironically, when David announces the capital sentence against Rechab and Baanah, he employs the same verb: "should I not *seek* his blood at your hands" (4:11: *hălô² ʾăbāqqēš*). What a surprise reversal! Ishbaal's executioners presumed David would laud their action. Instead, the king rejects the deed and refutes their reasoning—he never sought vengeance against Saul's house. Quite the contrary, he remained and will remain faithful to Saul and to his oath to preserve the lives of Jonathan's descendants.

As David begins to swear an oath, imprecating himself if he does not fulfill his word, Rechab and Baanah should be worried. After the introductory formula, "as the Lord lives," he describes the Lord as the one who has rescued his life from every distress. This aside reprises the theme of the David Narrative (see section 1.3 above) that was introduced in David's opening speech before Saul (1 Sam 17:37): "The Lord, who saved me from the paw of the lion and from the paw of the bear, will save me from the hand of this Philistine." We are nineteen chapters since that speech (with twenty-one chapters to go), and this reprise keeps the theme of the narrative in the mind of the reader: it is the Lord who delivers David, not Rechab, Baanah, or anyone else. He did not want Ishbaal dead, and he especially does not want the bloodguilt that results from that murder. David interrupts his oath to tell Rechab and Baanah the story of the Amalekite who claimed to have assisted Saul in his death. The bloodguilt for Saul's death did not fall on David's head, and the bloodguilt for Ishbaal's murder will not either. David then completes his oath, the gist of which is: "Just as I grabbed Saul's killer and executed him, so I will execute you."

David declares Ishbaal, whom Rechab and Baanah call David's "enemy" (2 Sam 4:8), to be "a righteous man" (4:11). Ishbaal, killed as he slept, was innocent and defenseless. (Presumably David has been informed offstage of the circumstances of the murder so that the narrator can keep us focused on the issues of the bloodguilt and David's fidelity to Saul's house.) David wants to ensure that Ishbaal's shed blood falls on Rechab and Baanah and not on him and his people. As in the previous scene, David must also be concerned about his alliance with the elders of Israel. His political skill, which preserved that alliance after Abner's murder, is needed again.

Rechab and Baanah arrived at David's court with the humiliated head of Ishbaal in hand, hoping to receive the king's gratitude and royal compensation. Instead, their corpses are hung in shame beside the pool at Hebron. When the Philistines disgraced the corpse of Saul by hanging it on the wall of Beth-shan (1 Sam 31:10-12), Saul's loyal subjects came to honor the king's remains with proper burial and mourning. The corpses of Rechab and Baanah are similarly dishonored but with no one to recover them, whereas the head of Ishbaal is honorably disposed. The respect that David accords Ishbaal's remains should signal to his loyal subjects that he was not complicit in their king's death and therefore the process toward a ratification of his alliance with the elders of Israel should proceed without disruption.

2.9 David Wears Saul's Crown (5:1-5)

2.9.1 Israel Anoints David as Their King (5:1-3)

STRUCTURE

A. The tribes of Israel come to David at Hebron (5:1a)
   B. Israel seeks a covenant with David (5:1b)
      C. David should be their shepherd and ruler (5:2)

A'. The elders of Israel come to the king at Hebron (5:3a)
   B'. The king makes a covenant with the elders of Israel (5:3b)
      C'. They anoint David as their king (5:3c)

The pattern here, described as "forward symmetry" by Jerome Walsh,[32] presents the story of David's anointing in two scenes. In the first scene,

---

[32] Jerome T. Walsh, *Style and Structure in Biblical Hebrew Narrative* (Collegeville, MN: Liturgical Press, 2001), 35–37.

"all the tribes" of Israel come to David, and in the second the "elders of Israel" come to the king. In the first scene, the tribes of Israel propose to have David as their shepherd; in the second scene the elders of Israel realize that design, anointing David as their king. The C' section looks back to 3:17-21 (see the structure of 3:7-27). Back then, David's plan to bring Saul's dominion under his sway was interrupted by Joab's murder of Abner. Now his efforts are realized.

COMMENTARY

The scene shifts from Abner's burial to the arrival of the tribes of Israel (those once loyal to Saul) in Hebron. They proclaim their unanimous support for Davidic rule by reminding David of their kinship with him: "We are your bone and flesh."[33] Their words echo Abner's appeal to Joab that led to a cessation of hostilities between Ishbaal's and David's forces: "How long will it be before you order your people to turn from the pursuit of their *kinsmen*?" (2:26). The tribes of Israel recall how David's military prowess served Saul's interests—"it was you who led Israel in war" (NJPS)—and then they quote God's words to David: "As for you [David], you will shepherd my people Israel." From the very beginning of David's story, the reader has known that this was David's destiny:

> The Lord said to Samuel, "How long will you grieve over Saul? I have rejected him from being king over Israel. Fill your horn with oil and set out; I will send you to Jesse the Bethlehemite, for I have provided for myself a king among his sons." (1 Sam 16:1)

Since his anointing, several characters in the story have come to recognize David's divine mandate. When David produces the corner of Saul's cloak as proof of his opportunity to assassinate him, Saul responds: "Now I know that you shall surely be king, and that the kingdom of Israel shall be established in your hand" (1 Sam 24:20). Abigail alludes to David's divine mandate when she blocks David's vendetta against her husband Nabal: "When the Lord has done to my lord according to all the good that he has spoken concerning you" (1 Sam 25:30). Abner decides to

---

[33] This formula functions as a preamble to a pledge of fidelity. Laban employs it when he greets Jacob ("Surely, you are my bone and my flesh" [Gen 29:14]), and its meaning is specified in the next verse (Gen 29:15): "because you are my kinsman" (*ʾāḥî*, literally, "my brother"). Abimelech employs similar language when he seeks the support of the lords of Shechem in his bid to become king (Judg 9:1-6): they should make him king because he is their bone and their flesh (Judg 9:2), and the lords agree by saying, "He is our brother" (Judg 9:3).

participate in David's mandate when he confronts Ishbaal's treason charge: "what the LORD has sworn to David, that will I accomplish for him" (2 Sam 3:9). Finally, in this scene, the people of Israel acknowledge David as their king. God's plan is coming to fruition.

The title with which the tribes of Israel honor David, "shepherd" (5:2), recalls his modest beginnings. When the prophet Samuel does not find God's choice for king among the sons that Jesse offers, he asks if there are any others. The youngest "is keeping the sheep," Jesse answers (1 Sam 16:11). When King Saul summons David into his service for the first time, he orders Jesse, "Send me your son David who is with the sheep" (1 Sam 16:19). When David travels to the battlefield where he will defeat Goliath, he leaves behind those sheep (1 Sam 17:20) only to be interrogated by his eldest brother Eliab as to their whereabouts (1 Sam 17:28). And David himself refers to his earlier occupation when he steps forward to fight Goliath: "Your servant used to keep sheep" (1 Sam 17:34). Thus, at the beginning of the David Narrative, we were reminded again and again of David's occupation as a shepherd. Then his earlier career is forgotten until this moment when it reappears as a metaphor for his leadership over Israel.[34]

The tribes of Israel also announce that David "will become leader [*nāgîd*] of Israel." When Samuel anointed Saul, he called Israel's first king a *nāgîd*.[35] That title is now transferred to David. Finally, the elders of Israel come on stage. Abner had met with them and, reminding them of their longtime aspiration to have David as their king, he had established an alliance between themselves and David (2 Sam 3:17). The ratification of that pact, delayed but not derailed by the murders of Abner and Ishbaal, is now accomplished. David is anointed king over Israel as Abner foretold. The youth David, who abandoned his flock of sheep to rout Goliath (1 Sam 17:20), has acquired a new flock, the people of Israel.

2.9.2 The Unification of Israel and Judah

From the time of his public display of grief for King Saul (2 Sam 1:11-12, 17-27) and his sending missives to the people of Jabesh-gilead (2:5-7), David has been trying to unify Judah and Israel under his rule. Now that he has succeeded (5:3), he will move his capital north to Jeru-

---

[34] The term "shepherd" as a metaphor for king appears in Ezekiel 37:24: "My servant David shall be king over them; and they shall all have one shepherd."

[35] Samuel anoints Saul with the words: "the LORD has anointed you ruler [*nāgîd*] over his heritage" (1 Sam 10:1).

salem, which is on the southern edge of Saul's territory. But within this unified kingdom, the old divisions will persist. Michal, David's wife and "daughter of Saul," will ridicule David's behavior as he brings the ark of the Lord into Jerusalem (6:20-23). Her derision points to an undercurrent of discontent among the remnants of Saul's regime who must now accept Davidic rule, symbolized by the ark's entry into David's capital. While fleeing Jerusalem, David meets Ziba, Mephibosheth's servant, who reports that Mephibosheth (Saul's grandson) has remained in Jerusalem hoping that the "house of Israel" would restore his father's kingdom to him (16:3). Ziba's claim (even if he is lying) offers further evidence that Judah and Israel were never fully unified under David. Shimei, a member of Saul's family (16:5-8), calls David a "man of blood," and interprets David's flight from Jerusalem as a vendetta for the "blood of Saul's house." Even though Shimei later retracts his harangue (19:16-23), his charges reveal the fissures in David's realm. In the end, the unified kingdom (was it ever really unified?) will collapse after the death of Solomon. King Jeroboam will rule over "all Israel" while King Rehoboam (scion of the Davidic line) will rule Judah (1 Kgs 12:20). The unification of Israel and Judah will be short-lived.

2.9.3 David's Regnal Years (5:4-5)

These verses signal the conclusion of act 2 of the David Narrative: David's rule in Hebron (1:1–5:5). As the curtain rose on this act, David received Saul's crown from an Amalekite messenger. As the curtain drops, that crown sits on David's head. The narrator combines David's years in Hebron with his regnal years in Jerusalem, an amalgamation that might have been more appropriate at the conclusion of his reign (where, in fact, it reappears [1 Kgs 2:11]). The proleptic news of David's long reign alludes to its successful conclusion. (Has the narrator spoiled the story by revealing the ending?) The reference to Davidic rule in Jerusalem bridges to act 3. The king is ready to relocate his court.

Chapter 3

ACT 3: DAVID ESTABLISHES HIS REIGN IN JERUSALEM
2 SAMUEL 5:6–8:18

3.1 Introduction

Act 3 tells the story of how David secures his capital and then rises to a world power. Immediately after he conquers Jerusalem, the Philistines attack. But David, with God's help, defends his capital, routing them twice (5:17-25). Then he moves the ark of God into his city (6:1-23), signaling to its inhabitants and especially to Michal, Saul's daughter and his wife, that he enjoys a particular relationship with God. The specifics of that relationship are announced in 2 Samuel 7 when God promises to establish David's royal dynasty forever. Then David begins to extend his dominion (8:1-14), defeating peoples whose territory borders his own and, finally, forming a government (8:15-18) in his capital city. As the curtain drops on act 3, David's rule is secure.

STRUCTURE

  A. David establishes Jerusalem as his capital (5:6-16)
    B. David fends off the Philistines' attack with God's help (5:17-25)
      C. David moves the ark to Jerusalem (6:1-23)
      C'. God's promise to David (7:1-29)
    B'. David attacks and defeats his neighbors with God's help (8:1-14)
  A'. David establishes his government in Jerusalem (8:15-18)

The act opens with David's capture of his new capital, Jerusalem, and it concludes with the establishment of his government (A/A') in that city. The Philistines attack David's nascent reign and are repelled with God's help (B), and later David attacks and routs them along with other nations, again with God's help (B'). The center of act 3 reveals critically important information about David's destiny and his relationship with the Lord: David transfers the ark of the Lord to the capital of his kingdom, and the Lord promises to establish that kingdom forever (C').

3.2 David Establishes Jerusalem as His Capital (5:6-16)

Given the place of Jerusalem in our biblical imagination, we might have expected a more extended treatment of this pivotal event in Israel's history. Instead, David seizes his future capital in three biblical verses that focus more on the "blind and lame" than on the military campaign. Why did David target Jerusalem? Did he consult God as he had before occupying Hebron (2:1)? Did he negotiate with the Jebusites prior to the attack? How did he strategize the city's capitulation? The narrator ignores our questions. His eye is focused on the ground upon which the future temple will be built. That hallowed terrain is now coming into David's possession.

The account of Jerusalem's capture can be divided into three sections followed by a caesura:

1. David conquers Jerusalem (5:6-8)
2. David secures his capital (5:9-10)
3. David builds a royal palace (5:11-12)
Caesura: A list of David's sons (5:13-16)

3.2.1 David Conquers Jerusalem (5:6-8)

STRUCTURE

A. The blind and the lame (5:6)
   B. Zion / city of David (5:7)
A'. The lame and the blind / the blind and the lame (5:8)

The mention of the blind and lame frames this scene's interpretive key: the introduction of two names for Jerusalem, Zion and city of David. David has captured Zion, the place where God will establish his dwelling. The title "city of David" anticipates the next scene when David attaches his own name to the city he has conquered.

COMMENTARY

The closing verses of act 2 foretold David's thirty-three-year reign in Jerusalem. That reign now begins. As the scene opens, Jerusalem belongs to the Jebusites (cf. Josh 15:8, 63 and Judg 1:21), whom the narrator qualifies as "the inhabitants of the land." That label recalls the classification of non-Israelite peoples whose land God promised to transfer to Moses:

> I will set your borders from the Red Sea to the sea of the Philistines, and from the wilderness to the Euphrates; for I will hand over to you *the inhabitants of the land*, and you shall drive them out before you.[1] (Exod 23:31)

When God first addressed Moses from the burning bush, he listed the Jebusites among the peoples whose land would be ceded to the Israelites:

> I have come down to deliver them from the Egyptians, and to bring them up out of that land to a good and broad land, a land flowing with milk and honey, to the country of the Canaanites, the Hittites, the Amorites, the Perizzites, the Hivites, and the Jebusites.[2] (Exod 3:8)

As Joshua prepared to enter the Promised Land, he dispatched spies to scout out Jericho. They reached the house of Rahab, who confessed that "all *the inhabitants of the land* melt in fear before you" (Josh 2:9), fulfilling God's word spoken to Moses. In 2 Samuel 5:6, the narrator, by tagging the Jebusites as "inhabitants of the land," recalls this divine plan and suggests that David's capture of Jerusalem from the Jebusites participates in the realization of this program announced at the burning bush. Nevertheless, despite God's promise that Moses would "drive out the inhabitants of the land" (Exod 23:31), the Jebusites continued to dwell and own property in Jerusalem during David's reign.[3] In fact, their presence in the David Narrative frames King David's public life in Jerusalem: his first act is to seize the Jebusite city, and his final act is to build the first altar in Jerusalem on land purchased from Araunah the Jebusite (2 Sam 24:21-24). After that, the elderly king retires to his bed (1 Kgs 1).

---

[1] NRSV (emphasis added). See Num 33:51-53 as well.

[2] The Jebusites are regularly included in lists of peoples to be driven out of the land. See, for example, Exod 3:17; 13:5; 23:23; 33:2; 34:11; and Deut 7:1.

[3] Solomon will conscript them for slave labor (1 Kgs 9:20-21).

The inclusion around this scene is an odd detail about "the blind and the lame." Read at face value, David's treatment of the blind and lame is rightly reprehensible to modern ears. In fact, their role in this scene makes little sense on the surface. The Jebusites employ this hyperbole— "even the blind and the lame will turn you back" (2 Sam 5:6)—to ridicule their aggressor. Furthermore, it is the Jebusite inhabitants, not the blind and the lame, who insist that David will be unable to enter the city. Why, then, does David focus his assault on "the blind and the lame" after his victory (5:8)? His order does not follow logically from 5:6, where the "blind and lame" served as a metaphor to amplify the Jebusites' battle rhetoric. Moreover, the exact meaning of the first half of 5:8 has left translators and exegetes puzzled for centuries.[4] The Hebrew text is obscure, and the LXX, Peshitta, and Targum versions offer different interpretations.

The second half of the verse is clear: the blind and lame shall not be admitted to "the house." To add to the curiosity of this passage, while calling our attention to the blind and the lame, the narrator provides few details about the conquest of the holy city, Jerusalem. The narrator's foreknowledge that the ark of the Lord will be transferred to Jerusalem explains the seemingly obtuse details in this brief scene. "The blind and the lame" are paired in Leviticus 21:18 in the context of regulations for persons performing religious functions. Any type of mutilation, including blindness or lameness, was an impediment to religious service at the altar. The specific mention of these two disabilities as Jerusalem falls into Israelite hands foreshadows the priestly rituals that will take place on this ground soon to be sanctified by the presence of the ark of the Lord. The narrator's concluding aside—"Therefore it is said, the blind and the lame shall not enter the house"—discloses his real interest. The "house" is the future temple (in 1 Kgs 8 the newly constructed temple is always referred to as a "house"), and his aside suggests that the origins of the restrictions regarding "the blind and the lame" derive from the very moment that Jerusalem, the city where the Temple will be built, was captured (though Lev 21:18 does not prohibit the blind and the lame from entering the Temple). The narrator, by referencing the religious practice of his own later time, ensures that his ancient audience grasps that this scene is about more than just the capture of another city.

---

[4] The NRSV renders it, "David had said on that day, 'Whoever would strike down the Jebusites, let him get up the water shaft to attack the lame and the blind, those whom David hates,'" whereas the NAB reads, "On that day David said: 'All who wish to attack the Jebusites must strike at them through the water shaft. The lame and the blind shall be the personal enemies of David.'"

At the center of this scene, two names for Jerusalem, Zion[5] and the city of David, are introduced for the first time in the David Narrative. The next appearance of these two names comes as Solomon prepares to dedicate the newly built temple in Jerusalem. Solomon's first act is to retrieve the ark of the covenant from Zion, the city of David (the place to which David will relocate the ark shortly), for its procession to the Temple:

> Then Solomon assembled the elders of Israel and all the heads of the tribes, the leaders of the ancestral houses of the Israelites, before King Solomon in Jerusalem, to bring up the ark of the covenant of the LORD out of the city of David, which is Zion. (1 Kgs 8:1)

The mention of these two names as David conquers the city foreshadows the day when the "house," into which the blind and lame cannot enter, will be dedicated.

3.2.2 David Secures His Capital (5:9-10)

With the city of the future temple now in Israelite hands, David puts his own name on the territory he has conquered. It now belongs to him.[6] He begins a building campaign to fortify his new capital from "the Millo inward." While the narrator assumes that we know what the Millo is (perhaps a defensive rampart[7]), what is clear is that David wastes no time in securing his new capital. The scene closes with the narrator's observation that the Lord is with David. That comment first appeared when Saul, tormented by an evil spirit, bid his servants to seek someone out to calm his restlessness with the music of a lyre (or harp, as tradition would have it). One of Saul's courtiers suggested that David could be of service:

---

[5] The title "Zion" often refers to God's dwelling on earth. See, for example, Psalms 9:11; 20:2; 50:2; and 65:1.

[6] A conqueror can name a city after himself. When Joab finishes his assault against the city of Rabbah, he orders David to fight alongside him, otherwise, he will rename Rabbah after himself, since he alone will have captured it (12:28).

[7] See Richard C. Steiner, "New Light on the Biblical Millo from Hatran Inscriptions," *BASOR* 276 (1989): 15–23. He suggests that the Millo was "an artificial terrace or mound, especially one built adjacent to the inside of a city wall" (p. 19). The Millo appears again in 1 Kings 9:15, 24 and 11:27.

> I have seen a son of Jesse the Bethlehemite who is skillful in playing, a
> man of valor, a warrior, prudent in speech, and a man of good presence;
> and the LORD is with him. (1 Sam 16:18)

The list of David's talents was complemented by the notation of God's
fidelity to him. Because David had just been anointed by Samuel at God's
insistence, that announcement was not news to the reader. But Saul, the
current, now rejected, anointed one could not perceive its foreboding.
The narrator repeated the phrase when David arrived at court, by which
point Saul was convinced of its veracity (1 Sam 18:12: "Saul was afraid
of David, because the LORD was with him") and wanted to eliminate
his potential rival. It was inserted yet again as David enjoyed increasing military success (1 Sam 18:14). But since the death of Saul (1 Sam
31), God has remained in the background, appearing only when David
inquired about the city to which he should return from his exile (2 Sam
2:1). Now, after the conquest of Jerusalem, the narrator repeats this comment, first spoken at Saul's court, in order to remind us of God's special
relationship with David.

3.2.3 David Builds a Royal Palace (5:11-12)

Hiram, king of Tyre,[8] introduced for the first time, sends cedar wood
and tradespeople to build a palace for David.[9] Their arrival provokes
David to deeper reflection, and the narrator allows us a fleeting, privileged glimpse into his inner thoughts. Since his anointing in 1 Samuel 16
we have known that David was destined to be king, and now, for the first
time, David recognizes his role in God's design for Israel. When other
characters in the story heralded his destiny, David did not react. Jonathan, in their final encounter, foresaw David's kingship (1 Sam 23:17), but
David offered no response. What did he think of Jonathan's prediction?
When Saul confessed that David would certainly become king (1 Sam
24:20), David was silent. Abigail, wife of Nabal, foretold that David
would be "prince over Israel" (1 Sam 25:30). But David said nothing.
While he knows that God answers his queries (1 Sam 23:4 and 2 Sam 2:1),
this is the first time that David acknowledges that the words spoken by

---

[8] The ancient city of Tyre was located about 165 kilometers (102 miles) north of
Jerusalem along the Mediterranean coast.

[9] The psalmist sings about the beauty of the cedars of Lebanon (Pss 29:5; 37:35;
92:12; and 104:16). In the Song of Songs the beloved likens the stature of her lover to
the cedars of Lebanon (Song 5:15).

Jonathan, Saul, and Abigail are being realized. The NAB translation "to know" in 5:12 seems a bit feeble given the import of this moment (the NRSV has "perceived"). Perhaps a better translation would be: "Thus David came to the full realization that the LORD had established him king over Israel."

3.2.4 Caesura: A List of David's Sons (5:13-16)

The last detail the narrator introduces before turning to the history of David's reign in Jerusalem is a list of the children born to him by his wives and concubines, who, unlike in the previous list (3:2-5), remain anonymous. The narrator reports that both sons *and daughters* were born to David, though the list may only include his sons, since his daughter Tamar (13:1), whose rape triggers a series of events leading up to Absalom's rebellion, is not mentioned. The narrator does not indicate if the names of the sons are in any particular order, as he did with the Hebron list. Should we assume that Solomon, David's successor, is the fourth born in Jerusalem (after the six sons born at Hebron)? With the exception of Solomon, the sons named here have no role in the David Narrative and are not mentioned again. The list functions as a caesura between the capture of Jerusalem and the story of David's reign in his new capital that is about to begin.

3.3 David Fends off the Philistines' Attack (5:17-25)

David's first act as king in Jerusalem will be to defend his city against a Philistine advance. The first battle of his life was against the Philistine champion Goliath (1 Sam 17). The first attack against his kingship will come from the Philistine camp again, and the outcome will be the same. God is on David's side!

STRUCTURE

    A. The Philistines come up for battle (5:17ab)
       B. Battle positions (5:17c-18)
          C. David's inquiry (5:19a)
          C'. The divine response (5:19b)
       B'. The battle (5:20)
    A'. The Philistines abandon their idols, which David carries off
       (5:21)

A. The Philistines come up for battle (5:22a)
  B. The Philistines' battle position (5:22b)
    C. David's inquiry (5:23a)
    C'. The divine response (5:23b-24)
  B'. David did as God commanded (5:25a)
A'. The Philistines are defeated (5:25b)

At the centers of these two parallel scenes, where we could expect the battle account, the narrator reports David's dialogues with God. His interests lie there. God directs both battles and, in the second, even orchestrates the military strategy. Whereas in the first scene the narrator briefly reports on the battle itself (5:20), in the second scene, the account of the battle is limited to reporting David's faithful observance of God's command.

COMMENTARY

News has reached the Philistines (we do not know how) that David has been anointed king of Israel. When King Hiram heard of David's election, he sent messengers and artisans to build David a palace (5:11). The Philistine reaction will be less cordial. As a fugitive, David had sought refuge with Achish, the Philistine ruler of Gath, and had taken up residence in Ziklag, a Philistine city (1 Sam 27:1-7). With Saul's death, he no longer needed Achish's protection and so he returned to Israel. We never learn how Achish reacted to David's betrayal.

This scene reports the first battle with the Philistines, Israel's principal enemy, after David's conquest of Jerusalem. The longstanding war between the Philistines and Israel had erupted into major battles before (1 Sam 4; 7:7-11) and during (1 Sam 13:1–14:23) Saul's reign, and Saul had died at the hands of the Philistines (1 Sam 31). The Philistine aggression in this scene is provoked not by the fact that David has secured Jerusalem, a potential strategic threat, but by David's anointing as king of Israel. Because their assault is against God's design for David, we reckon it has little chance of success.

The Philistines "go up" (2 Sam 5:17) for attack, reminding us that their cities were situated on the coastal plain along the Mediterranean Sea, and David descends to the "stronghold"; the just captured "stronghold of Zion" (5:7) springs to mind. But scholars, noticing that one normally *ascends* to Jerusalem (whereas David *descends* to this stronghold), suggest that the stronghold referred to here is the cave of Adullam (1 Sam 22:1), to which David fled to escape Saul. This cave, about twenty-seven kilometers (seventeen miles) southwest of Jerusalem, is called a "stronghold" in

1 Samuel 22:4.[10] But a precise geographical description of David's battle position is not the narrator's primary concern. The Philistines, marching toward Jerusalem, establish their offensive line in the valley of Rephaim, a valley mentioned in Joshua 15:8 as part of the western boundary of Judah (near the Hinnom Valley, southwest of Jerusalem). We expect the battle to ensue immediately, but instead, the narrator pauses the action so we can attend to David's conversation with God.

David does not engage in battle without first consulting the Lord. When the Philistines attacked the town of Keilah, he did not attempt to rescue the populace without divine sanction (1 Sam 23:1-5). In this scene, as then, the divine response comes swiftly, in contrast to God's silence before Saul's pleas the last time the Philistines attacked Israel (1 Sam 28:6). God refused to answer King Saul, whom he had rejected. But when David, the chosen one, seeks divine help against the Philistine threat, the response is immediate. He asks two questions: "Should I go up?" and "Will you give them into my hand?" God answers both of them: "Go up" and "I will certainly give the Philistines into your hand." David's inquiry illustrates an important theme in biblical theology: it is God who grants the victory. That lesson was learned long ago by Gideon who defeated the Midianites with three hundred troops who drank water from a nearby stream like a pack of dogs (Judg 7). By routing the Midianites with that crass bunch, God taught Israel that victory belongs to God alone (Judg 7:2). David knows and we know this battle theology and so he consults God while we listen in.

The battle is passed over without description. Once God has announced who will win, the actual details of the combat are hardly compelling—like watching the replay of a sporting event knowing the final score. In the post-battle summary, the narrator reports that the battlefield was renamed "Baal-perazim" (translated "lord of the breaches"). When David explains the meaning of this new name—"The LORD has burst forth against my enemies before me"—he generalizes his victory to include all his foes. His exclamation recalls the central theme of the David Narrative first announced in his speech before Saul: God delivers David (1 Sam 17:34-37a). It echoes the predictions of Jonathan (1 Sam 20:14-15) and Abigail (1 Sam 25:29), and it foreshadows David's speech near the end of his life when he sings about his deliverance by God (2 Sam 22; see section 1.3 above).

---

[10] For a discussion of the possible referents for the "stronghold" in 2 Samuel 5:17, see Christian E. Hauer, "Jerusalem, the Stronghold and Rephaim," *CBQ* 32 (1970): 571–78.

As the scene closes, the narrator takes us back to the battlefield where the Philistines have abandoned their idols. This concluding detail leaves the impression that the Philistines have recognized the power of the Lord and thus have left behind their once-revered religious icons, their "idols." David carries them off. But what did he do with them? When the Philistines captured the ark of the covenant from the Israelites, they placed it in the temple of Dagon (1 Sam 5:2) to celebrate Dagon's supposed victory over the Lord. After Saul's defeat and death, the Philistines carried the dead king's armor to the temple of Astarte (1 Sam 31:10). David does not yet have a temple where he could place these idols to celebrate the Lord's victory. The Chronicler, concerned with the orthodoxy of David's action for a later Jewish audience, reports that David ordered them burned (1 Chr 14:12), while our narrator appears indifferent to the question.

The second battle account complements the first with a few significant changes. The Philistines take up the same strategic position in the valley of Rephaim. David's location is not provided, which offers further evidence that the narrator is not focused on ensuring that we have a precise geographical picture of each side's battle position.[11] David makes inquiry again, and this time God strategizes with him as to the battle signal. Just before the narrator announces David's victory, he comments, "David did just as the LORD had commanded him," reprising a key theme in the David Narrative—the obedient David contrasts with the disobedient Saul. His comment looks back to the very first allusion to David's kingship during Saul's reign. The prophet Samuel, having anointed Saul, ordered the new king to travel to Gilgal and wait seven days until his arrival. Samuel was to bring the sacrifices with him and would show Saul what to do (1 Sam 10:8). But when Samuel failed to appear and Saul saw his grip over the army loosening, he offered the sacrifices himself (1 Sam 13:8-9). When Samuel finally arrived, he condemned Saul's disobedience:

> You have not kept the commandment of the LORD your God, which he commanded you. (1 Sam 13:13)

Precisely at this moment, Samuel informed Saul that God had decided on his replacement:

> [B]ut now your kingdom will not continue; the LORD has sought out a man after his own heart; and the LORD has appointed him to be ruler over his people, because you have not kept what the LORD commanded you. (1 Sam 13:14)

---

[11] By contrast, when Abner and Joab positioned their ranks for battle, the narrator described their positions in greater detail (2:12-13) so that the audience could visualize that neither side held a strategic advantage.

David is the one *after God's own heart* and the narrator exploits this battle scene to recall this theme (2 Sam 5:25): "David did just as the Lord had commanded him," unlike his deposed predecessor. Thus, the faithful David cannot be accused of usurping Saul's throne (see 1:2-16 and 4:8-12), even if Shimei son of Gera thinks otherwise (16:5-8). It was God who determined the transfer of the throne to David the very first time Saul disobeyed.

These two victories allow David to extend his territory to the region of Gezer, a town about thirty kilometers (nineteen miles) west of Jerusalem at the eastern edge of the coastal plain; they foreshadow David's future campaigns (reported in 2 Sam 8), when he will extend his influence even farther beyond the walls of Jerusalem.

3.4 David Moves the Ark of God to Jerusalem (6:1-23)

Joseph Conrad, in the preface to one of his novels, mused about the primary objective of his art: "My task which I am trying to achieve is, by the power of the written word to make you hear, to make you feel—it is, before all, to make you see. That—and no more, and it is everything."[12] David, having defended his city from Philistine attack, is now ready to transfer the ark of God to his new capital, and we are positioned along the parade route to observe the pageantry and enjoy the orchestra and choir. The narrator's art in this episode compels us to *see, hear, and feel* David's triumph!

Two events mar the festivities: the killing of Uzzah and the confrontation between David and his wife Michal. The quarrel between the king and his predecessor's daughter discloses the significance of this episode: because God preferred David over Saul, Michal's father, David has enjoyed the privilege of relocating the ark of God to his new capital. Only then does the reader grasp the meaning of the king's revelry before the ark.

STRUCTURE

   A. David gathers the people to bring up the ark, called by the name of the Lord of hosts. The celebrations begin (6:1-5)
     B. *Interruption*: Uzzah's death. The celebrations are suspended (6:6-11)
       C. The ark is brought into the city of David amid joy and sacrificial offerings (6:12-15)

---

[12] Conrad's preface to *The Nigger of the Narcissus* (1897).

B'. *Interruption*: Michal despises her husband, the king (6:16)
A'. The liturgy for the ark's reception: David blesses the people
    in the name of the Lord of hosts and the people go home
    (6:17-19)
Epilogue: The confrontation between Michal and David (6:20-23)

The center of this concentric structure focuses on *how* the ark entered
the city of David, namely, with proper religious solemnity. As the episode
concludes (A'), David blesses the people, invoking the divine title (6:18:
"the name of the LORD of hosts") that was introduced at the beginning
of the celebrations (6:2). When the crowd disperses, the celebration of
the ark's arrival into the city of David is concluded. The A C A' scenes
are replete with festive language that is absent in the "interruptions"
and the epilogue.

3.4.1 The Celebrations Begin (6:1-5)

STRUCTURE

A. David gathers the chosen men of Israel (6:1)
  B. David and the people set out to fetch the ark of God (6:2)
    C. The ark of God is readied for transport (6:3a)
  B'. Uzzah and Ahio guide the ark of God (6:3b-4)
A'. David and Israel rejoice (6:5)

As the curtain rises, David and the people of Israel have assembled (A).
As it drops, they have begun to sing and dance (A'). At the center of the
scene the main action gets underway: the ark departs from the house
of Abinadab.

COMMENTARY

David gathers *again* all the "chosen men" of Israel. Perhaps we should
consider the march against Jerusalem (5:6) or the battles with the Philistines (5:17-25) as the previous occasions when David summoned the
troops. The throng of thirty thousand allows for a spectacular display as
the ark begins its journey to Jerusalem, referred to as "the city of David"
three times in this episode (6:10, 12, 16). The king is moving the ark of
the Lord into his city.

The construction of the ark was ordered by God (Exod 25:10) immediately after the ratification of the covenant (Exod 20:22–24:18), and
upon its completion Moses "took the covenant and put it into the ark"

(Exod 40:20). The top of the ark is referred to as "the mercy seat," upon which God appears in a cloud (Lev 16:2).[13] The ark itself symbolizes God's fidelity to Israel (Josh 3:7-8), and it can be summoned when God must be consulted (Judg 20:27 and 1 Sam 14:18-19). It also plays a critical role in military operations. As the Israelites traveled through the desert after their flight from Egypt, the ark led the way:

> Whenever the ark set out, Moses would say, "Arise, O Lord, let your enemies be scattered, and your foes flee before you." (Num 10:35)

Israel's crossing of the Jordan River into the Promised Land mirrors the Red Sea crossing, except that at the Red Sea, it was Moses' raised staff and outstretched arm (Exod 14:16, 21) that divided the waters (the ark had not yet been constructed). At the crossing of the Jordan, it was the ark of the Lord that blocked the river's flow:

> So when those who bore the ark had come to the Jordan, and the feet of the priests bearing the ark were dipped in the edge of the water, the waters flowing from above stood still, rising up in a single heap far off at Adam, the city that is beside Zarethan. (Josh 3:15b-16a)

In the assault against Jericho, the Israelites marched around the city walls—soon to tumble down—with the ark (Josh 6). The ark went into battle with them against the Philistines (1 Sam 4:3), who captured it and quickly learned that it was best to restore it to its rightful owners (1 Sam 5:1–6:12). Upon the ark's reentry into Israel, it was deposited at the house of Abinadab and there it remained:[14]

> And the people of Kiriath-jearim came and took up the ark of the Lord, and brought it to the house of Abinadab on the hill. They consecrated his son, Eleazar, to have charge of the ark of the Lord. From the day that the ark was lodged at Kiriath-jearim, a long time passed, some twenty years, and all the house of Israel lamented after the Lord. (1 Sam 7:1-2)

---

[13] "In Israelite thought, Yahweh is imagined . . . sitting (albeit invisibly) on an immense cherubim throne located in the temple (1 Kgs 6:23-28; Isa 6:1-8), with his feet propped on the ark of the covenant, which serves as his 'footstool' (Pss 99:5; 132:7; 1 Chr 28:2)" (F. W. Dobbs-Allsopp, "R[az/ais]ing Zion in Lamentations 2," in *David and Zion: Biblical Studies in Honor of J. J. M. Roberts*, ed. B. F. Batto and K. L. Roberts [Winona Lake, IN: Eisenbrauns, 2004], 25).

[14] The ark of God is mentioned in 1 Samuel 14:18, but most scholars read the verse with the LXX ("'Bring the ephod,' for he carried the ephod") so that the ark never leaves the house of Abinadab.

Now David travels to the house of Abinadab to retrieve this most sacred symbol of Israelite religion for its relocation to his new capital, Jerusalem.[15]

Attempts to map out the ark's travels in 2 Samuel 6 will prove frustrating. We are told at the beginning of the episode that the ark is at the house of Abinadab "on the hill." On the basis of 1 Samuel 7:1, we know that Abinadab's house is near Kiriath-jearim (fourteen kilometers [nine miles] west of Jerusalem). The location of the threshing floor of Nacon, where Uzzah dies (2 Sam 6:7), is unknown. After the death of Uzzah, the ark is deposited in the house of Obed-edom the Gittite (a person from Gath). If we assume (with no evidence) that this Gittite lived near Gath, then the ark would be around forty kilometers west of Jerusalem (further away than when the episode began). But it is more reasonable to presume that Obed-edom was living as a foreigner nearby the threshing floor of Nacon. None of these geographical obscurities diminish in any way the principal aim of this episode, namely, the relocation of the ark to David's city.

The "new cart" on which the ark is transported is reminiscent of the new cart that the Philistines were required to construct for the ark's return to Israel (1 Sam 6:7), and it suggests that transporting the ark demanded exceptional deference from both Israelite and non-Israelite peoples. No ordinary cart was acceptable. The sons of Abinadab are introduced: Ahio is in front of the ark, leaving us to presume that Uzzah has taken up his fateful position at the back. As the scene closes, the celebrations begin. Thirty thousand people are dancing, playing instruments, and singing songs.

3.4.2 Interruption: Uzzah's Death. The Celebrations Are Suspended (6:6-11)

STRUCTURE

A. Uzzah and the ark: the ark arrives at Nacon (6:6)
   B. The Lord and Uzzah: the death of Uzzah (6:7)
      C. David, the Lord, and Uzzah: the threshing floor of Nacon is renamed (6:8)
   B'. The Lord and David: David's fear (6:9)
A'. David and the ark: the ark remains at the home of Obed-edom (6:10-11)

---

[15] 1 Samuel 4:1–7:2 and 2 Samuel 6 are sometimes referred to as the "ark narratives." The longer title for the ark ("the ark of the covenant of the LORD of hosts, who is enthroned on the cherubim") appears only in these passages.

The scene opens with the ark making its way toward the city of David. The first half of the scene focuses on Uzzah. At the center David and Uzzah are mentioned together and the location where Uzzah died is renamed. As the scene concludes, the focus is on David who decides that, for the moment, the ark should not be relocated to his capital. The lyres, harps, and tambourines fall silent as the ark is deposited at the house of Obed-edom.

COMMENTARY

The festive procession of the thirty thousand is brusquely interrupted by a burst of divine anger. Uzzah, whose father Abinadab had tended the ark, dies by the wrath of God, and the narrator does little to ease our shock. The ark has reached the threshing floor of Nacon, an unknown location, on its journey toward the city of David. The oxen appear to have jerked the cart, though the Hebrew verb, *šāmĕṭû*, is not easily interpreted as the different translations in the NRSV ("shook") and NJPS ("stumbled") indicate. Whatever happened, the unlucky Uzzah, positioned at the back of the cart, grabbed hold of the ark. The Lord's reaction to Uzzah's impromptu gesture was swift and with little explanation: God slew Uzzah because of *haššal* (according to the Hebrew text). At this critical juncture in the narrative, the Hebrew text preserves an incomprehensible term that appears only here in the Bible. For this reason the NRSV replaces the Hebrew word *haššal* with the explanation given in 1 Chronicles 13:10 ("because he put out his hand to the ark"). The rewriting of 2 Samuel 6:7 by the author of 1 Chronicles, the first person to interpret this inscrutable event for later generations, indicates that the Hebrew term *haššal* was as inexplicable for him as it is for us today.

Why did Uzzah have to die? His position behind the ark was mere coincidence. It could have just as easily been Ahio, his brother. Perhaps for the ancient reader the text was less troubling. But for us, the narrator seems far too dispassionate, far too withdrawn. We want answers from him. We want answers from God. As we read on, hoping to ease our anxiety, we join with biblical commentators who for centuries have tried to explain Uzzah's execution. *Numbers Rabbah* (fifth century) reports that "R[abbi] Johanan and R[abbi] Eleazar differ on their explanation for Uzzah's death. One says: He smote him on account of his error, and the other says: He smote him for having applied himself to his own needs in its [the ark's] presence."[16] The ancient rabbis swiftly dispatched Uzzah to "the next world" because he had the good fortune of dying beside the

---

[16] *Num. Rab.* 14.4; trans. Slotki (London: Soncino, 1983).

ark.[17] All turns out well. Aphrahat, a third-century Persian author and biblical scholar, thought that Uzzah was killed because he failed to follow the prescriptions for transporting the ark as outlined in Numbers 7:9: the ark should have been carried on the shoulders as seems to be the case later in 2 Samuel 6:13.[18] But this explanation does not account for why Ahio was not slain as well. Gregory of Nazianzus argued that God killed Uzzah "to preserve the sacred mystery associated with the ark."[19] These rabbis and early Christian authors strained to defend God's reaction by specifying Uzzah's crime. But their explanations, even though they reappear in modern commentaries, are not very satisfactory to modern readers. Uzzah's death remains an enigma and it lays bare the limits of the art of interpretation.

David's reaction—anger and fear—mirrors our own alarm. The NRSV captures in English the Hebrew constructions that distinguish God's anger from David's:

2 Samuel 6:7: The anger of the LORD was kindled against Uzzah.[20]
2 Samuel 6:8: David was angry.

Human expressions of anger at God are nowhere near as common as expressions of God's wrath against Israel. Still, human anger directed at God begins with Cain (Gen 4:5) who was angered by God's lack of regard for his sacrifice (another provocative text). Jonah becomes angry when, after all his efforts to preach condemnation to the Ninevites, God relents and does not punish them (Jonah 3:10–4:3). But in the Jonah story the reader is in a position quite different from this scene. We recognize that Jonah's anger is unwarranted and that God needs to teach him a lesson. But as David gazes on Uzzah's corpse, we are on his side. What lesson is gained by this slaughter? Perhaps a clue to illuminating the meaning of this scene comes at the climax when the place of Uzzah's untimely demise is named.

The location of Uzzah's death, Perez-uzzah, or, "the breach of Uzzah," memorializes God's reaction. This triple use of the word "breach" (He-

---

[17] *Num. Rab.* 14.4.

[18] Aphrahat, Demonstration Fourteen, §20, in I. Parisot, ed. *Aphraatis Demonstrationes*, Patrologia Syriaca 1 (Paris: Firmin-Didot, 1894). See Craig E. Morrison, "Scenes from First and Second Samuel retold in Aphrahat's Fourteenth Demonstration, 'Exhortatoria,'" *Parole de l'Orient* 36 (2011): 169–89.

[19] Gregory of Nazianzus, Oration 20, "On Theology, and the Appointment of Bishops," in *Gregory of Nazianzus*, ed. Brian E. Daley (London: Routledge, 2006), 110.

[20] The Hebrew expression *ḥrh* + *ʾap* is not restricted to God. Humans can "kindle their anger" as well (see Num 24:10).

brew *prṣ*) recalls the recent defeat of the Philistines against whom God also "made a breach" (translated literally):

> David came to Baal-perazim and David struck them [the Philistines] there. He said, "The LORD made a breach against my enemies before me like a breach of water. Because of this, that place is called Baal-perazim [lord of the breaches]. (2 Sam 5:20)

> David became angry because the LORD had breached a breach against Uzzah and that place was named Perez-uzzah [Uzzah's breach], to this day. (6:8)

In both scenes God intervenes to make a "breach" against a character and the sites are renamed to commemorate the divine outburst. In the first scene, the breach is against David's enemies, and David is victorious. In the second scene, the breach is against Uzzah, and David is furious and fearful. Though Uzzah's infraction is obscure (whereas the Philistines' crime is obvious), in both scenes God's "breach" results in a change of plans. The Philistines abandon their attack and David abandons his plans for the ark.

The narrator shifts immediately to David's inner thoughts: "How can the ark of the Lord come into my care?" He recognizes that the "breach" against Uzzah signals divine displeasure with his project to transfer the ark. When the Philistines absconded with the ark of the Lord, they suffered terrible hemorrhoids and the statue of their god, Dagon, was smashed to pieces (1 Sam 5). Now Uzzah lies dead for his ambiguous infraction against the ark. Has David committed an error too? Should he have consulted the Lord before relocating the ark? Neither we nor David have enough information to identify his misstep. But he is afraid: against whom might the Lord make the next breach? So the celebrations are suspended and the ark is deposited at the house of Obed-edom the Gittite. The scene closes with the news that Obed-edom's household was blessed by the ark's presence. That information is now on its way to David.

3.4.3 The Ark Is Brought into the City of David (6:12-15)

STRUCTURE

The good news reaches David (6:12a)
A. David brings up the ark with rejoicing (6:12b)
    B. The rituals (6:13-14)
A'. David and Israel bring up the ark with shouts and trumpets (6:15)

Verse 6:12a looks back to the previous scene to explain why David decided to recommence the ceremonies to relocate the ark. The liturgical actions at the center of the scene (sacrificing, dancing, and wearing the ephod) are framed by the "bringing up" of the ark with joy.

COMMENTARY

The household of Obed-edom the Gittite enjoys divine blessings and the messenger brings that news to David, citing the reason for Obed-edom's good fortune: the presence of the ark at his house. David takes this as a signal that the Lord's anger has abated and so resumes his plans. In this second attempt to relocate the ark, the narrator focuses on David alone—no mention is made of the thirty thousand who had travelled to Abinadab's house to fetch the ark at the beginning of the episode (6:1). This time sacrifices punctuate the ark's journey. When the people of Beth-shemesh received the ark from the Philistines, they too offered sacrifice (1 Sam 6:15). When Solomon relocates the ark from the city of David to his newly built temple, countless animals are sacrificed (1 Kgs 8:5). In this scene David sacrifices an ox and a fatling every six paces. The narrator is not worried about the practicalities of so many sacrifices, nor should we be. What is important is that the ark's arrival into Jerusalem is accompanied by unforgettable ritual. Should David have offered sacrifices the first time he tried to relocate the ark? Is this the negligence that provoked God to exact the death penalty from Uzzah and thereby suspend the ark's transfer? The narrator emits no clue.

King David dons the linen ephod, normally restricted to priests (1 Sam 2:28; 14:3; and 22:18) and performs priestly functions. The ephod (see Exod 28:6-14) "functioned symbolically to bring a human representative of the Israelite community into contact with the unseen God."[21] In 1 Samuel 23:9 David orders Abiathar the priest to bring the ephod when he inquires of God (though David normally seeks God's advice without it). When Samuel the prophet serves in the shrine at Shiloh, the linen ephod that he wears (1 Sam 2:18) signifies his priestly role that permits him to preside at sacrificial rituals (1 Sam 9:13-14). This vestment (David is the only king to don the linen ephod) signals David's office as priest-king, who offers sacrifice, distributes the portions of the sacrifice, and blesses the people (2 Sam 6:17-19). David's reign in Jerusalem is framed by his sacrificial liturgies: to celebrate the ark's transfer, David offers

---

[21] Carol Meyers, "Ephod," in *The Anchor Bible Dictionary,* ed. David N. Freedman (6 vols.; New York: Doubleday, 1992), 2:550.

up oxen and fatlings and at the end of his public life, he builds an altar in Jerusalem and offers up burnt offerings and peace offerings (24:25).[22]

To conclude the scene, the narrator adds two details—*shouts* and *trumpet blasts*—that underscore the significance of this event (6:15). The trumpet, made from a ram's horn and also known as a shofar, has both military and religious uses. It was sounded for the first time as God descended on Mount Sinai in a cloud (Exod 19:16). The shofar blasts and "shouting" (battle cries) that accompanied the fall of Jericho's walls celebrated God's victory on Israel's behalf (Josh 6:5). Now those same rituals greet the ark of the covenant of the Lord of hosts as it enters Zion, the city of David. The words of the psalmist echo in the background:

> God has gone up with a shout,
> the LORD with the sound of a trumpet. (Ps 47:5)

3.4.4 Interruption: Michal Despises Her Husband, the King (6:16)

Just as the ark of the Lord, led by the ephod-clad David, is entering the city, the narrator swings the camera toward a window from which we view a disgruntled Michal peering out. No tambourine in her hand— she despises the jubilant *king*. The Hebrew narrative underscores the simultaneity of the events: the glorious entrance of the ark and Michal's scornful glance.[23] What a contrast! This is only the second time in this episode that David is referred to as "King David" (he has been named thirteen times so far *without* his title). The introduction of his title offers a clue to decoding Michal's disdain (a fuller explanation comes in the epilogue), and another clue comes in the narrator's reference to her as "the daughter of Saul." On other occasions, Michal was referred to as David's wife (1 Sam 19:11 and 1 Sam 25:44),[24] but here and in the epilogue the narrator focuses on her parentage. What has caused Michal's affection for David to change so drastically? She once loved him (1 Sam 18:20), and when her father tried to kill him, she facilitated his escape (1 Sam 19:11-17). The narrator leaves us in suspense until the festivities are over.

---

[22] This presentation of David hints at another contrast between the king and his unfortunate predecessor. David can offer sacrifice as the ark enters Jerusalem, and we are sure that God is pleased. But when Saul offered sacrifices (1 Sam 13:9), disobeying the prophet Samuel's order (1 Sam 10:8), he lost his kingdom to David (1 Sam 13:14).

[23] See the discussion of Hebrew narrative in section 1.4.1.

[24] In 2 Samuel 3:13-14 David refers to Michal as "Saul's daughter" since that scene focuses on the agreement that King Saul made with the young David.

3.4.5 The Liturgy for the Ark's Reception (6:17-19)

STRUCTURE

A. The people bring in the ark (6:17a)
    B. David sacrifices, blesses, and distributes (6:17b-19ab)
A'. The people depart (6:19c)

COMMENTARY

After the brief appearance of Michal, the narrator swings the camera back to the main action. Three liturgical gestures celebrate the ark's arrival: (1) sacrifice, (2) blessing, and (3) the distribution of food. The ark is placed in a tent (a reference to the "tent of meeting"; see Num 7:89), and then David offers sacrifice in keeping with the prescriptions in Exodus 29:42:[25]

> It shall be a regular burnt offering throughout your generations at the entrance of the tent of meeting before the LORD.

These rituals echo the first sacrifices that were offered before the tent of meeting when the newly ordained Aaron blessed the people, offered a burnt offering and a well-being offering, entered the tent of meeting, and, upon exiting it, blessed the people again (Lev 9:22-23). While the description of David's rituals is less detailed, the priest-king offers burnt offerings and well-being offerings at the entrance of the tent of meeting where the ark now resides and then blesses the people *in the name of the Lord of hosts*, the title that was introduced at the beginning of this episode (6:2). The story of the ark's entrance into Jerusalem closes with a feast as the people enjoy a king's largess that includes bread, meat, and even raisins, a delicacy that the youthful *inamorata* in the Song of Songs solicits from her beloved (Song 2:5).[26] With these savory foods in hand, everyone heads home. The ark has arrived in David's city, and all are filled with joy. All but one.

---

[25] On what sort of altar did David offer these sacrifices? This question is ignored so that the story of the construction of the first altar in Jerusalem can be reserved until the very end of David's public life (2 Sam 24:25).

[26] After Solomon encounters God, who fulfills his request for a "listening heart" (1 Kgs 3:12), he returns to Jerusalem to offer burnt offerings and well-being offerings, and he provides a feast for his servants (1 Kgs 3:15).

3.4.6 Epilogue: The Confrontation between Michal and David (6:20-23)

STRUCTURE

A. The daughter of Saul (6:20a)
  B. Accusation (6:20b)
    C. God chose David over Michal's father (6:21)
  B'. David rejects Michal's accusation (6:22)
A'. The daughter of Saul (6:23)

The scene opens with an intended blessing for the daughter of Saul and closes with the notice that she remained childless. The center, which is framed by Michal's sarcastic accusation and David's equally sarcastic response, reprises the story of David's election as king.

COMMENTARY

As David moves toward his home, Michal is heading to meet him. Their confrontation seems to have happened in the street for all to see. David would have blessed his wife and his entire household as he had the people of Israel, but the daughter of Saul is in no mood for his blessing. This title for Michal, "daughter of Saul" (not "David's wife"), forms an inclusion that frames David's announcement at the center of the scene: the Lord chose him to replace her father. Had David simply wanted to underscore his status in Israel, the mention of his election would have sufficed. Instead, he reminds Michal of God's decision against her father. Only recently had David come to recognize his divine election (2 Sam 5:12), which has now received a public ratification by the transfer of the ark to his city. But the "daughter of Saul" will have none of it.

From her vantage point at the window, she saw not a king's triumph but instead a king exposing himself, acting like "riffraff," as the NJPS puts it (NRSV has "vulgar fellow").[27] The narrator does not describe David's attire as scanty or inappropriate. Just how was David exposing himself? We cannot know for sure. But Michal is angry. When the daughter of Saul refers to her husband as "the king of Israel," she alludes to the memory of her father who once bore that title. Her message to him is obvious: "You're no king," which is code for "My father made a better king than you!" Incensed that the ark of the Lord was led into Jerusalem by David and not by her father, she recognizes that David has solidified

---

[27] The Hebrew word behind the English "riffraff," *hārēqîm*, is used to describe the worthless troops that Abimelech hired to execute his own kin (Judg 9:4). Michal has launched a serious charge.

his authority over Israel. There is little chance for a Saulide successor to reclaim the throne now.

Her reprimand gives David the opportunity to make a short speech that interprets the meaning of the ark's transfer. He points to his election by God, by which he replaced Saul. The term he employs to describe his leadership, *nāgîd* ("ruler," not *melek*, "king"), was first spoken by God to Samuel when he informed him of his intention to select Saul as leader over Israel:

> Tomorrow about this time I will send to you a man from the land of Benjamin, and you shall anoint him to be ruler [*nāgîd*] over my people Israel. (1 Sam 9:16)

David appropriates that title (translated with "prince" in the NRSV in 2 Sam 6:21), bestowed by God on Michal's father, as he reminds her of his own divine election that deposed her father.[28] He wants her to know that he "danced before the LORD" (6:21) and *not* before her!

Now we understand Michal's disdainful glance from the window during the celebrations. The king's joviality was too much for the daughter of Saul. She once loved David (1 Sam 18:20) and, by saving his life, assisted in his election as king (1 Sam 19:11-17). But that love is now gone. She must know that she was the *only* condition that David demanded from the Saulide court when Abner came seeking an alliance with him (2 Sam 3:14). Ishbaal, her brother and a puppet successor to her father, ordered her abduction from her husband Paltiel, who followed her weeping (3:16), for her return to David. Paltiel's tears leave open the possibility that Michal had similar feelings for him. David has treated her as little more than a trophy that he won and then lost when Saul, her father, put him to flight. But at his first opportunity he demanded that trophy, Michal, back. Now she despises the king for dancing before the ark, which to her looks like dancing on her father's tomb.

The narrator, who has little empathy for Michal, has the last word: Michal died childless. By introducing that detail, the narrator implies a causal connection—divine retribution for her sneering glance and flippant remarks before God's chosen one. Moreover, her childlessness means that David's successor cannot be a Saulide descendant and ensures that Samuel's pronouncement to Saul that God had torn the kingdom from him and given it to someone better than he (1 Sam 15:28) is absolute. With this closing remark, the narrator dismisses Michal from the David Narrative. We never hear of her again.

---

[28] The title *nāgîd* looks forward to the next scene when God speaks to David about his election as the *nāgîd* (7:8).

3.5 God's Promise to David (7:1-29)

The normally fast-paced action of the narrative is suspended briefly so that we can attend a private audience that God grants David. The episode's literary genres (an oracle and a prayer), along with its unique themes and language, signal its special function in the David Narrative. For the first time our point of view hovers above a particular event in David's life. With events such as his flight from Saul, David's battles, or his dispute with Michal, we watched the scene unfold before us. Here, we are given a bird's-eye view into God's design for Israel's history and, in particular, how David's kingship is woven into that history that now embraces eternity. Up to this point, God's conversations with David have been pithy responses to specific inquiries such as whether Saul would attack Keilah (1 Sam 23:10-12) or whether he should pursue the Amalekite raiders (1 Sam 30:8). Now God makes his longest speech in the David Narrative. We have known about the special relationship between God and David from the moment that Samuel warned Saul that God had found his replacement, a person "after his own heart" (1 Sam 13:14) who would be better than he (1 Sam 15:28). We watched David's anointing at God's order (1 Sam 16:1-13), and recently David himself recognized his destiny (2 Sam 5:12). But until this moment God and David have not spoken on the subject.

In the David Narrative, this is the only time that the key events in Israel's history are reprised. The review serves to herald the next installment in that history: the establishment of David's house and throne forever. This divinely directed history was last reviewed by the dying Joshua, who recounted the events from Abraham's migration to Canaan up to Israel's arrival in the Promised Land (Josh 24:2-13). Now God extends this history to include David's throne and his royal line. In the brief opening scene (2 Sam 7:1-3) David notes the disparity between his cedar house and God's house, a tent. He intends to remedy that situation. As the dialogue between David and God develops, a play on the word "house" (appearing fifteen times) emerges. The house, namely, the Temple, that David intended to build for God becomes a house, namely, a royal line, that God will build for David. God seems to enjoy the wordplay. We should too.

STRUCTURE

This episode can be divided into three scenes:

1. David and Nathan: David proposes a "house" for the ark of God (7:1-3)

2. Nathan and God: the divine oracle
   a. God, who redeemed Israel, decides on his house (7:4-7)
   b. (*wĕʿattâ*) God will build a house for David (7:8-17)
3. David and God: David's response
   a. David praises God's redemptive acts (7:18-24)
   b. (*wĕʿattâ*) David's prayer (7:25-29)

The second and third scenes are in parallel. The first section of each scene recalls God's salvific acts with specific reference to the liberation from Egypt, and the second section presents God's promise to build a house for David that will last forever. In each scene, the second section is introduced with *wĕʿattâ* (translated in the NRSV with "Now therefore" in 7:8 and with "And now" in 7:25), signaling a consequence based on the premise set forth in the first section.

3.5.1 David and Nathan: David Proposes a "House" for the Ark of God (7:1-3)

When David conquered Jerusalem, the narrator, who, along with his readers, lived after the Temple had been built, was more focused on the capture of the site for the future temple than on the battle for Jerusalem. He called the newly conquered Jerusalem "Zion" (see 5:7), a reference to the place of God's dwelling, and closed the scene with a reminder of the custom that the blind and the lame were not to enter "the house," that is, the Temple (5:8). David now proposes to build that "house" for the ark of God that he just brought to his capital. At present David is dwelling in his house and the Lord has given him rest. The two phrases in the opening verse, joined by "and," imply causality: David enjoys peace in the realm and the comforts of his palace *because* the Lord has given him rest from his enemies. Indeed, it was God's military counsel that determined the defeat of the Philistines (5:19, 23), and in the scenes that follow this episode David is again victorious with God's help (8:6, 14). But the narrator's evaluation of the security of David's throne seems a bit rosy. More battles lie ahead. Unlike the previous conflicts, however, where David played defense (5:17 and 5:22), in future campaigns he will be the aggressor. After attacking and defeating the Philistines (8:1), he will garner a series of victories against the Moabites, Edomites, and others (8:2-14). His son Solomon will appeal to these battles to explain why, during David's reign, the construction of the Temple had to be postponed:

> You know that my father David could not build a house for the name of the LORD his God because of the warfare with which his enemies surrounded

him, until the LORD put them under the soles of his feet. But now the LORD
my God has given me rest on every side; there is neither adversary nor
misfortune. (1 Kgs 5:3-4)

During Solomon's reign, the geopolitical situation will improve. Not
only will God give Solomon the same "rest" that he gave to David,
but there will be neither "adversary nor misfortune" to impede the
Temple's construction. David never enjoyed this degree of "rest" from
his enemies, as Solomon explains, and therefore he could not build the
Temple.

The notice that David enjoys rest from his enemies recalls the covenant in which God promised to give Israel rest from its adversaries (Deut
12:10 and 25:19), to fight Israel's battles (Deut 3:22), and to bestow on
them the Promised Land:

> When the LORD gives rest to your kindred, as to you, and they too have
> occupied the land that the LORD your God is giving them beyond the
> Jordan, then each of you may return to the property that I have given to
> you. (Deut 3:20)

This divine promise frames Joshua's life. In his opening speech, Joshua
recalls Moses' words:

> Remember the word that Moses the servant of the LORD commanded you,
> saying, "The LORD your God is providing you a place of rest, and will give
> you this land." . . . [A]ll the warriors among you shall cross over armed
> before your kindred and shall help them, until the LORD gives rest to your
> kindred as well as to you, and they too take possession of the land that the
> LORD your God is giving them. (Josh 1:13-15a)

Near the end of his life Joshua summons the Reubenites, the Gadites,
and the half-tribe of Manasseh to announce that the covenantal promise
has been fulfilled:

> You have observed all that Moses the servant of the LORD commanded you
> and . . . have been careful to keep the charge of the LORD your God. And
> now the LORD your God has given rest to your kindred, as he promised
> them. (Josh 22:2-4a)

Just before Joshua's farewell speech, the narrator reminds us again that
the promise made to Moses has been fulfilled:

> A long time afterward, when the LORD had given rest to Israel from all
> their enemies all around, and Joshua was old and well advanced in years
> . . . (Josh 23:1)

The setting for Joshua's speech resembles the setting for this episode: a circumstantial clause (Joshua is old; David dwells in his palace) is coupled with the notice that God has given Israel rest from its enemies. The replay of covenantal language at this point in the David Narrative signals to the audience that God's covenant with Israel is under discussion.

At the center of this opening scene, David, having noticed the disparity between his cedar palace (King Hiram's gift in 2 Sam 5:11) and God's tent, consults with Nathan, who is introduced here for the first time and is called a "prophet," the only information given about him. In this role, he enjoys immediate access to the king like the prophets Elijah (1 Kgs 18:17) or Isaiah (2 Kgs 20:1). Nathan's later appearances come at moments when God's plan for David and his successor Solomon is at risk of collapse. When the death penalty looms for the king after he takes Bathsheba, Uriah's wife, and then orchestrates Uriah's murder, Nathan offers the king clemency (2 Sam 12:13), and so God's plan, announced in this chapter, endures. When Solomon is born, Nathan renames David's son Jedidiah, meaning "Beloved of the LORD" (12:25). As David lies on his sickbed, Nathan informs the king that Adonijah has announced his claim to the throne (1 Kgs 1:11-27), and then he proceeds to ensure Solomon's succession (1 Kgs 1).

The Hebrew word *yĕrî'â*, translated "tent" (2 Sam 7:2) in the NRSV, is the term used for the Lord's tabernacle that was built in the Sinai desert (Exod 25–31).[29] God, *not* Moses, initiated the construction of the tabernacle. David's reference to the ark's housing as the *yĕrî'â*, "tent," recalls that construction and foreshadows God's reaction to David: as in Exodus, so now, God alone decides on the design for the ark's dwelling and when it should be built. Thus, David's offer to build a temple is going to be declined. But for the moment, we are impressed with David's piety that prompts him to propose a proper temple for the Lord. David's first word to Nathan, "see," focuses the prophet's attention (and ours) on the incongruity between the royal palace and the ark's tent so that Nathan infers David's plans. The prophet, who seems to have the authority to commend the plan, gives his consent, reminding the king that God is with him, the same remark that the narrator made after David's conquest of Jerusalem (2 Sam 5:10).

David is referred to as "the king" three times in this opening scene in contrast with the preceding chapter in which the narrator referred to him as "David" twenty times and only twice as "King David" (6:12, 16) and never by the title "king" alone. These references to David's title foreshadow the theme of the upcoming oracle: God is about to extend the covenant with Israel to include the king and his "house."

---

[29] The term *yĕrî'â* in Exodus 26:1-13 describes the curtains that are to be woven for the tabernacle.

3.5.2 Nathan and God: The Divine Oracle (7:4-17)

God's longest speech in the David Narrative is divided into two sections: 7:4-7 and 7:8-17. The first section sets out the problem ("Are you the one . . . ?") and the premise for the upcoming announcement regarding David's throne. The second section, which begins with *wĕʿattâ* (7:8 "Now therefore"), draws a conclusion.

3.5.2.1 GOD DECIDES ON HIS HOUSE (7:4-7)

STRUCTURE

Setting (7:4)
A. A house for God ("should you [singular] build a house for me?") (7:5)
 B. The people of Israel (7:6ab)
  C. God moving about (7:6c)
   D. Tent and tabernacle (7:6d)
  C'. God moving about (7:7a)
 B'. The people of Israel (7:7b)
A'. A house for God ("you [plural] did not build a house for me") (7:7cd)

The inclusion (A/A') in God's speech focuses on David's intention to build the Temple. The B/B' and C/C' sections recall how God traveled with the "people of Israel" as they wandered through the desert before they entered the Promised Land. At the center lies the issue that has provoked the divine response: the tent, which David proposes to replace with the Temple.

COMMENTARY

As the previous scene closed Nathan consented to David's plan: "go and do." Now God orders Nathan to "go," meaning "go back," reversing Nathan's course in order to reverse David's plans. It is not the king's decision to build a house for the ark and God wastes little time in letting him know. Why does God not speak directly to David as in the recent battle scenes when God strategized the defeat of the Philistines (5:23-24)? In this scene there is much more at stake than the outcome of a single battle. God is about to shape the course of Israel's history and to reveal David's destiny. Thus the "word of the LORD," which in the books of Samuel comes only to prophets, now comes to the prophet Nathan for delivery to David.

The messenger formula, "Thus says the LORD" (7:5), common in prophetic literature to introduce divine speech, appears for the first of five times in the David Narrative. It is spoken four times by Nathan (twice here [7:5, 8] and twice after David's affair with Bathsheba [12:7, 11]) and once by the prophet Gad after David's crime of ordering the census (24:12). It signals to the reader that the words that follow belong to the sender, in this case God, and that the prophet is a mere conduit.[30] The oracle begins with a rhetorical question: "Are *you* the one to build me a house to live in?" God is not seeking information from David. The king has overstepped his authority and the rhetorical question corners David into proffering a negative answer: "No, in fact, I am not the one to build a house for God." The Hebrew strongly emphasizes the subject pronoun, "you" (ʾattâ), to underscore the contrast between David's role and God's role: *I* (God [not *you* David!]) led the people of Israel out of Egypt, *I* have traveled about among them, and *I* appointed people to shepherd Israel. This speech sets forth the premise—God, not David, guides Israel's history—for the argument in the next section (7:8-17).

The interpretive key to this discourse lies at its center. The "tent and tabernacle" recall the establishment of this movable structure as the ark's abode. It was God who determined its construction and who appointed its furnishings (Exod 25:9): "According to all that I show you concerning the construction of the tabernacle and the construction of all of its furniture, thus shall you do." Has David forgotten God's direct involvement in the design of this structure that has housed the ark for the last few centuries? God did not raise the question with David just as he had never raised it with any of the leaders of Israel. Thus, the question of a new abode for the ark is settled, and so the divine oracle could have ended here. But God has more to say.

3.5.2.2 GOD WILL BUILD A HOUSE FOR DAVID (7:8-17)

STRUCTURE

    A. Thus will you (Nathan) say (7:8a)
        B. What God did and will do for David (7:8b-9)
            C. What God will do for his people (7:10-11a)
                D. I will give you rest (7:11b)
                    E. The Lord will make you a house (7:11c)

---

[30] The messenger formula is not limited to divine speech. In Genesis 32:4 Jacob employs it when he sends messengers to Esau: "Thus says your servant Jacob."

D'. When you rest with your ancestors (7:12a)
C'. What God will do for David's kingdom (7:12bc-13)
B'. What God will do for David's successors (7:14-16)
A'. Thus Nathan spoke (7:17)

At the center of this section, when God promises to build a "house" for David, the discourse shifts momentarily into the third person and the name of the Lord (YHWH) appears twice. After this climax, the word "forever," *ʿôlām* (v. 13), appears seven times, reiterating that God's plan for David is eternal. In the frame around the center (C/C' and D/D' sections), God makes specific promises to Israel and to David's kingdom. The B/B' sections parallel what God (underscored by the use of the personal pronoun *ʾănî*, "I" [7:8b, 14]) did and will do for David. The oracle is framed by the messenger formula and the narrator's comment that Nathan had been faithful to the divine message (A/A').

COMMENTARY

Having laid out his premise, God now draws a conclusion (introduced with "Now therefore" [7:8]). The messenger formula ("thus you will say") is followed by God's reference to David as his "servant." David may be king of Israel, but to God he is a servant, and David, in his prayer before God, will apply that title to himself nine times (7:18-29). Referring to oneself as a "servant" is a normal expression of politeness when a person of lower status addresses a superior.[31] The longer title for God in 7:8, "the LORD of hosts," is used sparingly in the David Narrative. David called upon God under this title when he confronted Goliath (1 Sam 17:45), and it appeared in 2 Samuel 6 in the title for the ark (2 Sam 6:2) and in David's blessing over the people (6:18). It is used most often in prophetic books (appearing over sixty times in Isaiah). This divine title, coupled with the messenger formula, underscores the solemnity of this discourse. Never before has God spoken this way to David.

God's speech opens with the personal pronoun "I," which is not required since Hebrew verbs indicate their subject. The Hebrew phrase may be rendered "It was I who took you" to express the contrast between David and God that is signaled by the use of the first-person pronoun.[32] It was God, not David, who made David the *nāgîd* (translated "prince"

---

[31] Absalom, David's son, refers to himself as a "servant" when addressing the king, his father (13:24).

[32] For a discussion of this construction, see Bruce K. Waltke and M. O'Connor, *An Introduction to Biblical Hebrew Syntax* (Winona Lake, IN: Eisenbrauns, 1990), 16.3.2d.

in the NRSV) over his people. The title *nāgîd* appears for the first time in the Bible in 1 Samuel 9:16 when God tells Samuel to anoint the one whom he will present to him as ruler (*nāgîd*) over Israel. As Samuel anoints Saul in 1 Samuel 10:1, he bestows that title on him (translated "ruler" in the NRSV). Its use in this oracle reminds the reader that God has transferred Saul's title to David, as David has just reminded his wife Michal (2 Sam 6:21). God informs David that he has been with him on his travels, cutting off the power of his enemies. We witnessed that divine protection in 1 Samuel 18–31 when God guarded David from Saul's machinations and more recently when David routed his principal adversary, the Philistines. Now David learns from the mouth of God what we have known since the day he was anointed by Samuel. The four first-person-singular verbs focus our attention on God as the sole actor in David's life and in Israel's history: *I* [God] *took . . . I was with . . . I cut off . . . I will make. . . .* David would still be with his flocks but for God's design.

As the oracle draws closer to the center and to the promise of a royal line for David, the focus shifts from what God has done to what God is about to do for David and for the people of Israel. God will make David's name great (2 Sam 7:9b), echoing the language of the covenantal promise to Abraham in Genesis 12:2.[33] The promise to "plant" the people on their land, the Promised Land, recalls the ancient victory hymn in Exodus 15: God acquired the people and "planted" them (Exod 15:16-17) on his own mountain.[34] The future tenses in 2 Samuel 7:10-11 suggest that God's plan for the people of Israel has not yet been fully realized until this moment when God makes David the *nāgîd* over the people of Israel. But there is still more.

At the center of the passage (7:11c), the oracle shifts from first- to third-person discourse, signaling the formality of God's pledge to David (after this decree, the oracle shifts back to the first person) and demanding the reader's full attention. David had imagined a house of cedar for God. God imagines a house for David—a Davidic line of kings. The oracle then introduces new terminology—"kingdom," "throne," "establish," and "forever." God will establish the Davidic throne and the kingdom will dwell secure forever. The focus is not on David's successor, who is not named, but on the promise of an eternal, royal line.[35] The reader waits until 1 Kings 1 to learn who might be the

---

[33] Genesis 12:2: "I will make of you a great nation, and I will bless you, and make your name great, so that you will be a blessing."

[34] The prophet Jeremiah also employs the metaphor of "planting" (Jer 11:17) to describe how God bestowed the land on the people of Israel.

[35] In this episode neither God nor the narrator reveals Solomon's name (which the narrator certainly knows), even though Solomon's life is intertwined with that

undisclosed subject of the sentence "He shall build a house for my name" (7:13).[36] The question that provoked the divine oracle, David's decision to build the Temple, is now closed. The word "house" appears eight more times in this episode—always in reference to David's lineage.

In 7:14 the personal pronoun *ʾănî*, "I," again underscores God's personal relationship to the king who will succeed David: "It is I who will be a father to him" (translation mine). David's son may sit on the throne, but God, not David, will be his father.[37] The oracle then alludes to the crises that will beset the Davidic kingdom. God will chastise David's descendants for their iniquities by raising up enemies against them, including Jeroboam, the first king of the northern kingdom of Israel. So, as the oracle hints at the sundering of David's kingdom (1 Kgs 11:11), it also assures David that God will not remove his "steadfast love" (*ḥesed*) from David's offspring as he removed it from Saul. The divine speech closes with a reaffirmation of the promise that David's kingdom will endure forever.

The modern reader knows that David's kingdom is not eternal. The Babylonians will destroy the Temple that David's son will build and King Zedekiah, the last king to sit on David's throne, will be taken into exile to Babylon along with King Jehoiachin (2 Kgs 24–25). But the oracle makes no mention of these events (see 3.6 below: "The Promise to David Reprised in 1 Kings and Psalm 89"). The narrator signals that the oracle is over by indicating that Nathan has been faithful in transmitting the divine message (7:17).

---

of Nathan the prophet. Nathan appears immediately after Solomon's birth to name him Jedidiah (12:25), meaning "beloved by God," and later he thwarts Adonijah's succession to David's throne and thus engineers Solomon's anointing as king (1 Kgs 1). Adonijah might have succeeded his father but for Nathan's intervention. For now, God leaves us in suspense as to which of David's sons (already named in 2 Sam 3:2-5 and 5:14-16) will be his successor.

[36] When Solomon decides to build the Temple, he claims his role in God's promise to David: "the LORD said to my father David, 'Your son, whom I will set on your throne in your place, shall build the house for my name'" (1 Kgs 5:5).

[37] This theme of "divine adoption" of the king appears in ancient Near Eastern literature, as Levinson notes (citing Ps 89:27-28): "Yahweh similarly affirms the Davidic monarch, both legally adopting him and appointing him his earthly counterpart as head of the divine council" (Bernard M. Levinson, "The Reconceptualization of Kingship in Deuteronomy and the Deuteronomistic History's Transformation of Torah," *VT* 51 [2001]: 513).

3.5.3 David and God: David's Response (7:18-29)

David's response to this divine promise is divided into two sections:
(1) 7:18-24, David praises God; and (2) 7:25-29, David's prayer.

3.5.3.1 DAVID PRAISES GOD'S REDEMPTIVE ACTS (7:18-24)

STRUCTURE

The setting (7:18ab)

First rhetorical question: "Who am I?" (7:18c)
Second rhetorical question: "What is my house?" (7:18d)
    What God did for David (7:18e-19)
Third rhetorical question: "What more can David say?" (7:20a)
    God has made known to him his plan (7:20b-21)

David praises God (7:22)

Fourth rhetorical question: "Who is like your people?" (7:23a)
    What God did for the people of Israel (7:23bc-24)

The four rhetorical questions that structure this section provoke David to
further reflection on God's interventions into his own life and into Israel's
history. The first three questions underscore the relationship between
David and God. The fourth question focuses on the people of Israel.

COMMENTARY

The brief staging describes David "sitting" (*yšb*) before the Lord,
presumably in the tent that contains the ark that he just relocated to his
city. At the beginning of the episode, David was "sitting" (*yšb*) in his
cedar palace while the ark was "sitting" (*yšb*) in a tent (7:2). The question
that triggered God's speech is now resolved (David's heir will build the
Temple) and David has quit his palace to "sit" (*yšb*) in the tent that he
had intended to replace with the Temple.

The king utters four rhetorical questions that engage the reader to consider appropriate answers for them. With his first two questions, "Who am
I?" and "What is my house?" David acknowledges his own triviality before
God's majesty and confirms the theme of Nathan's oracle (7:4-17): God is
the primary actor in the life of this shepherd-king.[38] God has brought David

---

[38] Responding to God, Moses marks his lower social status with respect to Pharaoh with the same idiomatic expression: "Who am I that I should go to Pharaoh

to this point—crown and capital city—as David now acknowledges (7:18). In addition, God has granted David a glance into the distant future so that he might see the role that his "house" will play in Israel's history through an eternal dynasty that David will sire. Then, praising God, he acknowledges that this legacy is minuscule when compared with God's grandeur and uniqueness: "there is no one like you" (7:22). The meaning of the last part of 7:19, rendered accurately in the NRSV with "May this be instruction for the people, O Lord GOD!" is obscure.[39] Perhaps David supposes that God's covenant with him is to be an "instruction" for future generations. No more is said about that proposal. The third question, "What more can David say?" again acknowledges the king's insignificance before God's grand design for Israel's history; he can add nothing since God knows him through and through. His prayerful stance echoes Psalms 94:11, "The LORD knows our thoughts," and 139:1, "O LORD, you have searched me and known me," among others. God has made known his heart to David, an experience that also evokes praise from the psalmist:

> The counsel of the LORD stands forever,
> the thoughts of his heart to all generations. (Ps 33:11)[40]

Nathan had told David: "Go, do all that you have in your heart [*bilbābĕkā*, translation mine]." Now David, whom God chose long ago "according to his heart" (1 Sam 13:14), praises God for making this promise to him according to "his heart." God's "heart" has prevailed over David's "heart" that desired to build the Temple. The rhythm of the rhetorical questions is interrupted by a doxology (7:22) in which David, the legendary composer of the book of Psalms, appeals to poetic language to praise God who is without equal.[41]

---

and bring the Israelites out of Egypt?" (Exod 3:11). David responds similarly to Saul's offer of his daughter in marriage (1 Sam 18:18): "Who am I . . . ?"—a polite acknowledgment of King Saul's superior status (even though we know that David is God's choice for king).

[39] The NRSV and the NJPS note that the Hebrew is "uncertain." The REB omits the phrase while the NAB emends the text: "this too you have shown to man, Lord GOD!"

[40] As this psalm verse suggests, the Hebrew word *lēb*, normally translated "heart," connotes more our English word "mind," the place of thought, than the English meanings normally associated with "heart."

[41] The language of David's doxology appears in Psalm 71:19:
> Your righteousness, O God, reaches to the heavens.
> You who have done great things,
> O God, who is like you?
>   (translation mine)
See also Jeremiah 10:6 and Isaiah 45:5, 21.

   The fourth question, "Who is like your people?" shifts the prayer
from what God has done for David to what God has done for the people
of Israel as David reprises Israel's rescue from Egypt that was mentioned
in the divine oracle (7:6). This review prepares for a new element that
will now be included in salvation history: the establishment of David's
throne forever. A generation later, when Solomon recalls God's promise
at the dedication of the Temple, David's kingship will have become im-
mortalized in Israel's national story:

> Since the day that I brought my people Israel out of Egypt, I have not
> chosen a city from any of the tribes of Israel in which to build a house,
> that my name might be there; but I chose David to be over my people
> Israel. (1 Kgs 8:16)

David's pronouncement, "you, O LORD, became their God," echoes covenantal language, though the word "covenant" (*bĕrît*) never appears in
2 Samuel 7.[42] Near the end of his life, when David looks back on his
encounter with God in 2 Samuel 7, he defines God's promise to him as
an "everlasting covenant":

> Is not my house like this with God?
> For he has made with me an everlasting covenant [*bĕrît ʿôlām*]. (23:5)

3.5.3.2 DAVID'S PRAYER (7:25-29)

STRUCTURE

A. Double imperative ("establish" and "do") + jussive ("let it be
      great") + "forever" (7:25-26a)
   B. The Lord is God over Israel (7:26b)
      C. What God has done for David ("uncovering the ear")
            (7:27ab)
         D. God builds David a house (7:27c)
      C'. David's response to God ("to pray this prayer")
            (7:27de)
   B'. "You are God" (7:28)
A'. Double imperative ("be willing" and "bless") + jussive ("let it
      be blessed") + "forever" (7:29)

---

[42] God, in his covenant with Abraham, announces, "I will be their God" (Gen 17:8).

This section of David's prayer has a concentric structure. David opens and closes his prayer with two imperatives and a jussive. The Hebrew root *dbr* ("word" and "to speak") appears three times in 7:25 and again three times in 7:28-29. At the center of this section the divine promise is reiterated: God will build David a house. The closing verse (7:29) reprises the central revelation of this chapter and is translated below literally so that its structure may be apparent:

> A. Now then, be willing and bless
>> B. the house of your servant
>>> C. to be forever before you
>>>> D. for you Lord GOD have spoken
> A'. by your blessing, be blessed
>> B'. the house of your servant
>>> C'. forever.

The D section of this final verse underscores that the blessings that have graced and will grace David's life have come to him only because God "spoke."

COMMENTARY

As in Nathan's oracle, the shift in the argument is signaled with "now then" (*wĕʿattâ*). Having recalled the redemption of Israel from Egypt and the eternal establishment of the people of Israel (7:18-24), now David celebrates a new development in salvation history, entreating God to confirm his word by establishing the Davidic kingdom forever. He praises God for revealing this design to him, or, in the Hebrew idiom, for "uncovering his ear" (7:27). The Hebrew root *dbr* (which lies behind the verb "to speak" [*dibbēr*] and the noun "word" [*dābār*]) appears six times in David's prayer, three times in 7:25 and three times in 7:28-29, and in all cases, either God is the speaker or the word is his. Such language replays a theme from Nathan's oracle: God is the sole actor in Israel's history and in David's life. The initial proposal that provoked this oracle and prayer—the proposed temple—is long forgotten.

David's prayer celebrates the efficacy of the "word of the LORD," a theme that will be developed in 1 and 2 Kings. When a "man of God" announces God's word to Jeroboam, he refuses to eat and drink at Jeroboam's table because he has been so ordered by the "word of the LORD" (1 Kgs 13). Later he is tricked into eating by an old prophet from Bethel, and, soon after, he is met by a lion and killed. Shocking as the scene is, this story and others like it in the books of Kings confirm the theme of David's prayer: the word of the Lord does not go unfulfilled. Psalm singers (Pss 33:4; 56:10; and 119:89) and prophets (Isa 55:11 and 66:5) join in David's praise of the divine word:

> He sends out his command to the earth;
> his word runs swiftly.
>
> He declares his word to Jacob,
> his statutes and ordinances to Israel. (Ps 147:15, 19)

Together with poets and prophets, David bids God to fulfill his word and grant him the promised dynasty that will last forever.

3.6 The Promise to David Reprised in 1 Kings and Psalm 89

One question gnaws at the reader. David's throne is, in fact, not eternal. The narrator makes no allusion to the coming Babylonian invasion that will obliterate the Davidic throne (2 Kgs 25:8-21); nor does he offer a comment on the incongruence between the future ruin of David's kingdom and God's unconditional, eternal promise. Even though the crimes of David's successors (7:14b) will provoke divine ire, the promise will endure: "But I will not take my steadfast love from him" (7:15). Or will it? Subsequent references to this promise, including David's own recollection of it, annex a condition:

> Then the LORD will establish his word that he spoke concerning me: "*If* your heirs take heed to their way, to walk before me in faithfulness with all their heart and with all their soul, there shall not fail you a successor on the throne of Israel." (1 Kgs 2:4)

The requirement to "walk before me in faithfulness" was not mentioned in 2 Samuel 7. This condition appears again in 1 Kings 8 when Solomon prays before the Temple:

> Therefore, O LORD, God of Israel, keep for your servant my father David that which you promised him, saying, "There shall never fail you a successor before me to sit on the throne of Israel, *if* only your children look to their way, to walk before me as you have walked before me." (1 Kgs 8:25)

God's response to Solomon also rewrites the promise to David with a condition:

> As for you, *if* you will walk before me, as David your father walked, with integrity of heart and uprightness, . . . then I will establish your royal throne over Israel forever, as I promised your father David, saying, "There shall not fail you a successor on the throne of Israel." (1 Kgs 9:4-5)

The apparent ambiguity between the promise given in 2 Samuel 7 without conditions and later rehearsals of that promise with conditions is elucidated by the poetry of Psalm 89.[43] The poet, who knows of the Babylonian destruction of Jerusalem and the deportation of the last Davidic king, recasts the eternal promise made to David in 2 Samuel 7 with the conditions mentioned in 1 Kings 2:4; 8:25; and 9:4-5:

> Forever I will keep my steadfast love for him,
> and my covenant with him will stand firm.
> I will establish his line forever,
> and his throne as long as the heavens endure.
> If his children forsake my law
> and do not walk according to my ordinances,
> if they violate my statutes
> and do not keep my commandments,
> then I will punish their transgression with the rod
> and their iniquity with scourges;
> but I will not remove from him my steadfast love,
> or be false to my faithfulness.
> I will not violate my covenant,
> or alter the word that went forth from my lips. (Ps 89:28-34)

While the psalmist echoes the theme of God's punishment in 2 Samuel 7:14-15 ("When he commits iniquity, I will punish him"), the covenant with David endures despite the failure of David's descendants to meet its conditions.

The psalmist, like our narrator, knows that the Davidic line in Jerusalem will come to an end. But has the promise been annulled? The poet faces this question head on:

> But now you have spurned and rejected him;
> you are full of wrath against your anointed.
> You have renounced the covenant with your servant;
> you have defiled his crown in the dust. (Ps 89:38-39)

In this hour of destruction and exile, the psalmist concludes with a plea to God to remember the "steadfast love" he promised to David:

---

[43] There has been some discussion as to which text, 2 Samuel 7:4-17 or Psalm 89:19-37, contains the original form of the oracle. Nahum M. Sarna argued that the oracle in Psalm 89 is a "deliberate and original exegesis on the part of the psalmist, who has adapted an ancient oracle to a new situation" (Nahum M. Sarna, "Ps 89: A Study in Inner Biblical Exegesis," in *Biblical and Other Studies*, ed. A. Altmann, Brandeis Texts and Studies 1 [Cambridge, MA: Harvard University Press, 1963]: 29–46).

Lord, where is your steadfast love of old,
which by your faithfulness you swore to David? (Ps 89:49)

The psalmist's hope for the restoration of the Davidic throne may explain
why the narrator in 2 Samuel 7 makes no allusion to the future destruction
of David's city and his royal line. Both poet and narrator trust that the
Babylonian exile is but a momentary punishment, while the promise that
God made to David remains eternal. The poet pleads for the restoration of
the Davidic throne while our narrator recounts the unconditional promise
to David without comment. While his narrative art does not permit a
plea like that of the psalmist, his silence on the incongruence between the
promise and the coming destruction of Jerusalem, which he will recount,
witnesses to his hope that David's kingdom will one day be restored.

3.7 David Attacks and Defeats His Neighbors with God's Help (8:1-14)

The narrator's art in this chapter—a rapid succession of victories
with David as the sole actor—allows us to observe the ascent of the shepherd-king onto the world stage. Victories over the Philistines, Moabites,
Edomites, and Arameans are woven into a single episode in order to
demonstrate the narrator's purpose expressed by his refrain: "the Lord
gave victory to David [and to David alone] wherever he went." God,
who just promised to bestow on David a great name (7:9), is already
making good on his word.

STRUCTURE

1. David's victories (8:1-6)
    David strikes (*nkh*) the Philistines (8:1)
    David strikes (*nkh*) the Moabites (8:2ab)
        Refrain 1: The Moabites became servants to David,
            bearers of tribute (8:2c)
    David strikes (*nkh*) Hadadezer (8:3-4)
    David strikes (*nkh*) the Arameans (8:5)
        Refrain 2: David establishes garrisons in foreign terri-
            tory (8:6a)
        Refrain 1: The Arameans became servants to David,
            bearers of tribute (8:6b)
        Refrain 3: The Lord gave victory to David wherever he
            went (8:6c)

2. David and the plunder (8:7-14)
   David takes gold from Hadadezer's servants and bronze
   from Hadadezer's town (8:7-8)
   David receives tribute from King Toi (8:9-10)
   David dedicates all the plunder to the Lord (8:11-12)
   David defeats the Edomites (8:13)
   Refrain 2: David establishes garrisons in foreign terri-
   tory (8:14a)
   Refrain 3: The Lord gave victory to David wherever he
   went (8:14b)

This episode divides into two sections: David's victories and his handling
of the plunder. The first verse functions as an overture as it introduces the
two verbs that guide our reading: David "strikes" (*nkh*) his foes and then
"takes" (*lqḥ*) plunder. Second Samuel 8:2-6 reports three more victories,
employing the verb *nkh*, "to strike," each time (the four appearances of
nkh are rendered with four different verbs in the NRSV), and 8:7-14, beginning with *lqḥ*, "to take" (used twice in this section), reports on what
David did with the plunder that he took. Three interlocking pairs of
refrains integrate the whole unit.

COMMENTARY

The transition to this episode, marked by the expression *wayĕhî 'aḥărê
kēn* (NRSV: "Some time afterward"), indicates that an unspecified period
of time has passed since God's promise to David in the previous episode.[44] The narrator presents a series of campaigns that read more like a
list of accomplishments than a war chronicle. Where and when did these
battles occur? What was David's victory strategy? Did he consult the
Lord? What losses did he sustain? Previous reports of battles with the
Philistines (5:17-21, 22-25) included a few details such as their locations
and battle strategies. But in this chapter even these details are suppressed
so that our attention might be focused on David, the sole actor.

In the ancient Middle East, kings went to war in the springtime, when
the rains stopped.[45] (It is difficult to move an army through the mud of

[44] See Charles Conroy, *Absalom Absalom! Narrative and Language in 2 Sam 13–20*,
Analecta Biblica 81 (Rome: Biblical Institute Press, 1978), 41–42.

[45] David sends Joab to lay siege to Rabbah "in the spring of the year" (11:1), according to the NRSV. The REB, NAB, and NJB provide a more literal translation—"at
the turn of the year," a reference to spring.

a cold winter rain.) Did David defeat the Philistines, the Moabites, King Hadadezer, the Arameans, and the Edomites in a single season? Unlikely. These campaigns must have happened over several years, though the rapid-fire list of victories creates the impression that David was fighting on all sides at the same time—a miraculous military feat that confirms the narrator's repeated interjection: "The LORD gave victory to David wherever he went." At times, the narrator seems to be overcome with admiration for David.

The opening scene, a hurried account of David's victory over the Philistines, gives the impression that the king singlehandedly overwhelmed Israel's principal adversary (as when he killed Goliath in 1 Sam 17). Just after his conquest of Jerusalem, David, still trying to fortify his city, came under two Philistine attacks (5:17-21, 22-25). Back then, his defensive maneuvers, with God's advice, brought him victory. Now David goes on the offensive, appropriating "Metheg-ammah," the meaning of which is unknown. The Chronicler, the first interpreter of 2 Samuel 8:1b, rendered it "Gath and its villages," suggesting that a major Philistine city came under Davidic rule (1 Chr 18:1). The Peshitta also interprets it as a place name, though a different one: "Ramath-gama" or "the hill of Gama." The Vulgate's interpretation, *frenum tributi*, "a bridle of tribute," associates the meaning of Metheg-ammah with the tribute that David received from other defeated populations. Despite this obscurity, the meaning of this scene is lucid. David defeated the Philistines and took "Metheg-ammah," whatever it was, from them. He "subdues" them just as the prophet Samuel did after the Philistines returned the ark of the Lord to Israel (1 Sam 7:13).

Next David routs the Moabites (a people who lived on the plateau on the other side of the Jordan), extending his authority to the east just as he has done to the west against the Philistines. (The fact that, during his flight from Saul, David had deposited his parents with the king of Moab [1 Sam 22:3-4], then an ally, seems to have been forgotten.) The scene focuses on David's treatment of the captured Moabites; nothing of the battle is reported. The meaning of David's actions—measuring prisoners of war with ropes to determine their fate—is uncertain. The wearing of ropes can be a sign of penitence (in 1 Kgs 20:31 Ben-hadad wears ropes on his head when he begs Ahab to spare his life), but using ropes to adjudicate captives appears only here in the Bible. Whatever its ancient meaning, it is clear that David swiftly subdued the Moabites, who lay prostrate before him awaiting a life or death sentence from their vanquisher. This brief scene concludes with the narrator's report that the Moabites became David's servants, bearing him tribute. This is the first time in his life that he achieves such a decisive victory over an enemy.

In the next campaign the narrator expands on the penalty David exacts from his foe. He strikes Hadadezer of Zobah,[46] who was heading off to renovate his monument along the Euphrates River, a region over which he must have exercised considerable authority (later Hadadezer conscripts the Arameans who live beyond the Euphrates to fight against David [2 Sam 10:16]).[47] Again, no information is provided about the battle, its location, its strategies, or the casualties among David's troops. The focus is on the scale of David's victory: twenty thousand infantry troops and seventeen hundred cavalry were captured along with a near thorough defeat of the charioteers. Still, Hadadezer's people are not reduced to tribute-bearing servants like the Moabites, and Hadadezer will remain a threat as he and his allies will engage David again in battle (10:15-19). Nevertheless, David has scuttled a major military power.

Our attention shifts to the Arameans of Damascus, a people who had allied themselves with Hadadezer in battle. David defeats them too, killing twenty-two thousand, and then establishes garrisons around Damascus, extending his dominion over Hadadezer's allies. The Arameans, like the Moabites, become David's servants and bear him tribute. After these four victories, the narrator interjects a comment for our reflection: "The LORD gave victory to David wherever he went" (8:6). When we heartily agree, the narrator's craft is a success! Only with divine help could David have achieved so handily this rapid series of decisive victories. The narrator, again ignoring the details of the battle, focuses on the gold and bronze that David received from Hadadezer and from his cities, Betah and Berothai (their precise locations are unknown). The plunder now becomes the critical stage prop for the rest of this episode.

Up to this point (8:8), David has defeated his adversaries and then exacted tribute. Now tribute comes to him without a battle. King Toi of Hamath sends his son Joram (not an ordinary court messenger) with salutations for King David along with gold, bronze, and silver, because David has defeated Hadadezer, Toi's enemy. Hamath, Toi's capital, is about 450 kilometers (280 miles) north of Jerusalem. The narrator's comment that "David made a name for himself" (8:13; translation mine) recalls God's promise to make David's name great (7:9). The narrator seems to suggest that David is achieving greatness by his own power,

---

[46] Zobah is perhaps in the north Biqa Valley in Lebanon (see Wayne T. Pitard, "Zobah," in *ABD*, 6:1108).

[47] David's swift dispatch of Hadadezer suggests that the battle in which he defeated Hadadezer's allies and his Aramean mercenaries, which is recounted later in 2 Samuel 10:15-19, had already happened. But the narrator's focus in this episode on David's multiple victories and his dedication of the bountiful plunder prevails over these chronological inconsistencies.

though, by his handling of the plunder (see below), David acknowledges that God is winning for him. David's name rivals that of King Hadadezer who ruled from Damascus to the Euphrates. David's influence extends north toward Hamath, east toward the Euphrates, southeast toward Moab, and west toward the cities of the Philistines. Soon he will conquer Edom, a kingdom that lies south of Moab. We might expect a report of David's victory celebrations in Jerusalem, the seat of this new world power. Instead, the narrator wants us to know what David did with the plunder, a seemingly insignificant matter in light of his recent military successes. The gold and bronze taken from Hadadezer are brought to Jerusalem, and, together with the tribute from King Toi, they are dedicated to the Lord. The Hebrew verb *qdš*, "to dedicate," appears *twice* in 8:11 as David dedicates the plunder from *all* the nations to the Lord. What is going on?

David's pious handling of the booty recalls that critical moment during Saul's reign when the hapless king failed to handle properly the plunder he seized from the Amalekites and so lost his throne to David (1 Sam 15). God had promised Saul victory over the Amalekites and given explicit orders that *all* the plunder was to be destroyed (1 Sam 15:3). But the disobedient Saul and his troops retained some of the plunder for themselves (1 Sam 15:19). That was Saul's final act of disobedience. Immediately afterward, the prophet Samuel was ordered to anoint David as Saul's replacement. David's handling of the plunder signals that he knows that his victories come only with God's help. So, instead of leading victory parades through his capital city, the faithful David dedicates the plunder, including the plunder taken from the *Amalekites*, to the Lord. But David did not engage the Amalekites in battle! The devout dedication of the Amalekite plunder to the Lord ensures that we associate David's actions with Saul's fall from grace. It is as if David went back to the story of Saul's dethroning in 1 Samuel 15, gathered up that Amalekite plunder that Saul failed to handle properly, and finally ensured that it too was dedicated to the Lord. He, not Saul, is the rightful king of Israel.[48]

David's final campaign, against the Edomites,[49] leads to another huge casualty count. Large casualty counts are not uncommon in the historical narratives of the Bible. Modern readers rightfully wonder what to make

---

[48] David also receives tribute from the Ammonites with whom he is, at present, an ally (see 10:1-2). The narrator offers a summary of David's victories that anticipates his future defeat of the Ammonites (10:6-19).

[49] In 2 Samuel 8:13 the Hebrew text reads "Aram," a confusion of two similar Hebrew letters, *daleth* and *resh* (1 Chr 18:12 reads "Edom"). Edom lies southeast of the Dead Sea, over one hundred kilometers (sixty-two miles) south of Jerusalem, and some scholars would locate the "Valley of Salt" in that region.

of them when scholars estimate that the population of Jerusalem in the Solomonic period was between four thousand and sixty-four hundred (even the population of Jerusalem ca. 700 BCE was only between 15,500 and 24,800).[50] In the David Narrative such numbers first appear when the women who come out to meet David after his contest with Goliath sing that David had slaughtered "his ten thousands" (1 Sam 18:7). In 2 Samuel 8:5 David kills twenty-two thousand Arameans, and later he will slaughter another forty thousand of them (10:18), a number that was labeled "suspicious" by H. P. Smith over a century ago.[51] Near the end of his life, David learns that 1.3 million soldiers live in his realm (to which must be added women, children, and men of nonmilitary age). Israel Abrahams in the *Encyclopedia Judaica* expresses the scholarly consensus that "Biblical numbers are not always intended to be taken at their face value. They are often used indefinitely—as round figures—or rhetorically, for emphasis or in a hyperbolic sense."[52] Henri Matisse, quoting Delacroix, titled his 1947 essay "Exactitude Is Not Truth."[53] Matisse argued that the representation of forms depended "on the profound feeling of the artist before the objects that he has chosen, on which his attention is focused, and whose spirit he has penetrated."[54] Our narrator, like an impressionist artist, is not trying to represent with exactitude the casualty counts or the size of David's army. His "feelings" are focused on "the objects that he has chosen," namely, David and God's predilection for David, his servant. The casualty counts witness to our narrator's awe for these two "objects," whose truths he seeks to penetrate through his art.

Did David sustain any casualties in this battle that saw eighteen thousand dead Edomites? The narrator leaves the impression that he did not, adding to the evidence that the Lord was with David wherever he went. The location of the battle, the Valley of Salt, is not known with certainty and the issue is irrelevant to the narrator's purpose. David reigns supreme in the territories surrounding his capital, establishing military outposts as far south as Edom and reducing those populations to servitude. The flashback to this battle in 1 Kings 11 reveals that the narrator knows that Joab, who fought alongside David, was responsible

---

[50] David Tarler and Jane M. Cahill, "David, City of" in *ABD*, 2:67.

[51] Henry P. Smith, *A Critical and Exegetical Commentary on the Books of Samuel*, The International Critical Commentary (Edinburgh: T & T Clark, 1899), 316.

[52] Israel Abrahams, "Typical and Important Numbers," in *Encyclopaedia Judaica* (Jerusalem: Keter, 2007), 15:334.

[53] The essay was reprinted in English in the 1948 catalogue for the Philadelphia Museum of Art that presented a Matisse exhibition. See Jack Flam, ed., *Matisse on Art* (Berkeley/Los Angeles: University of California Press, 1995), 179.

[54] Ibid.

for some of the casualties.[55] But the narrator withholds that information
for now so that we keep focused on David alone. God bestowed these
several victories on him, not on Joab. The narrator closes with a refrain
that again exposes what motivates his craft: God gave the victory to
David. On that day long ago when he faced Goliath, David professed
before Saul that he enjoyed God's favor: "The LORD, who saved me from
the paw of the lion and from the paw of the bear, will save me from the
hand of this Philistine" (1 Sam 17:37). His victory over Goliath was just
the first in a string of divine interventions that now have propelled the
shepherd-king onto the world stage.

3.8 David Establishes His Government in Jerusalem (8:15-18)

Davidic rule is now sufficiently secure that the king can establish a
government and so the narrator pauses the action to list its members.
Even today, the first act of a newly elected head of state is the formation
of a government. When the Queen of Sheba arrives at Solomon's court,
she marvels at his authority:

> The Queen of Sheba perceived all the wisdom of Solomon, the house that
> he had built, the seating of his courtiers, and his attending servants. (1 Kgs
> 10:4-5a; translation mine)

By noting the "seating order" of his top officials, namely, the structure
of Solomon's government, she recognizes that Solomon's rule is stable.
By contrast, the rebel Absalom will begin to establish a government by
appointing Amasa as military commander (2 Sam 17:25), but this will be
a crisis appointment as he attempts to secure his father's throne. He dies
before he can appoint the members of his government. As soon as David
quashes the rebellions of both Absalom and Sheba, he will reestablish his
government and the narrator provides a second, similar list of its chief
members (20:23-26), assuring us that his throne is once again secure.

Thus, what appears at first glance as a rather insignificant list of
courtiers is, in fact, a critical milestone in David's public life. At the time
of his anointing (1 Sam 16), the formation of a government was out of
the question. Though he became a rising courtier in Saul's entourage,

---

[55] 1 Kings 11:15-17a: "For when David was in Edom, and Joab the commander of
the army went up to bury the dead, he killed every male in Edom (for Joab and all
Israel remained there six months, until he had eliminated every male in Edom); but
Hadad fled to Egypt with some Edomites."

marrying the king's daughter (1 Sam 18:27), when Saul felt threatened by him, he was forced to flee. God's choice for king had no government and his subjects included "everyone who was in distress, and everyone who was in debt, and everyone who was discontented" (1 Sam 22:2). Gradually, David came to exercise command, securing the allegiance of the sons of Zeruiah (1 Sam 26:6)—Joab, Abishai, and Asahel—who would become his military commanders. He also had Abiathar as his priest (1 Sam 22:20-23 and 30:7). But this was hardly a stable government. With Saul's death, events hastened toward the establishment of a Davidic administration. The fugitive king returned to Hebron and was anointed king by the people of Judah (2 Sam 2:3-4). Abner, Saul's general, joined David's side, and Saul's son and successor, Ishbaal, was murdered. David relocated his capital to Jerusalem and, after fending off Philistine attacks, he brought the ark of the Lord into his city. Finally, having received God's promise of an eternal throne, he extended his dominion far beyond the walls of his capital, acquiring the great name that God promised him. Now the once shepherd-king is ready to form a stable government.

The narrator opens with a comment on the nature of Davidic rule: "David administered justice [*mišpāṭ*] and equity [*ṣĕdāqâ*] to all his people" (8:15). This is high praise since *mišpāṭ* and *ṣĕdāqâ* often describe divine justice (see, for example, Isa 33:5; Jer 9:24; and Ps 99:4), and thus Davidic rule should be considered a manifestation of God's justice on earth. The narrator's comment prepares us for what is to come in the next episode: the king who rules with *mišpāṭ* and *ṣĕdāqâ* keeps faith (*ḥesed*) with the surviving members of the house of Saul, according to the promise he made to Jonathan in 1 Samuel 20:14-15. Near the end of his life, David sings that he wants to be remembered as a king who ruled with justice:

> The God of Israel has spoken,
> the Rock of Israel has said to me:
> One who rules over people justly [*ṣaddîq*],
> ruling in the fear of God,
> is like the light of morning. (2 Sam 23:3-4a)

In this list and in the later list in 20:23-26 Joab comes first. As chief of the army, he is unquestionably the most powerful person at court, perhaps more powerful than the king (see the discussion of Joab's character in section 1.4.3 above). He can disregard royal orders (murdering Absalom in 18:14) and can order the king into battle (12:27-28).[56] Jehoshaphat,

---

[56]Abner, King Ishbaal's general, reminds King Ishbaal that he keeps the king on his throne (3:8).

mentioned for the first time, will remain David's recorder throughout his reign (see 20:24) and will join Solomon's court (1 Kgs 4:3). Seraiah, the secretary, is also mentioned in the second list (20:25; written Sheva[57]) and the division of labor between the secretary and the recorder is left to our imagination. David's priests, according to this first list, are Zadok and Ahimelech but in the second list, they are Zadok and Abiathar (20:25). Zadok, mentioned for the first time, will remain loyal to David during Absalom's rebellion (15:24-29) and during Adonijah's attempt to claim his father's throne (1 Kgs 1:8). Ahimelech, *son* of Abiathar, is otherwise unknown. The priest Ahimelech, *father* of Abiathar, was executed by Saul for collusion with David (1 Sam 22:18), but his son, Abiathar, escaped to David (1 Sam 22:20) and, like Zadok, remained loyal to David during Absalom's rebellion (15:24-29), but later he allied himself with Adonijah (1 Kgs 1:7). Numerous scholars suggest that the reading in the Hebrew text, "Ahimelech, son of Abiathar" (so the NRSV), in 2 Samuel 8:17 is corrupt and prefer "Zadok and Abiathar" (with the REB and the NJB), thus harmonizing this list with the later one in 20:23-26. But this textual confusion rests quietly in the passage, which is focused not so much on an accurate list of names as on proclaiming that David's reign is now stable enough to establish a government.

Benaiah son of Jehoiada, one of David's most trusted subordinates and a fierce warrior, appears in the second list as well (20:23). When Joab and Abiathar join Adonijah's faction, Benaiah remains loyal to David (1 Kgs 1:8), accompanying Nathan and Zadok to anoint Solomon as David's successor (1 Kgs 1:38-39). Benaiah's loyalty to Solomon is exemplified in 1 Kings 2 when, in three different scenes, he discharges Solomon's orders, executing Adonijah (1 Kgs 2:25), Joab (1 Kgs 2:34), and Shimei (1 Kgs 2:46) and replacing Joab as military commander (1 Kgs 2:35). Benaiah was "over"[58] the Cherethites and the Pelethites, David's most loyal guard that springs into action in moments of crisis. They march out with the king when Absalom's rebellion forces him to abandon Jerusalem (2 Sam 15:18), they assist in the pursuit of the rebellious Sheba son of Bichri (20:7), and they are present (with Benaiah) when Zadok anoints Solomon as David's successor. The narrator presumes we recognize them

---

[57] Seraiah, Sheva (20:25), and Shavsha (1 Chr 18:16) are thought to be the same person. See J. Maxwell Miller and John H. Hayes, *A History of Ancient Israel and Judah* (Louisville, KY / London: Westminster John Knox Press, 1986), 187.

[58] Most English translations report that Benaiah was "over" the Cherethites and the Pelethites. This reading is borrowed from 1 Chronicles 18:17: "Benaiah son of Jehoiada was over [ʿal] the Cherethites and the Pelethites" (reading ʿal where 2 Sam 8:18 reads a *waw*). The Hebrew text in 2 Samuel 8:18 reports that Benaiah, the Cherethites, the Pelethites, and David's sons were priests.

and opts not to clutter the story by explaining their role to us. Finally, David's sons were priests, inheriting their father's role as the priest who donned the linen ephod, offered sacrifice and blessed the people when the ark of the covenant was transferred to Jerusalem (6:13-14 and 6:17-19).

Act 3, which opened with David's conquest of Jerusalem, now closes with the Davidic government extending its rule from Jerusalem in every direction. The relocation of the ark of the Lord to Zion, the city of David, celebrated David's special relationship with God who preferred him over Saul and promised him an eternal lineage. The House of David is now enshrined in God's covenant with the people of Israel. The king stands at the apex of his power.

Chapter 4

ACT 4: DIVINE RESCUE FOR A BEGUILED KING
2 SAMUEL 9–20

4.1 Introduction

Act 3 closed with the establishment of David's government, after his victories over neighboring states, and this act will close with the reestablishment of that government. But in between King David will be beguiled several times and nearly lose his throne. This act opens with David exercising his authority over the remnants of the house of Saul as Mephibosheth is given permanent residence at the royal palace. David acts in accord with the oath that he made with Jonathan. Immediately afterward, he subdues the Ammonites (2 Sam 10). But the threats to his throne from within his court will prove far more menacing than the Philistines or the Ammonites. He is forgiven for his affair with Bathsheba and his subsequent murder of Uriah (12:13), after Nathan beguiles him with a parable about a ewe lamb. David's missteps continue when Amnon rapes Tamar and David fails to punish Amnon. Absalom beguiles David with a tale about a sheep-shearing festival to which the king sends his sons, including Amnon, whom Absalom promptly has killed and then flees. Fooled by a phony widow, David consents to Absalom's return to Jerusalem. Finally, David falls for Absalom's ruse to go to Hebron, a decision that could have cost David his life. But it does not, only because, at the climax of this act, God will intervene to ensure Absalom's ruin, and the beguiled king is rescued. After a second rebellion is put down, David is able to reestablish his government in Jerusalem and act 4 comes to a close.

4.2 David's Fidelity to His Covenant with Jonathan (9:1-13)

Act 3 closed with the notice that David ruled with justice and equity. The opening episode of act 4 illustrates why the king merited such high praise: David shows the "kindness of God" (9:3) to a surviving Saulide descendant. In the account that follows, a major subplot in the David Narrative, the story of the covenant between David and Jonathan, comes back on stage: Jonathan is dead and David is about to fulfill his part of their agreement.

STRUCTURE

> A. David's intention (9:1)
>> B. The king speaks to Ziba (9:2-5)
>>> C. Mephibosheth does obeisance (9:6)
>>>> D. David fulfills his covenant with Jonathan (9:7)
>>> C'. Mephibosheth does obeisance (9:8)
>> B'. The king speaks to Ziba (9:9-11)
> A'. David's intention is accomplished (9:12-13)

The D section at the center, framed by Mephibosheth's expression of obeisance (C/C'), reveals the narrator's reason for including this episode within the David Narrative: David fulfills the promise that he made long ago to Jonathan, Saul's son. In a first exchange with Ziba (B), David discovers the whereabouts of Jonathan's son so that he may "show the kindness of God" to him, and in their second exchange David outlines the specifics of his act of "kindness" (B'). The entire episode is framed by David's intention to be faithful to Jonathan's son (A) and the narrator's concluding remark that he had done so (A'). Up to and including the center of this episode David's statement "I will show kindness" is repeated three times. From the center until the end of the episode the decree that Mephibosheth will eat at the king's table is repeated four times. At the center (D) the two matters converge: David's expression of kindness means that Mephibosheth will eat at the king's table. The narrator is attentive to the proper use of David's royal title. In 9:1-2a he refers to David by name, but when Ziba arrives he prefers the title "king" (9:2b-4). He switches back to David's name with Mephibosheth (9:6-7) even though Mephibosheth greets David with deference ("your servant"). When Ziba comes back on stage, so does the title "king" (9:9-11).

COMMENTARY

David's request for information regarding Saul's descendants opens this episode. No setting is provided. It seems we are meant to imagine that the king is addressing the courtiers that were just listed in 8:16-18, though we are left to wonder which of them executed his inquiry and went to fetch Ziba. This paucity of detail keeps our attention focused on the narrator's objective, which is to portray David's fidelity to his promise to Jonathan. One word in David's opening question is unexpected. Why does the king ask if there is anyone *left* in Saul's house? His focus on those *still remaining* allows some redaction critics to argue that this episode once followed the account of the execution of seven of Saul's descendants (now recounted in 21:1-14). The way David articulates his question seems to presume their deaths. Adding to this evidence, when Saul's descendant, Mephibosheth, finally appears, David assures him that he has nothing to fear (9:7). Mephibosheth could be afraid because he knew of the deaths of Saul's descendants reported in 21:1-14 and was expecting to share his cousins' fate. Moreover, this episode, were it to follow the execution of seven Saulide descendants, could illustrate how King David secured his throne by sequestering Mephibosheth, a remaining claimant, under his court's watchful eye. This evidence, though by no means conclusive,[1] triggers the question as to the function of the Mephibosheth story in its present location, separated from the account of the deaths of Saul's descendants and following the establishment of David's court. The narrator knows that David will enjoy a long reign and will see his son succeed him, and therefore he also knows that Mephibosheth's claim to the throne poses absolutely no threat to David. When, in his final discourse to Solomon, David identifies potential threats to his son's throne, he names Joab and Shimei but not Mephibosheth (1 Kgs 2:5-9). From the narrator's point of view, the Mephibosheth episode, were it once about putting a claimant to David's throne under house arrest, no longer needs to serve that purpose. It can be used to portray David as a king who remained faithful to his covenant with Jonathan—the king's first order of business after establishing his government.

The story of the covenant between David and Jonathan began back in 1 Samuel 18:1-5 when the two were seen together for the first time. The soul of Jonathan was said to be "bound" with David's (1 Sam 18:1), and, though the reason for Jonathan's admiration for David was not disclosed, we could imagine, without any comment from the narrator, that Jonathan, like us, had been astounded by David's recent defeat of

---

[1] In 21:1-14 David knows of Mephibosheth's existence (21:7), whereas his question in 9:1 presumes his ignorance of this Saulide descendant.

the giant Philistine, Goliath (1 Sam 17). At their first meeting, the particulars of their covenant were not disclosed, though Jonathan's gestures in 1 Samuel 18:4 (conferring on David his outer clothes, his sword, bow, and belt) suggested he had made himself David's vassal, even conceding to him his right of succession. When David is forced to flee from Saul's murderous schemes, he finds Jonathan and in their exchange (1 Sam 20:12-17), in which Jonathan employs the covenantal term *ḥesed* (translated "kindness" in 2 Sam 9:1), we learn more about their pact:

> May the LORD be with you, as he has been with my father. If I am still alive, show me the faithful love of the LORD; but if I die, never cut off your faithful love [*ḥesed*] from my house, even if the LORD were to cut off every one of the enemies of David from the face of the earth. (1 Sam 20:13c-15)

Jonathan, praying that God will be with David while acknowledging that God is no longer with his father, appeals to David to remain loyal to his descendants. David bids Jonathan to discover Saul's intentions toward him during the next day's new moon festivities (1 Sam 20:5-7), and they develop a plan for Jonathan to signal to David their next rendezvous. At the festive meal, Saul, angered by David's absence, throws his spear at Jonathan (1 Sam 20:33), who then heads out to meet David (a moment captured most poignantly by Rembrandt's *David and Jonathan* [1642]). The two reaffirm their covenant:

> Then Jonathan said to David, "Go in peace, since both of us have sworn in the name of the LORD, saying, 'The LORD shall be between me and you, and between my descendants and your descendants, forever.'" He got up and left; and Jonathan went into the city. (1 Sam 20:42)

They meet for a final time while David is hiding from Saul in the Wilderness of Ziph (1 Sam 23:15) and Jonathan declares that David (not he) will be Saul's successor (1 Sam 23:17), thus confirming, at last, our hunch as to why he conferred his weapons on David the day they first met (1 Sam 18:4). For the third time they affirm their covenant (1 Sam 23:18) and Jonathan departs never to see David again. The news of the existence of Jonathan's son, Mephibosheth, inserted just after Abner's murder (2 Sam 4:4), evoked the memory of David's promise to show "the faithful love [*ḥesed*] of the LORD" (1 Sam 20:14) to that son. When David, in his opening question in this episode, retrieves the word *ḥesed*,[2] his covenant with Jonathan springs to mind.

---

[2] Unfortunately, the NRSV is not consistent in its translation of *ḥesed*: in 2 Samuel 9:1 it is translated as "kindness" but in 1 Samuel 20:14 it is translated as "faithful love."

The narrator pauses the action to inform us of Ziba's existence, delaying the appearance of Mephibosheth, so we can attend to David's exchange with Ziba in which David repeats his earlier question. Ziba, who was once a trusted member of Saul's court, responds to David's summons with (literally) "your servant" (rendered in the NRSV with "at your service"). Not only is Saul's servant now loyal to David, but this is the *first* time in the David Narrative that David receives such a deferential form of address. When David addressed King Saul for the first time in 1 Samuel 17:32, he employed this polite expression to refer to himself: "David said to Saul, 'Let no one's heart fail because of him; your servant will go and fight with this Philistine.'" He applied it to himself (and his men) again when he sent messengers to Nabal (1 Sam 25:8), when he addressed King Achish of Gath (1 Sam 27:5; 28:2; 29:8), and when he addressed God (1 Sam 23:11 and 2 Sam 7:20-29). Now, one of David's subjects, a one-time member of Saul's court, addresses him with this deferential greeting. This detail bridges the opening episode of act 4 with the closing episode of act 3: the shepherd who long ago referred to himself as "your servant" before King Saul has become head of state in Jerusalem (8:15-18) and thus merits the deference worthy of a king.

While addressing Ziba, David expands on his opening question: his desire to express his "kindness" (9:1; *ḥesed*) to Jonathan's descendants becomes "the kindness [*ḥesed*] of God" (9:3). This modification brings David's words into closer conformity with Jonathan's appeal in 1 Samuel 20:14, "show me the faithful love [*ḥesed*] of the LORD." Ziba tells David of the existence of the son but never says his name, focusing instead on the son's injury to which the narrator again directs our attention at the end of the scene (9:13).[3] Any concern Ziba might have that David could harm Mephibosheth is put to rest by David's opening declaration that he seeks to express his faithfulness to Jonathan's son.[4] That son had found refuge with Machir son of Ammiel, whom we assume was a valued member of Saul's court. He will become an equally valued member of David's court.[5] The location of Machir's town, Lo-debar, is not known with certainty, but, on the basis of 17:27, it would seem to be near Mahanaim,

---

[3] The Hebrew expression for his injury, *nĕkēh raglāyim* (NRSV: "he is crippled in his feet"), occurs only in 4:4 and 9:3.

[4] Ziba will meet David again as the king abandons Jerusalem, fleeing from Absalom's rebels. He informs the king that Mephibosheth has remained in Jerusalem hoping to receive his father's throne. But Ziba's yarn seems far-fetched and the evidence hints at his duplicity (see 16:1-4 and 19:24-30), leaving us with the impression that Ziba is an opportunist looking to ingratiate himself with the king.

[5] Machir and others will assist David with provisions as he flees from Absalom (17:27).

where Abner crowned Ishbaal king over Israel (2:8). Located within the territory that Saul once governed, Mahanaim would be a logical place to hide a Saulide claimant to David's throne.

Mephibosheth's nurse had escaped with him (4:4), then a five-year-old boy, upon learning that Saul (his grandfather) and Jonathan (his father) had been killed in the battle with the Philistines (1 Sam 31:1-7). We can assume that she recognized that the child's life, a claimant to the throne, could be at risk. That brief account also explained how Mephibosheth became disabled (he fell while running away and was left crippled), and it may also imply that, though he is a direct descendant of Saul, his injury had compromised his hope of assuming the throne. The closing line of David's capture of Jerusalem echoes in the background: "Therefore it is said, 'The blind and the lame shall not come into the house'" (2 Sam 5:8). Could Mephibosheth ever assume the throne? When David flees Jerusalem to escape Absalom's rebels, Ziba informs David that Mephibosheth has remained in Jerusalem hoping that Absalom would return his father's throne to him (16:3). Since David does not question Mephibosheth's eligibility, it appears that in David's worldview Mephibosheth's infirmity did not impede his claim to the throne.

David sends messengers and has Mephibosheth brought to him. Mephibosheth's reaction to the royal escort is not revealed, but his remark to David in 19:28 ("all my father's house were doomed to death before my lord the king") suggests that he feared that his execution was imminent. Arriving at court, he is presented with his full name, "son of Jonathan, son of Saul," which underscores his claim to his grandfather's throne. But the potential claimant falls prostrate before King David and refers to himself with the same deferential title that Ziba uttered: "your servant." Mephibosheth's terror is confirmed by David's words: "Do not be afraid." Jonathan's son then learns what we already know: David intends to fulfill the covenant he made with Mephibosheth's father, Jonathan, an agreement that for Mephibosheth is entirely new information.

David will return to Mephibosheth all the land that belonged to his grandfather Saul. Is Mephibosheth going to rule over that territory? No. The grandson shall eat at David's table always, an idiomatic expression to signal that Mephibosheth will remain at David's court, enjoying the privileges of the palace.[6] When David summons Ziba back on stage and informs him of this agreement—"All that belonged to Saul and to all his house I have given to your master's grandson"—the word "all" conjures up Saul's most prized possession, the crown. That will remain in David's hands, as Jonathan had foretold (1 Sam 23:17). Mephibosheth is granted

---

[6] In his final discourse, David commends the sons of Barzillai to Solomon, exhorting him to "let them be among those who eat at your table" (1 Kgs 2:7).

rights over the harvest of his grandfather's land, but David will remain king over that land. Ziba is ordered to work the land in order to provide the disabled Mephibosheth with an income (he has a son, Mica), while Mephibosheth himself enjoys a king's largess. Three times David emphasizes that Mephibosheth will *"always"* eat from the royal table (9:7, 10, 13). When the Babylonian king releases King Jehoiachin from prison, the Judean king too is allowed to "eat food always" (2 Kgs 25:29, my literal translation) with the Babylonian king, but similar to Mephibosheth, he is not given permission to return to rule Judah. The privilege of eating at the king's table seems like house arrest.

Jonathan's son responds to the king's decree with another act of obeisance and, adding to his earlier expression of deference ("your servant"), refers to himself as "a dead dog." When Ishbaal accused Abner of having a sexual relationship with Saul's concubine, Abner sarcastically likened himself to a dog's head (2 Sam 3:8). This metaphor is among the most self-deprecating expressions. While it can be translated into English without difficulty because it is not that offensive in contemporary Western culture, the third-century Jewish author of Targum Jonathan (the translation of the Hebrew Bible into Aramaic) could not render literally the word "dog" into his Aramaic-speaking world because it was too vulgar. So he translated this verse with: "What is your servant that you should look upon *an ordinary man* like me." (The insult "dog" remains offensive today in some Middle Eastern cultures.) We might imagine that Mephibosheth looked around at David's palace thinking that all this could have been his. But in this scene he is presented as powerless to realize his ambitions, if he has any.

The king repeats his decree regarding Mephibosheth to Ziba, adding that it is Ziba's duty to execute his order. Background information on the number of sons and servants in Ziba's household (9:10) suggests that he is up to the task, and he declares his readiness to fulfill the king's command. His shift in allegiance from Saul to David is captured in the Hebrew text. David said to Ziba: "You . . . shall work the land for him . . . so that your lord's [*ădōnêkā*, i.e., Saul's] grandson may have food to eat" (9:10; translation mine). Ziba answered: "According to all that my lord [*ădōnî*, i.e., David] the king commands his servant, so your servant will do" (9:11; translation mine). David refers to Saul as Ziba's master but Ziba acknowledges David as his new master.

Meanwhile, Mephibosheth, eating at the king's table "like one of the king's sons," is accorded a high rank at court—the same as David's own sons, but *without* the right of succession. The narrator tells us that Mephibosheth had a young son named Mica. If Mephibosheth were to return to Saul's throne, that son could succeed him. But Mica is never heard from again. As the narrator takes his leave of Mephibosheth, he has us stare at his infirmity: "Now he was lame in both his feet." Later on, that condition will be critical for determining whether or not Mephibosheth joined Absalom's rebels or remained loyal to David. When, having observed David in this scene, we admire the king whose first act was to fulfill his covenant with Jonathan, the narrator has accomplished his purpose.

4.3 David Subdues the Ammonites with God's Help (10:1-19)

The extension of David's authority that began in 8:1-14 continues in this episode. Hanun, a new Ammonite king, comes onto the world stage and his foolishness results in a new balance of power among world leaders that is once again dominated by David. David's earlier victories demonstrated that God was winning for him "wherever he went" (8:6, 14). At the center of this episode David's commander Joab prays for that same divine assistance—"may the LORD do what seems good to him" (10:12)—and his prayer is heard. Our ubiquitous narrator shifts rapidly between royal courts and opposing armies, omitting information that we might find useful, in order to keep us focused on the purpose of this account: God is on David's side. Two verbs, "to see" and "to send," dominate the episode. The first and second scenes are dominated by "sending" envoys and then troops. The second and third scenes are dominated by "seeing" the battle strategies and their outcomes. The episode (10:19) concludes with a Hebrew wordplay: Hadadezer's kings "see" (*wayyir²û*) that they are defeated and the Arameans "fear" (*wayyîrĕ²û*) to help the Ammonites again.

The episode comprises three scenes:

Scene 1: A diplomatic embarrassment for David (10:1-5)
Scene 2: Joab's victory over the Ammonites (10:6-14)
Scene 3: David's victory over Hadadezer and the Arameans (10:15-19)

The first scene reports the humiliation of David's envoys at the Ammonite court by King Hanun. The second and third scenes report the defeat of the Ammonites and their allies by Joab and David. Scenes 2 and 3 parallel each other. Scene 2 opens with the Ammonites "sending" for mercenaries, and scene 3 opens with Hadadezer "sending" for the Arameans, who lived beyond the Euphrates. Just as Joab defeats the Arameans hired by the Ammonites, so David defeats the Arameans summoned by Hadadezer. The major difference in the second and third scenes is that Joab's speech is not repeated by David, but its theology is presumed: God helps David wherever he goes (8:6, 14).

4.3.1 A Diplomatic Embarrassment for David (10:1-5)

STRUCTURE

Setting (10:1)
A. David sends envoys (10:2)
  B. Hanun hears accusations against the envoys (10:3a)
   C. The accusations (10:3b)
  B'. Hanun believes the accusations and humiliates the envoys
    (10:4)
A'. David sends word to the envoys (10:5)

The text is structured around the accusations made by Hanun's court-iers against David's envoys that result in the hostilities reported in the two scenes that follow. This scene begins and ends at David's court; the events at the center take place at Hanun's court. The Hebrew root *šlḥ* ("to send") appears five times. Four times it is a *qal* verb and David is the subject (10:2, 5 and twice in 10:3). Once Hanun is the subject (10:4) and the verb is *piel*, the factitive sense of which is captured in the NRSV with "sent away." The envoys sent by David are sent away by Hanun.

COMMENTARY

David suffers a diplomatic outrage when Hanun humiliates his en-voys that we know were sent in good faith. The episode begins with the formula *wayĕhî ʾaḥărê kēn*, indicating that an indeterminate period of time has passed since David introduced Mephibosheth into his court (9:1-13). The narrator then provides the essential background information: Nahash, king of the Ammonites is dead, and his son, Hanun, has succeeded him. David will send envoys to Hanun to pay his respects at his father's passing. During this transition of power in the Ammonite kingdom, neighboring states could attack the inexperienced king. When the Philistines heard that David had been anointed king over Israel, they immediately attacked (5:17), and when Ahab died, the Moabites rebelled against Ahaziah, Ahab's son (2 Kgs 1:1 and 3:5). Thus, David will assure the dead king's heir that good relations between their two kingdoms will continue.

David's desire to express his "loyalty" to Hanun replays the Hebrew word *ḥesed* (translated "kindness" in 2 Sam 9:1) from the previous epi-sode, which recounted David's expression of *ḥesed* toward Mephibosheth. Just as David was loyal to his private agreement with Jonathan, so will he be loyal to his international agreements by sending an entourage of public mourners to pay his respects to his recently deceased ally. In the Bible such gestures of sympathy can be a private/personal or public/

diplomatic affair. David consoles Bathsheba after the death of their son (12:24). Jacob, believing that his son Joseph is dead, mourns and his children rise to comfort him (Gen 37:34-35). In this scene, David honors a dead king with an official entourage, similar to what we see at state funerals today. Unfortunately, David's plan to strengthen his alliance with the Ammonite kingdom is scuttled by Hanun's unseasoned leadership, resulting in needless hostilities.

How had King Nahash expressed his loyalty (*ḥesed*) to King David? Nahash had been defeated by Saul after he threatened the people of Jabesh-gilead, who remained ever loyal to Saul, their liberator, even after his death, secretly removing his corpse from the walls of Beth-shan (1 Sam 31:11-12).[7] Since Nahash has not been mentioned in the David narrative until now, we rely on David's opening remark that presupposes an alliance between himself and Nahash. A bit more information from the narrator would have been helpful, and the fact that the narrator is mum indicates that the history of their alliance is not requisite for understanding this scene. The narrator, always reluctant to clutter his story with details not directly relevant to his purpose, leaves us to suppose that, because Nahash was Saul's enemy, he had become David's ally.

We journey with the mourning cortege until they reach the Ammonite territory. Before the exchange of official greetings, the scene shifts to Hanun's court, where the approach of David's envoys is under discussion. The new king receives unsolicited advice from his courtiers who argue that David's emissaries are a threat to the dominion of the newly crowned king. Their choice of words, "to search" and "to spy," insinuate that David is preparing for a military assault,[8] and their rhetorical questions put the fledgling king on the defensive: "Do you really think . . . ," implying: "Are you so naïve as to think . . . ?" They pressure him to demonstrate that he grasps David's real intentions, leaving him little room to maneuver. When Rehoboam assumes Solomon's throne (1 Kgs 12:1-19), the rebel Jeroboam solicits from the new king a reduction in the heavy labor that his father laid upon the people. Rehoboam's more senior courtiers encourage him to attend to Jeroboam's request, but his younger courtiers advise to the contrary and the young king foolishly follows the advice of the latter, resulting in a rebellion that sunders his kingdom. Hanun too receives bad counsel from heavy-handed courtiers, and he lacks the ability to evaluate it: he never speaks during the entire scene! His inexperience at governing his father's court is egregious. All

[7] The NRSV inserts a lengthy addition from 4QSam[a] between 1 Samuel 10:27 and 11:1 that explains the threat that Nahash posed to Saul's dominion.

[8] In Judges 18:2 the Danites sent scouts "to spy out" and "to search" the land of Israel in preparation for an attack to secure the territory for themselves.

the while we know that David's intentions are wholly upright; he represents no threat. Hanun's folly turns an ally into an enemy!

David's official delegation never receives a royal audience to convey their expressions of condolence to the new king, and so the reader is aghast when Hanun himself shaves off half their beards and cuts off their garments at the hips. Driver imagines that the "half" here "is not half in length, but half in breadth," rendering them utterly ridiculous, since wearing a beard was presumed in the biblical world.[9] The Hebrew term *šēt* (10:4, translated "hips" in the NRSV) may refer to the buttocks; the prisoners captured by the king of Assyria are led away "naked and barefoot, with buttocks [*šēt*] uncovered" (Isa 20:4). With a beard half-shaved and bare buttocks, the emissaries must now travel back to David's court. Let David take that!

Upon learning of this outrage, David orders his envoys to remain at Jericho until they have become decent, thus saving himself the public embarrassment of their arrival at court. A needless war will now ensue—the price of Hanun's stupidity.

4.3.2 Joab's Victory over the Ammonites (10:6-14)

STRUCTURE

Setting the stage: the decisions of the Ammonite court (10:6)
A. David sends Joab from Jerusalem (10:7)
  B. Preparations for battle (10:8-10)
      a. Ammonite battle arrangements (10:8a)
        b. Aramean battle arrangements (10:8b)
        b'. Joab's battle arrangements against the Arameans (10:9)
      a'. Joab's battle arrangements against the Ammonites (10:10)
  C. Joab's speech (10:11-12)
  B'. Outcome of Battle (10:13-14a)
        b". Joab defeats the Arameans (10:13)
      a". Joab defeats the Ammonites (10:14a)
A'. Joab returns to Jerusalem (10:14b)

---

[9] When Joab grabs Amasa's beard to murder him, the narrator does not pause to explain that Amasa wore a beard (2 Sam 20:9). In Isaiah 7:18-25, the king of Assyria becomes "God's razor" that shaves "the beard" of God's adversaries (Isa 7:20)—an expression of divine punishment.

The scene opens by paralleling the military moves of the adversaries: the Ammonites "send" (10:6), and David "sends" (10:7); the Ammonites array their troops (10:8), and Joab arrays his troops (10:9). At the beginning of the scene the Ammonites "see" that they have become odious to David (10:6), and at the end of the scene the same Ammonites "see" that their Aramean ally has fled, and they flee as well (10:14). Joab too "sees" his losing predicament (10:9), but his prayer (the center of the scene) promises victory. The slightly lopsided structure (the B section is twice the length of B') of the scene is an effective narrative device: the preparations for battle and the uneven troop strengths are presented in detail, but once Joab invokes God, the scene comes to a swift, victorious conclusion.

COMMENTARY

The narrator returns us to Hanun's court where the Ammonites recognize that their mistreatment of David's envoys has been received as an act of aggression. The Hebrew word translated in the NRSV with "they had become odious"[10] signals an impending conflict.[11] The Ammonites muster their allies and hire Aramean mercenaries, who will be the first to flee when Joab's troops approach (10:13). The Arameans and King Maacah come from the Transjordan area, north of Jerusalem.[12] Tob is about nineteen kilometers (twelve miles) southeast of the Sea of Galilee.[13] But the narrator is not offering us a geography lesson. By listing the allies and the number of their troops, we grasp the overwhelming force against which David's forces, whose numbers are not given (but we imagine they are significantly less), must now contend. David dispatches his commander Joab,[14] who was recently named to that post (8:16), to fight the first of two wars with the Ammonites.[15]

The Ammonite army arrays at the gates of their city (presumably Rabbah, named in 12:26-29), while their allies—the narrator lists them yet again—remain in the open country. The narrator's laconic description of the initial battle maneuvers (he is really interested in Joab's prayer)

---

[10] It is used to describe the stinking Nile (Exod 7:21) when all the fish died (the first plague).

[11] After Saul (really Jonathan) defeats the Philistine garrison, Israel recognizes that it has become "odious" to the Philistines (1 Sam 13:4) and war ensues.

[12] Beth-rehob, according to Judges 18:28, is near the territory of Dan in the north of Israel. Zobah is perhaps in the north Biqa Valley (Lebanon), and Maacah is along the northern boarder of Israel.

[13] P. Kyle McCarter, *II Samuel*, Anchor Bible 9 (Garden City, NY: Doubleday, 1984), 271.

[14] See section 1.4.3 above.

[15] The second war begins in the next episode (2 Sam 11:1).

leaves the impression that Joab was drawn toward the Ammonite army defending the city gates when he was ambushed by the Aramean mercenaries in the fields. Surrounded (10:9) and outnumbered, it seems that Joab has been snookered. As the tension is about to peak—we expect the slaughter of Joab's forces—the narrator pauses the action so that we can attend a strategy meeting between Joab and his commanders. The troops will have to fight on two fronts. Joab will pit his best men against the Aramean mercenaries while the rest of the army, under the leadership of his brother Abishai (see 2:18-32), will contend with the Ammonites.

Joab's speech, the center of this scene and episode, is the narrator's primary focus. The front that succeeds in advancing against the enemy will come to "help" (*yšʿ*, translated thus in the NRSV in this scene) the front that is losing.[16] The verb *yšʿ*, common in military contexts (see Josh 10:6 or 2 Kgs 16:7), portends the divine rescue that is about to take place. It last appeared in 2 Samuel 8:6, 14 where God was its subject: "The LORD *gave victory* [*yšʿ*] to David wherever he went." Though Joab is referring to human *help*, such help will not be necessary as God will provide the *help*, meaning the victory. So *help* will come, not according to Joab's battle strategies, but according to God's will.

Joab rouses his troops to victory with a direct imperative, "be strong!" and a cohortative (the speaker includes himself in the command), "let us be courageous." Despite their perilous predicament, he reminds them that they are fighting for their people and for God's cities. Finally, and most important, Joab prays, bidding God to do what seems best.[17] Like David (see 5:17-25), Joab knows that the victory is bestowed upon Israel by God. When five Amorite kings beset the Gibeonites, Joshua's ally (Josh 10:3-4), God did more damage to the Amorites with hailstones than the Israelites did with the sword (Josh 10:11). Joab bids God to do the same for him now. The conclusion to the scene comes quickly. When Joab's forces array, the Arameans run away (they are, after all, mercenaries). There is no battle and there are no casualties. God has received Joab's prayer and the enemy has fled. When the Ammonites see that their Aramean hires have fled, they follow their lead, running back into their city. The conquest of that city will wait for another day (2 Sam 12:29); for now, Joab returns to Jerusalem. The abrupt ending serves the narrator's purpose. The details about troop movements and Joab's strategy created tension and delayed the scene's climax, namely, Joab's prayer. But as soon as God was invoked, Joab, though outnumbered and forced

---

[16] But what happens if both fronts are losing? That troubling question is ignored.

[17] Eli, the priest of Shiloh, prays the same prayer when the young boy Samuel reveals to him the vision he has had during the night (1 Sam 3:18; see also Judg 10:15 and Ps 119:65).

to fight on two fronts, received divine help. Whether offstage or onstage, God wins Israel's battles.

4.3.3 David's Victory over Hadadezer and the Arameans (10:15-19)

A. The Arameans see their defeat and regroup (10:15)
   B. Hadadezer sends for reinforcements (10:16ab)
      C. Shobach comes to fight (10:16c)
         D. David's battle preparations (10:17ab)
            E. The Arameans array (10:17c)
               F. The battle (10:17d)
            E'. The Arameans flee (10:18a)
         D'. David's victory (10:18bc)
      C'. Shobach dies (10:18de)
   B'. Hadadezer's allies see their defeat and sue for peace (10:19ab)
A'. The Arameans are afraid to fight for the Ammonites (10:19c)

    The scene opens with the Arameans, allies of Hadadezer, "seeing" ($r\mathord{\check{}}h$) that they are defeated and regrouping for battle (A). It ends with the Arameans "afraid" to support any more Ammonite military initiatives (A'). Hadadezer's allies, who were ready to serve him (B), will not do so again (B'). The D/D' sections report David's preparation for the military campaign and his subsequent victory. The brief but decisive battle with the Arameans sits at the center of this scene (F) and is framed by verbs "to array" and "to flee" (E/E' sections). As in other battle scenes, the troop movements are parallel: The Aramean troops *assemble* ($\mathord{\check{}}sp$), they come from *across* ($\mathord{\check{}}br$) the Euphrates, and they *come* ($bw\mathord{\check{}}$) to Helam (10:15-16); David assembles ($\mathord{\check{}}sp$) all Israel, they cross ($\mathord{\check{}}br$) the Jordan River, and they come ($bw\mathord{\check{}}$) to Helam (10:17).

    Instead of joining Joab's victory celebrations in Jerusalem, we observe the Arameans in their defeat. They will regroup to fight yet again. Hadadezer (from Zobah in 8:3), defeated by David in 8:3-8, comes back on stage (the narrator does not account for his sudden return). Some scholars argue that David's defeat of Hadadezer's allies in this scene logically occurred before David finally struck him down, which was reported earlier (see 8:3-6). The narrator remains undisturbed by this apparent chronological muddle. To reorder these events into a more logical sequence would harm the narrator's primary purpose—a portrait of a victorious David who was saved by God.

Hadadezer rallies the Arameans from beyond the Euphrates at Helam under the command of Shobach, Hadadezer's general, who appears only in this scene. Helam, an unknown location, must be in the Transjordan area given that David crosses the Jordan River to engage the Arameans (10:17). We suppose that Hadadezer enjoyed considerable authority in the region of the Euphrates (his destination in 8:3) whence he draws his troops. David learns of the Aramean troop movements and summons his army to meet Hadadezer at Helam. The battle is almost comic: the Arameans array, fight, and run away, just as they did in the previous scene (10:13). As in 2 Samuel 8, the focus is on a victorious David rather than on the details of the battle. Though God is not mentioned—David neither consults God nor evokes the divine name (as Joab did)—the refrain from 2 Samuel 8, "The Lord gave victory to David wherever he went," resounds in the background. God, evoked or not, is unquestionably on David's side as evidenced by the huge number of Aramean casualties. When David kills Shobach, Hadadezer's commander, Hadadezer's allies recognize their defeat, sue for peace, and become David's minions. They join other conquered peoples (the Moabites [8:2] and the Arameans of Damascus [8:6]) who have been put into David's service.

The episode concludes (2 Sam 10:19) with a wordplay on the Hebrew verbs, *rʾh*, "to see," a verb central to this passage, and *yrʾ*, "to fear." In the Hebrew text of this verse the two verbs are identical in form and have almost the same pronunciation.[18] Hadadezer's allies "saw" (*wayyirʾû*) that they were defeated and the Arameans "feared" (*wayyîrĕʾû*) to help the Ammonites again. Had the Arameans been "afraid" of defeat at the beginning of the scene, instead of "seeing" their defeat (10:15), they could have avoided 40,700 casualties. Likewise, had the Ammonites in 10:6 "feared" that they had "become odious to David," instead of "seeing" as much, they too could have saved themselves heavy losses.

The narrator's final remark that the Arameans would not *help* (*yšʿ*) the Ammonites again replays the Hebrew word "to help" from Joab's speech at the center of the second scene. Joab had planned for the winning flank to *help* (*yšʿ*) those on the losing flank (10:11). In fact, God (often the subject of *yšʿ*), who received Joab's prayer, helped the Israelite forces win. Thus the Arameans come to a prudent decision about their alliance with the

---

[18] Hebrew "they feared" can be spelled two ways: *wayyîrĕʾû* (see Gen 20:8) and *wayyîrĕʾû* as in this verse. The "defective" spelling in this verse ensures that the two verbs, "they saw" and "they feared," are graphically identical.

Ammonites, given that God *helps* (*yšʿ*) David (see 8:6, 14, where *yšʿ* is trans- lated in the NRSV with "gave victory"; see also section 1.3 above). A new balance of power on the world stage emerges. King Hanun had abused David's emissaries and then mustered Aramean mercenaries to defend himself. But he cannot do so again. Isolated and significantly weakened, his capital will be conquered by David in the next episode (12:26-31). The Arameans, decisively beaten, never confront David's forces again.

These battles, spawned by a vapid, stupid king (even the Trojan War, sparked by Paris' abduction of Helen, had a more credible provocation) and resulting in thousands of hapless casualties, are now over; and we may be left distraught by their huge costs and God's role in them. A careful reading of these battles reveals that our narrator was not focused on the gruesome bloodshed—the battles were passed over with little detail.[19] But still, there remains a sense of discomfort that apologetic explanations do not readily satisfy, especially in light of the appalling wars of the twentieth century. A poem, Robert Frost wrote, "begins in delight . . . and ends in a clarification of life—not necessarily a great clarification, . . . but in a momentary stay against confusion."[20] The nearly three millennia of human warfare since the day that thousands of Arameans died on the battlefield testifies to the fact that the horrific costs of David's wars have not yet brought about the "momentary stay against confusion" for which Frost yearned.

4.4 The Story of David, Bathsheba, and Uriah (11:1–12:31)

> *Your faith was strong but you needed proof*
> *You saw her bathing on the roof*
> *Her beauty and the moonlight overthrew you*
> *From "Hallelujah" by Leonard Cohen*

Desire, lust, love, marriage, intrigue, murder, cover-up, despair, and mourning meld together in this tragic episode in which two people die and our hero's fragility is exposed for the first time. In 1599 George Peele, in his *The Love of King David and Fair Bethsabe*, gave voice to David's pas- sion for the voluptuous Bathsheba that the biblical narrator leaves to our own imaginations. Rembrandt (*Bathsheba at her Bath*, 1654) and Genti-

---

[19] Later in 18:6-8, when Absalom's rebels are defeated, the narrator provides no description of the battle itself.

[20] Robert Frost, "The Figure a Poem Makes," in *American Poetry and Poetics*, ed. by Daniel G. Hoffman (Garden City, NY: Doubleday, 1962), 443.

leschi (*David and Bathsheba*, 1640) cast this episode's most erotic scene across their canvases. Thomas Hardy novelized the wife of Uriah in the desirous Bathsheba Everdene in *Far from the Madding Crowd* (1874). In the early 1950s, David (played by Gregory Peck) and Bathsheba (played by Susan Hayworth) appeared in cinemas (*David and Bathsheba*, 1951). Today in the Fraumünster Church in Zürich, David and Bathsheba look down on tourists from a Chagall window that depicts the descent of the New Jerusalem. Music, art, literature, and film are just a few of the media that have animated this classic of biblical narration.

Details of this tale are dispensed begrudgingly. Divine disapproval probably began as soon as David "took" Bathsheba, Uriah's wife, the first time (11:4), but we only learn of it once Uriah is dead and Bathsheba has moved into the palace. Did Uriah refuse to go home because he suspected that David had slept with his wife? Did Joab guess the reason why the king wanted one of his military officers dead—and it had to look like a battle casualty? Did Bathsheba surmise that David had ordered her husband's elimination? If Uriah had gone home to his wife, would David have forgotten about her? We read on hoping for answers, but the story, which rebuffs a simplistic interpretation, ends without disclosing its intrigues. For David's admirers, his crimes are embarrassing. Even the narrator, who later celebrates the memory of David's fidelity to the Lord, must, on one occasion, confess the disgrace of this entire episode: "David did what was right in the sight of the Lord, and did not turn aside from anything that he commanded him all the days of his life, except in the matter of Uriah the Hittite" (1 Kgs 15:5). When the Chronicler came upon this story, he simply skipped it (see 1 Chr 20:1-2). It was a tale best forgotten. But he was wrong. Who cannot see his or her own moral ambiguity reflected in these two chapters that plumb the depths of human passion, power, intrigue, depravity, and self-deception?

STRUCTURE

This episode is concentrically organized in eleven scenes:

A. David sends Joab and the army to attack Rabbah (11:1)
   B. David sleeps with Bathsheba, the wife of Uriah (11:2-5)
      C. David and Uriah: David arranges Uriah's death (11:6-13)
         D. David to Joab: Uriah must die (11:14-17)
            E. Joab to David: Joab's news comes to David (11:18-25)
               F. David ushers the wife of Uriah into his house. The Lord is displeased (11:26-27)

E'. Nathan to David: God's news comes to David
    (12:1-7a)
D'. Nathan to David: the child will die (12:7b-15a)
C'. David and the child: God ensures the child's death
    (12:15b-23)
B'. David sleeps with Bathsheba, his wife (12:24-25)
A'. Joab and David conquer Rabbah (12:26-31)

The story of David, Bathsheba, and Uriah is framed by the battle against
the Ammonite capital, Rabbah. As the episode begins, David dispatches
Joab and the army to besiege the city. As it concludes, the Ammonite
capital capitulates to David. The B/B' episodes recount the two times
that David sleeps with Bathsheba, who conceives each time. Episodes
C and D recount the successful plot to kill Uriah while C' and D' report God's response to David's crime: the child will die. The E/E' sections contrast David's reaction to the death of Uriah to his reaction to
Nathan's parable about the slaughter of a ewe lamb. The turning point
in the episode (F) comes when we learn of the divine reaction to these
events. God will turn David's "happily ever after" into an atonement
ceremony.

4.4.1 David Sends Joab and the Army to Attack Rabbah (11:1)

The episode opens without reference to David's regnal year or how
much time has passed since he vanquished the Ammonites in the previous episode. A temporal clause announces the setting: it is springtime,
the beginning of the dry season in Israel, when kings go to war.[21] No
commander would choose to drag an army through the mud of the rainy,
cold Israelite winters. We can assume that the humiliation that David's
envoys suffered at the hands of the Ammonites (10:4) occurred during
the winter and that David had immediately dispatched Joab, despite
the weather, to give a swift, out-of-season response to this diplomatic
outrage. Joab had forced the Ammonites back into their capital city,
Rabbah (10:7-14). Now spring has arrived and David can launch a more
systematic campaign against Rabbah, the Ammonite capital.

---

[21] The Hebrew expression in 2 Samuel 11:1, *těšûbat haššānâ*, "the turn of the year"
(NRSV: "spring of the year"), appears in 1 Kings 20:22 when an anonymous prophet
warns the king of Israel that at this time of year—*těšûbat haššānâ*—he will come under
attack from the king of Aram.

The narrator opens with piercing satire: it is the time when kings go to war, so our king stays home, sending Joab and all Israel out for battle.[22] Later, in the battle with Absalom's rebels, David will plan to join his troops on the battlefield, but his soldiers will protest, insisting that David should remain safe in the city (18:3). But in this scene neither Joab nor the troops suggest that the king should remain in Jerusalem, and so, swayed by the narrator's opening remark, we suspect that David should have led his army into battle. Our suspicions are confirmed at the conclusion of the David-Bathsheba episode when Joab, now fed up with the stay-at-home king, orders David into the battle theater (12:28). An ancient scribe, transmitting the Hebrew text of 2 Samuel 11:1, noticed the implied disapproval of David in the narrator's opening remark and so, in an effort to protect David, inserted into the Hebrew word "kings" an *aleph* (changing the consonantal text from *hmlkym* to *hmlʾkym*) so that it would read "messengers," resulting in the text: "At the turn of the year, the time when messengers go out, David sent Joab . . ." While the insertion of the *aleph* does not result in a great deal of sense (Joab is hardly David's messenger), it makes David's action appear less irresponsible. A later scribal notation in the Masoretic Text indicates that the *aleph* should not be read and thus restores the original meaning "kings" to the text. Thus, Joab marches out to punish Rabbah with all Israel in tow while the king stays home in Jerusalem.

The first verb in the scene, "to send" (*šlḥ*), introduces a key leitmotif in this episode. In every case but one David is either the sender or the receiver of messengers.[23] The only instance in which David is not directly involved in the sending or receiving of messengers comes when God sends Nathan (12:1), and that decisive "sending" determines the unexpected dénouement of David's hasty marriage to Bathsheba. By sending and receiving, David is able to remain in his palace while directing events until a disgruntled Joab orders him into battle (12:28). From heaven God

---

[22] While most English translations agree that the meaning of the Hebrew verb "to go out" (Hebrew *yṣʾ*) in this context connotes "to go out for battle," the words "for battle" do not appear in the Hebrew text.

[23] His royal sending authority allows him to achieve his various and changing objectives. He sends Joab against the Ammonites and against their city, Rabbah (11:1). He sends messengers to find out about the "woman" (11:3) and then sends to have Bathsheba brought to him (11:4) for their tryst. David sends for Uriah (11:6) and then sends him back (11:14) with his death warrant in hand. After Uriah's murder, David sends again for Bathsheba (11:27). Others send word to David: Bathsheba sends word to him of her pregnancy (11:5); Joab sends word to David of Uriah's death (11:18); and, finally, Joab sends word from the battle front (12:27), ordering David to lay siege to Rabbah.

exercises divine authority by sending his messenger, Nathan, with the verdict on David's hasty marriage. The "sending" leitmotif establishes four locations for the action, two onstage (the palace and the battlefield) and two offstage (Uriah's house and heaven).

4.4.2 David Sleeps with Bathsheba, the Wife of Uriah (11:2-5)

STRUCTURE

A. (11:2)
1. David rises from his bed
2. He sees a woman
3. She is bathing
4. The woman is beautiful
   B. David sends and inquires (11:3a)
      C. The wife of Uriah (11:3b)
   B'. David sends and takes (11:4a)
A'. (11:4bcd-5)
1. She comes to him
2. David takes her to his bed
3. Why she was bathing
4. The woman is pregnant

At the center of the scene, David learns not only the name of the woman that he spied but also her current marital status and her particular relationship to the crown. Not only does the king desire a married woman, but her husband is among his foremost officers, whom David has just sent off to war. The consequences of his actions in this scene will drive the subsequent events in the rest of this episode. The news of Bathsheba's identity (C) is framed by David's "sending": he sends and inquires (B), and then he sends and takes (B'). In the A section we observe Bathsheba bathing, but we must wait until the A' section to learn why she is bathing. As the scene opens, David rises from his bed (*miškābô*) (A) to which he will soon take the wife of Uriah (*wayyiškab*) (A').

COMMENTARY

We assume it is now evening of the day that David dispatched his army to Rabbah. As the curtain rises, David is lying alone on his bed, the main prop on stage. The narrator continues his subtle criticism of David by repeating the term "time" (*ʿēt*) from 11:1: The "time of the year" when kings go to war is now "the time of the evening" (NRSV: "late one afternoon") when the king is resting. David rises to stroll on his roof terrace from which he spies a bathing woman. When the narrator pauses the action to observe that "the woman was very beautiful," we are standing beside David, gazing at her with him. The narrator, who knows *why* she was bathing, leaves us in the dark for the moment. The sensuality of this scene is only faintly acknowledged: a bathing woman, unaware that she is being observed by her liege and her husband's commander. In *The Love of King David and Fair Bethsabe* (1599), George Peele imagines the poetry David uttered as he attends to the woman of his passion:

> What tunes, what words, what looks, what wonders pierce
> My soule, incensed with a sudden fire
> What tree, what shade, what spring, what paradise,
> Enjoyes the beautie of so faire a dame?[24]

Two leitmotifs are introduced in this scene. The Hebrew root *škb*, "to lie down" (11:4), appears eight times in 2 Samuel 11–12. In this opening scene, David *lies* with Bathsheba. By contrast, in the next scene, Uriah *lies* down at the gate of the palace and not with Bathsheba his wife. Eventually David *lies* on the ground (12:16), and finally, as the episode draws to a close, David *lies* with Bathsheba (12:24), who is now accepted by the narrator (and God) as David's legitimate wife. A second leitmotif, *lqḥ*, "to take," is also introduced. David *takes* Bathsheba (11:4) to bed, but after Uriah's murder he sends and *gathers* her (11:27: *ʾsp* [NRSV: "brought her"] not *lqḥ*, "take") to his household.[25] This less aggressive language lends legitimacy and magnanimity to David's gesture: the king marries the widow of one of his commanders who perished in battle (but we know that Uriah was murdered by David). But when God refers to David's marriage to Bathsheba (Nathan's speech in 12:7b-12), he reprises the verb "to take" (12:9 and 12:10) not "to gather." The narrator's choice of words in this scene, "David *took* her" (11:4), foreshadows the divine sentence to be handed down for David's crimes: as David *took* the wife of another man so God will *take* David's wives and give them to another (12:11).[26]

The answer to David's inquiry about the woman comes in a rhetorical question: "Is this not Bathsheba, the wife of Uriah?" Is the messenger implying that David should have recognized the wife of one of his military officers? Is David only pretending not to recognize the lovely Bathsheba? The narrator is mum. Bathsheba is not married to some

---

[24] George Peele, *The Love of King David and Fair Bethsabe* (London: The Malone Society Reprints, 1912), lines 53–56.

[25] In 1 Samuel 25:42 the verb *lqḥ* is not used when Abigail becomes David's wife.

[26] Later, Absalom will have sexual relations with David's concubines (16:22).

anonymous infantryman. Known as "the Hittite," though his name is distinctly Hebrew,[27] Uriah is a member of David's military elite known as "the Thirty" (23:39). The king desires the wife of one of his chief officers. Is this another reason that David was happy to evacuate the palace of any military personnel, including Bathsheba's husband? Again, the narrator is silent. Could David take the wife of one of his soldiers with impunity? On two occasions, Abraham fears that rulers more powerful than himself would execute him in order to seize Sarah, his attractive wife (Pharaoh in Gen 12:10-16 and King Abimelech in Gen 20:2[28]). David acts like one of those potentates in this episode: he seizes the beautiful wife of one of his minions and then has the husband executed. His infraction is codified in Deuteronomy 5:21, "Neither shall you covet your neighbor's wife," and Deuteronomy 22:22, "If a man is caught lying with the wife of another man, both of them shall die, the man who lay with the woman as well as the woman." Though Deuteronomy is edited after David's reign, when Nathan accuses David of having taken Uriah's wife and David confesses his sin, both the prophet and the king accept that the death penalty is the expected punishment, and so Nathan offers the king clemency (2 Sam 12:13): "You shall not die."

The narrator's pithy but careful description of the tryst between David and Bathsheba underscores David's responsibility: *He* took her, *she* came, *he* slept with her, and *she* went home. Though women can be the subject of the verb *škb*, "to sleep with someone,"[29] David is presented as the main actor at this critical moment. And even if Deuteronomy 22:22 declares that both of them deserve death, Bathsheba's responsibility is overlooked as the narrator keeps the focus on David: *he* took Bathsheba, the wife of Uriah, and *he* slept with her, not vice versa.

Only after their night together does the narrator reveal why Bathsheba was bathing: she was completing the ritual purification after her menstrual cycle. (According to Lev 15:19-24, this is a period of seven days.[30]) Why was this information, which the narrator knew at the beginning of the scene, withheld until now? Isaac ben Judah Abravanel (1437–1508) explains that Bathsheba was in the cycle when she was most fertile.[31] He is followed by several modern commentaries such as Henry P.

---

[27] According to Hans W. Hertzberg (*I and II Samuel*, trans. J. S. Bowden [Philadelphia: Westminster Press, 1960], 310), the title Hittite may designate his family roots.

[28] In both scenes God intervenes to block these adulterous relationships.

[29] In Genesis 19:30-38, Lot's daughters, who are responsible for the sexual encounter with their drunken father, are the subject of the verb *škb* (Gen 19:33).

[30] David P. Wright and Richard N. Jones, "Discharge," in *ABD*, 2:205.

[31] Uriel Simon, "The Poor Man's Ewe-Lamb: An Example of a Juridical Parable," *Bib* 48 (1967): 213.

Smith, who writes that the narrator's comment shows "why conception followed."[32] Some modern scholars cite the Talmudic tractate *Niddah* (31b), which notes that conception is most possible after purification.[33] But neither Talmudic tractates nor modern medicine offers insights into the mind of the ancient narrator regarding when a woman was most likely to conceive. This news, delayed until now, ensures we know who has fathered Bathsheba's child. And Bathsheba knows too and so she sends word of her pregnancy to David and not to her husband Uriah. Her washing (11:2: *rḥṣ*) in this scene foreshadows David's washing (12:20: *rḥṣ*) after the son she bears him dies. Bathsheba has just washed herself after her seven days of impurity. David will wash himself after his seven days of atonement.

We learn of the pregnancy first from the narrator and then from Bathsheba. These are her only words in the entire David-Bathsheba episode. As a character, she is a mere agent ("the performer of an action necessary to the plot"[34]). We learn nothing about her reaction to the traumatic events that transpire: her husband's death and the suffering and death of her child. Second Samuel 11–12 is not about Bathsheba; it is about David.[35] As the scene closes, the king has a crisis on his hands. If only she had not become pregnant!

4.4.3 David and Uriah: David Arranges Uriah's Death (11:6-13)

STRUCTURE

Setting the stage (11:6-7)
A. David's first attempt to have Uriah sleep with his wife, but Uriah "did not go down to his house" (11:8-9)
   B. Uriah swears an oath (11:10-11)
A'. David's second attempt to have Uriah sleep with his wife, but Uriah "did not go down to his house" (11:12-13)

---

[32] Henry P. Smith, *A Critical and Exegetical Commentary on the Books of Samuel*, The International Critical Commentary (Edinburgh: T & T Clark, 1899), 317.

[33] See, for example, McCarter, *II Samuel*, 286.

[34] Adele Berlin, *Poetics and Interpretation of Biblical Narrative* (Winona Lake, IN: Eisenbrauns, 1988), 27.

[35] But we have not heard the last of Bathsheba. In 1 Kings 1, during Adonijah's rebellion, she will play a critical role in seating her son Solomon on David's throne.

COMMENTARY

David, who from his palace sent Joab (and the then unmentioned Uriah) into battle (11:1), moves quickly to resolve his predicament, summoning Uriah back to Jerusalem. The narrator moves aside to let us observe the events as they unfold without his comment. To fetch Uriah back to Jerusalem, David has to contact Joab, his commander, who complies with the royal order without question. (Does Joab wonder what is going on?) When Uriah arrives at court, the king, feigning interest in the siege of Rabbah, makes small talk: How's Joab? How's the army? How's the war? After this inane conversation (the narrator skips Uriah's answers), the king gets down to business: Go home and sleep with your wife! What is Uriah thinking? "Why did the king summon *me* from the field to learn about the war? Why doesn't he pose his questions directly to Joab?" Later Uriah will tell David that he is baffled by the king's behavior. For now, the king orders the soldier "to wash his feet," a euphemism, the meaning of which Uriah reveals the next day: "Should I lie with my wife?" (11:11). The king hopes that if Uriah sleeps with his wife just once, he will accept Bathsheba's future child as his own, even if the child is born several weeks earlier than expected and has David's ruddy complexion.

Uriah exits the court and a present from the king follows him. Why did not David himself bestow the royal gift before Uriah departed? The present is borne by court spies who will trail after Uriah and then report back to the king. The gift-bearers, apparently cognizant of what really matters, inform the king that Uriah did not go home (11:10). David does not bother to ask what happened to the gift. The narrator, informing us (not David) that Uriah spent the night at the palace gate, begins to develop Uriah as a foil[36] to David: the faithful Uriah slept at the entrance to the palace along with his master's guard, whereas the deceitful David slept with Uriah's wife in the very palace Uriah now defends. As David descends from immorality to villainy, Uriah garners our admiration and then our pity.

We pass immediately to the next day when David addresses Uriah (11:10). Continuing his performance for Uriah, David fakes astonishment

---

[36] The term comes from *Hamlet* (act 5, sc 2, lines 193–95):
I'll be your foil, Laertes. In mine ignorance
Your skill shall, like a star i' th' darkest night,
Stick fiery off indeed.
It refers to the reflective metal placed behind a jewel to reflect its brilliance (see M. H. Abrams, *A Glossary of Literary Terms* [Boston, MA: Thomson, Wadsworth, 2005], 234). Uriah's faithful continence is the reflective foil that makes the crime of David's taking of Uriah's wife smolder ever more shamefully in the eyes of the reader.

at Uriah's refusal to go home: "You have just come from a journey."[37] Is David so focused on the crisis of Bathsheba's pregnancy (and an eventual charge that he took his neighbor's wife) that he has forgotten about the battle for Rabbah? Uriah reminds the king about the nature of the "journey" from which the king has summoned him: "The ark and Israel and Judah remain in booths; and my lord Joab and the servants of my lord are camping in the open field." David stands corrected by his foil whose response suggests that the faithful soldier finds the whole situation quite peculiar.[38] How can the king bid him to sleep with his wife? He will refuse the royal order while the Lord's ark is in the field. We know that the combat position of the ark was not a problem for David when he slept with Uriah's wife. David's options are dwindling. He can hardly accuse Uriah of disobeying a direct order to sleep with his wife without the soldier becoming suspicious.[39]

If only Uriah had followed the king's order that he have sex with his wife! Instead, he swears on David's life that he will not follow the king's command. What bitter irony: Uriah swears on the life of his wife's seducer that he will not follow the seducer's order to sleep with his wife. These are his last words on stage! Now David sees little chance that Uriah will wittingly have sexual relations with his wife. So in a few months Uriah will grasp why he was summoned from the battlefield by the king and told to have sex with his wife. And David will be accused of taking another man's wife and will be sentenced to death.[40] The king cannot allow that to happen. Recognizing that his scheme is scuttled, David decides to send him back to the battlefront as the faithful soldier desires. But first Uriah should pass another day in Jerusalem. The narrator is again silent on David's scheme and so we wait along with Uriah to see how the morrow will unfold. What if Uriah is drunk? Lot's two daughters made their father so drunk that he had sexual relations with them (Gen 19:30-38). So David will get Uriah drunk, hoping that the inebriated soldier will forget his oath (and the war) and rush off home

---

[37] The Hebrew term "journey" (*derek*) is rarely used to describe a military expedition. *ThWAT* (2:301) lists two other occasions where it seems to have this sense (1 Sam 15:20 and 18:14).

[38] First Samuel 21:5-6 alludes to the practice that soldiers on the march would abstain from sexual relations.

[39] Is Uriah already suspicious of a tryst between David and Bathsheba? The narrator teases us by not providing enough information to decide.

[40] The gravity of this charge is illustrated by Genesis 12:10-16 and 20:1-7. In each case, a major ruler risks execution by God when he takes another man's wife. In these accounts, both rulers are innocent of their crime as they did not know that Sarah was Abraham's wife.

to his wife. When this maneuver fails too, the phrase "Uriah did not go down to his house" echoes like a refrain. The narrator leaves us with a final contrast between David and his doomed foil. Uriah goes out *in the evening* (11:13) and lies down *on his bed.* The drunken soldier remains faithful to his oath and does not seek out his wife for sex. Recently a sober king arose *in the evening* from *his bed* and saw Uriah's wife bathing and sought her out for sex. We leave Uriah "lying with" (*škb ʿim*) the servants of his lord and not with his wife, with whom David had lain (*škb ʿim*) in the previous scene. Uriah's fidelity brings David's crime into sharp relief.

4.4.4 David to Joab: Uriah Must Die (11:14-17)

STRUCTURE

A. What David does (11:14)
  B. David's plan (11:15)
A'. What Joab does (11:16)
  B'. David's plan is executed (11:17)

This scene is composed of two parallel events, each of which begins with the stage-setting construction *wayĕhî.* The first event establishes the plan of action that should conclude with Uriah's death. Then the plan is executed and Uriah dies.

COMMENTARY

It is the next day, and David has learned offstage what we already know: the drunken Uriah kept his oath and was not tempted to have sex with his wife, Bathsheba. So David composes a letter to Joab, the contents of which are kept from us until the missive is already in Uriah's hand. Could not David have employed the services of a court messenger to send a letter to Joab? Was such a bald exploitation of Uriah really necessary? The image of the faithful Uriah marching back happily to rejoin the troop remains in our minds. He is as faithful as David is nefarious. The scene brings to mind an unforgettable moment in English literature, when Rosencrantz and Guildenstern present to the English king their missives that they think demand "the present death of Hamlet" (act 4, sc. 3, line 66). That event happens offstage though the audience cannot help but imagine their faces as the order for their execution is read out. We have little pity for these two pawns of King Claudius, who tried to play Hamlet as one would play a pipe (act 3, sc. 2, lines 335–41). But we feel an intense pity for

Uriah. Though perhaps ingenuous, he is an innocent victim who, because he preferred to remain with his comrades and not to consort with his wife, now bears the royal missive that provides the strategy for his demise.

The narrator, who could have simply informed us that David sent a letter to Joab to ensure Uriah's immediate death, instead presents David's exact instructions. Would not Joab, who beguiled and murdered Abner and later will kill Amasa, have known how to take care of the king's problem without such details? It would seem so. But the details of the letter ensure that we hold David fully responsible for Uriah's execution. Joab must make the death look like a battle casualty, and there is to be no slipup, no chance of Uriah's survival. Our empathy for Uriah increases along with our revulsion for David. Imagine the face of Uriah as he turns to see that his comrades-in-arms have withdrawn their support from him. Did Uriah grasp David's scheme just before he died?

The action moves rapidly; we never see Uriah hand over the royal letter and the battle is recounted summarily: the Ammonites come out of the city, they fight, and some of David's men are killed along with Uriah. We learn in the next scene that the strategy was quite foolish, but it was necessary to secure Uriah's elimination. Some of David's men were lost too. This seemingly minor detail, which the narrator opted to include, reveals that Joab, in order to accomplish the king's directive, had to sacrifice other men as well—all this to cover the king's tryst with the now-pregnant Bathsheba. Our beloved hero has become a ruthless tyrant.

4.4.5 Joab to David: Joab's News Comes to David (11:18-25)

STRUCTURE

A. Joab prepares the messenger for the king (11:18-19)
    B. Condition: David's possible, furious reaction (11:20-21)
A'. The messenger reports to David (11:22-24)
    B'. David's actual, calm reaction (11:25)

Joab hypothesizes the king's angry response in the protasis of a condition that includes five questions:

A. Protasis: "if the King becomes angry and says" (11:20a)
    B. Question 1 (11:20b)
        C. Question 2 (rhetorical) (11:20c)
    B'. Question 3 (11:21a)
        C'. Question 4 (rhetorical) (11:21b)

B". Question 5 (11:21c)
A'. Apodosis: "then you shall say" (11:21d)

The first and fifth questions are introduced by synonymous, interrogative adverbs in Hebrew (both translated with "why" in the NRSV) and followed by the same Hebrew verb (*ngš*), translated in the NRSV with "go so near." The fifth question repeats the first one. The second and fourth questions, both introduced with *hălô*, are rhetorical questions. The B' question, "Who killed Abimelech son of Jerubbaal?" alludes to Joab's real question for David: "Who killed Uriah?"

COMMENTARY

As the scene opens, Joab, David's dodgy, clever commander, is preparing his messenger to report his defeat by the Ammonites. The narrator, who passed rather quickly over the details of Uriah's death, wants us to attend to the details of Joab's instructions to his messenger. The messenger should be prepared for the king's fury at the news of Joab's defeat. But we know that David will not, in fact, become enraged and that Joab knows it too. So what is going on? At this moment, David's interest in the battle against Rabbah lies solely in learning of Uriah's demise. Does Joab hope that by instructing the messenger to announce first the defeat and to delay the news of Uriah's death, he can dupe David into betraying his real interests to his courtiers? What will the courtiers think when David's rage at the defeat is swiftly and visibly placated by the news of Uriah's death? Will they wonder how the death of Uriah could have calmed the king's anger so speedily? If nothing else, the court may suspect the king's complicity in this defeat, lessening Joab's responsibility. That may be just what Joab has in mind.

Joab employs a conditional clause (if . . . , then . . .) that is composed of a lengthy protasis (the "if" clause), which includes five questions, and a pithy apodosis (the "then" clause). The first, third, and fifth questions seem, at first glance, to be seeking information. But the first and third questions are, in fact, answered by the second and fourth rhetorical questions. Thus, the first question, "Why did you approach the city to fight?" could be taken to be a question seeking information. But it is followed by the rhetorical question: "Did you not know that they would shoot from the wall?" This rhetorical question (which demands an affirmative answer) corners the addressee who now realizes that the first question really meant, "You should not have approached the city for battle." The third question (Who killed Abimelech son of Jerubbaal?) followed by the fourth (rhetorical) question really means, "You should have remembered how Abimelech was defeated." The final question, "Why did you approach the wall?"

repeats the first question, the answer to which is now clear. The addressee has little room for maneuvering or explaining and is forced to admit that this military strategy was doomed to failure. Because those at court will not know the real reason for this strategy, Joab could appear incompetent.

Joab retells elements of Abimelech's story in a different key from what we read in Judges 9:50-54, where there is no mention of a "wall" or "archers." It is a tower in Thebez that Abimelech would have set ablaze when a resourceful woman tossed a millstone from atop the tower onto his head. The narrator of Judges, who does not pronounce on the foolishness of Abimelech's strategy, allows the dying Abimelech a final word (addressed to his amour-bearer): "Draw your sword and kill me so that history will not record: 'A woman killed him.'" Ironically, his private wish to avoid what for him would be a ghastly epitaph becomes, in fact, his public memorial: a clever woman triumphed over Abimelech. Joab recasts this story, presuming that he can be accused of having imitated Abimelech's folly in his attack on Rabbah. Thus, Joab's third question, "Who killed Abimelech?" alludes to Joab's real question for David: "Who killed Uriah?"

If the king becomes angry, as the messenger rightly expects, then the messenger should tell him that Uriah, whose name here is prefixed with the title "your servant," is dead. That title underscores that David, now a tyrant, has murdered one of his own. The messenger (and those troops listening to Joab's instructions) may be wondering how the news of Uriah's death will ameliorate the king's rage. Joab could have instructed the messenger to tell David immediately of the death of Uriah and then to proceed with the full account of the battle. Instead, he orders the messenger to recount the details of the battle first. If the king objects to Joab's battle strategy, then the messenger should tell him that Uriah is dead. If events go according to Joab's plan, the messenger, along with David's court, will observe the king's immediate change of disposition and wonder how the news of Uriah's death remedies the defeat. By tripping up the king publically, Joab can protect his own reputation as a military commander.

The messenger arrives and makes his report as he was ordered. The battle account is immediately followed by the report that some of David's men were killed, including Uriah. The messenger does not pause for the court (and us) to observe the king's initial reaction to the defeat, to learn whether David would have raged against Joab's foolish strategy. But the messenger does provide more information about the battle. It seems that the Ammonite troops drew David's men from the field toward the gate of the city so that they might be cut down by the archers along the wall. The strategy, patently incompetent, was necessitated by David's order, and though the messenger appears to be ignorant of the significance of the details in his missive, the reader hears again that the royal order required that other troops be sacrificed to achieve Uriah's murder.

David's reaction to the defeat is obviously muted, bringing into sharp relief the disparity between the expected royal reaction and his actual reaction. He poses none of the five possible questions hypothesized by Joab. His casual remark, *che sarà, sarà*, "the sword devours here and there," is hardly appropriate given the loss of his troops. While it reveals how important to him was the death of Uriah, the messenger and courtiers must be wondering what is going on. The king's cool reaction contrasts with his fury at the taking of the poor man's beloved sheep in the upcoming parable from the prophet Nathan (2 Sam 12:5-6). For the moment, David has developed into a heartless fiend, much like Shakespeare's Macbeth. The harm created by both of them continually increases. King Duncan's murder leads to Banquo's murder and finally to the gratuitous slaughter of Macduff's wife and children. David's desire for another man's wife has resulted not only in Uriah's murder but also in the murder of other troops loyal to David. To all this, the king reacts with *che sarà, sarà*.

David employs a Hebrew idiomatic expression to inform his commander that he should not be overly disappointed by the defeat (11:25): "Let the affair not be a bad thing in your eyes" (*ʾal-yēraʿ bĕʿênêkā ʾet-haddābār*, translation mine).[41] David's phony platitude is only for the messenger since Joab knows why the defeat was necessary and does not need the king's consoling remarks. The narrator will replay David's words at the climax of the David and Bathsheba episode when he reports God's displeasure with these events (11:27): "the affair which David had done was bad in the eyes of the LORD" (*wayyēraʿ haddābār . . . bĕʿênê YHWH*; translation mine). This immediate recasting of David's words contrasts his reaction with God's reaction: David tells the messenger to inform Joab that he should not be too upset about the loss of life and the death of Uriah. But God is upset with the entire affair![42]

4.4.6 David Ushers the Wife of Uriah into His House. The Lord Is Displeased (11:26-27)

The scene immediately shifts to Bathsheba, who has learned of her husband's death. The narrator continues to refer to the new widow as

---

[41] The idiom occurs, for example, in 1 Samuel 8:6, to describe Samuel's reaction to the people's request for a king: "The affair displeased Samuel" (see also Gen 21:11 and 1 Sam 18:8).

[42] Unfortunately, the play on this idiom is lost in most English versions (NIV, NJPS, NRSV, REB, NAB, NJB) because the two phrases are rendered differently.

the *wife of Uriah*, reminding us that she was married to another man. Pregnant with the king's issue, does Bathsheba wonder about the circumstances of Uriah's timely death? Was her husband really just another chance casualty of war? A clue to her disposition may lie in the narrator's description of her brief and perfunctory mourning. When Sarah died (Gen 23:2), Abraham went to mourn Sarah and *to weep for her*. When Jacob died, even the Canaanites remarked on the depth of the Israelites' grief (Gen 50:10-11). When David learns of the deaths of Saul and Jonathan, he tears his clothes (2 Sam 1:11), mourning, weeping, and fasting until evening. He follows Abner's bier, weeping at his grave and singing a lament (3:31-35). David's cry for his dead son Absalom will be heard by the victorious troops (18:33; 19:3-4). By comparison, Bathsheba appears to have given Uriah's death short shrift. There is no weeping, no sung lament, no tearing of clothes, no sackcloth, no fasting, and no description of his burial. Her dispassionate mourning concludes promptly and is focused more on the removal of her mourning garb (11:27) than on her donning it. The mourning rites are presented as little more than a necessary public ritual before her transfer to the palace.

David *sends* for Bathsheba a second time, repeating the leitmotif (*šlḥ*) from the last time he *sent* and *took* (*lqḥ*) Bathsheba (11:4; see the discussion there). This time he *sends* and *gathers* (*ʾsp*) her into his household (NRSV: "David sent and brought her"). Their adulterous liaison has remained a secret and so David can publicly *gather* the widow of one of his fallen soldiers into his palace. Bathsheba becomes his wife, bears a son that everyone takes to be Uriah's (though Joab is probably suspicious about the child's paternity), and the story is over. David's crimes of adultery and murder remain undiscovered. Having married the beautiful Bathsheba, David has written the conclusion for this story: "and they all lived happily ever after." But God, who till now has remained offstage, is not happy. The divine displeasure, which probably began as soon as David bedded Bathsheba and only increased with Uriah's murder, bursts onstage: "But the thing that David had done displeased the Lord." What is God going to do?

4.4.7 Nathan to David: God's News Comes to David (12:1-7a)

STRUCTURE

1. The Lord sends; Nathan comes and speaks (12:1a)

    A. The rich man and the poor man (12:1b-3a)
      B. The treatment of the ewe lamb (12:3b)
    A'. The rich man and the poor man (12:4)

2. David reacts (12:5-6)

3. Nathan issues a pronouncement (12:7a)

This scene and the following one (12:7b-15a) share the same structure: Nathan speaks, David reacts, then Nathan responds. In this scene Nathan weaves a story, and in the next he announces God's oracle. In this scene David denies, and in the next he confesses. In this scene Nathan accuses, and in the next he offers a word of clemency. The center of Nathan's "parable" focuses on the special care that the ewe lamb enjoyed. That lamb is the subject of five verbs.

COMMENTARY

Nathan appears for the second time without any reintroduction from the narrator (see 7:1-3), who also withholds any description of the scene's setting. Details of what Nathan the prophet was doing when God interrupted his day would only clutter the hurried opening of this scene and God's charge cannot abide such a delay. God's message to Nathan is not revealed to us now,[43] so we wait to learn its content at the same time as David does, although, because we know of God's displeasure, we sense that it is not good news. This divine act of "sending," the only instance in the David and Bathsheba episode in which David is not directly involved, determines the outcome of this episode, an outcome that David is not expecting.

Nathan prefaces the divine oracle, which begins in 12:7b, with a fable of his own.[44] His yarn is often labeled a "parable," though, given the context in which it appears, it has a limited scope of meaning—what Richard M. Eastman has labeled a "closed parable." An "open parable" has "a designed instability" and is constructed with "opaque, irreducible details as to block the final verification of any one hypothesis." "The reader is hindered from endorsing any one character or any one theme."[45] Were Nathan's parable not in this narrative context, it would be less "closed" as a parable. But within the David and Bathsheba story, the reader is

---

[43] In some cases the theme of the divine discourse is revealed to the prophet (and to us) before it is communicated to the addressee. In 1 Kings 21:19 we learn of the divine message (the dogs will lick up the blood of Ahab) with Elijah the prophet before it is communicated to Ahab.

[44] Nathan's yarn is not introduced with the messenger formula, "thus says the LORD," which introduces the divine speech in 12:7. It is his own creation.

[45] Richard M. Eastman, "The Open Parable: Demonstration and Definition," *College English* 22, no. 1 (October 1960): 17.

guided to specific applications between the characters and events in the parable and the characters and events in 2 Samuel 11. David hears Nathan's story not as a parable but as a legal case requiring the king's judgment. Because we have been informed of God's displeasure and of Nathan's divine mandate, we know that the legal case is a fabrication, and so from the start we are interpreting Nathan's words in light of David's tryst with Bathsheba and the murder of Uriah, while the beguiled David acts in his public role as final arbiter.

The parable opens with two men, one rich, the other poor. The rich man's wealth was in flocks and herds. The poor man had nothing but a single ewe lamb that he had acquired. The center of the parable focuses on the treatment of the ewe lamb. Nathan could have immediately shifted to the arrival of the traveler and the slaughter of the poor man's lamb, but instead, he details the poor man's affection for the ewe lamb. We observe how the poor man raised the lamb, which is the subject of the verbs that follow (all of which, because they are feminine,[46] encourage the Hebrew reader to make the association with Bathsheba): the lamb matured, she ate from his food, drank from his cup, lay in his lap, and was like a daughter to him. By slowing the action, Nathan, the narrator, has us visualize the poor man's exaggerated care for the lamb.[47] This hyperbolic description links the poor man with Uriah and the ewe lamb with Bathsheba. In the final phrase, "she was like a daughter to him" (*wattĕhî lô kĕbat*; 12:3), Hebrew readers hear in the Hebrew word "daughter" *bat*, the first syllable of Bathsheba's name ("Bathsheba" means "daughter of Sheba"), and they complete the word in their minds: "that lamb was like a *Bath[sheba]* to him." After this lengthy focus on the lamb's nurturing, the parable comes to a swift conclusion: a traveler has arrived, and the rich man does not want to take one of his own animals, despite their great number, so he takes the poor man's lamb to cook for the traveler.

The parable lacks closure. How did the poor man react when the rich man came and seized his beloved lamb for slaughter? A description of the poor man weeping for his ewe lamb would allow a release for our pent-up feelings of empathy for him. By denying us a catharsis, Nathan imprints on our minds the image of the poor man imploring the rich man to spare his ewe lamb and then mourning as his prize possession, which was like a daughter to him, was seized to be roasted for a stranger's dinner. Our rage toward the rich man is quickly transferred to David.

---

[46] Verbs in Hebrew are also classified by gender.

[47] A similar device appears in the Good Samaritan parable (Luke 10:30-35). The priest and Levite pass by the wounded man very quickly (each receives three verbs). But when the Samaritan arrives, the narrator slows the action and offers a detailed description of his care for the injured person.

The kind of animal, a ewe lamb, that Nathan chooses for his parable is not accidental. The female sheep is an animal that can be sacrificed for the expiation of sin:

> If the offering you bring as a sin offering is a sheep, you shall bring a female without blemish. You shall lay your hand on the head of the sin offering; and it shall be slaughtered as a sin offering at the spot where the burnt offering is slaughtered. (Lev 4:32-33)

Leviticus 13–14 treats questions of impurity arising from skin diseases, including the rubrics for the purification ceremony (Lev 14). Once the person is declared clean (Lev 14:7), he is allowed back into the camp. After seven days he bathes and washes his clothes. On the eighth day, the one who has been cleansed brings to the priest two male lambs and a ewe lamb (Lev 14:10). The priest slaughters one of the lambs as a guilt offering, putting some of the blood of the lamb on the one who has been cleansed.

This expiatory function of the ewe lamb illuminates the meaning of David's actions in the scenes that follow, after he confesses his sin to Nathan (2 Sam 12:15b-23). David's courtiers will stand by the king as his condemned son becomes ill and will expect him to perform mourning rites after the child dies (they have no idea what he is doing). But David will perform some of the rubrics of the expiatory liturgy described in Leviticus 14. He will lie on the ground seven days, and once the child is dead he will change his clothes, bathe, and anoint himself (actions that recall the anointing that the newly cleansed person receives from the priest in Lev 14:14-20). Thus, the "ewe lamb" in Nathan's parable, a sacrificial animal of expiation, foreshadows David's eventual atonement for his crimes against Uriah.

Other elements of the parable replay the leitmotifs (see 2 Sam 11:2-5) in this episode. The lamb is said to lie (*škb*) on the poor man's lap. The image of Bathsheba, who before the tryst with David used to lie with Uriah, leaps to mind. The rich man *takes* (*lqḥ* appears twice in 12:4) the poor man's ewe lamb just as David *took* Bathsheba (11:4). When his ewe lamb is taken, the poor man is given no choice in the matter. So too, Uriah was given no choice when Bathsheba was taken. Other aspects of the parable, though they have no direct parallel with the events in 2 Samuel 11, shape our reaction to David's crime. The description of the poor man's treatment of the ewe lamb allows us to imagine the extraordinarily tender love that Uriah had for Bathsheba. Given what we know about Uriah's fidelity to David and to the Lord, we can readily imagine that he was equally devoted to his wife. In the parable, the poor man watches as his dear ewe lamb is taken and cooked for dinner while Uriah was unaware when his ewe lamb, Bathsheba, was taken by David. The *slaughter* of the ewe lamb brings Uriah's murder to mind. Like an innocent ewe lamb, he slept at the door of the palace and refused to have sexual relations with his wife because his fellow soldiers (David's troops) were arrayed for battle. On David's order, he was slaughtered.

As King David sees it, Nathan has brought a legal case before the king, who must defend the rights of the defrauded poor man. Later a fake widow will plead for the life of her only surviving son before the king (14:4-11). In both cases the king gives credence to the pretenders by pronouncing on their cases and even swearing an oath. His outrage against the rich man contrasts with his lackadaisical reaction to the battle losses against Rabbah and the death of Uriah (11:25). The slaughter of the ewe lamb infuriates the murderous king, who appears to have compartmentalized his crimes and is oblivious to their significance. We wait for Nathan to spring the trap.

When David swears that the rich man shall pay with his life, we remember the hapless Uriah who swore an oath and, even when made drunk by David, kept his word. The death sentence, an obvious exaggeration for the crime against the poor man, alludes to the sentence that should fall on David's head for having taken his neighbor's wife, slept with her and murdered her husband. The king then decrees a penalty that agrees with Exodus 22:1: the rich man, who took a lamb that was not his and slaughtered it, must restore four lambs to the poor man. Then Nathan identifies the man whom the king has just condemned: "you are the man." As we hear Nathan bellow the news, we imagine David's reaction as he grasps that Nathan's legal case was bogus and that the prophet (and God) knows that he seized Bathsheba and murdered Uriah. Will the sentence that David pronounced on the rich man be carried out on him?

4.4.8 Nathan to David: The Child Will Die (12:7b-15a)

STRUCTURE

1. Nathan's (God's) speech
   A. Messenger formula + what God did for David (especially giving wives) (12:7bc-8)
      B. Accusation: "you despised" (12:9a)
        C. You killed Uriah by the sword (12:9b)
          D. You took his wife (12:9c)
        C'. You killed Uriah by the sword (12:9d)
      B'. Punishment for despising God (12:10)
   A'. Messenger formula + what God will do now (take David's wives) (12:11-12)

2. David reacts (12:13a)

3. Nathan issues a pronouncement (12:13b-14)

4. Nathan leaves (12:15a)

The structure of this scene parallels the preceding one: Nathan speaks, David reacts, and then Nathan responds. At the center of the oracular text is the accusation: David *took* Uriah's wife, which is framed by the double mention of Uriah's murder. The B/B' sections accuse David of despising God by doing evil in God's eyes (B), which is then specified in the (B') section as taking the wife of Uriah the Hittite as his own wife (B'). The A section reviews all that God did for David, especially the transfer of Saul's wives. In the A' section God announces a fitting retribution: God will *take* David's wives and give them to his neighbor. David reacts to this oracle and Nathan, after a final word, departs.

COMMENTARY

Having informed David that he is the rich man in the parable, Nathan launches into a divine oracle (the formula, "thus says the LORD," signals that the words that follow are no longer his). The narrator does not reveal David's immediate reaction to Nathan's revelation, though we imagine that David's mask of denial falls with the realization that the legal case he just decided is really a parable that interprets his life. The oracle, by beginning with the emphatic first-person pronoun, "*I* anointed you," recalls the divine oracle in 7:5-16, in which God also employed the first-person pronoun when addressing David (7:8, 14). In 2 Samuel 7 it underscored God as the primary protagonist in the history of Israel. Now it underscores God as the primary protagonist in David's life. As in 7:5, the solemn messenger formula, "Thus says the LORD," introduces divine speech, though this oracle includes a longer title for God: "Thus says the LORD, the God of Israel." The oracle in 2 Samuel 7 reviewed the key events in Israel's history under God's direction. This oracle reviews the key events of David's life under God's direction: his anointing (1 Sam 16), his rescue from Saul (1 Sam 18–31), and the transfer of Saul's kingdom to him (2 Sam 3:6–5:5). It was God who deposed King Saul and then ordered Samuel to fill up his horn with oil and to anoint one of Jesse's sons (1 Sam 16:1). The mention of God's rescue (*nṣl*) of David from Saul reminds the reader of the main theme of the David Narrative (see section 1.3 above). David would not have become king or held on to the throne without God's continued rescue from the trials he has confronted and any review of David's life, however brief, must include that theme.

God reminds David that the transfer of Saul's kingdom also included Saul's wives. This may be a reference to David's marriage to Ahinoam (1 Sam 25:43), who, Jon D. Levenson has argued, is the same person as Ahinoam, the daughter of Ahimaaz, Saul's wife (1 Sam 14:50).[48] The narrator may presume that she was transferred to David, since a deposed or defeated king's wives are part of the booty that transfers to the victor. When King Ben-hadad of Aram threatens King Ahab, he sends messengers to Ahab to tell him, "Your silver and gold are mine; your fairest wives and children also are mine" (1 Kgs 20:3). The rebel Absalom has sexual relations with David's concubines to demonstrate to all Israel that he has usurped his father's throne (2 Sam 16:20-23). When Bathsheba approaches Solomon to ask for David's concubine, Abishag, for Adonijah, Solomon's brother, the king retorts, "Ask for him the kingdom as well" (1 Kgs 2:22). Solomon recognizes that Adonijah's possession of the dead king's concubine would threaten Solomon's claim to the throne, and so he orders Adonijah's immediate execution just for asking (1 Kgs 2:24).[49] Thus, though the transfer of Saul's wives is not explicitly reported in the account of David's accession to the throne, we are meant to assume as much and so God now refers back to it. God put Saul's wives in David's "lap" (ḥêq), a term that hearkens back to Nathan's parable: the poor man's ewe lamb slept in his lap (ḥêq, 2 Sam 12:3; NRSV reads "bosom"). Were this not enough, God would have welcomed any further request from his servant David. But David preferred to seize his neighbor's wife in secret.

God summarizes the indictment: David has despised God by doing what is evil in God's eyes (12:9). The oracle replays here the last line of 2 Samuel 11, when David believed that his story with Bathsheba was happily concluded, but the narrator informed us that the whole affair was "evil in God's eyes" (11:27). Now David learns that God has not been duped by the plot to murder Uriah. The Ammonites were mere instruments to accomplish David's intrigue. The double charge of Uriah's murder, "You have struck down Uriah the Hittite with the sword," and "[you] have killed him," frames the center of the oracle: "[you] have taken his wife to be your wife." God never refers to Bathsheba by name; she remains Uriah's wife. God also rejects the term "to gather" (ʾsp) that appeared in 11:27 to describe David's inclusion of Bathsheba into the palace household in preparation for his marriage to her, preferring instead the verb "to take" (lqḥ): just as David "took" Bathsheba to his

---

[48] Jon D. Levenson, "1 Samuel 25 as Literature and as History," *CBQ* 41 (1978): 11–28; see also Jon D. Levenson and Baruch Halpern, "The Political Import of David's Marriages," *JBL* 99 (1980): 507–18.

[49] It is for this reason that Ishbaal charges Abner with usurpation by accusing him of having sexual relations with Saul's concubine, Rizpah (2 Sam 3:6-11).

bed (11:4) and the rich man "took" the poor man's ewe lamb (12:4), so God accuses David of having "taken" Uriah's wife.

God now turns to the punishment.[50] In the oracle in 2 Samuel 7, God played on the word "house." Now God plays on the word "sword." Just as David killed Uriah "with the sword," now that sword will not depart from his house; God will wield it against David forever. The expression forever (*'ad 'ôlām*) echoes the promise made to David in 2 Samuel 7 where it appeared seven times. God had promised that David's house would stand "sure forever" (7:16). But now, because of this crime against Uriah, the house of David will be forever beset by troubles. The rebellions of Absalom (2 Sam 15–19) and of Sheba son of Bichri (2 Sam 20) jump to mind, but the oracle also foreshadows the crises and eventual destruction that await the Davidic line in the distant future. In 12:11 another messenger formula ("thus says the LORD") introduces the specifics of the divine verdict that suits the crime: just as David took Uriah's wife, God will take David's wives and will give them to another who will lie with them before all Israel (the leitmotif *škb*, "to lie down," appears again). David's seizure of Bathsheba was done in secret but God will seize David's wives before "all Israel" and "before the sun." Absalom will have sexual relations with David's concubines in a tent pitched on the palace roof (16:20-22), a place that is "in the sight of this very sun," and "before all Israel," as God now predicts.

Finally, David speaks, confessing his sin. What will be his fate? When Saul plainly confessed his sin (1 Sam 15:30) and pleaded for forgiveness, the prophet Samuel would have none of it. God had rejected him. Will David now suffer the same fate? Will God regret having established David's throne as he regretted having chosen Saul as king? Is the promise to David (in 2 Sam 7), who stands convicted of murder and of taking his neighbor's wife, to be annulled? Elements of David's crime and confession parallel Saul's (1 Sam 15:10-31). The prophet Nathan accuses David of having despised the "word of God" (2 Sam 12:9) just as the prophet Samuel accused Saul of having rejected the "word of God" (1 Sam 15:26). Both David and Saul confess their guilt (Saul confesses twice: 1 Sam 15:24 and 15:30) and from both God takes something to give to another. In David's case it is his wives. In Saul's case it is the kingdom:

> And Samuel said to him [Saul], "The LORD has torn the kingdom of Israel from you this very day, and has given it to a neighbor of yours, who is better than you." (1 Sam 15:28)

---

[50] The Hebrew particle *wĕʿattâ* in 12:10 introduces a conclusion based upon the preceding premise (see 7:8).

I [God] will take your wives before your eyes, and give them to your neighbor, and he shall lie with your wives in the sight of this very sun. (2 Sam 12:11)

Nathan's oracle does not threaten God's promise to David in 2 Samuel 7, even though the transfer of the king's wives to another can imply as much. Absalom will be the agent of this divine punishment: he will have relations with David's concubines, but God will *not* confer the kingdom upon him. David will not be deposed. God's promise endures as Nathan offers a word of clemency to the penitent David, commuting the death penalty that David and the audience expected. (Saul pleaded for such clemency from Samuel but never received it.) David will not die, but the child born to him and Bathsheba will not live. In the divine oracle in 2 Samuel 7, Nathan announced to David that his successor would build the Temple (7:13). This child has no chance of fulfilling that promise or of laying claim to David's throne.[51] With that Nathan goes home.

4.4.9 David and the Child: God Ensures the Child's Death (12:15b-23)

David's son lies deathly ill. The laconic narrator, ignoring Bathsheba's anguish, focuses on David's actions and his worried courtiers, whose reaction to David, a seemingly superfluous detail, is key to interpreting the meaning of this scene.

STRUCTURE

A. The Lord acts (12:15b)
  B. David reacts to the child's illness; he lies on the ground (12:16)
    C. The elders fail to understand; David refuses to eat (12:17)
      D. The servants fail to understand David's behavior (12:18)
        E. David asks a question (12:19ab)

---

[51] The MT reads: "because you have scorned the enemies of the LORD." The Hebrew scribal tradition added "the enemies" to avoid the phrase, "You have scorned the LORD."

A'. The Lord has acted (12:19c)
  B'. David reacts to the child's death; he rises from the ground
       (12:20ab)
    C'. They set food before him; David eats (12:20c)
      D'. The servants question David (12:21)
        E'. David explains his behavior and asks a question
             (12:22-23)

This scene is divided into two parallel sections. As soon as God's
verdict on the child is exacted, the king reverses his rituals. In the A/A'
sections the Lord acts, first striking the child, then killing him. In the B
section David interrupts his routine, throwing himself on the ground
and fasting. In B' section he rises from the ground, washes, and begins
his normal routine. In the C section the elders bid David to rise and eat
but he refuses. In the C' section they bring food and he eats. In the D/D'
sections David's courtiers observe his actions, they fail to understand
what he is doing and ask questions, first of themselves, then of David.
In the E section David asks his servants about the child (he wants to
know whether God has acted). In the E' section David asks his servants
if he can now do anything to save a dead child (only David knows why
the child is dead).

COMMENTARY

As promised, the Lord strikes the child with illness and, while the
child and mother suffer offstage, we observe David. The Hebrew verb
ngp, "to strike," is often associated with divine castigation that leads to
the death of an individual (1 Sam 26:10) or a military defeat (Judg 20:35
and 1 Sam 4:3). It describes God's plagues against the Egyptians (Exod
8:2 and 12:13). After Abigail impedes David from killing her husband,
the Lord strikes (*ngp*) Nabal and he dies (1 Sam 25:38). In these two cases,
God intervenes, breaking the will of another person (Pharaoh and Nabal)
and "striking" his adversary, thus demonstrating divine authority over
the situation at hand. Similarly here, God intervenes to punish David,
ruining David's plan to live happily ever after with Bathsheba and the
child born by his seizure of another man's wife. The narrator, reflecting
the divine judgment, continues to refer to Bathsheba as Uriah's wife. The
moment to recognize the marriage has not yet arrived.

Why does David fast and lie on the ground? Nathan announced the
divine penalty against the child without equivocation; there is little to
do. What appears to others as David's plea for the life of the child is,
in fact, his act of penance. Perhaps God will accept his contrition and
not exact the penalty for his sin from the newborn child. When King

Ahab, with Jezebel's help, seizes Naboth's vineyard, the prophet Elijah condemns King Ahab and promises the destruction of his kingdom: "I will sweep you away" (1 Kgs 21:21; translation mine). But when Ahab repents, putting on sackcloth and fasting, God commutes the sentence: "Because he has humbled himself before me, I will not bring the disaster in his days" (1 Kgs 21:29). Similarly, when Hezekiah falls sick, he is informed by the prophet Isaiah that his death is imminent (2 Kgs 20:1-5), but when he prays, albeit with words that David cannot say at this moment—"Remember, O Lord, that I have walked before you in truth"—God receives Hezekiah's prayer and revokes Isaiah's original pronouncement, and the king is healed.[52] So David implores God not to exact the penalty that Nathan has announced, a penalty that should have fallen on him.

The members of David's court are at a loss to understand what the king is doing. Courtiers often imitate a king's mourning rituals. When the news of Saul's death reaches David, he tears his clothes and all those with him do the same (2 Sam 1:11). When the news of the supposed deaths of David's sons reaches the court, again the king tears his garments and his servants follow suit (13:31). But in this scene, the courtiers do not join in David's fast. They must be wondering why the king is making such a fuss over Bathsheba's child, *the son of Uriah*. If some of the courtiers, such as the messenger who was sent to fetch Bathsheba from her bath, know more about the child's pedigree, the narrator does not tell us. They surround the penitent king, reaching down to pull him up off the ground. But he refuses to rise and will not eat. As the narrator presents them, they know nothing of the king's crime and thus cannot grasp the meaning of his actions. But we know that David is not merely appealing to God for the sake of a sick child.

The earliest interpretations of this scene (4QSam[a] and many Greek manuscripts) tried to clarify David's behavior by adding in 12:16 that David lay down "in sackcloth." But that addition makes David's actions explicitly penitential,[53] and the courtiers would rightly become suspicious. Why would the king put on *sackcloth* to pray for the life of Uriah's son? Instead, the Hebrew text is purposely vague so that the courtiers interpret his gestures as a ritual to implore God for the life of the child. Their apprehension about David's reaction to the news that Uriah's son has died (the narrator has us eavesdrop on their deliberations) testifies to the intensity of David's despair that perplexes them. But they express

---

[52] David is not in the same position as the upright Hezekiah who reestablished proper worship, eradicating foreign religious practices.

[53] The defeated Ben-hadad presents himself to King Ahab in sackcloth to express his regret and to seek clemency from the king (1 Kgs 20:31-32).

no inkling that the child is the king's progeny or that the king is atoning for his crime of having seized his neighbor's wife and murdered her husband. But we know that David's gestures—fasting and lying on the floor—are acts of penance and atonement.

The king finds himself "lying" (*škb*) alone on the ground, the penultimate use of the Hebrew verb *škb* in this episode. It first appeared in the tryst between David and Bathsheba (11:4). Uriah, despite David's orders to lie with his wife (*škb* in 11:11 where Uriah refers to the royal command), lies down (*škb*) with his fellow soldiers (11:9). Now David has descended from the comfort of his bed (and Bathsheba) to the ground. The final appearance of *škb* appears in the next scene when David can return to his bed with Bathsheba (12:24).

On the seventh day the child dies. That number of days is another signal that atonement and purification is the proper interpretation of David's actions. The seven days that the Lord kept the child alive ensured that David would complete a seven-day period of purification as the book of Leviticus prescribes.[54] As the servants do not understand any of this, they worry that David could become despondent when the child dies: he could even do harm to himself! Their fear underscores the disparity between what we know (David's crimes) and what they know (that Bathsheba's child is Uriah's son). When he sees his courtiers whispering together and probably glancing toward him with disconcerted frowns, he knows that the child is dead. His penance has not been accepted; the divine penalty has been exacted. To him, the news comes as no surprise, whereas the courtiers remain baffled.

So the king rises. He washes himself, anoints his body, changes his clothes (presumably not changed for seven days), enters the house of the Lord[55] to worship, and then eats. Again, we are not surprised that David eats as soon as the news comes that the child is dead, since his atonement is over. But his servants are appalled; fasting is part of a mourning ceremony (David, mourning for Abner, swore that he would not eat until the evening [3:35]). In their minds, David seems to be performing the mourning ceremony backward: "What have you done? You fasted

---

[54] A person with a skin disease remains confined for seven days. The malady is checked after seven days, and, if the blemish has not spread, then the person is confined for another seven days and released (Lev 13:2-8). Similarly, persons made impure by touching a corpse remain impure for seven days (Num 19:11).

[55] The "house of the LORD" is normally a reference to the Temple, which has not yet been built (see 2 Sam 7). So we presume that David entered the tent where the ark of the Lord is housed at present. The narrator is not disturbed by this apparent inconsistency, perhaps because the issue at stake in this scene is David's prayer after his penance and not the question of the Temple.

when the child was alive, but when the child died you rose and ate." But we know that David was atoning for his sins and imploring God not to exact the penalty from the child. His prayer has not been heard. The child is dead, and so he rises to eat. David's "washing" himself further indicates purification after atonement. He washes himself just as Bathsheba washed herself after the seven days of her purification. The anointing alludes to the anointing of the cleansed leper in Leviticus 14:17-18 (see section 4.4.7 above).

In response to the courtiers' inquiries David equivocates. He is hardly going to disclose to them that Bathsheba's child was his and that he was atoning for his adultery and the murder of one of his loyal soldiers. Instead, he explains his actions as a plea for divine intervention on behalf of a deathly ill child. He begins with the question "Who knows?" as if he were entirely in the dark as to the outcome. His statement to the servants, "the LORD may be gracious to me," sounds to them like an innocent prayer. But David always knew that the child was doomed and that there was little chance that his prayer would be granted.[56] By his response the king admits to himself that God did not hear his plea and the child died as expected. But the servants, who expect David, who was inconsolable before the death, to mourn now that the child is dead, are unable to interpret David's behavior, and the narrator wants us to hear their perplexity. They have not understood him from the beginning of this scene. But we have. And by focusing on their confusion the narrator compels us to grasp the significance of this scene: David has atoned for his sin.

4.4.10 David Sleeps with Bathsheba, His Wife (12:24-25)

With his penance completed, David goes to console Bathsheba, whom the narrator refers to as David's wife for the first time (12:24), a signal that God has accepted the king's atonement. Any lingering concern that God might depose him, as he did Saul, is now set to rest. The reappearance of Bathsheba reminds us that much of her story has happened offstage. Her reactions to her tryst with the king, to the death of her husband, and now to her son's seven days of suffering and death were not recounted. The narrator has kept the focus on David, who now sleeps with Bathsheba a second time, and the verb "to lie," *škb*, appears for the final time in this episode. Their first encounter in the royal bed (and the first appearance

---

[56] Do the servants question David because of suspicions about the child's paternity? The narrator is silent.

of *škb*) led to David lying (*škb*) on the ground in penance. He returns to
his bed and to his now-legitimate wife, who conceives a second time.
Their first son was never named, but this son receives two names, one
from David[57] and one from God. The first son died according to God's
decree, but this son is loved by God. When Nathan came to David the
last time, God was displeased (11:27). Now he comes with good news:
God is delighted. Not only has God's promise to build David a "house"
(7:11b-15) not been altered, but the fulfillment of that promise is underway: David's successor, the one who will build the Temple that David
had envisioned (7:1-3) and God wants (7:13) has been born. Solomon
will remain offstage until it is time for him to assume the throne (1 Kgs
1). This is David's story.

Nathan's four appearances in the David Narrative are linked to the
question of David's successor. The first time he appeared, he promised a
Davidic line of kings with a particular focus on the immediate successor
who would build the Temple:

> When your days are fulfilled and you lie down with your ancestors, I will
> raise up your offspring after you, who shall come forth from your body,
> and I will establish his kingdom. He shall build a house for my name, and
> I will establish the throne of his kingdom forever. (7:12-13)

His second appearance ensured that the child born to David and the
"wife of Uriah" would *not* be the successor about whom he spoke in
7:12-13. That child would die (12:14). His third appearance in this scene
hints that this child may be the successor. The narrator did not recount
a visit from Nathan at the birth of any other of David's children. In fact,
the individual births of these children were not recounted except for two
lists of David's descendants (3:2-5 and 5:14-16). So the visit from Nathan
at the birth of Solomon and the announcement of God's name for the
child, Jedidiah ("Beloved of the LORD"), bodes well for this son. Our
suspicions about his destiny are confirmed when Nathan appears for the
last time in the David Narrative to ensure that Solomon ascends to his
father's throne (1 Kgs 1:11-40). After the David and Bathsheba episode,
the question of David's successor will come to center stage. In 2 Samuel
15, Absalom will attempt a coup d'état, and in 1 Kings 1, Adonijah will
declare himself David's rightful successor (1 Kgs 1:5), garnering support
for his ascension to the throne from members of David's court, including
Joab, the most powerful member of that court. But Nathan will engineer
Solomon's succession. He will not go directly to David, who will be so
old that the lovely Abishag will have been brought in to keep him warm

---

[57] The *qere* in the MT has Bathsheba name her son.

in bed, but to Bathsheba to warn her that if Adonijah becomes king, she and her son will be at risk. The two of them will stage the report of Adonijah's succession to King David, who will declare Solomon as his rightful successor, ordering the priest Zadok and the prophet Nathan to anoint Solomon king and to cry out: "Long live King Solomon!" (1 Kgs 1:34). In the end, Adonijah will confess to the queen mother, Bathsheba, that Solomonic rule was "from the LORD" (1 Kgs 2:15).

4.4.11 Joab and David Conquer Rabbah (12:26-31)

The riveting events at the palace have kept the siege of Rabbah out of mind. That battle returns to center stage as the David and Bathsheba episode draws to a conclusion.

STRUCTURE

A. Joab assails Rabbah (12:26)
   B. Joab commands David (12:27-28)
A'. David takes Rabbah (12:29)
   B'. David obeys Joab's order (12:30-31ab)
Conclusion: David and the army return to Jerusalem (12:31c)

Two events comprise this scene. Joab orders David to finish the battle against Rabbah, and David does as ordered. The entire David-Bathsheba episode concludes as David returns to Jerusalem.

COMMENTARY

The episode opens with the final assault against the city of Rabbah. Joab, no longer pestered by royal requests to fake a defeat, takes the city with ease. The scene shifts quickly to his message for David, which contains three parts: a report on the current state of combat, an order for David, and a threat. He has captured the "city of water," probably a reference to the city's water supply.[58] Cut off from water, Rabbah will soon capitulate. He commands David to muster his own troops for a decisive breach against the city. Can the chief army officer order the king about? When David established a favorable alliance with Abner, Saul's general, Joab murdered Abner, thwarting David's hopes for an orderly

---

[58] See McCarter, *II Samuel*, 312.

assimilation of Saul's kingdom under his dominion (see 3:12-39). Back then David admitted that he could do nothing to retaliate against Joab:

> Today I am powerless, even though anointed king; these men, the sons of Zeruiah, are too violent for me. (3:39)

David must wait until he lies on his deathbed to engineer the revenge for that murder (1 Kgs 2:5-6). In this scene Joab exercises his power over the king a second time. Does he know about the recent events back at the palace? The narrator, who could answer our questions, again remains silent—too silent for us, his inquisitive readers. If Joab has learned that Bathsheba, once wife to Uriah, is now David's wife, then he knows why he had to make Uriah's death look like a war casualty. He also knows that David has used him to help secure the wife of one of his soldiers. Accomplishing the king's bidding required him to adopt a battle strategy that made him look like Abimelech, whose own stupidity resulted in his death at the hands of a resourceful woman (see 2 Sam 11:21 and Judg 9:50-54). Moreover, Joab had to lose other men along with Uriah in order to accomplish the king's pleasure. Now, as this scene begins, Joab, without any more royal interference, conquers the city in the swiftness of a single biblical verse. He threatens that if the king does not join him in the battle, he will take Rabbah and will put his own name on the city. When David took Jerusalem, he immediately renamed it the "city of David" (2 Sam 5:7). Thus Joab informs David that Rabbah will become the "city of Joab."

Though to our ears Joab's threat seems treasonous, David obeys. What choice did the king have? Were Joab to reveal David's plot to murder Uriah, what loyalty could David command from his troops? Conspiracies against the king by his military officers were not unknown in ancient Israel. Pekah, a military commander in Israel's court at Samaria, conspires against King Menahem, kills him, and rules Israel for twenty years (2 Kgs 15:23-27). So David complies with the order of his chief military officer: he gathers the troops that remained in Jerusalem and heads to Rabbah. He finishes the assault against the city and conquers it, confiscating the crown from Milcom's head,[59] which the narrator pauses to describe so that we grasp the significance of David's victory. (Hanun, the Ammonite king who provoked the hostilities with David [2 Sam 10:1-5], is not mentioned.) He also secures a great deal of plunder from the Ammonite kingdom (anticipated in 8:12). Finally, like the

---

[59] The MT reads "their king" (*malkām*). Samuel R. Driver (*Notes on the Hebrew Text and the Topography of the Books of Samuel* [Oxford: Clarendon, 1913], 226) suggests "Milcom," which appears in several Greek manuscripts.

populations conquered in 2 Samuel 8, the Ammonites become David's servants, though this time the narrator describes the tasks of the enslaved laborers. Their instruments are no longer swords, bows, and arrows but saws, axes, and kilns. David has avenged himself against the Ammonites who foolishly humiliated his envoys (10:4).

David's swift victory reminds us that God is back with him, giving him victory wherever he goes (see 8:6, 14). When David atoned for his sin and pleaded for the life of the child, God *did not* hear his prayer. Saul, after his sin (1 Sam 15), pleaded with God who *did not* listen to him (1 Sam 28:6). Shortly thereafter, Saul was killed in battle (1 Sam 31:1-6). Had the Lord abandoned David as he did Saul, then David would certainly have lost the battle against the Ammonites, just as Saul lost against the Philistines. Thus, the scene of David's victory complements the preceding scene with Bathsheba, assuring the reader that David is set right with God who gives him victory again, just as God had done in the past. So David and his army return to Jerusalem as the curtain falls on this masterpiece of historical narrative.

4.5 The Rape of Tamar and a Brother's Revenge (13:1-39)

Hanging in the National Gallery in Washington, DC, is a painting by Giovanni Francesco Barbieri (known as Guercino) with the harmless title, *Amnon and Tamar* (1649–50). It has been placed beside another of his works titled *Joseph and Potiphar's Wife* (1649–50) and together the two masterpieces form a diptych. In *Amnon and Tamar*, Guercino brings us into Amnon's bedroom immediately after the rape: Amnon and Tamar have risen from a disheveled couch and Amnon is pushing Tamar out of his room. Tamar's determined glance and pointed finger urge Amnon to reconsider his decision, but Amnon's fists are clenched and his left arm is raised, ready to push Tamar out of the canvas and out of his life. This revolting scene when viewed beside the moment of aggression against Joseph (Gen 39:11-12) underscores Tamar's agony: Joseph escaped the grasp of Potiphar's wife, but Tamar was raped.

This biblical episode can be divided into two sections: the rape itself (2 Sam 13:1-22) and Absalom's revenge and flight (13:23-39). Aspects of the two sections parallel each other: in each a plan is hatched, King David is consulted, and then violence erupts. David plays a key role by providing Amnon access to Tamar and later, when informed of Amnon's crime, he fails to exact justice for Tamar. That failure incites Tamar's brother Absalom to take matters into his own hands, foreshadowing his appropriation of the role of "judge" in 2 Samuel 15 as he organizes

Giovanni Francesco Barbieri, called Guercino (1591–1666). *Amnon and Tamar* 1649–1650. Oil on canvas. Courtesy of the National Gallery of Art, Washington DC.

his usurpation. Had David exercised his authority to punish Amnon for his violent crime he might have averted the rebellion that would nearly destroy his reign. Nathan had recently warned David that God would stir up troubles from within his own house (12:11). Those troubles are about to begin.

4.5.1 The Rape of Tamar (13:1-22)

Tamar's rape is unbearable to read. Because the narrator provides us with so much preliminary information about Amnon's scheme, we watch in dread as the childlike Tamar approaches her predator, ready to hand-feed him with her fresh baked delicacies. Today, our growing understanding of the violence of rape illuminates and conditions our reading of this episode. In some societies sexual violence is addressed more openly, and those who would keep the issue out of the public eye are themselves suspect and their interests in secrecy called into question. Tamar, the virgin, was unprepared for the manipulations of her attacker, her half brother, the king's firstborn and heir to the throne.

STRUCTURE

A. The characters and their relationships (13:1-3)
  B. Planning the rape (13:4-7)
      a. Jonadab's advice to Amnon (13:4-5)
      b. David provides Amnon access to Tamar (13:6-7)
    C. Tamar's actions (13:8-9)
      D. Tamar comes into the inner room (13:10)
        E. The dialogue before the rape (13:11-14a)
          c. Amnon orders Tamar (13:11)
          d. Tamar protests (13:12-13)
          e. Amnon will not listen to Tamar (13:14a)
           F. The rape (13:14b)
        E'. The dialogue after the rape (13:15-16)
          c'. Amnon orders Tamar (13:15)
          d'. Tamar protests (13:16ab)
          e'. Amnon will not listen to Tamar (13:16c)
      D'. Tamar is thrown out (13:17-18)
    C'. Tamar's actions (13:19)
  B'. The aftermath of the rape (13:20-21)
      a'. Absalom's advice to Tamar (13:20)
      b'. David's reaction (13:21)
A'. New relationships among the characters (13:22)

This meticulously constructed scene places the rape at the center. It opens with a description of the relationships among the characters (A), and when it closes some of these relationships are permanently ruptured (A'). In the B section David ensures Amnon access to Tamar and is later (B') enraged by the violence. The C/C' sections focus on Tamar's actions: her care for her brother before the rape and then her gestures of grief after the rape. In the D section Tamar comes into Amnon's bedroom, and in the D' section she is thrown out. The center (F) is framed by the verbal confrontation between Amnon and Tamar (E/E' sections).

4.5.1.1 THE CHARACTERS AND THEIR RELATIONSHIPS (13:1-3)

STRUCTURE

A. Tamar and Amnon (13:1)
  a. Tamar is Absalom's sister (13:1a)
  b. Amnon desires her (13:1b)
 B. Amnon is sick about her (finite verb + infinitive) (13:2a)
  C. Tamar is a virgin (13:2b)
 B'. Amnon cannot touch her (finite verb + infinitive) (13:2c)
A'. Amnon and Jonadab (13:3)
  a'. Jonadab is Amnon's friend (13:3a)
  b'. Jonadab is very crafty (13:3b)

The inclusion in this scene is signaled in Hebrew by *lĕ* + a personal name (13:1: *lĕʾabšālôm*, "belonging to Absalom"; and 13:3: *lĕʾamnôn*, "belonging to Amnon"): Absalom has a sister and Amnon has a friend. The center of the passage reveals the complication that Amnon must overcome if he is to satisfy his lust: Tamar is a virgin. The center is framed by two impersonal Hebrew verbs, "it was distressful" (*wayyēṣer*) and "it was impossible" (*wayyippālēʾ*), followed by infinitive complements that describe Amnon's feelings and his predicament.

COMMENTARY

The battles fought thus far in the David Narrative have taken place on the international stage. Now the battles move inside the palace. The rape of Tamar and Absalom's rebellion (beginning in 15:1) are family affairs. The narrator signals that some time has passed since the David-Bathsheba story (*wayĕhî ʾaḥărê kēn*; see the discussion on this Hebrew construction in section 3.7 above) and introduces new characters. Absalom is mentioned first, even though he does not appear until later in this story, since he is the protagonist for the next seven chapters. Then Amnon and Tamar, characters of lesser importance in the David Narrative, are brought on stage. Finally, the narrator mentions the "crafty" Jonadab, who enjoys two appearances in this chapter (here and 13:32-33). Amnon is David's firstborn son, and Absalom is David's third son (3:2-3). David's second son, Chileab, receives only a birth notice and is never mentioned again. If he is presumed dead, or incapable of assuming the throne, then the main characters in this story are the two eldest sons in line to the throne.[60] (There

---

[60] By 1 Kings 1, Adonijah will be the eldest surviving son of David. Seeking to marry Abishag, he speaks to the queen mother, Bathsheba (1 Kg 2:15): "You know

is no indication in the narrative that they are aware of Solomon's special relationship with God [12:25]). Tamar is David's daughter by Maacah, and Jonadab is David's nephew. Familial language, such as "brother" (ʾāḥ), occurring twelve times in this episode, and "sister" (ʾāḥôt), occurring nine times, underscores the internecine nature of this conflict. Even as Amnon is about to rape Tamar (13:11), he calls her his sister, and Tamar, in her refusal, refers to him as her brother. The modern reader waits for the narrator to raise the question of incest, but he never does. As noted in the introduction (see section 1.4.2 above), the text can raise contemporary questions that were outside the narrator's purview. When Tamar asserts that the king will allow Amnon to marry her (13:13), we can assume that in the narrator's mind incest is not part of Amnon's crime.[61]

The presentation of Tamar is restricted to the details essential to the episode: she is beautiful and, more important, a virgin. (The narrator leaves us to discover for ourselves that Tamar, who will refuse Amnon, is also a very determined woman.) The Hebrew term bĕtûlâ can refer to a woman who has never had sexual relations or to an unmarried woman. In this episode the former meaning is intended since after the rape Tamar loses her status as a royal "virgin" daughter, though she remains unmarried (she tears the "long robe with sleeves" that once signaled her status in society [13:18-19]). The narrator presumes that we understand that the virgin daughters of the king were protected from unsolicited advances from men, including their brothers and half brothers. As we learn later from Tamar's protest, Amnon could have sought the king's permission to marry her (13:13). Since he never explored this option, it would seem that from the beginning his intention was an illicit sexual encounter that became rape when Tamar refused. For this reason, the ordinary translation "to love" for the Hebrew verb ʾhb in 13:1 (NRSV: "Amnon fell in love with her") and elsewhere in this story is hardly appropriate. Amnon does not "love" Tamar. She is a beautiful woman and he desires her, or, better, he is fixated on her, infatuated with her,

---

that the kingdom was mine, and that all Israel expected me to reign; however, the kingdom has turned about and become my brother's, for it was his from the LORD." He assumes that as the eldest he should have ascended to the throne. Since Bathsheba does not contest his claim, it is safe to presume that at this point in the narrative, Amnon was first in line to the throne followed by Absalom.

[61] For a further exploration of this question, see Calum M. Carmichael, *Sex and Religion in the Bible* (New Haven/London: Yale University Press, 2010), 135–57. Deuteronomy 27:22 forbids a man from sleeping with his sister, but, as Carmichael writes, "the lawgivers disapproved of what they found in some of their nation's traditions because the narratives condoned relationships that the lawgiver judged to be incestuous" (p. 140).

and lusting after her. But he needs a way to gain access to her. Enter the conniving Jonadab, Amnon's cousin.

4.5.1.2 PLANNING THE RAPE (13:4-7)

The action in this scene begins when Jonadab questions Amnon, whose dejected countenance has caught his attention. His title for Amnon highlights the contrast between Amnon's status as "the king's son" and his present state as "poor" or "helpless" (Hebrew: *dal*; NRSV: "haggard") and he wants to know why the heir to the throne appears so dejected day after day. Amnon discloses his dilemma to Jonadab. He is infatuated with Tamar, the sister of Absalom his brother (again, the NRSV's translation "in love" for Hebrew *ʾhb* in 13:4 is inappropriate). The Hebrew word order of Amnon's response to Jonadab underscores his fixation on Tamar (translated literally): "Tamar, the sister of Absalom my brother, I desire." His mention of Tamar includes her relationship to Absalom, who is next in line to the throne after him. "So just marry her" would seem to be the most obvious recommendation (incest is not an issue, see above), especially since we later learn that Tamar says that David would have granted the request (13:13). But Jonadab has grasped that Amnon does not intend marriage. He wants sex, and he needs a scheme to gain access to Tamar, the king's protected virgin daughter and his half sister. Jonadab suggests that he feign sickness to draw the king's attention so that he can request that Tamar come to his aid. (In this same meeting, Amnon could have asked David for permission to marry Tamar.) The close contact between victim and predator will permit a more violent option if his proposal for sex is refused.

The first part of Jonadab's plan unfolds as he foresaw. The king comes to visit Amnon, once "sick" (13:2: *ḥlh*) because of his fixation on Tamar, now feigning sickness (13:6: *ḥlh*) in order to get his hands on the king's virgin daughter, his half sister. David, duped by Amnon's plot, sends his virgin daughter into his son's clutches (13:7). Jonadab's plan has met with immediate success, and we fear that the rest of the scheme will proceed as designed. The beautiful Tamar will consent to sex or be raped if she will not. This ancient story anticipates the insights of modern research: the predator is often a family member or good friend. Tamar, like the majority of rape victims, knows her attacker: "women are least safe at home, and least safe with friends, acquaintances, and family."[62]

---

[62] Anna C. Salter, *Predators: Pedophiles, Rapists and Other Sex Offenders: Who They Are, How They Operate, and How We Can Protect Ourselves and Our Children* (New York: Basic Books, 2003), 81. In the United States, 62 percent of rape victims know their attacker.

Amnon expands Jonadab's advice when King David arrives. Jonadab had advised Amnon that he should ask the king to send Tamar to him with explicit instructions (13:5): she should make food in front of him and allow him to eat from her hand. The image of Amnon lying in bed, fed from Tamar's hand is sensual enough. But when David comes to his son's sickbed, Amnon specifies the food he wants her to make: "Let my sister Tamar come and make a couple of cakes" (*ûtĕlabbēb . . . lĕbibôt*). Amnon's desired food has provoked much discussion. P. Kyle McCarter suggests dumplings and, on the basis of rabbinic literature, provides the recipe. He concludes that what Amnon is asking for is "enheartening dumplings, perhaps a traditional food for the sick."[63] Hans Wilhelm Hertzberg suggests that what Amnon wants is his "favorite dish," i.e., what his heart desires (the Hebrew root of *lĕbibôt* "cakes" and "heart" [*lĕb*] is the same).[64] The precise delicacy that Tamar prepared for Amnon will probably remain obscure. More important is the wordplay on the Hebrew name for this food.[65] In the love poetry of the Song of Songs 4:9, the lover employs the same Hebrew verbal root to appeal to his beloved bride: "You have aroused me sexually" (*libbabtinî*).[66] This alternative meaning captures the duplicity of Amnon's request, and the Hebrew reader perceives in the name of the food an allusion to Amnon's sexual arousal and his true intentions. But David only hears that Amnon wants a special treat while he is sick. Whether David should have detected these sexual overtones (he knows Amnon wants her to feed him as he lies in bed) is left to the reader to decide. David complies with Amnon's request and Tamar is sent to Amnon.

4.5.1.3 AMNON REALIZES HIS INTENTION (13:8-19)

As Tamar comes onstage Amnon has already taken up his position on his bed. Our hearts sink. The narrator delays the moment of the rape so that we can observe the innocent Tamar preparing the food as the king

---

[63] McCarter, *II Samuel*, 322.

[64] Hertzberg, *I and II Samuel*, 323.

[65] See also the discussion in McCarter, *II Samuel*, 322.

[66] Richard Hess discusses the meaning of this Hebrew word in Song 4:9: "The question of its meaning is tied up with whether it is based on a positive meaning such as 'you have aroused me sexually, you have given me virility' (where the heart conveys the idea of arousing the emotions), or whether it may carry a privative meaning such as 'you have stolen my heart'"; see Richard S. Hess, *Song of Songs*, Baker Commentary on the Old Testament Wisdom and Psalms (Grand Rapids, MI: Baker Academic, 2005), 113, note m.

ordered. She is the subject of six active verbs (13:8-9): she takes dough, kneads it, makes cakes, bakes them, takes a pan, and pours them out. Our empathy for her grows as she attends to her sick brother and we wait for him to pounce. She trusts Amnon; she has no reason not to— "misplaced trust is the predator's most powerful resource."[67] When the pseudo-patient, refusing to eat, orders everyone out, we know what is coming. But his victim is completely in the dark. He orders her to bring the food into an inner room so that she might feed him by hand. This inner room, *ḥeder* in Hebrew, is associated with the bedchamber since it is often followed by the term *miškāb*, "bed" (Exod 8:3 [MT 7:28]; 2 Sam 4:7; and elsewhere). Tamar obeys, and we go in with her as she carries the food she has prepared for her predator. Amnon's plan has worked; he now has his long-awaited, private access to the lovely virgin daughter of the king. As Tamar brings the *lĕbibôt* toward Amnon's mouth, the predator throws off his sickly disguise and reveals his true intentions. In an instant, Tamar recognizes that Amnon is not sick. On the contrary, he is strong.

Amnon did not move immediately to rape her. Grabbing her, he invites "his sister" to his bed, fully expecting that she will accede to his proposition. Unlike Shechem, who, without discussion, seized Dinah and forced her to have sex with him (Gen 34:2), Amnon has set the stage: the servants are outside, he and Tamar are in an inner room, and his sickness provides them with a pretext to be alone together. Now Tamar can consent to the tryst and return home. Who will know of it? But the narrator's earlier, curt description of Tamar's character overlooked her most notable quality. She is a woman of resolve, quite prepared to reject Amnon's advances with a quadruple refusal: "no, my brother," "do not force me," "such a thing is not done in Israel," and "do not do anything so vile" (13:12). Uncompromisingly, she defends her resistance: she would have to bear her reproach and her brother would be considered a rogue. Then she proffers a solution that would allow her to come to his bed: Amnon should speak to the king about marrying her; she is certain he will approve. (A modern reader may reasonably wonder why Tamar would agree to share Amnon's bed after his initial grab.) But we know that Tamar's plea, which was always an option for Amnon (and for the scheming Jonadab), was never his intention, though it remains his obligation after the rape to wed her (discussed below). Had Amnon wanted a public relationship with Tamar, he could have asked David for permission to marry her instead of faking a request to gain access to her. He wanted her to consent to this secret affair, and he is prepared to deal with her

---

[67] Gavin de Becker's "Foreword" in Salter, *Predators*, xi.

should she refuse. Tamar is the first one to use the language of rape. When she pleads, "do not force me," she employs the same Hebrew verb that described Shechem's rape of Dinah (Gen 34:2: *ʿnh*).

When Tamar warns Amnon that "such a thing is not done in Israel," she appeals to the custom that, as she explains, a virgin daughter of the king needed the king's permission to wed. Thus, raping her will render him a "scoundrel," in Hebrew, a *nābāl*. The Hebrew term recalls Nabal, the unfortunate husband of Abigail (1 Sam 25:14), the meaning of whose name Abigail explained to an angry David: "Nabal [*nābāl*] is his name, and folly [*nābāl*] is with him" (1 Sam 25:25). By threatening Amnon with that title, Tamar unwittingly foreshadows that Amnon will share Nabal's fate (see 1 Sam 25:37). He too shall die. But Amnon cannot appreciate the premonition that we hear in this appellative, and, given that Tamar will not consent, he rapes her. The narrator, determined that we see Tamar as an innocent victim, describes Amnon overpowering her (NRSV: "being stronger than she" [13:14]), indicating that she continued to resist. Current research describes how both rapists and the general population can justify the rape by shifting some or all of the responsibility onto the victim.[68] The narrator, as if anticipating that alibi, ensures that we assess Tamar to be a wholly innocent victim.

Immediately after the violence, Amnon is filled with deep loathing for Tamar. While, modern studies note that the reactions of rapists after the rape are varied,[69] once the rapist has proven his domination (as in Amnon's case), the victim is of no use.[70] Amnon's rage is compounded by Tamar's earlier rejection—he wanted her, but she never wanted him. So now Amnon treats Tamar cruelly. His loathing surpasses his original lust and so, just as he ordered her to "come and lie" (two imperatives) with him, now he orders her to "rise and get out" (two imperatives). He is a sadistic raper, who seeks "revenge and punishment from another person by the use of violence and cruelty."[71] But once again his violence does not silence Tamar. Her dismissal, she contends, would be a still greater wrong. Because he has violated her, he is obliged to marry her and bring her into his household, observing the law in ancient Near Eastern cultures, including Israel:[72]

---

[68] Linda B. Bourque, *Defining Rape* (Durham, NC/London: Duke University, 1989), 68–74.

[69] John M. MacDonald, *Rape: Offenders and Their Victims* (Springfield, IL: Charles C. Thomas, 1971), 70.

[70] Salter, *Predators*, 83.

[71] Ronald M. Holmes, *Sex Crimes* (Newbury Park/London/New Delhi: Sage Publications, 1991), 79.

[72] Samuel Greengus, "Law," in *ABD*, 4:247.

> If a man meets a virgin who is not engaged, and seizes her and lies with her, and they are caught in the act, the man who lay with her shall give fifty shekels of silver to the young woman's father, and she shall become his wife. Because he violated her he shall not be permitted to divorce her as long as he lives. (Deut 22:28-29)

But Amnon will have none of it, and, when she refuses to leave, he orders her thrown out and the door locked. Given the Tamar we have met in this story, she will come right back inside to claim her rights unless the door is bolted. The innocent virgin entered the room ready to nurse her sick brother at his bedside. Now she is thrown out of that room against her will.

At this point the narrator pauses to inform us of the particular garment worn by the virgin daughters of the king. (Such background information is necessary as this prop will soon be used onstage.) The special status of a "virgin daughter of the king" in society was signaled by a special robe, called a *kĕtōnet passim* (NRSV: "a long robe with sleeves"). The same garment was worn by Joseph (Gen 37:3) and signaled his special status among his brothers. The narrator then focuses our attention again on Tamar's actions; she is the subject of five active verbs (13:19): she took ashes, she tore her robe, she put her hands on her head, she went along, and she cried out. Those hands that once "took" (*lqḥ*) dough now "take" (*lqḥ*) ashes. She will publicly declare the violence she has endured with gestures often associated with mourning.[73] Perhaps Tamar's public protest will force Amnon to observe the law by unbolting the door to claim her as his wife. If not, her public outcry should force King David to adjudicate her claim against Amnon.

4.5.1.4 THE AFTERMATH OF THE RAPE (13:20-22)

Absalom now comes onstage for the first time. We do not know whence he comes or where he encounters Tamar. (Is she still sitting in front of the locked door of Amnon's house?) No one else appears to have heeded her wailing. Instead of asking the obvious question, "What has happened to you, Tamar?" his inquiry—"Has Amnon your brother been with you?"— suggests that he knew all along that Amnon posed a threat to her. But now the woman, who vehemently rebuffed Amnon's aggression, is unable to speak. Her wailing is her final sound on stage. Absalom

---

[73] David tore his garments upon learning of the deaths of Saul and Jonathan (see 2 Sam 1:11), and mourners put dust on themselves (see Isa 61:3; Jer 6:26; Job 2:8) with loud wailing (see Ezek 27:30).

surmises what has happened, and he advises her to keep the event to herself and not to take it to heart. She should remember that Amnon is her brother (and first in line to David's throne). Absalom's advice to Tamar horrifies us, especially since we know of the plot that led up to the rape (Tamar and Absalom do not). Contemporary research into sexual abuse reveals that "secrecy is the life blood of sexual aggression."[74] Only about 10 percent of all rapes are ever reported.[75]

As inappropriate to modern readers as Absalom's words are, they are also ominous, much like the words of Friar Laurence to the weeping Juliet:

> Hold, then; go home, be merry, give consent
> To marry Paris. (act 4, sc. 1)

How can Juliet go home and be merry with Romeo banished on pain of death? How can Tamar quiet down and not feel the impact of the violence she has suffered? Because both Friar Laurence and Absalom have a plan to address their respective crises. And in Tamar's case, as Jonadab reveals at the end of the story (13:32), from the day Amnon raped his sister Absalom was determined to kill Amnon. (We do not know how Jonadab knows this.) Thus, though on one level Absalom's words to Tamar are vapid, on another level Absalom's calmness in the face of such violence signals that he has resolved how to avenge this act. Amnon shall pay with his life. For now, Absalom bides his time. We say goodbye to Tamar here. She lives in Absalom's house as a "desolate woman," in Hebrew a *šōmēmâ*, the same term that is used for the destroyed city of Jerusalem that, in Lamentations 1:13, is personified as a desolate woman.

The scene now shifts to David, who, having learned of the rape, becomes "very angry" (*ḥrh*). He may have forgotten that he ordered Tamar into her predator's presence, but we have not. Just recently he became furious (*ḥrh*) at a rich man who had absconded with the poor man's ewe lamb. For that imaginary victim, David angrily demanded justice: the rich man, who deserved death, would have to make a fourfold restitution (2 Sam 12:5-6). Now the same Hebrew verb reports David's fury at the news that his virgin daughter has been raped by his firstborn son. But this time, no recompense will be made to a real victim. The king's refusal to act contrasts with the swift justice he will dispense for the phony widow of Tekoa who feigns mourning in the next episode (14:8). It seems that the king is better at imaginary justice than real justice. Tamar's case is not heard because, as the NRSV reports, David loved

---

[74] Salter, *Predators*, 4.
[75] Holmes, *Sex Crimes*, 75.

Amnon, for he was his firstborn (13:21).[76] We stand with Absalom, who is appalled by David's favoritism that protects the predator. The king, who should have ordered Amnon to marry his victim and to take her into his household, fails to act, even though his own command led to the violence against his daughter.

The closing lines of this scene introduce another leitmotif into the David Narrative: the king's affection for his sons clouds his royal judgment. Once Amnon is dead, David transfers his affection to Absalom (13:39); Joab will exploit this to engineer Absalom's return to court. When father and son reunite, it is the father who will kiss the son, not a grateful son who will kiss his forgiving father (14:33). As a father, David will be pleased to have his son back home, but as king, he will fail to recognize that he has just rehabilitated a future rebel. Even during the rebellion, David's affection for Absalom will remain unchanged.[77] The conflict between a king and a usurper is, in David's heart, a struggle between a father and his son. While the narrator allows us a glimpse into the depth of David's despair after Absalom's murder (18:33), we never learn if Absalom (or Amnon) returned his father's affection. The narrator presents their relationship from David's perspective. In this scene, David's affection for Amnon is a tragic flaw that stirs Absalom to rebel. The future strife that will beset his kingdom could have been avoided had the father been able to call his son Amnon to account for the crime against Tamar.

Absalom, realizing that the king will not hear Tamar's cause, will assume the role of judge for his sister, usurping the king's role and foreshadowing the moment he establishes himself as judge at Jerusalem's city gate (15:2-6) in preparation to usurp the crown. The narrator does not comment on the extent to which David's failure to adjudicate Amnon's crime prompted Absalom to seize his father's throne. We are left to decide that question for ourselves. The episode concludes with the narrator's comment that the rapport between Absalom and Amnon was forever ruptured. No further communication took place between them because, as the narrator reminds us, Absalom remained focused on the fact that Amnon had raped his sister. He hated him. It is Absalom's move.

---

[76] This explanation, which appears in most English Bibles, is taken from the LXX.

[77] When the rebel Absalom is about to be defeated, the king bids his generals: "Deal gently for my sake with the young man Absalom" (18:5).

4.5.2 *Absalom's Revenge (13:23-39)*

The story of Absalom's revenge against Amnon replays in a different key the events and themes of Tamar's rape. Both Tamar and Amnon unwittingly enter the homes of their attackers, and the violence against them happens around food. Both victims are made available to their assailants by King David. The previous scene centered around the rape. At the center of this scene Jonadab informs David that Amnon was murdered for that rape. The Hebrew text alerts its readers to the parallels between these two scenes in the opening line of this account of Absalom's revenge. The previous scene opened with the background information that Absalom had a sister (13:1: *hyh + l* + Absalom). This scene opens with the same construction (13:23: *hyh + l* + Absalom) to report that Absalom had sheep shearers. But in one aspect these two scenes stand in sharp contrast: whereas the narrator provided a lengthy description of Tamar's care for her predator before she was raped, little attention is paid to Amnon before he is murdered. Amnon is not an innocent victim.

STRUCTURE

A. Absalom and the king (13:23-27)
  Inclusion. Absalom invites all the king's sons to celebrate with him (13:23)
  a. Absalom petitions the king (13:24)
  b. The king refuses Absalom (13:25a)
  c. Absalom "presses" the king (13:25b)
  a'. Absalom petitions the king (13:26a)
  b'. The king questions Absalom (13:26b)
  c'. Absalom "presses" the king (13:27ab)
  Inclusion. Absalom makes a king's feast (13:27c)
  B. Absalom acts (13:28-29a)
    C. Flight and a first report to the king (13:29b-31)
      d. The king's sons flee (13:29b)
      e. Report and mourning (13:30-31)
      D. Jonadab's report (13:32-33)
        f. "Let not . . ."
        g. All the king's sons are not dead
        h. Only Amnon
        E. Jonadab informs the king of Absalom's motives: because Amnon raped Tamar (13:32b)
      D'. Jonadab's report (13:33)
        f'. "Let not . . ."
        g'. All the king's sons are not dead

h'. Only Amnon
C'. Flight and a second report to the king (13:34-36)
d'. Absalom flees (13:34a)
e'. Report and mourning (13:34b-36)
B'. Absalom acts (13:37-38)
A'. Absalom and the king (13:39)

Justice for Tamar, which should have been the king's responsibility, was only delayed, not denied. In the B/B' sections the narrator focuses on Absalom, his execution of Amnon and then his flight. The C/C' sections describe the two moments of mourning, the first when the king errone-ously believes that all his sons are dead and the second when he learns that only Amnon is dead. At the center of the scene (D), Jonadab appears again to correct the report that all the king's sons are dead. The critical news of Jonadab's report appears at the turning point of the scene: David learns that Absalom murdered Amnon because he raped his sister (E).

COMMENTARY

Absalom harbored a grudge against Amnon for two years until he saw an opportunity to exact his revenge. (The narrator ensures that we know that the passage of time did not diminish Absalom's resolve.) It is now sheep-shearing season, a time for celebration. When the fugitive David sought provisions from Nabal during the sheep-shearing season, he expected a welcoming reply because he had come at a festive time (1 Sam 25:8). Absa-lom will host a sheep-shearing festival at his house in Baal-hazor, twenty kilometers (twelve miles) north of Jerusalem, thus drawing Amnon onto his home turf, just as Amnon drew Tamar onto his home turf. Absalom seeks his father's unwitting collaboration with his scheme just as Amnon did.

The scene (2 Sam 13:24-27) then shifts to the court in Jerusalem as we attend a meeting between David and Absalom. Absalom makes his seemingly harmless proposal to the king: he wants the king and his brothers to attend his sheep-shearing party. We see father and son, king and future rebel, onstage together for the first time. David addresses Absalom with the informal, familial title "my son," a title that forms an inclusion to Absalom's presence in the David Narrative. Absalom is mentioned for the final time when David cries out for him after his death: "my son, my son" (eight times!).[78] Thus, the future rebel's entrance onto and exit from the stage of history is framed by his father's affection that

---

[78] The title "my son" appears five times in 2 Samuel 18:33 and three times in 19:4. Its appearance in this scene is the first hint of the king's inordinate affection for Absalom.

the title, "my son," expresses. By contrast, Absalom never addresses David informally with "my father." In this scene, Absalom chooses a most deferential form of address, "will the king . . . please go," referring to himself not as "your son" but as "your servant." With this degree of politeness, Absalom underscores his public relationship with David as the king and distances himself from his familial relationship with him as his father.[79] As an ordinary father in Israel, David would not have had the authority to adjudicate the crime against his violated daughter, but as king he should have defended the rights of his subject Tamar.

As in the account of Tamar's rape, David knows far less about his interlocutor's intentions than does the audience. When the king declines the invitation to come to Absalom's festivities, the narrator reports that Absalom "pressed" (*prṣ*) him to no avail. What was Absalom's initial plan? Given the pressure he applied to David, it seems that he intended to kill Amnon in the king's presence. Such a public crime would have brought Absalom and the king into a direct confrontation over the king's failure to exact justice for Tamar. But that altercation never happens since the king refuses to attend, though the narrator adds that he gave Absalom "his blessing." Such irony! The king blesses the party at which his first-born son is to be murdered. David's initial response forces Absalom to tip his hand a bit. He specifically wants Amnon to attend the festivities (just as Amnon specifically wanted Tamar to care for him). David's question, "Why should Amnon go?" suggests that his suspicion is aroused. Should the king have suspected Absalom's plot against Amnon two years after Tamar's rape? Jonadab, David's nephew, knew that Absalom was still seeking revenge for this crime (13:32). Absalom, ignoring the king's query, "presses" again (*prṣ*) for Amnon's presence at the festivities and the king acquiesces. The narrator, who knows of the coming rebellion, closes this opening scene with the remark that Absalom "made a feast like a king's feast."[80] The future usurper is already throwing royal parties. We listen in on Absalom's orders to his servants. Just as Amnon engineered the rape of Tamar, so Absalom orchestrates Amnon's murder. The servants should wait until Amnon's heart is merry (*lēb tôb*) with wine. Then his guard will

---

[79] See Craig E. Morrison, "Politeness," in the *Encyclopedia of Hebrew Language and Linguistics*, forthcoming.

[80] In 13:27 many English versions read with the NRSV: "Absalom made a feast like a king's feast." The phrase is taken from the LXX. Driver was unsure if this reading was original (*Notes*, 302), but now it seems that the addition has traces in 4QSam[a] along with a gap sufficient to include the reconstructed Hebrew text (E. C. Ulrich, *The Qumran Text of Samuel and Josephus*, Harvard Semitic Monographs 19 [Missoula, MT: Scholars, 1978], 85).

be down. In case they are afraid to murder the king's firstborn son, they should remember that the order comes directly from him.[81]

When Tamar tried to stop Amnon from raping her, she warned him that he would be considered a scoundrel, in Hebrew, a *nābāl* (see 2 Sam 13:13). That epithet recalled the death of Nabal, the husband of Abigail, whose fate Amnon is about to share. There are several parallels between that story (1 Sam 25) and the murder of Amnon:

1. Both scenes take place during sheep-shearing season (1 Sam 25:2; 2 Sam 13:24).
2. Nabal and Absalom hold celebrations that are fit for a king (1 Sam 25:36; 2 Sam 13:27).
3. Just before their deaths, Nabal and Amnon have hearts merry with wine (*lēb tôb*; 1 Sam 25:36; 2 Sam 13:28).
4. Both Nabal and Amnon (labeled a *nābāl*) die.

Had Amnon recognized the foreshadowing allusion to Abigail's husband in the epithet *nābāl*, he might have halted his violence against Tamar and thus averted Absalom's revenge.

The account of Amnon's execution is summarily presented. We do not see the victim arrive, sit at table, and begin enjoying the meal as we saw Tamar arrive and begin kneading dough. Tamar was raped on-stage. Amnon is killed offstage so that we do not hear a cry for help or an appeal for mercy that could stir feelings of compassion for him. Our sympathies remain with Tamar and her avenging brother. As soon as Amnon is dead, the narrator turns our attention to the king's sons, the potential heirs to the throne, who mount their mules to flee the scene.[82] They suppose that they will be his next victims as he secures his place as David's sole successor. Only the reader, Absalom, and Jonadab know that Absalom does not intend to harm them.

The narrator brings us into David's court to attend the news arriving from Absalom's house. The first account reports that all the king's sons are dead. There are no survivors (and therefore no successors to David's throne except Absalom). The king immediately initiates the mourning ceremony for his dead sons, tearing (13:31; *qrʿ*) his clothes just as Tamar tore (13:19; *qrʿ*) her clothes after she had been raped and expelled from Amnon's house. Later, when the king finally learns that only Amnon is dead, he weeps aloud (13:36), as Tamar cried out (13:19) after the rape.

---

[81] When Saul gave the order to murder Ahimelech and his entire house, his servants refused to do so (1 Sam 22:17). Absalom wants to avoid that possibility at the moment when Amnon is a ready victim.

[82] Mules were used by nobles (see 2 Sam 18:9 and 1 Kgs 1:33).

The king, who failed to hear Tamar's case, now imitates her rituals of mourning. But his mourning must be brief, as the king must defend himself from the imagined threat Absalom presently poses to his crown. Enter Jonadab once again. The misintelligence allows David's nephew the chance to speak, not only to rectify that earlier report, but also to persuade the king of Absalom's singular motivation. (The narrator ignores the question of whence came this rumor that all the king's sons had been killed.)

Jonadab, who once advised the dead Amnon on how to get access to Tamar, now advises the king about the circumstances of Amnon's murder: all the king's sons are not dead, and, more important, Absalom is not attempting a coup d'état. Amnon is the only casualty, victim of a revenge killing. When Jonadab recalls Amnon's crime against Tamar, he uses the explicit term for rape (ʿnh), reminding the king of the violence for which Amnon was *not* held responsible. That violence is not diluted with expressions such as "to lie with" (škb ʿim), which could suggest that Tamar was partially responsible for their sexual encounter. Amnon raped Tamar and so Absalom killed him. To this he could have added: "because you, O king, did nothing to punish Amnon for this crime!" The center of this scene insists that we grasp the king's failure. For this reason Absalom, as he foments rebellion, will establish himself as judge in Israel (15:2-6), intending to accomplish for the Israelites what his father, the king, failed to accomplish for his sister, Tamar: were he a judge in Israel, the claims of victims would be heard (15:4). Ironically, Jonadab consoles (13:33) David with the same advice that Absalom gave to Tamar (13:20): "Don't take it to heart." True, David should not "take to heart" the exaggerated news that Absalom has murdered all his sons. He should, however, take to heart the fact that Absalom has exacted revenge from Amnon because the king failed to act in Tamar's defense.

The report of Absalom's flight interrupts the events at court. Twice the narrator directs our attention to Absalom's escape (13:34, 37) as we observe David in mourning. A limitation of narration is that, unlike a stage production, two scenes cannot be presented simultaneously. Charles Dickens masterfully works to overcome this limitation by juggling three concurrent scenes as *A Tale of Two Cities* draws to a close: (1) the Manettes' flight from Paris, (2) Miss Pross and Mr. Cruncher at the Manettes' abandoned apartment, and (3) Madame Defarge drawing near to her mortal encounter with Miss Pross. Dickens and the biblical narrator employ the same narrative technique: a refrain in the background. Dickens interrupts repeatedly the dialogue between Miss Pross and Mister Cruncher with the refrain, "Madame Defarge . . . drew nearer and nearer" so that as we listen to Miss Pross and Mister Cruncher chatter, we see Madame Defarge making her way through the streets of Paris toward them. Similarly, as we listen to the report of Amnon's murder and observe the king's grief, the narrator's refrain, "Absalom fled," holds that simultaneous event in the background.

Jonadab's report is confirmed by the sentinel just as the king's sons reach the court unharmed. Jonadab insists that the king observe the accuracy of the first part of his announcement—only Amnon is dead—and thus accept the veracity of the second part of his report, that Absalom killed Amnon in revenge for his sister's rape. But how does Jonadab know this and why is he given such a prominent role in this scene? (He was not at the sheep-shearing festivities and Absalom would hardly have confided in him.) Before Jonadab met Amnon, he was described in Hebrew as *ḥākām* (13:3), the base meaning of which is "wise." The NRSV prefers "crafty," which aptly describes Jonadab's advice before Tamar's rape (the NJPS chooses "clever"; the REB and the NJB opt for "shrewd"). But perhaps "perceptive" is a more appropriate gloss for *ḥākām* since it describes Jonadab's interventions in both scenes. In the previous scene Jonadab perceived Amnon's dejection and inquired about it. In this scene he keenly notes that Absalom's desire for revenge against Amnon has not abated even after two years. This quality makes him a foil to David, who failed to recognize Absalom's plot against Amnon and, as we shall see, is beguiled too often. The narrator never calls David *ḥākām* (but see 14:20 where the phony Tekoite widow flatters David with this Hebrew word).

Meanwhile, Absalom is heading north to Geshur, an area in the Golan, about one hundred kilometers (sixty miles) north of Jerusalem. He seeks refuge with Talmai, the king of Geshur, his maternal grandfather (3:3). David makes no attempt to extradite the murderer for punishment, though, at the same time, the narrator's comment that Absalom's time in Geshur lasted only three years hints at his eventual return to Jerusalem. The leitmotif of David's affection for his sons closes the episode. The king who could not punish Amnon the rapist now yearns (so the NRSV) for Absalom the murderer.[83] This ominous closing remark comes from a narrator who knows well that David should have left Absalom to die in Geshur. The king's affection for Amnon has resulted in a family tragedy. His affection for Absalom will nearly destroy his reign.

[83] At this critical juncture (13:39) where, according to the NRSV, David seems ready to rehabilitate Absalom, the Hebrew text is very obscure. Where the NRSV describes David as "yearning for Absalom," the NJB reads "his [David's] anger against Absalom subsided." The latter translation lessens David's desire to see his son.

4.6 Joab Brings Absalom Back to Court (14:1-33)

Joab, the protagonist in this episode, manipulates David into reinstating Absalom to his court. The events climax not when the father greets his fugitive son but when the king detects Joab's machinations at work. By then it is too late; the king, again beguiled, has already given his word.

STRUCTURE

A. Joab's plan: he sends the wise woman to the king, putting words in her mouth (14:1-3)
> B. The woman manipulates the king to reconsider Absalom's exile (14:4-17)
>> C. The king recognizes Joab's role and changes his mind on Absalom's exile (14:18-20)
> B'. The king executes his decision on Absalom's exile (14:21-28)
>> (*Interruption*: an introduction to Absalom [14:25-27])
A'. Absalom's plan: he sends Joab to the king, putting words in his mouth (14:29-33)

As the scene opens, Joab notices that the king is focused on his son, and he devises a plan to bring Absalom back to Jerusalem (A). The episode concludes when Absalom devises a plan to see the king and the king is reconciled with his once banished son (A'). The B/B' sections balance the woman's manipulations with David's order to fetch Absalom. At the center of the text, the king, while unmasking the woman's charade and recognizing Joab's maneuvers, changes his mind on the question of Absalom's exile. While Joab is off fetching Absalom, the narrator interrupts the story to provide the reader with some background information about Absalom. Even though Joab is not always onstage, his scheme, which is ultimately successful, drives the events in this episode.

4.6.1 Joab's Plan (14:1-3)

The episode opens with a short introduction to the main characters about to appear. Joab, the main protagonist, is mentioned first. He has noticed what the narrator told us as the previous scene closed: David is thinking about Absalom. As we watch the events unfold, from the arrival of the Tekoite widow to the burning of Joab's barley field, our awareness of the king's predilection toward his fugitive son remains in the background. David's affection for Absalom will render David a complex and, at times, unheroic character as we observe how that affection muddles his ability to command and nearly leads to his ruin.

The scene abruptly shifts to Joab's summoning a woman from Tekoa[84] who is "wise," the same attribute (*ḥākām*) that was recently ascribed to Jonadab (13:3), David's foil, because he, not David, perceived Absalom's desire for revenge against Amnon. Now this unnamed, wise woman will outwit David. Joab's detailed instructions (six imperatives) ensure that the king will be swayed by the imposter's phony grief-stricken appearance, a disguise that appeals to his own grief for his exiled son. When the wise Tekoite woman agrees to Joab's scheme without comment, she joins the parade of persons who have beguiled David thus far: Nathan with his phony parable, Amnon with his fake illness, and, most recently, Absalom with his sheep-shearing festival that was really a murder plot. The reader's sense that by this point David should be more suspicious of people coming to him with requests may explain why Joab chooses a counterfeit widow to beguile David. Why should the king suspect that a Tekoite woman, dressed as a mourner, is a scam?

In the past Joab was quite willing to confront the king.[85] But now he appears to have reckoned that a direct challenge to David on the Absalom question would be ineffective, as the widow explains (14:20) as soon as David recognizes Joab's scheme: Joab knew that he had to approach the question in a roundabout way. The NJPS translates the first part of 14:20 with, "It was to conceal the real purpose of the matter" (the NRSV reads: "In order to change the course of affairs"). But why is Joab so interested in rehabilitating Absalom? The Joab we have met thus far would hardly be concerned with the king's broken heart or the plight of a banished son. His own interests must be foremost in his mind and so we wait for them to emerge as the episode unfolds.

Before Tamar was raped, we listened to Jonadab's advice as it was given to Amnon (13:5). In this scene the narrator withholds the precise words that Joab put into the widow's mouth (14:3) so that when she reaches David, while we know more than David, we still have much less information than Joab and the wise woman. The suspense builds as we wait to see how the phony mourner's tale corresponds with Joab's observation that David's mind was focused on Absalom (14:1), and as his plot becomes clear to David, it also becomes clear to us.

---

[84] Tekoa is about sixteen kilometers (ten miles) south of Jerusalem.

[85] Joab rejected the king's alliance with Abner (3:24-25), and he ordered the king into battle against Rabbah (12:27-28).

4.6.2 The Woman Manipulates the King (14:4-17)

STRUCTURE

A. The first exchanges
   a. The woman calls to the king (14:4)
   b. The king responds (14:5a)
   a'. The woman explains her plight (14:5b-7)
   b'. The king responds (14:8)

B. The central exchanges
   a. The woman explains the bloodguilt question (14:9)
   b. The king responds (14:10)
   a'. The woman calls upon the king to swear an oath (14:11a)
   b'. The king responds (14:11b)

A'. The last exchanges
   a. The woman again calls to the king (14:12ab)
   b. The king responds (14:12c)
   a'. The woman explains her new plight (14:13-17)
   b'. [No response from the king!]

The scene can be divided into three sections. Each one, except the last, contains two exchanges: the woman initiates and the king responds. The A/A' sections can be divided into two parts, the woman calls for the king's attention (14:4: "Help, O king"; and 14:12: "Let your servant speak") and the king grants her permission to speak. In the second part of the A/A' sections the woman then explains her predicament. At the center (B) the woman draws the king into an oath that determines the outcome of their dialogue. The scene is abruptly interrupted (14:17) when the king sees through the widow's charade and so ceases to react to her ploys.

COMMENTARY

The scene shifts immediately to the arrival of the woman, whose immediate access to the king is not explained by the narrator. Like Joab and Absalom who will follow her, she shows her obeisance to the king by prostrating before him. "Help, O king," she cries out, begging for deliverance from her dire situation. But we know that she is Joab's mouthpiece and that it is Absalom who needs royal deliverance. The king gives her leave to speak, and she argues her case. She is a widow who had two sons. They fought and one killed the other. She underscores that no one was present to separate them, implying that, had someone been there, the fratricide would not have occurred. Amnon's murder jumps to mind. Absalom wanted the king to attend his sheep-shearing party in which he was planning to attack Amnon (13:24). The king not only refused the invitation but also facilitated Amnon's presence at Absalom's party. (Is Joab, through the woman, accusing David of complicity in the death of Amnon?) The Hebrew word that the woman employs to name the person who could have intervened to save her dead son is *maṣṣîl*, "a deliverer, a rescuer" (14:6), from the verbal root *nṣl*. Had David acted as a *maṣṣîl* for Amnon, he might have saved his life and avoided the present troubles. This Hebrew root reappears when the wise widow reports that she came to the king hoping he would "deliver" (*nṣl*) her from those who would kill her surviving son (14:16). At that point in their dialogue, David, who failed to deliver Amnon, has already delivered her son from the vendetta of the bloodguilt. For her fictitious son David becomes the *maṣṣîl* that he failed to become for his own son.

The woman reports that the members of her clan are demanding the life of the murderer, her only surviving son. In the background is the notion of the blood avenger's right to retaliation for the wanton murder of a member of the clan. In such cases, the killer had no right to protection in one of the asylum cities (Exod 21:13-14). When the Gibeonites come to David, demanding the execution of seven of Saul's descendants as an expiation for Saul's crimes against them, David complies in order to lift the bloodguilt that has brought famine to his kingdom (2 Sam 21:1-9). The king accepts the widow's assessment of her situation without disputing the blood avenger's right, even though exacting the bloodguilt will leave the woman childless. Her yarn does not apply directly to the conflict between Amnon and Absalom; it forgets that Amnon was not a mere victim of a conflict between two brothers, though the vengeance that Absalom exacted exceeded the expected punishment for rape. The narrator has not reported that Amnon's brothers were demanding Absalom's life for the murder of Amnon, and though his flight to Geshur seems to suggest as much, we wait until Absalom's final words in this episode to learn that bloodguilt was indeed involved (14:32): "Now let me go into the king's presence; if there is guilt in me, let him kill me!"

The woman describes her remaining son as the "heir" who must continue her husband's name.[86] Absalom is not David's sole heir nor is he the only one who can propagate David's name on the earth. But her words, which are not her own, reveal that in Joab's mind Absalom is David's "inheritor." Joab's motives for fabricating this scene are now emerging. He is establishing himself as the person upon whom Absalom

---

[86] Her words foreshadow Absalom's future since his name will not continue on the earth. He dies with only a monument to his memory (18:18).

must depend in order to reenter the king's good graces. Abner, Ishbaal's chief military officer (the same position that Joab holds in David's court), was responsible for putting Ishbaal on Saul's throne (2:8-9). When Ishbaal accused Abner of attempting to usurp the throne, his general did not deny the accusation or beg forgiveness. Instead, he reminded the king of his power over him (3:8): "[I] have not given you into the hand of David." Now Joab wants to be the king-maker for David's oldest son and apparent successor, Absalom. His first step is to facilitate Absalom's return to court, ensuring, at the same time, that Absalom knows who is pulling David's strings.

In contrast with the justice denied to Tamar, justice comes swiftly for this woman and her make-believe son. The king orders her to go home—he has ruled in her favor, and she can leave. But she has not yet attained her desired outcome and so she ignores the royal order. She shifts the conversation to the question of the "bloodguilt" incurred by the unjustified murder, transferring it from her guilty son and from the king, who has heard her plea, to herself and her father's house. The avenger of blood can now seek her life in exchange for that of her murdered son instead of her living son. Could the king nullify the right of the blood avenger to exact vengeance from the wanton murderer? In the case of the Gibeonites (21:1-9), David did not have the option. But in this case, it seems he does (certainly Joab thinks he has this authority), though bloodguilt legislation does not designate a particular person with the competence to do so.[87] And while David does not specify how he will handle the rights of the avenger of the bloodguilt, he decides in her favor, rescuing her from any further retaliation. If David can save the woman's son from automatic, retributive justice, then what about his own son, Absalom?

The widow, whose present, albeit fake, mourning exemplifies the king's yearning for his son, also foreshadows the king's eventual mourning for Absalom after he is murdered by Joab. Later, during Absalom's rebellion, David's instructions to his commanders, Joab, Abishai, and Ittai, echo the widow's concern for the life of her imaginary son: "Deal gently for my sake with the young man Absalom" (18:5). The woman's repeated use of the appellation "my son" (14:11 and 14:16) is the same title that David uses for Absalom, beginning in 13:25 when he greets him for the first time and more dramatically in 18:33 and 19:4 when he cries out for his dead son as he ascends the gate. David allays the woman's remaining concerns by *swearing an oath*: "As the LORD lives, not one hair of your son shall fall to the ground." This oath formula ("not a hair of

---

[87] In Numbers 35:22-28 "the congregation" is permitted to decide questionable cases of murder.

the head"), which appears elsewhere (1 Sam 14:45 and 1 Kgs 1:52), fore-shadows Absalom's death with bitter irony—not a hair from Absalom's head will fall to the ground since he is murdered as he hangs entangled by his long hair in an oak tree.

With the oath sworn, it seems that the woman has achieved Joab's objective. The king has exercised his authority to lift the bloodguilt, and if he can nullify the blood vendetta against an imaginary son, what about his own son Absalom? In order to raise this question in David's mind she seeks permission to address the king further. After Nathan finished his parable, he immediately confronted David with its correct interpretation (2 Sam 12:7: "You are the man!"). Our wise woman opts for a more circuitous route to bring the king around, challenging him with a question: "Why then have you planned such a thing against the people of God?" Her interrogation must come as a surprise to the unsuspecting king who was probably expecting yet another impediment to the rescue of her only son. Nathan's parable (12:1-4) was intended to force David to confess his crimes with Bathsheba and against Uriah. The widow's story, which has successfully beguiled David into absolving her imaginary son, should now force him to reconsider his own son's status as an exile in Geshur. In case David has not yet figured out the woman's ruse, her second charge unmasks her motives: having just sworn an oath to protect her son from a bloodguilt vendetta, has the king not convicted himself since he has not lifted the banishment of his own son who is under a similar vendetta? As we grasp her purpose, so does David.

The woman continues: life is fragile and death is part of life, but God does not seek death. Just as God preserves life, so God also devises ways to restore the banished back into the community. Her theology leaves David with a question: if God devises ways to bring the banished home (14:14), why does the king devise ways to keep his own son banished from his kingdom (14:13)? Her true motives now exposed, the widow appeals to her fable about her imaginary son (14:15). If we are confused by the flow of this dialogue, we are joined by numerous scholars who argue that the Hebrew text of 14:15-17 has been jumbled during its transmission and that these verses belong to the woman's original story and should be placed after 14:7.[88] But if we read the text as it is presented in all the ancient witnesses and modern English translations, it seems that the wise woman is drawing out the parallel between what David has done for her pseudo-son and what he must do for his real son. The story of her fictitious son collapses into the story of David's real son. Thus, when the woman claims that she addressed the king so that he might

---

[88] The word *wĕ‘attâ*, "now then," at the beginning of 14:15 should introduce a logical conclusion to 14:13-14, but it does not.

fulfill her request (in reality Joab's request), we are now certain (and so is David) that her real request was to have David restore Absalom to court.

The Tekoite woman, disguised no longer, expresses her hope that David will deliver her, a masquerading widow, and her imaginary son from those who would obliterate them from the "heritage of God" (in Hebrew *naḥălâ*)—a reference to the people and land of Israel that God has chosen.[89] Now David should recognize that the language of "deliverance" (the Hebrew verbal root *nṣl*), reprised from 14:6 (the two fighting sons had no one to "deliver" them from their rage and so one murdered the other), accuses him of having failed to deliver his son Amnon from his brother's attack. Her artificial fear that she and her son would be eliminated from the heritage of God aptly applies to Absalom, who at present lives in the kingdom of Geshur (13:37)—expelled from the heritage of God. She closes her speech with a prayer that the king's oath may give her rest. In fact, the oath he has sworn will give rest to his own heart that longs for Absalom. Her flattering exclamation—"my lord the king is like an angel of God"—has a sarcastic tone. Had David the wisdom of an "angel of God" he would have been more circumspect about the woman's scam and would not have been so easily maneuvered into swearing an oath. Joab's clever fabrication that taught the king that he could lift the sanction against his own son is hardly a sign of David's angelic discernment. And so the wise woman beguiles David yet again. (Did David believe her?) Finally, she prays that God may be with David (Saul [1 Sam 17:37] and Jonathan [1 Sam 20:13] wished David the same years ago). The balanced exchange between the wise woman's pleas and the king's rejoinders regarding her fictitious son comes to an abrupt end. The king has caught on.

4.6.3 The King Recognizes Joab's Role (14:18-20)

We expect the king to respond to the woman's question regarding Absalom: "Are you telling me that I should save my own banished son just as I saved your fictitious one?" Instead, the king brusquely changes the subject, asking a question that is prefaced with a royal directive that the wise woman should not withhold the truth. (He now appreciates her resourcefulness and wants to avoid further digressions.) In a comical reversal of roles, the woman, who had bowed to the ground before the

---

[89] See Deuteronomy 4:20: "The LORD took you and brought you out of the smelting furnace, from Egypt, to become a people, his possession [*naḥălâ*], to this day" (translation mine). See also Deuteronomy 9:26 and 1 Kings 8:51.

king, begging to be allowed to speak, now gives the king leave to address her, albeit with proper deference: "Let my lord, the king, speak." The king wants her to confirm Joab's involvement in her charade. It is more logical to suppose that Absalom was behind her masquerade, and the narrator does not explain why the king supposed that Joab was involved. (Joab had perceived the king's predilection for Absalom, but we have little reason to suppose that the king would have confided his feelings to him.) She confesses Joab's involvement, reprising the narrator's words from 14:3, "he . . . put all these words into the mouth of your servant" (14:19), and then offers a vague explanation for Joab's maneuvering, though the exact meaning of the ancient Hebrew idiom is not apparent to modern readers. The NJPS interprets the phrase to mean that Joab hatched this indirect approach to conceal his true intentions from the king. The NRSV interprets the phrase more benignly: Joab wanted to change the course of events with regard to Absalom. Whatever the phrase means, Joab's real intentions—becoming the power behind Absalom's eventual rule—remain concealed from David.

As quickly as the wise woman sheds one charade she dons another, flattering David with grandiose remarks about his authority: "one cannot turn right or left from anything that my lord the king has said." Joab has had little difficulty turning to the right or left of the king's intentions, murdering Abner and nearly ruining David's strategy to rule over Saul's kingdom (3:27). Later he will execute Absalom, defying the king's direct order to "deal gently" with the rebel (18:5). Such flattery, as G. K. Chesterton noted, praises people "for the qualities they have not got":

> A man may say that a giraffe's head strikes the stars, or that a whale fills the German Ocean, and still be only in a rather excited state about a favourite animal. But when he begins to congratulate the giraffe on his feathers, and the whale on the elegance of his legs, we find ourselves confronted with that social element which we call flattery.[90]

In fact, David does not possess the authority reflected in the widow's panegyric. She closes with a tribute that can be likened to congratulating "the giraffe on his feathers": "My lord," she declares, "has wisdom like the wisdom of the angel of God to know all things that are on the earth." David is, in fact, dangerously gullible. In this scene, his gullibility has not resulted in serious damage to his reign, but in the next episode Absalom will sit at the city gate for *four years* fomenting his rebellion while the king, who the woman declares has the "wisdom of the angel of God," fails to take notice of this thing happening "on the earth." Just

---

[90] G. K. Chesterton, *Heretics* (New York: Garden City, 1905), 203–4.

as her phony widowhood duped David, her flattery obstructs David from interrogating her further. She is indeed wise.

4.6.4 *The King Executes His Decision on Absalom's Exile (14:21-28)*

The scene shifts so abruptly that the wise woman is not even given an exit. Joab appears (we are left with the impression that he was listening at the door), and the pace of the narrative quickens. Absalom will soon be back at court, since David unceremoniously lifts the sanction on his son as the wise woman taught him he could do. In his order to Joab, he refers to Absalom as "the young man," introducing into the narrative another significant title for Absalom (besides "my son") that links this scene to the next time David issues a direct order to Joab to protect "the young man Absalom" (18:5).[91] In this episode Joab obeys, but in 2 Samuel 18 he deliberately violates David's order. For now Joab bows down to David in gratitude, knowing that his strategy, which began when the widow bowed down to David in 14:4, has met with success. This is the only time that the general bows to the king in the David Narrative (more flattery?). Such obeisance, a bit out of character for him, is complemented by his brief discourse ("Today your servant knows that I have found favor in your sight, my lord the king") that reveals just how much he wanted to achieve his goal. *He* will bring Absalom back to court, and the king's son will know who engineered his return.

4.6.4a Interruption: An Introduction to Absalom (14:25-27)

As soon as Joab departs, David issues a restriction regarding Absalom's rehabilitation for all his courtiers to hear: he refuses to see his son (literally, "he will not see my face"[92]). Since we know that David longs

---

[91] When David assembles the troops, he gives specific orders to Joab, Abishai, and Ittai concerning "the young man Absalom" (18:5). The man who sees Absalom hanging from the oak tree and refuses to kill him reminds Joab of David's direct orders concerning "the young man Absalom" (18:12). Then, after the defeat of Absalom's troops, when Ahimaaz reaches David, David's first question regards the "young man Absalom" (18:29). And, finally, when the Cushite reaches David, the king again asks about "the young man Absalom" and the Cushite responds by employing that same title for Absalom (18:32).

[92] Seeing the ruler's face is an expression of acceptance. The disguised Joseph sends his brothers back to Egypt with the request that they return with their youngest

to see Absalom (13:39–14:1) and will eventually kiss him when he finally does see him (14:33), we sense that his decree does not spring from his heart. His refusal to see Absalom is a public display of his displeasure that is intended to satisfy those courtiers and family members who would have avenged Amnon's murder. The action is then paused for Absalom's formal introduction into the narrative (a bit delayed, since we have already met him). In 1 and 2 Samuel such introductions are reserved for major characters. When Saul appears before Samuel for the first time, the narrator pauses the action for a brief description: Saul was very tall and unique among the entire people (1 Sam 10:23-24). Likewise, his successor, David, is described as ruddy and handsome with lovely eyes (1 Sam 16:12). Now Absalom is presented as stunning from head to toe, the most handsome in all Israel. While this introduction signals the pending role he will have in the narrative, does it mean that this good-looking prince is next in line for the throne? We know about God's predilection for Solomon (2 Sam 12:24) and that God intends for one of David's own sons to succeed him (7:12), but which son will it be?

The focus on Absalom's personal grooming may seem a bit strange to the modern reader,[93] but within the narrative, this information foreshadows the scene in which he dies. Absalom's lovely hair becomes entangled in an oak tree (18:9), leaving him suspended from its branches and an easy target for Joab's spear. The very hair that Absalom was so proud of that he announced its weight after his annual barbering[94] becomes the instrument of his downfall. The narrator also mentions Absalom's descendants, another notification that is normally reserved for kings. Once Saul has consolidated his rule as king of Israel, the narrator lists his sons and daughters (1 Sam 14:49). Likewise, the narrator lists David's offspring in two groups, those born in Hebron (2 Sam 3:2-5) and those born in Jerusalem (5:13-16). Other important characters, such as Joab or Abner, are not accorded a notification of their offspring as they are not in line for the throne. On the basis of this interlude, it seems the narrator wants us to entertain the possibility of Absalom's succession to David's throne.

---

brother. When their father, Jacob, objects to sending Benjamin with them, his brothers remind their father that if Benjamin does not join them, they will not see the man's (Joseph's) face (Gen 43:3, 5 and 44:23, 26).

[93] In biblical narrative such seemingly harmless details are never irrelevant. In 2 Samuel 13:1 the only characteristic that the narrator gave to Tamar was her beauty, a detail that was critical to the story as it unfolded.

[94] Authorities estimate "two hundred shekels by the king's weight" to be somewhere between two and five pounds.

This list of Absalom's descendants is inconsistent with the later notice that after his death he had no son to continue his name (18:18). Perhaps we are to assume that his sons died or were killed in the rebellion, but the narrator could have said as much. It is noteworthy that while Absalom's sons remain anonymous, his one daughter is named. In the notification of Saul's descendants, first the sons were named, then the daughters (1 Sam 14:49). In the list of David's descendants, his daughters were not named at all. But in this list of Absalom's offspring, we ignore his sons to focus on the daughter whom Absalom had named Tamar. She, like her aunt, Absalom's sister (13:1), is very beautiful. This detail calls to mind the tragic circumstances of the once beautiful Tamar who now dwells "desolate" in her brother's house, the same house where Absalom will reside as he waits for an audience from the king. As if to remind himself and the king of what Amnon did to his sister, he named his only daughter, David's granddaughter, after his violated sister. The interlude closes with the news that Absalom returned to Jerusalem and did not see the king's face. His isolation dragged on for two years—the same length of time that Absalom had held his grudge against Amnon.

4.6.5 Absalom's Plan (14:29-33)

The scene shifts to Absalom's house where it is two years later and David has observed his decree not to see his anathematized son. Now Absalom wants to gain readmittance to the court and so he summons Joab, who refuses to come. After a second summons, Absalom recognizes that his overtures are useless. While the narrator withholds Joab's motivations, it seems that Joab intends to teach Absalom that he alone can open the door into the king's presence and that Joab will come to Absalom when *he* decides and not before. It must serve Joab's interests as king-maker to hold the out-of-favor Absalom, David's eldest son, in such a precarious position as long as possible. But the burning of his barley field gains Joab's attention and signals that Absalom will not be trifled with. A third missive is not required for Joab to present himself at Absalom's house. Ignoring the earlier two letters sent from Absalom, he addresses only the question of the burnt barley field. Absalom reminds Joab and, at the same time, informs us, of the contents of his letters that confirm our suspicions that Joab had deliberately refused to grant Absalom access to the king. Now Absalom puts words into Joab's mouth, just as Joab once put words into the wise Tekoite's mouth.

Absalom's message to the king confirms that a bloodguilt vengeance was the reason for his self-imposed exile. When the phony widow spun her yarn, the narrator remained silent on the extent to which Absalom was under the same threat as her pseudo-murderer son. Now, frustrated by his long banishment from court, he declares, "if there is guilt [*ʿāwōn*] in me, let him kill me" (14:32). In Lamentations 4:13[95] and Isaiah 59:3[96] the Hebrew term *ʿāwōn* (translated with "iniquity" in reference to the addressee's guilt or culpability) is linked to the shedding of blood. We are now certain that the invented son in the woman's fable allegorized Absalom's situation. But Joab knows and we know that David will not execute the bloodguilt vengeance. Even after Absalom's rebellion and David's own acknowledgment that Absalom would kill him (2 Sam 16:11), he cannot bring himself to harm his son (18:5). His affection for Absalom muddles his reasoning.

This final scene draws the story of Absalom's return to court (14:1-33) to a conclusion. Joab, who noticed David's grief over two years ago (14:1), delivers Absalom's message to David, who promptly summons Absalom to court. Joab's first appeal to the king on Absalom's behalf, through the wise woman, met with success (14:2-20). His second direct approach to the king also met with success (14:21-23). Now his third maneuver enjoys the same success. He has rehabilitated Absalom and, more important, ensured that Absalom knows this. When Mephibosheth approached David, he prostrated himself in fear (9:6-7). Absalom does the same, though without fear. As we fully expect, David kisses Absalom. The narrator's description of their reunion underscores that the father kissed his son, not that the two of them kissed or that the repentant son kissed the generous father. The father's feelings for the son are paramount. Very shortly the treacherous son will be kissing his future allies (15:5) as he incites a rebellion against his father.

4.7 Absalom Foments Rebellion (15:1-12)

The seeds of Absalom's rebellion were sown when Amnon raped Tamar, Absalom's sister, and the king failed to hold Amnon responsible (13:21). Absalom, the rebel protagonist in this episode, now moves against the king, his father. This episode can be divided into three scenes. In scene 1 (15:1-6) Absalom appropriates for himself judicial authority in Israel, meting out justice at Jerusalem's gate. Having created new alliances, he

---

[95] "It was for the sins of her prophets and the iniquities [*ʿăwōnôt*] of her priests, who shed the blood of the righteous in the midst of her."

[96] "For your hands are defiled with blood [*baddām*], and your fingers with iniquity [*beʿăwōn*]."

deludes David (scene 2, 15:7-9) and then lays the groundwork for the rebellion (scene 3, 15:10-12).

4.7.1 Absalom at the Gate (15:1-6)

STRUCTURE

A. Introduction: Absalom gathers military resources (15:1)
  B. Absalom and the plaintiff's suit for justice (*mišpāṭ*) (15:2a)
    C. Absalom calls to the plaintiff (15:2b)
      D. Absalom acknowledges the claim, but justice cannot be done (15:3)
        E. Absalom's ambitions (15:4a)
      D'. Justice would be done were Absalom judge (15:4b)
    C'. Plaintiffs bow down to Absalom (15:5)
  B'. Absalom and the plaintiff's suit for justice (*mišpāṭ*) (15:6a)
A'. Conclusion: Absalom has succeeded in garnering political support (15:6b)

At the center of this passage Absalom expresses his desire for an official role in Israel. He contrasts the absence of justice for the plaintiffs under King David with his readiness to preside over the judicial process were he judge in the land (D/D' sections). Absalom calls to the plaintiffs (C), who bow down in obeisance to him (C'). They had come to the king seeking justice (B), but Absalom appears to resolve their claim (B'). As the scene opens, Absalom is acquiring military assets (A). As it closes, he has acquired the hearts of the people (A').

COMMENTARY

An indefinite period of time has passed since David readmitted his son Absalom to court. The narrator, by means of a Hebrew reflexive phrase, *lô*, "for himself," ensures that we grasp that Absalom acquired the chariots, horses, and fifty running men at his own initiative and for his own use. These resources were not awarded him by the king; in fact, we sense that his father has no idea what he is up to. What is going on? The narrator's view of Absalom's military assets reprises the threat uttered by the prophet Samuel to the Israelites, who had demanded a king for themselves (1 Sam 8). Upset by their insistence, Samuel appealed to God who advised him to accede to their request. But first, God, through Samuel, warned the people about the practices (*mišpāṭ*) of their future king:

He said, "These will be the practices [*mišpāṭ*] of the king who will rule over you. He will take your sons and he will set them for himself [*lô*] in his chariots and as his horsemen and they will run before his chariots. He will set them for himself [*lô*] as chiefs of the thousands and chiefs of the fifties." (1 Sam 8:11-12; translation mine)

Samuel concludes his discourse by predicting the suffering that the people will endure because of their desire for a king (1 Sam 8:18): "And in that day you will cry out because of your king, whom you have chosen for yourselves; but the LORD will not answer you in that day." Neither Saul nor David oppressed their dominions as Samuel foretold, but now, for the first time, the narrator, by reprising the specific terminology of Samuel's speech (*lô*, "for himself"; *mišpāṭ*, "practice, judicial process"; *merkābâ*, "chariot"; *rwṣ*, "to run"), casts Absalom's self-initiated rise to power as a fulfillment of Samuel's prophetic warning.[97] This presentation of Absalom's rise should leave us anxious. What is he planning to do with his entourage of chariots, horsemen, and fifty men running ahead of him?

The king's son rises early every morning to take up his position at one of the gates of Jerusalem where legal disputes are settled.[98] The narrator ensures that we observe that Absalom's activity had become a daily routine ("he used to," *wĕqātal*, beginning in 15:2). The plaintiffs arrive seeking a hearing from the king, just like the wise woman from Tekoa, who approached the king and received such a hearing (14:4-17). But Absalom interrupts this process, redirecting them to himself. Without his intervention, we suppose that they, like the Tekoite woman, would have reached the king. Before inquiring about their suits, he asks their city of origin. Upon learning that the person is from one of *the tribes of Israel*, he immediately gives credence to the claim. In the David Narrative, the expression "tribes of Israel" last appeared in 5:1 to refer to the people who were once loyal to Saul and had now come to anoint David as their king. In the scene that follows this one, as Absalom garners support for his usurpation, he sends his covert messengers throughout "all the tribes of Israel" (15:10). Our hunch that Absalom is seeking to make contact

---

[97] The narrator reprises Samuel's speech again when Adonijah announces that he is David's successor: "Now Adonijah son of Haggith exalted himself, saying, 'I will be king'; he prepared for himself chariots and horsemen, and fifty men to run before him" (1 Kgs 1:5).

[98] The prophet Amos (5:15) exhorts his audience to establish justice (*mišpāṭ*) at the gate. In Ruth 4:1-2 Boaz prepares the legal proceedings to "redeem" Ruth, inviting ten men (witnesses) to sit with him *at the gate*. See D. A. McKenzie, "Judicial Procedure at the Town Gate," *VT* 14 (1964): 100–104.

with lingering supporters of the Saulide line will be strengthened later when, in a stunning scene, the fleeing David is confronted by a member of Saul's clan, Shimei son of Gera, who accuses him of having the blood of Saul's family on his hands and of having usurped Saul's throne (16:8). The plaintiff, referring to himself as "your servant," addresses Absalom with polite deference. But in the David Narrative such politeness is normally reserved for the king.[99] Absalom has already usurped the deferential language that is accorded his royal father.

Absalom's endorsement of the plaintiff's complaint without any discussion reveals that his primary purpose at the gate is to build alliances. Justice is secondary. He dismisses the obvious option of escorting the plaintiff to the king and instead laments that there is no one to hear the plaintiff's case. They must return home without justice—the king has failed them. Absalom's charge is very serious in a world where the king is legislator, judge, and executor in the land. The king's alleged absence creates disorder in an ancient society that cannot function without him. Odysseus' twenty-year absence from Ithaca creates a series of crises in his household that worry the reader who yearns for Odysseus' homecoming. Odysseus himself is apprised of the upheaval at home when he consults the spirit of Teiresias in the underworld.[100] He must get back to Ithaca. The plaintiffs coming to Jerusalem leave satisfied that their case was heard by Absalom but also aware that the king is not exercising his judicial authority in society. Absalom is lying—the king just recently adjudicated the cause of the (albeit fake) Tekoite widow (14:4-17)—but the king *did not hear* Tamar's just claim against Amnon and so for her and Absalom the accusation against the king has merit.[101] There was "no one deputed by the king to hear" (15:3) *her* case because of the king's affection for Amnon (13:21).

At the center of this passage (15:4) Absalom designates himself as judge for the plaintiffs. The NRSV translation, "If only I were judge in the land," captures the rhetorical sense of the Hebrew, which literally reads, "Who will make me judge in the land?" The immediate answer to Absalom's question is that his father could appoint him as judge. But by addressing his question to the plaintiffs, who have just learned that their suits cannot be heard by the crown, he invites them to consider

---

[99] When Mephibosheth presents himself to King David, he refers to himself as "your servant" (9:6), as do Jonadab (13:35) and the Tekoite widow (14:6).

[100] Cf. Homer, *The Odyssey*, trans. A. T. Murray, The Loeb Classic Library (Cambridge, MA: Harvard University Press/London: William Heineman, 1919), book 11, lines 115–17: "thou shalt find woes in thy house—proud men that devour thy livelihood, wooing thy godlike wife, and offering wooers' gifts."

[101] Earlier the narrator remarked on the justice and equity of Davidic rule (8:15).

him as judge, eliminating their need to see the king. The narrator is silent about David's knowledge of Absalom's activity at the gate, which went on for four years. But can the king be entirely in the dark? When his son Adonijah asserts his claim to the throne, David is old and ailing, and the narrator explains that David never inquired as to why Adonijah was building up his own military force (1 Kgs 1:5-6). But as Absalom gathers his allies at the city gate, the unsettling question of the king's knowledge of his activities is critical (discussed below). For now, the plaintiffs leave Jerusalem without an audience from the king but with the knowledge that if Absalom were judge, their complaints would have received a public hearing.

When the plaintiffs bow down in obeisance to Absalom, the rebellion is underway. Normally this kind of obeisance is reserved for God, the king, or the prophet Samuel. David shows such obeisance to Saul (1 Sam 24:8); Abigail shows it to David (1 Sam 25:41); Saul shows it to the ghost of Samuel (1 Sam 28:14); Mephibosheth shows it to David (2 Sam 9:6); and, in the previous chapter, the Tekoite woman, Joab, and Absalom show their obeisance to the king. The plaintiffs, who were diverted from their journey to David's court at Absalom's invitation, are now bowing down to the king's son instead of to the king. By "kissing" the persons who come to him, Absalom secures future alliances.[102] There is a deep irony in these gestures: just six verses ago Absalom prostrated himself before David and David kissed him (14:33) to celebrate their reunion. Now Absalom is creating conspirators with a kiss.

In 15:6 the narrator closes with a summary of the scene, repeating that Absalom diverted plaintiffs who were heading to the king for a judicial hearing. The NRSV reports that "he stole the hearts of Israel." The English expression "to steal the heart" can imply that Absalom won over the people of Israel by his action. But this positive connotation is not intended here. The narrator, no friend to Absalom (he labels Absalom's actions a "conspiracy" in 15:12), does not want to present Absalom's scheming as a victory over a negligent king. The expression "to steal the heart" (*gnb* + *lēb*) appears only three times in the Bible, here and in Genesis 31:20, 26 where it describes Jacob's hiding from Laban his intention to flee.[103] In Genesis 31:20, 26 the NRSV renders the expression with "to deceive," a translation that may be closer to the meaning here, namely, that Absalom duped the people of Israel into trusting him.

---

[102] Jonathan and David kissed (1 Sam 20:41) as an expression of the alliance between them.

[103] In Genesis 31:20, 26 it is in *qal* whereas in 2 Samuel 15:6 it is in *piel*.

4.7.2 Absalom Goes to David (15:7-9)

STRUCTURE

A. Absalom asks permission (15:7)
    B. The vow (15:8)
A'. Absalom obtains permission (15:9)

COMMENTARY

The judicial proceedings at the gate, under Absalom's direction, went on for four years, after which he presented himself to David with a request to go to Hebron.[104] Given the length of time that Absalom spent undermining Davidic rule, the question of David's awareness of Absalom's scheming cannot be avoided. It is critical to the entire David Narrative. If we sense that after four years the king should have perceived Absalom's treachery, then sending him to Hebron is an outrageously foolish decision. And if David behaves with such disregard for his own safety and for the security of his realm, then his leadership is unsound. How can he allow Absalom out of his sight? This is the same Absalom who sought the king's assistance to ensure Amnon's presence at his sheep-shearing party (albeit over six years ago in narrative time, but less than two chapters ago for us). Moreover, David himself worked the same ruse on Saul when, in order to discover Saul's malicious designs, he plotted with Jonathan to beguile Saul with a story about his receiving permission from Jonathan to attend a family festival at Bethlehem (1 Sam 20:6). Now Absalom spins a similar tale. If the king allows Absalom to go to Hebron, should he be dismissed as a fool who, by his own incompetence, nearly lost his crown? The narrator sees the question and needs to convince us that David was in the dark about the goings-on at the gate (including the obeisance of his subjects to his son) in order to protect him from that charge. So, when Absalom finally goes to Hebron, two hundred Jerusalemites accompany him, who, the narrator insists, went with Absalom in good faith (2 Sam 15:11).[105] They had no idea that Absalom had been creating allies each morning at the city gate, and, by extension, we assume that the king too was completely unaware of Absalom's treachery.

---

[104] There is a problem (15:7) in the Hebrew text, which reads "forty" years (see the NJPS). The Syriac version, the Vulgate and some Greek manuscripts, which read "four" instead of "forty," are followed in most translations. The number forty contradicts the notice that David reigned thirty-three years in Jerusalem (5:5).

[105] In 15:11 the narrator employs two expressions to underscore their naïveté: They went innocently and knowing nothing about "the whole matter" (translation mine), i.e., the usurpation.

Absalom greets the king without the gestures of obeisance that he showed upon his restoration to court (14:33) and requests the king's permission for his journey to Hebron (the city of his birth [3:2-3]) to fulfill a vow he made to the Lord while still in exile: "If the LORD will indeed bring me back to Jerusalem, then I will worship the LORD in Hebron." It is a clever pretense since a vow once made must be kept, as the story of Jephthah's daughter (Judg 11:29-40), horrific as it is to modern readers, teaches. Why he needs to fulfill the vow *in Hebron* (his birthplace), a city thirty kilometers (nineteen miles) south of Jerusalem, is not made explicit, and David does not inquire. But if Absalom is drawing support for his rebellion from the remnants of Saulide supporters, then his journey to Hebron represents a critical strategic move. With the main center of Saulide support north of Jerusalem and Absalom's rebels south of the city, Jerusalem can be attacked from two sides. Absalom's invented excuse further shields David from the accusation of wanton negligence: how could he impede his son from fulfilling a vow that obviously was received by God since Absalom is back in Jerusalem. But we have the impression that Absalom is lying since we know that it was Joab, not God, who intervened to rehabilitate Absalom. Meanwhile the narrator, who can reveal a character's lies (cf. 1 Kgs 13:18), remains silent.

We suspect that David's ill-advised permission to Absalom has been clouded by his affection for his son that was first mentioned in 2 Samuel 14:1 when Joab noticed that David was focused on his then-exiled son. But the intensity of that affection is grasped only after the rebellion is quashed. Even though the son would have killed his father, the father wails for his dead son (18:33 and 19:4), whom he would have preserved alive (18:5), despite the threat that the rebel son would have posed to his reestablished reign. Two royal dictates—the imprudent order to the troops at the end of the rebellion to take Absalom alive (18:5) and the equally unwise decision in this scene to send Absalom to Hebron—frame the subplot of David's uncritical love for his rebel son. That love, which in any other setting would be a virtue, could have rendered him a tragic hero, whose downfall is not "due to villainy but to some great flaw."[106] (This ancient account of David's nearly tragic flaw represents a groundbreaking exploration into the complexity of human fallibility.) In the end, David's

---

[106] Aristotle, *The Poetics*, trans. William Hamilton Fyfe, rev. ed., The Loeb Classic Library (Cambridge, MA: Harvard University Press/London: William Heineman, 1932), book 18, line 6. Fyfe translated *di' hamartian megalēn* with "to some great flaw." The revised translation by Stephen Halliwell renders the Greek with "by a great error," noting that the word "*Harmatia . . .* could cover a range of possible factors in tragic agency" (Aristotle, *The Poetics*, trans. Stephen Halliwell, The Loeb Classic Library [Cambridge, MA/London: Harvard University Press, 1995], 70).

flawed affection for his son does not turn him into a tragic hero because God intervenes in 17:14 (see below). As the scene closes, the father bids his son, "Go in peace," when, in fact, his son goes for insurrection. These are the father's final words to his son. The two never meet again.

4.7.3 The Rebellion Begins (15:10-12)

Absalom wastes no time. "Secret messengers" are dispatched "throughout all the tribes of Israel" to sound trumpets that will signal the inauguration of Absalom's reign.[107] The narrator implies that these messengers also make contact with those plaintiffs from the tribes of Israel (15:2) whose complaints were received by Absalom because the king was supposedly unavailable. Absalom must secure their loyalty as his insurrection begins. The two hundred Jerusalemites who follow Absalom represent the oblivious Jerusalem populace and their king (discussed above). Absalom sends for one of David's counselors, Ahithophel, whom we meet for the first time. When David later learns of his betrayal, he acknowledges the significant threat that this turn of events poses to him in Absalom's court (15:31). Ahithophel's role as counselor foreshadows the theme of advice giving that will dominate the first part of the story of the rebellion.[108] And when Absalom errs on the choice of whose advice to follow (so willed by God), his downfall is inevitable. Ahithophel comes from the town of Giloh, whose precise location is not known (the town is listed in Josh 15:51 among other cities, including Debir, which is about thirteen kilometers [eight miles] southwest of Hebron). If Giloh is in the vicinity of Debir, then Absalom has gained the support of a leader from the south of Judah. Ahithophel's motives for betraying David are not disclosed. Such information could compromise our image of David (did Ahithophel consider David incompetent?).

Absalom signals his usurpation by offering sacrifice just as his brother Adonijah will do later when he announces his right to succeed his father (1 Kgs 1:9). For those two hundred naïve Jerusalemites in attendance, Absalom's sacrifices represent the fulfillment of his vow, but in reality they signal that his coronation festivities have commenced. Absalom's attempt to seize the throne before his father's death has parallels in Israel's later history that reports two kinds of usurpation:

---

[107] In 1 Kings 1:34 David orders the trumpet sounded to signal Solomon's enthronement (against Adonijah the usurper): "blow the trumpet and say, 'Long live King Solomon.'"

[108] This is the first of *seventeen* times that the Hebrew verb "to give counsel" (*yʿṣ*) or the noun "advice" (*ʿēṣâ*) appears in the story of Absalom's rebellion.

1. A usurper outside the royal line conspires against the king, murders him and then succeeds him, as in the case of Shallum son of Jabesh, who murders King Zechariah and seizes his throne (2 Kgs 15:10). The northern kingdom, as it collapses, endures several usurpations of this sort.

2. The king's own courtiers rebel against him, murder him, and place the king's son on the throne. King Joash (2 Kgs 12:20-21), King Amaziah (2 Kgs 14:19-21), and King Amon (2 Kgs 21:23-24) die at the hands of their courtiers but are succeeded by their own issue.

Absalom's rebellion is similar to the second type of usurpation since he enjoys some support among David's courtiers, most notably from Ahithophel. As the narrator concludes the entire episode (2 Sam 15:1-12), he discloses his opinion of these developments: Absalom's coronation is a "conspiracy" (*qešer*). This Hebrew term appears regularly in 1–2 Kings to describe the intrigues at court that result in royal assassinations and usurpations.[109] King David has a rebellion on his hands.

4.8 God Rescues David from Absalom's Rebellion (15:13–20:3)

Is Absalom's rebellion merely a story about who will succeed King David? Can Shakespeare's *Hamlet the Prince of Denmark* be reduced to a succession narrative? While the question of succession lurks in the background of the play ("Popp'd in between the election and my hopes"[110]), reading *Hamlet* as a story about succession to the Danish throne ignores the baffling complexity of this experiment in English theater. So too, the reduction of Absalom's rebellion to a question of succession bankrupts the inventive experiment of this ancient masterpiece. The account of the battle between a king and a usurper is overwhelmed by the conflict between a father and his son. God will rescue the father, who is his chosen king, from his own tragic flaw: his affection for his son that bests his political acumen and nearly ruins his reign.

God's promise in 2 Samuel 7—"When your days are fulfilled and you lie down with your ancestors, I will raise up your offspring after you"—looms in the background of this rebellion. Is this how David's days are to be fulfilled? David himself wonders as much when he orders

---

[109] See, for example, 1 Kings 15:27; 16:9; 2 Kings 12:20 (MT 12:21); 14:19; 15:10, 25; and 21:23.

[110] *Hamlet*, act 5, sc. 2, line 66.

Zadok to return the ark of the covenant to Jerusalem: "If I find favor in the eyes of the LORD, he will bring me back and let me see both it and the place where it stays" (15:25). Until we learn that God has rendered foolish Ahithophel's good counsel (17:14), thus granting David's prayer (15:31), David's future is in doubt. For this reason the narrator details the advice-giving scenes in Absalom's court (16:20–17:14), scenes that could have easily been summarized in a few words, so that we might grasp for ourselves that God alone rescued David from the usurping Absalom.

God's role, understated in this episode, is disclosed by a seemingly insignificant detail: the crossing of the Jordan. The narrator employs the Hebrew root ʿbr, "to cross" (in various nominal and verbal forms), to report David's flight from Jerusalem, his crossing of the Jordan, and his reentry into Jerusalem. It appears over thirty times in these chapters (in the rest of 2 Samuel ʿbr appears only twenty times), and when the order comes that David should cross the Jordan (17:16), the verb ʿbr is reinforced by a Hebrew infinitive absolute that draws the reader's attention to this critical moment: the king is about to cross out of the land of Israel. Once Absalom is defeated, David's crossing back over the Jordan echoes the Israelites' first crossing over the Jordan under Joshua's leadership (Josh 1–4). Both David and Joshua cross the Jordan and come to Gilgal (Josh 4:19; 2 Sam 19:40). Both are assisted by women who prevaricate to save the mission: Rahab in Joshua 2:1-21 and the woman of Bahurim in 2 Samuel 17:20. Both episodes include the ark of the covenant, though David prevents the ark from crossing out of Israel (15:25). In the account of Joshua's crossing, God's role is explicit, determining Joshua's every move: "the LORD spoke to Joshua son of Nun. . . . 'Now proceed to cross the Jordan, you and all this people, into the land that I am giving to them, to the Israelites'" (Josh 1:1-2). God does not explicitly direct David's every step, but the leitmotif of crossing the Jordan, because it echoes Joshua's crossing, signals that God is with David, just as he was with Joshua.

STRUCTURE

The story of Absalom's rebellion can be divided into five episodes:

A. David's flight from Jerusalem (15:13–16:14)
   B. The victorious Absalom and his counselors (16:15–17:14)
      C. David reaches Mahanaim (17:15-29)
   B'. The rebellion is crushed and Absalom is executed (18:1–19:8abc)
A'. David's reentry into Jerusalem (19:8d–20:3)

As the rebellion grows, David flees the city, abandoning his palace to the care of ten concubines (15:16). This rebellion is officially over when David reenters the city and places the ten concubines under house arrest (20:3). Those women function as a literary inclusion to the story of Absalom's rebellion. At the center of the story David reaches Mahanaim and is welcomed into the city, foreshadowing his eventual victory.

4.8.1 David's Flight from Jerusalem (15:13–16:14)

The story of David's flight from Jerusalem can be divided into two parts. In the first section (15:13-31) David looks back to Jerusalem, praying for God's help and strategizing for his eventual return to the city. In the second section (15:32–16:14) David, having passed over the Mount of Olives, meets three individuals, Hushai, Ziba, and Shimei. The first two are allies; the third comes to accuse and insult the fugitive king.

4.8.1.1 DAVID AND HIS ALLIES EXIT JERUSALEM (15:13-31)

We can hear the alarms sounding in Jerusalem as we follow David's hurried exit through the gates of the city that he conquered ten chapters ago. Into this fast-paced action, the narrator inserts three interludes to allow us to visualize two events in the background: (1) the troops marching and (2) David and the people weeping as they cross over to the Mount of Olives. Just outside the city David meets Ittai the Gittite, whose loyalty he secures, and Zadok the priest, whom he orders to bring the ark back to Jerusalem, praying that the ark's return might foreshadow his own. As he abandons his city, he receives the ominous news that his trusted counselor, Ahithophel, has betrayed him (the first of four interruptions regarding Ahithophel).

STRUCTURE

David orders his courtiers to flee Jerusalem (15:13-17)
    Interlude: the troops are marching out (15:18)
David questions the loyalty of Ittai the Gittite (15:19-22)
    Interlude: The people are weeping as they pass through the Kidron Valley (15:23)
David orders Zadok to take the ark back to Jerusalem (15:24-29)
    Interlude: David and the people are mourning (15:30)

First interruption regarding Ahithophel: David learns of Ahithophel's betrayal (15:31)

4.8.1.1a David Orders His Courtiers to Flee Jerusalem (15:13-17)

The news of the events in Hebron reaches David as a messenger reports what we already know: the "heart" of the people of Israel has gone over to Absalom (see 15:6). David makes no attempt to defend the city or to prepare an assault against Absalom in Hebron. He chooses flight, ordering his court to abandon the city immediately lest Absalom overtake them. The narrator, by employing the Hebrew verb *mhr*, "to make haste," to modify the action, has us visualize the furious activity in the city before Absalom's impending arrival. While the narrator does not offer an assessment of the magnitude of the rebellion, it must be fairly widespread since David determines that, for the moment, his only defense lies in flight. Furthermore, he has no illusions about his son's intentions—Absalom will allow him no escape. Jerusalem will be an open city when the rebels arrive, thus preserving it from Absalom's sword.[111] The scene closes by locating David at what most English translations refer to as "the last house" (the meaning of the Hebrew *bêt hammerḥāq* is uncertain). Modern readers are not yet sure where David is or in what direction he is heading.

Before David vacates his palace, the narrator focuses on a rather strange event involving ten concubines whom the king leaves behind to care for his house. This detail is framed by the double notice that everyone else followed David out of the city:

> So the king left, followed by all his household,
> > except ten concubines whom he left behind to look after the house.
> The king left, followed by all the people. (15:16-17a)

The peculiarity of David's action (very odd for today's readers), along with its narrative framing, suggests that it should not be overlooked. These women will reappear when, in order to signal the success of the coup d'état to the people of Jerusalem, Absalom has sexual relations with them (16:21-22). More important, the "ten concubines" function as a literary inclusion to the entire story of Absalom's rebellion. When David returns to his palace and places these women under house arrest, the curtain drops on Absalom's rebellion (20:3).

---

[111] David's haste foreshadows how, after the rebellion is quashed, a contrite Shimei will "make haste" to him to seek his pardon (19:17).

4.8.1.1b Interlude: The Troops Are Marching Out (15:18)

STRUCTURE

A. All (*kol*) the servants
  B. passed by (*'br*)
    C. him
A'. all (*kol*) the Cherethites, all (*kol*) the Pelethites, and all (*kol*) the
    six hundred Gittites
  B'. passed by (*'br*)
    C'. the king

The first phrase is paralleled by the second phrase, which specifies the
particular groups of servants who passed in front of the king.

COMMENTARY

This is the first of three interludes that interrupt the story of David's
flight in order to present events concurrent to the main line of the narrative. They are signaled in the Hebrew text by an initial clause that does
not begin with a verb (in contrast to a *wayyiqtol* clause that normally
indicates the progression of the narrative; see section 1.4.1 above). In
this verse, a circumstantial clause (*wě X qātēl*) shifts our attention from
David's initial preparations for flight to other simultaneous events. As
David heads out of the city toward the last house (the previous scene),
where he will challenge the loyalty of Ittai the Gittite (the next scene),
the reader should see (and hear) in the background the Cherethites, the
Pelethites, and the Gittites marching out of the city. In the account of
Absalom's rebellion, the narrator often employs this Hebrew clause type
(*wě X qātēl*) to help us visualize the various stages on which simultaneous events are occurring.

The Cherethites and Pelethites, mentioned earlier in 8:18, are troops
under the direction of Benaiah, a high-ranking member of David's court
(see 8:15-18). The Gittites (from Gath, one of the five Philistine cities) are
a group of soldiers who are loyal to David. (After the death of Uzzah,
David entrusted the ark of the Lord to the house of Obed-edom, the
Gittite [6:10]). Not all Gittites were equally loyal—Goliath, the Philistine champion, also came from Gath. This interlude also introduces the
Hebrew word *'br*, "to cross over," which will be central to David's flight
from and reentry into Jerusalem (see section 4.8 above, on 15:13–20:3).
The repetitive use of *'br* in the Hebrew text is lost in English translation,
since to mirror it would render the translation excessively dull.

4.8.1.1c David Questions the Loyalty of Ittai the Gittite (15:19-22)

STRUCTURE

A. David orders Ittai: double imperative ("go back and stay back") (15:19a)
   B. Reasons for the orders (15:19b-20a)

A'. David orders Ittai: double imperative ("go back and take back") (15:20b)
   B'. Ittai swears an oath (15:21)

A". David orders Ittai: double imperative ("move ahead and march on") (15:22a)
   B". Ittai marches on (15:22b)

The three double imperatives that David issues structure this passage. The first two commands would have Ittai return to Jerusalem. But when Ittai swears an oath of allegiance, David issues new orders, and Ittai joins the king's retinue.

COMMENTARY

Ittai, the commander of the six hundred Gittites who are currently passing in front of David (15:18), appears for the first time. David questions him and orders him back to Jerusalem. In his conversation with Ittai, David cleverly refers to Absalom as "the king" ("The king said to Ittai . . . go stay with *the king*"), putting the Gittite commander to the test. Will Ittai unwittingly acknowledge Absalom's kingship? David has good reason to be careful: he himself intends to plant spies in Absalom's court. Ittai could be Absalom's informant in his own camp. David justifies his order: Ittai is a recently arrived foreigner and so his loyalty is questionable. Their conversation mirrors the scene in which David and his six hundred men (1 Sam 27:2) joined the forces of Achish, a Philistine leader, to fight against Israel. Then David was the foreigner and the Philistine commanders rejected his participation in their campaign. When Achish informed David of the Philistines' protest, David objected (1 Sam 29:8): "But what have I done? What have you found in your servant from the day I entered your service until now, that I should not go and fight against the enemies of my lord the king?" We know that while he was in Philistine territory David conducted raids against various peoples, always keeping his exploits hidden from Achish (see 1 Sam 27:8-11). Though Achish trusted David, praising him as "an angel of God," he acceded to the objection of his Philistine commanders and so David and his

six hundred troops departed. As we are about to see, Ittai's response to
David will be markedly different from how David responded to Achish.

David informs Ittai that he would have to wander about with him
when David himself does not know where he is going. (David probably knows the direction he is heading, but he is not yet ready to trust
that information to Ittai.) He orders him back to Jerusalem in the Lord's
steadfast love and faithfulness (*ḥesed weʾĕmet*).[112] This is the same alliance-
building language that appeared in 2 Samuel 2:6 when David tried to
bring the citizens of Jabesh-gilead into a pact with him (see also Josh
2:14). The Gittite responds to David's expression of loyalty to him with
an oath: the fact that "the king" does not know whither he flees does not
deter him. He is ready to risk his life for "the king" (he rejects David's
reference to Absalom as "king" in 15:19), and this oath convinces David
to allow Ittai to "cross over" (*ʿbr* again) with him. (When David was a
foreigner in Philistine territory he never swore an oath of fealty to Achish [1 Sam 29:8].) Ittai comes back on stage in 2 Samuel 18:2 when David
organizes his troops against Absalom's forces. He will remain loyal to
the oath he swears in this scene.

4.8.1.1d Interlude: The People Are Weeping as They Pass through the Kidron Valley (15:23)

This second interlude again breaks the progression of the narrative (*wĕ
X qātēl*) to provide background information concurrent to the main event
line. While David is challenging Ittai's loyalty (the previous scene), we
learn that the entire land is weeping (the expression occurs only here in
the Bible). This interlude introduces a lament motif into the story of Absalom's rebellion: the people loyal to David adopt expressions of mourning. In the next interlude (15:30), David himself is weeping and walking
barefoot with his head covered. Soon he will meet his friend Hushai, who
comes with his clothes torn and dirt on his head (15:32). And once the
rebellion is over, David meets Mephibosheth (Jonathan's son whom he
brought to court in 2 Sam 9), who did not care for his physical appearance or wash his clothes from the time that David left the city (19:24).
These intermittent references to acts of mourning, when viewed together,
depict David's retreat from Jerusalem as a communal or national lament
that begins in this verse with the personification of the land weeping.[113]

---

[112] The NRSV, along with most English translations, reads with the LXX: "may the
LORD show steadfast love and faithfulness to you."

[113] A similar metaphor occurs in Job 31:38: "If my land has cried out against me,
and its furrows have wept together . . ."

Communal laments call upon God in a time of national crisis (see Pss 44, 74, 79, 80, and 83). The book of Lamentations records Israel's communal response to the tragic destruction of Jerusalem: "the elders of daughter Zion" sit on the ground with dust on their heads (Lam 2:10). Personified as a woman, Jerusalem weeps (Lam 2:11) and is clad in torn clothes that expose her nakedness (Lam 1:8). Through these rituals, the people acknowledge their infidelity, express contrition, and seek forgiveness. Similarly in this interlude, the people express their grief over the tragedy that has befallen their city. But what sin has brought on this national crisis? While the narrator does not accuse David of having incurred God's wrath, very shortly Shimei son of Gera will charge David with the deaths of members of Saul's family (16:7-8), which leads David to acknowledge that Absalom's insurrection may witness to God's rebuke (16:10): "If he is cursing because the LORD has said to him, 'Curse David . . .'" When David orders the ark of the covenant back to Jerusalem, he concedes that, if God no longer wants him to be king, he is prepared to accept the divine prerogative (15:25). His worry about the meaning of Absalom's uprising explains why he and his followers exit Jerusalem as mourners doing penance.

As in the first interlude (15:18), the Hebrew verb *ʿbr*, "to cross," reappears three times in this verse: the people are "crossing over," the king is "crossing over" the Kidron valley, and the people are "crossing over" toward the desert (the NRSV employs three different English verbs). The Kidron valley, just east of Jerusalem, indicates that David is heading toward the Mount of Olives. He is still dangerously close to the city.

4.8.1.1e David Orders Zadok to Take the Ark Back to Jerusalem (15:24-29)

STRUCTURE

A. The ark is leaving the city (15:24)
 B. David orders Zadok to return (*šwb*) the ark to the city (15:25a)
  C. David explains why (15:25b-26)
 B'. David orders Zadok and others to return (*šwb*) to the city (15:27)
  C'. David explains why (15:28)
A'. The ark returns to the city (15:29)

COMMENTARY

The opening of this scene bridges the preceding interlude with David's conversation with Zadok. While we imagine the crowd exiting the city, the Hebrew particle *wĕhinnēh* (translated "lo" or "behold" in the King James Bible) at the beginning of 15:24 focuses our attention on Abiathar, Zadok, and the Levites, who are carrying the ark of the covenant of God into flight.[114] Their procession, which adheres to the directives for transporting the ark in Deuteronomy 10:8, recalls the first time that the ark crossed the Jordan into the land of Israel (Josh 3:6), when Joshua ordered the priests to carry (*nś'*) it and pass over (*'br*) before the people. The narrator borrows some of that vocabulary now to recount the ark's departure from Jerusalem as the people "cross over" (*'br*) from David's city to the Kidron valley. When David began his reign in Hebron, the ark was still at the house of Abinadab (placed there in 1 Sam 7:1). Once he had conquered Jerusalem, he transferred the ark to his royal city (see 2 Sam 6). The confrontation with his wife Michal, daughter of Saul, at the end of that episode witnessed to the fact that the arrival of the ark in Jerusalem signaled the consolidation of David's rule over Saul's dominion (6:20-23). The ark's exit from Jerusalem in this scene portends David's defeat by forces that are still loyal to Saul, as Shimei's cursing suggests (16:8) and, if we are to believe Ziba, Mephibosheth hopes (16:1-4). David had wanted to provide the ark a proper dwelling (7:1-3), but God intervened, blocking his plan but promising him an eternal line to succeed him. Now that ark, symbol of God's approval of Davidic rule, is exiting the City of David with the fugitive king. Has God altered the promise made to David in 2 Samuel 7? The narrator bids us to read on.

The "king"[115] initiates the dialogue with Zadok (15:25). He and Abiathar (priests in David's court; 8:17) are to become David's operatives in Jerusalem. And once Absalom is dead, David will contact them to prepare for his reentry into his city (19:11). Later Abiathar will support Adonijah's claim to the throne (1 Kgs 1:7), but Zadok will remain loyal to David and Solomon (1 Kgs 1:8). As this scene unfolds, David orders Zadok to bring the ark back to Jerusalem. The narrator allows us to hear David's rationale, which, though brief, is critical for understanding his flight. If he has not lost God's favor, then he, like the ark that he now orders back, will return to Jerusalem. But if the rebellion is a sign that God no longer sustains him, then he accepts the divine judgment.[116] His

---

[114] In 15:24 the NRSV adds Abiathar (he is not mentioned in the Hebrew text) with Zadok to coordinate with 15:29 where both Zadok and Abiathar are mentioned.

[115] In the narrator's mind David never ceases to be king over Israel. (Of course, the narrator knows the outcome of the rebellion.)

[116] David's words to Zadok reprise the theme of his trust in divine rescue that David announced in his opening speech before Saul (1 Sam 17:37): "The LORD who saved me from the power of the lion and the power of the bear will save me from the power of this Philistine" (translation mine; see section 1.3 above).

confession reveals why "the land" is weeping (2 Sam 15:23) and why David himself and his friend Hushai, whom he is about to meet, bear the signs of mourning. God's wrath against him may have brought about his flight from the city.[117] A second time David addresses Zadok, now called "the priest,"[118] ordering him back to Jerusalem so that he and Abiathar, along with their sons, Jonathan and Ahimaaz, can become his informants in the city under Absalom's rule. He specifies a rendezvous point where he will await their communication.[119] As the scene concludes, the ark heads back to its place to await the return of the one who first brought it to Jerusalem.

4.8.1.1f Interlude: David and the People Are Mourning (15:30)

This third interlude in the story line (*wĕ X qātēl*) pauses the action to describe David's departure with his people. As the ark makes its way back to Jerusalem, David crosses the Kidron Valley and is ascending the Mount of Olives.

STRUCTURE

1. David
    A. went up, weeping
        B. head covered
            C. walking barefoot
2. The people
        B'. heads covered
    A'. went up, weeping

---

[117] In 21:1-14, God's wrath punishes the land with a famine because of Saul's transgression.

[118] The phrase *hărô'eh 'attâ* in 15:27 is problematic. The MT reads either "Are you a seer?" or "Are you looking?" Most English translations read with the LXX, "Look." The NJPS notes that the meaning of the Hebrew is uncertain and suggests the gloss "Do you understand?"

[119] The *ketib* in the MT reads "fords," whereas the *qere* reads "desert" or "steppe." The *qere* reading coordinates with 17:16, "the steppe of the wilderness," though several Hebrew manuscripts read "the fords of the wilderness" (cf. *BHS*). The question is not critical to the story. What is important is that David informs Zadok of his location, even though that location remains obscure in the Hebrew text.

COMMENTARY

David appears to be heading toward the Transjordan region. He is barefoot, weeping, and has covered his head. The people, following his lead, do the same (though they are not barefoot) as they ascend the Mount of Olives. The mourning gestures, mentioned briefly in the previous interlude (15:23), now become explicit and express David's humiliation at the hands of Absalom. In Esther 6:12, the humiliated Haman hastens to his house in mourning with his head covered. The prophet Jeremiah describes the people of Judah, who have been disgraced by a divinely warranted drought, as covering their heads to signify their shame (Jer 14:3-4) and proclaiming a communal lament (Jer 14:7-9). The meaning of walking barefoot is illuminated by Isaiah 20:3-4 in which the prophet foresees that the king of Assyria will lead away his Egyptian captives "naked and barefoot." David is humiliated from head to toe. This reversal of royal attire expresses his penance. Has God abandoned his current choice for king as he abandoned Saul?

4.8.1.1g First Interruption Regarding Ahithophel: David Learns of Ahithophel's Betrayal (15:31)

The narrator interrupts the story (the first of four interruptions that focus on Ahithophel) to inform David that one of his chief counselors has betrayed him, information we already know (15:12).[120] David's situation is worsening. The narrator again discloses his opinion of this rebellion, labeling the rebels "conspirators," just as earlier he referred to the uprising as a "conspiracy" (15:12). All we know about Ahithophel is that he was one of David's counselors and that he comes from Giloh, a town south of Jerusalem in the vicinity of Hebron. As in 15:12, the narrator sheds no light on why Ahithophel defected. But the narrator wants us to hear David's reaction, namely, his prayer that God "turn the counsel of Ahithophel into foolishness." He recognizes that Absalom has acquired a wise ally in Ahithophel. When God does indeed intervene, it is not to render Ahithophel's advice foolish but to render Absalom a fool for failing to follow Ahithophel's wise counsel (17:14). But for the moment we do not know whether God will receive David's supplication. So we wait as the suspense builds.

David's prayer, presented as a brief soliloquy to the audience, is critical for understanding the episode of Absalom's rebellion. When God effects David's prayer, rendering Ahithophel's wise counsel foolish in

---

[120] The information is introduced with *wĕ X qātal* not *wayyiqtol*.

the eyes of Absalom, he rescues David from defeat (a key theme in the David Narrative; see section 1.3 above). David's prayer also signals that the "advice-giving" scenes that follow are crucial for understanding the function of Absalom's rebellion within the entire David Narrative. While the battle that restores David to the throne will be reported summarily, the narrator will devote much time to the scenes where Absalom seeks advice, since his defeat comes when God effects David's prayer concerning that advice. Once God acts, the rebellion's failure and David's return are assured.

4.8.1.2 THE FUGITIVE KING MEETS ALLIES AND A FOE (15:32–16:14)

David's flight is punctuated by his encounters with three people:

1. David and Hushai (15:32-37)
2. David and Ziba (16:1-4)
3. David and Shimei (16:5-13)

4.8.1.2a David and Hushai (15:32-37)

STRUCTURE

A. Hushai intends to go with David (15:32)
   B. David's speech to Hushai (15:33-36)
A'. Hushai turns back to Jerusalem (15:37)

David's speech is framed by Hushai's arrival and departure. As the scene begins, Hushai is leaving Jerusalem with David. As it ends, he has reversed course.

COMMENTARY

Just as David reaches the summit of the Mount of Olives, where, the narrator adds, people used to worship God, he meets Hushai. (David has just taken advantage of this once holy place to pray that God render Ahithophel's advice foolish.) Hushai is the first of several individuals who come out to greet David and are introduced with the Hebrew construction *liqra*ᵓt, "to meet." As David flees from Jerusalem, he meets— *liqra*ᵓt—Hushai and then Ziba (16:1). (When Shimei son of Gera comes out to condemn David [16:5-13], *liqra*ᵓt is not used.) As he returns to Jerusalem, the people of Judah (19:15), Shimei (19:16), and Mephibosheth

(19:24) come to meet—*liqra᾿t*—him. During his flight, the narrator focuses our attention on the approach of Hushai (15:32), Ziba (16:1), and Shimei (16:5) by the use of the particle *hinnēh* (once translated "behold") so that we observe their approach at the same moment as David does.

Hushai is an "Archite," a people mentioned in Joshua 16:2, whose land, located southwest of Bethel, became part of the territory of Benjamin.[121] Thus, even though Hushai comes from a region once governed by Saul, he is now fiercely loyal to David, expressed by his mourning attire: torn clothes and dirt on his head. When David mourned the deaths of Jonathan and Saul, he tore his clothes (2 Sam 1:11), and when the messenger came to Shiloh to report to Eli the news of the Israelite defeat and of the deaths of Hophni and Phinehas, he too arrived with torn clothes and an earth-smudged head (1 Sam 4:12). Thus Hushai, presenting himself as a mourner, acknowledges that Absalom's uprising is a defeat for David, and he wants David to know whose side he is on.

David's speech to Hushai is at the center of the scene. David ordered Ittai and Zadok back to Jerusalem with a series of imperatives, but to Hushai, "his friend" (15:37), he gives no direct order. He sets out two conditions for Hushai and, presuming Hushai's loyalty, expects him to get his gist. But he leaves Hushai free to decide. First he tells Hushai that if he goes into flight with him, he will be a "burden"—the Hebrew term refers quite literally to a load for transport. How exactly Hushai would be a burden for David is not explained and the loyal Hushai does not ask questions.[122] But if he returns to Jerusalem and declares his loyalty to Absalom, then he can *foil* (the Hebrew verb is *prr*) Ahithophel's advice. (Again, David is certain that Ahithophel will provide Absalom with astute counsel.) And, in fact, at the moment when the narrator reports on God's intervention into the events, the same verb is used: "the LORD had ordered the foiling [*prr*] of Ahithophel's advice" (17:14; translation mine). Thus, in this place where, the narrator reminds us, God was worshiped (15:32), God is indeed listening in the background to David's plan and will act accordingly.

In the second part of this speech, David informs Hushai of other trustworthy collaborators who are already in Jerusalem. But because Hushai will have access to Absalom's inner court, he will learn the rebels' strategy. That information should be passed on to Zadok and Abiathar who will send Ahimaaz and Jonathan to inform David. (Zadok knows

---

[121] Siegfried S. Johnson, "Archite," in *ABD*, 1:359.

[122] As David returns to Jerusalem, he invites Barzillai to come with him, but Barzillai declines the king's offer, explaining that he would only be a "burden" to him (19:35). He then elucidates how he would be a "burden": he is old and his senses are in full decline.

where David will be holed up.) The narrator suppresses Hushai's consent, giving the impression that David's friend instantly agreed and reversed course for Jerusalem. The scene closes with a flash ahead to the simultaneous arrivals of Hushai and Absalom in Jerusalem. But we continue to travel with David as Hushai makes his way back to Jerusalem.

4.8.1.2b David and Ziba (16:1-4)

Hushai exits and immediately Ziba comes to meet (*liqra³t*) David just as he passes beyond the summit of the Mount of Olives and his beloved Jerusalem passes out of sight. (The Hebrew construction *wě X qātal* in 16:1 captures the combination of events occurring at nearly the same time.) Again the Hebrew particle *hinnēh* in 16:1 focuses David's attention (and ours) on Ziba's approach and the gifts he bears.

STRUCTURE

Setting (16:1)
A. The king's question (16:2a)
   B. Ziba's response (16:2b)
A'. The king's question (16:3a)
   B'. Ziba's response (16:3b)
A". The king's decree (16:4a)
   B". Ziba's response (16:4b)

COMMENTARY

Ziba, the servant of Mephibosheth, is under David's order to work the lands that once belonged to Saul for the benefit of Mephibosheth, the son of Jonathan, whom David brought under the protection of his court (2 Sam 9). The provisions, described in detail, that Ziba offers are the fruits of that land, and, for the moment, we assume that Mephibosheth is behind this generous gift. Ziba declares himself on David's side, providing the barefoot king with a donkey to ride (see the discussion in 19:24-30), a more dignified form of transport for the king.[123]

The king immediately asks, "Where is Mephibosheth?" (We are wondering too.) David's precise wording—"Where is your master's

---

[123] In 1 Kings 1:33 David gives orders for Solomon to ride his own mule (the Hebrew word is not the same as in 2 Sam 16:2) when Solomon descends to the Spring of Gihon for his anointing as king.

son?"—alludes to the fact that the king would have no relationship with Mephibosheth or Ziba were it not for his covenant with Jonathan, Mephibosheth's father and son of Saul, Ziba's master (see the discussion of 9:1-13 above). We also know that Mephibosheth, who is disabled (4:4), would have required assistance to flee Jerusalem with David. In his response, Ziba offers more information than David's question asked. The simple answer is that Mephibosheth remained in Jerusalem. But then the provisions in Ziba's hands would be an expression of Mephibosheth's loyalty: unable to flee with the king, Mephibosheth delivers his support through his servant Ziba. So the gift-bearing Ziba indicts his master: Mephibosheth has remained in Jerusalem hoping to be restored to his grandfather's throne.[124] (Ziba's assertion, which David does not dispute, confirms our suspicions that Absalom drew a significant amount of support from forces once loyal to Saul.) If David believes Ziba, he should imagine that Ziba tried to help his disabled master to flee, but Mephibosheth refused. The provisions are Ziba's gift while Mephibosheth is a traitor.

Ziba's explanation for Mephibosheth's absence seems implausible. Even though there is evidence that Absalom drew support for his rebellion from the remnants of Saul's region (15:1-6), it seems unlikely that "King Absalom," would relinquish his dominion over Saul's territory. But for now, David has little reason (or time) to interrogate Ziba further, and so the question of his veracity will remain suspended until Mephibosheth comes onstage and we hear his side of the story. The fleeing David bestows Mephibosheth's lands on Ziba (a decision he will need to revisit after he hears from Mephibosheth in 19:24-30), but the decree has no effect, since the fugitive king is not even in possession of his own property. For the moment David needs to make an ally of Ziba, whose final words ("I have found favor") celebrate his craftiness that has met with success. Once Absalom is dead, Ziba will reappear among those rushing to accompany the victorious David back to Jerusalem (19:17), but he never speaks again.

4.8.1.2c David and Shimei (16:5-13)

The longest of David's three meetings is with Shimei, who is still loyal to Saul. He accuses David of crimes about which we have heard nothing up to this point in the David Narrative.

---

[124] The Hebrew reads *ʾābî*, "my father," but Hebrew does not distinguish between "father" and "grandfather" (see Ernst Jenni and Claus Westermann, *TLOT*, trans. Mark E. Biddle [Peabody, MA: Hendrickson, 1997], 1:3), so Mephibosheth must be referring to Saul, his grandfather. Mephibosheth's father, Jonathan, never received his father's crown.

STRUCTURE

A. David is fleeing; Shimei reviles David and throws stones (16:5-6)

  B. Shimei's insults: "the LORD has returned [*hēšîb*] on you" (16:7-8)

   C. Abishai's request (16:9)

    D. David's interpretation of this event: God sent Shimei (16:10)

   C'. Response to Abishai's request (16:11)

  B'. David responds to Shimei's insults: "the LORD will return [*wĕhēšîb*] to me" (16:12)

A'. David continues to flee; Shimei continues to revile David and to throw stones (16:13)

This scene is framed by David's flight and Shimei's insults and stone throwing, actions that continue in the background as we listen to the dialogue. In the B section Shimei declares that Absalom's rebellion testifies to the fact that God has "returned" on David all the blood he shed in the house of Saul. But in the B' section David prays that God might "return" to him good instead of Shimei's abuse. In the C/C' sections Abishai seeks David's permission to kill Shimei, but David refuses. At the center is David's short speech that explains his penitential behavior (weeping and walking barefoot): God told Shimei to revile him. The Hebrew verb "to revile" (*qll*) appears eight times in this scene.

COMMENTARY

As David arrives at Bahurim he encounters Shimei (the *hinnēh* clause focuses our attention on Shimei's approach). Bahurim, a town just east of Jerusalem, is where Abner told Michal's weepy husband (Abner had retrieved Michal from him as a condition for his audience with David) to go back home (3:16) while he continued on to Jerusalem. It seems to be a town along the border of the territory once ruled by Saul. As he reaches Bahurim, David is greeted by this member of Saul's family who reviles him while hurling stones at him and his entourage. Not everyone in Bahurim, however, is hostile to David. Later a husband and wife from Bahurim will protect David's secret envoys from capture as they travel with critical news about Absalom's planned assault against the fugitive king (17:15-20).

The narrator allows us to hear in full Shimei's stark accusations (he could have reduced Shimei's speech to a brief summary). David is a "scoundrel" (the NRSV's translation for Hebrew *ʾîš habbĕliyyāʿal*[125]), a label that also has political connotations. The narrator applies it to Sheba son of Bichri (20:1), an insurrectionist who attempts an unsuccessful rebellion against David. That nuance may capture Shimei's intent here: David is an insurrectionist who rebelled against Saul. He then labels him a "man of blood," a phrase properly translated "murderer" in many English versions. Finally, he employs a technical expression to imply that David usurped Saul's throne when he accuses him of ruling in Saul's place.[126] The usurper is now condemned to flee because, as Shimei sees it, God is avenging the blood that David shed. Shimei's accusation that David murdered members of Saul's house puts a new spin on David's succession to Saul's throne and on the reason why Absalom drew support among the "tribes of Israel" (see 15:1-6). Can this be true?

The narrator allows Shimei to speak without commenting on the veracity of his denunciation or the credibility of his character. Recent scholarship has given some credence to Shimei's claims. Baruch Halpern writes that "the fate the Saulides suffered at David's hands was a very live issue indeed at the time of the Absalom revolt, late in the reign."[127] Steven L. McKenzie too suggests that Shimei's viewpoint "may well have a basis in history"[128] and agrees with others who suggest that David may even have had a hand in Saul's death.[129] A number of scholars argue that Shimei's charges presuppose that David had already executed Saul's sons in reparation for the bloodguilt owed the Gibeonites, an event that the narrator recounts much later (21:1-14). That information could explain why even David wonders whether God has mandated Shimei's accusations (16:10). We too can wonder, given the quick success of Absalom's rebellion, if Shimei was not expressing a dissent that was widely held among the remnants of the Saulide regime.[130] At the very least, our narrator, usually

---

[125] The term is not easily translated by a single English word. Abigail used it to describe her husband Nabal in 1 Samuel 25:25 (translated "ill-natured" in the NRSV) because he foolishly rejected David's request for assistance (1 Sam 25:10). It is also applied to the two men who, in a legal proceeding, falsely accused Naboth of cursing God and the king (1 Kgs 21:13). The charge of these two "scoundrels" (in the NRSV) resulted in Naboth's wrongful execution.

[126] The Hebrew phrase by itself is ambiguous: it can refer to a legitimate succession (see 10:1) or chronicle a coup d'état (see 2 Kgs 15:14, 25, 30).

[127] Baruch Halpern, *David's Secret Demons: Messiah, Murderer, Traitor, King* (Grand Rapids, MI: Eerdmans, 2001), 86. McCarter (*II Samuel*, 373) also raises the question.

[128] Steven L. McKenzie, *King David: A Biography* (New York: Oxford University Press, 2000), 110.

[129] McKenzie, *King David*, 136.

[130] See K. L. Noll, *The Faces of David*, JSOTSup 242 (Sheffield: Sheffield Academic Press, 1997), 126. If the events in 21:1-14 did occur before Absalom's rebellion, then

a friend to David, has allowed Shimei to raise the question of the king's legitimacy by chronicling this scene during David's flight.

The circumstances of Saul's demise were reported in 1 Samuel 31 and in 2 Samuel 1. When an Amalekite warrior informed David of how he had helped dispatch the mortally wounded king, David ordered him executed for having shed the blood of the Lord's anointed (1:14). By declaring the Amalekite messenger responsible for his own execution, David asserted his own innocence in Saul's death, even though he enjoyed its political benefits. Does Shimei not believe this account? Does he not know that David refused two opportunities to eliminate King Saul (1 Sam 24:4 and 26:8)? When Joab summoned Abner back to Jerusalem, the narrator paused the action to inform us that David had no idea what Joab was plotting (2 Sam 3:26), absolving him of this crime. When David learned of Abner's murder, he immediately proclaimed his innocence: "I and my kingdom are forever guiltless before the LORD for the blood of Abner son of Ner" (3:28). David's explicit declaration of his innocence *before God* contrasts with the accusations we learn about now, leaving us in a quandary.

The narrator casts a measure of doubt on the veracity of Shimei's remarks by reporting the dialogue between David and Abishai. Abishai would, with David's leave, kill Shimei, whom he upbraids as a "dead dog," often an expression of self-deprecation that here is used as an insult (see above for a discussion of this slur in 3:8). Abishai's intention to kill Shimei recalls the opportunity he and David had to kill Saul. The two scenes have striking parallels.

1 Samuel 26:8-11	2 Samuel 16:9-12
26:8a Abishai speaks to David.	16:9a Abishai speaks to David.
26:8b Abishai comments on the situation at hand: God has given Saul into David's hand.	16:9b Abishai comments on the situation at hand: Why should Shimei revile the king?
26:8c Abishai proposes to David that he kill David's enemy.	16:9c Abishai proposes to David that he kill David's enemy.
26:9 David prevents Abishai from killing Saul.	16:10a David prevents Abishai from killing Shimei.
26:10 David invokes God to impede Abishai.	16:10b David invokes God to impede Abishai.
26:11 David invokes God a second time.	16:11-12 David invokes God a second time.

---

the narrator's decision to recount them after the rebellion is another way to shield David from Shimei's accusations. To this point in the David Narrative, David is not responsible for the death of any member of Saul's family.

The echo of 1 Samuel 26:8-11 undermines Shimei's accusations. David did not give Abishai leave to kill Saul then, and he does not give him leave now to kill Shimei. Just as David preserved Saul's life long ago, now he preserves the life of a member of Saul's family. Just as he reminded Abishai that the length of Saul's life was in God's hands, now he impedes him from executing Shimei by suggesting that God has sent Shimei to revile him. This speech, appearing at the center of the scene, reveals David's own interpretation of his flight from Jerusalem. The NJPS translation of 16:10 is closer to the Hebrew ("He is abusing [me] only because the LORD told him to abuse David") than the more hopeful NRSV translation ("If he is cursing because the LORD has said to him, 'Curse David'"), which leaves open the possibility that God did not send Shimei to revile him.[131] David's admission suggests that his gestures of mourning and humiliation are acts of atonement for his sin,[132] though the precise content of that sin remains ambiguous.

As David explains his reasoning, he expands his audience to include everyone present, not just Abishai. What are Shimei's charges, he laments, in light of a rebellion that is led by his own son? David's reference to Absalom as his own "issue" (ʾăšer yāṣāʾ mimmēʿay[133]) links this scene to God's promise to him in 2 Samuel 7, the only other time this phrase appears in the David Narrative. Nathan had announced to David that after his death, God would raise up his descendants, "his very own issue" (ʾăšer yēṣēʾ mimmēʿêkā), to succeed him (7:12), establishing his house and throne forever. The echo of that promise now underscores a deep irony in David's words. One of David's *own issue*, in whom God's promise might have been fulfilled, now seeks his life. If 2 Samuel 7 is the zenith of David's reign, this scene is its nadir. David orders that Shimei be left alone as he is not speaking his own word but may well be a divine messenger, like Nathan who first announced that David's *own issue* would sit on his throne. While we have no reason to believe that Shimei enjoys a divine mandate similar to Nathan's, David cannot be sure. The Hebrew text contains a play on the word "son," *bēn*. David seems to be saying,

---

[131] The Hebrew verbal root *qll* can be translated "to curse" or "to abuse/to revile." I have chosen the latter meaning (with the NJPS) since "to curse" in the Bible can include a divine invocation as when Joshua invokes God to pronounce a curse (using the Hebrew root *ʾrr*) on anyone who would rebuild Jericho (Josh 6:26). In this case, Shimei does not invoke God; rather he reviles or mocks David for the maledictions that he believes God has already brought upon him.

[132] David's confession supports the argument that the events in 21:1-14 happened before Absalom's rebellion.

[133] The NRSV's "my own son" does not render the expression literally. The NJPS reads, "my own issue."

"my son [*bĕnî*], [i.e., the one who should be by my side] wants to kill me, how much more this *ben haymînî* [Benjaminite, which translated literally means, 'son of my right hand,'] who is not my son, wants to do me harm" (a free rendering of the Hebrew text in 16:11).

As he listens to Shimei's curses, David utters another prayer (16:12). His previous prayer begged God to render Ahithophel's advice to Absalom foolish (15:31). Now he prays that God might see his "distress" (so the NRSV) and return to him good in place of Shimei's insults. At this critical moment in the David Narrative, the Hebrew text is problematic. Most English translations follow the Greek, Peshitta, and Latin versions, which read "my affliction/distress." The Hebrew consonantal text reads "my guilt" (*ketib*: *ᶜwny*); the Masoretic Text instructs us to read "my eye" (*qere*: *ᶜyny*). We are confronted with three possible readings, all of which enjoy a degree of canonical status: David bids God to look "into his eye," or "upon his distress," or "upon his guilt." The last reading is the most problematic and the other two readings can be explained as later interpretations that wanted to protect David from admitting a crime. If David admits "guilt" then perhaps he is confessing to at least some of Shimei's indictment. The ambiguity here is tortuous and commentators who would consider David a usurper read "my guilt." Others who lean toward David's legitimacy read "my affliction." The ambiguous text thwarts our demand for expository clarity and without a convincing solution for this reading, the question of David's legitimacy will continue to tease readers of the David Narrative for centuries to come. After Absalom's defeat, Shimei runs to David to beg forgiveness and asks David not to remember his "guilt," employing the same word (*ᶜāwōn*, 19:19 [MT 19:20]) as in this scene. This reuse of that term argues in favor of the *ketib* reading ("my guilt") here: David worries about his own possible guilt as he listens to Shimei's charges, but in the end, it is Shimei who confesses that he, not David, bears guilt for calling David a murderer.

In his final statement, David places his destiny in God's hands, reprising a central theme of the David Narrative (discussed in section 1.3 above) that was introduced the day that David stood before Saul: "The LORD, who saved me from the paw of the lion and from the paw of the bear, will save me from the hand of this Philistine" (1 Sam 17:37). David prays to God, who, as we shall see, hears his prayer, in contrast to Saul, whose prayers went unheeded (1 Sam 28:6). At the end of his public life David will celebrate his rescue by God in song:

> In my distress, I called to the LORD
> To my God, I called.
> From his temple he heard my voice
> My cry reached his ears. (2 Sam 22:7)

As the scene concludes, there is no change in the situation: David continues his escape and Shimei continues to revile him, throwing stones at him and tossing dust in the air. But we have been changed by these accusations regarding David's legitimacy as Saul's successor.

4.8.1.3 THE CONCLUSION OF DAVID'S FLIGHT FROM JERUSALEM (16:14)

This verse concludes the episode (15:13–16:14) that began when David ordered his officials to abandon Jerusalem. The narrator ignores David's precise location (we might like to know how far he is from Jerusalem[134]), wanting instead to focus on the weariness of David and his troops. Very soon Ahithophel will advise Absalom to attack immediately (17:1-2), knowing that David will be weary from his flight from Jerusalem, and we will grasp that Ahithophel's advice is exactly right, confirming that he does provide Absalom with brilliant counsel just as David had feared. Had the usurping king listened to Ahithophel, his rebellion could have proved victorious. We leave a weary David at this unknown location and return to Jerusalem just as Absalom is arriving uncontested into the city.

4.8.2 The Victorious Absalom and His Counselors (16:15–17:14)

The four scenes that comprise this section report the advice that the usurping king solicited and received (the Hebrew root y‘ṣ, "to give counsel," appears over ten times). The decisive moment comes when God intervenes against Ahithophel's wise advice and Absalom's fate is sealed. These events eclipse the details about the rebellion itself: How many rebels were involved? How did Absalom's forces conquer Jerusalem? Did the remaining Jerusalemites put up some resistance? What was the shape of Absalom's emerging court? The narrator ignores our questions in favor of the dialogue between the usurper and his two counselors, Ahithophel and Hushai. The second and third interruptions regarding Ahithophel appear in this episode. In 15:31 David learned that his counselor Ahithophel had joined the rebellion (first interruption), and he prayed that God might render foolish Ahithophel's counsel. That

---

[134] The NRSV adds "at the Jordan" on the basis of the Greek manuscript b (Lucianic) and Josephus. But the textual witnesses for this reading are few. And the narrator is interested not in David's location but in the fact that at this point in the flight he is weary. Thus, "at the Jordan" is a later, clarifying addition to the text and the MT is preferred.

prayer lies in the background as we observe Absalom soliciting advice from Ahithophel and Hushai. Will God answer David's prayer? The narrator adds to the suspense with a second interruption: Ahithophel's counsel was like divine advice! But when, in the third interruption, God foils Ahithophel's advice, we know that David will be victorious.

STRUCTURE

A   Absalom and Hushai (16:15-19)
    B. Absalom and Ahithophel: first counsel (16:20-22)
Second interruption regarding Ahithophel (16:23)
    B'. Absalom and Ahithophel: second counsel (17:1-4)
A'. Absalom and Hushai (17:5-14a)
Third interruption regarding Ahithophel (17:14b)

4.8.2.1 ABSALOM AND HUSHAI (16:15-19)

The narrator returns to the scene when Hushai arrived in Jerusalem just as Absalom was entering the city (15:37). All the Israelites arrive with Absalom, but Ahithophel's presence is given special notice. The narrator links this scene to the previous dialogue between David and Hushai by referring to Hushai as "David's friend" (16:16), just as he did when Hushai departed from David (15:37). Hushai greets Absalom by crying out twice "Long live the king!" signaling his approval of the rebellion.[135] This is the only time we hear Absalom acclaimed king (the narrator never accords him this title). Absalom is rightly surprised by Hushai's cry of loyalty. His questions—"Is this your loyalty to your friend? Why did you not go with your friend?"—reveal that he is aware of the kinship between David and Hushai. Absalom is suspicious. He should have listened to his instincts and put Hushai under guard until his loyalty could be verified. But Hushai immediately allays Absalom's doubts, responding to him with a double entendre (16:18): "No; but the one whom the LORD and this people and all the Israelites have chosen, his I will be, and with him I will remain."

The unwitting Absalom interprets Hushai's words—"whom the LORD and this people and all the Israelites have chosen" (16:18)—as a profession of loyalty to him. But we, aware that David is the one whom God has

---

[135] Hushai's laudation will be heard again when Adonijah's followers proclaim his succession to David's throne with "Long live King Adonijah" (1 Kgs 1:25). When Samuel presents Saul to the tribes of Israel as their king, the people announce their approval with "Long live the king" (1 Sam 10:24).

chosen, hear another meaning. In 1 Samuel 16 the Hebrew verb *bḥr*, "to choose," appears three times, and each time it introduces one of Jesse's sons whom God has *not chosen* so that when the youngest son, David, is retrieved from the flocks, it is clear that he is the divine choice. David himself, in his dispute with his wife Michal, declares that God has chosen him (2 Sam 6:21). And while the verb *bḥr* does not appear in 2 Samuel 7, God's promise to David confirms that he is God's choice for the throne in Jerusalem. Hushai's declaration of loyalty for the one whom *all Israel* has chosen (16:18) echoes Abner's speech when David assumes the kingship over Saul's dominion (3:12, 21) and *all Israel* comes to Hebron to anoint him king over Israel (5:1, 3). So Absalom mistakes Hushai's words as a sign of loyalty to him while we enjoy his duplicitous claim of fealty. Hushai is indeed showing loyalty to his friend (David), but Absalom fails to see it. When Hushai insists that his loyalty flows from the fact that Absalom is the king's son, we are reminded that the king and the rebel are also father and son. The scene ends without a reaction from Absalom, but we are left with the impression that Absalom remained somewhat mistrustful of Hushai. God's intervention is going to be necessary.

4.8.2.2 ABSALOM AND AHITHOPHEL: FIRST COUNSEL (16:20-22)

Absalom turns to Ahithophel, David's trusted advisor, for help: "Give us your counsel; what shall we do?" He does not appeal to Hushai, who is offstage until Absalom calls him back in 17:5. The usurper has appropriated his father's palace but cannot decide what his first royal act should be without consultation. When David received Saul's crown (1:10), he "inquired of the LORD" (2:1), who told him to go to Hebron where the people of Judah would anoint him king. The rebel Absalom, who leads what the narrator has branded a "conspiracy," cannot consult God for advice on how to finish off David, God's chosen king. So he asks Ahithophel who, we are about to learn, was just like consulting "the oracle of God" (16:23). If God does not hear David's prayer to render Ahithophel's advice foolish, there is little hope for David.

Ahithophel counsels Absalom to have sexual relations with the ten concubines that David left to care for his house (15:16), explaining that when all Israel hears of it, they will know that Absalom has made himself "odious," as the NRSV translates, to his father.[136] The NJPS translation—"when all

---

[136] The NRSV's overly literal translation is unhelpful. This Hebrew root (*bʾš*) does mean "to stink" (as the Nile does in Exod 7:18), but the expression "to be odious to someone" or "to make oneself odious to another person" is not part of everyday English usage.

Israel hears that you have dared the wrath of your father"— captures the significance of Absalom's sexual relations with these women. By seizing the deposed king's concubines, Absalom will demonstrate to the Jerusalemites that he has usurped his father's throne. When Ishbaal accused Abner of having sexual relations with Saul's concubine Rizpah in 3:7 (see the discussion there), he was accusing him of treason: attempting to sire an heir by the dead king's concubine that could usurp Ishbaal's throne. In 1 Kings 2:13-25 when Adonijah seeks Abishag, David's concubine, as his wife, Solomon perceives the request as a threat to his throne and orders Adonijah executed just for asking. Thus, Absalom, by having sexual relations (in a semipublic fashion) with David's concubines, announces the success of his usurpation. Ahithophel adds that the news of Absalom's appropriation of these women will serve to encourage those who are on his side: they will know that David is not coming back to Jerusalem.

Absalom accepts without discussion Ahithophel's counsel, and the narrator brings us up to the roof (presumably of the palace) to the pitched tent into which Absalom enters with the concubines. Apart from the expression of his virility, Absalom also seeks to produce an heir to his throne, and he does so on the same roof from which David once spied the lovely Bathsheba bathing (the mother of the true heir). The details of this scene recall Nathan's rebuke of David after his tryst with Bathsheba:

> I will raise up trouble against you from within your own house; and I will take your wives before your eyes, and give them to your neighbor, and he shall lie with your wives in the sight of this very sun. For you did it secretly; but I will do this thing before all Israel, and before the sun. (12:11-12)

Indeed, trouble has erupted within David's own house as David's concubines are brought out on the roof of the palace ("before all Israel" and in broad daylight) to be given to Absalom (not "to your neighbor" as Nathan foresaw). By not responding immediately to David's prayer to frustrate Ahithophel's advice, God has allowed Absalom's rebellion to achieve this level of success with the result that the words of Nathan the prophet are fulfilled. But this is the apex of Absalom's victory over David. God is about to act.

4.8.2.3 SECOND INTERRUPTION REGARDING AHITHOPHEL:
AHITHOPHEL'S COUNSEL COMES FROM GOD (16:23)

The narrator interrupts these advice-giving scenes to provide more background information on Ahithophel. His advice was like the word of one "who consulted an oracle of God." The exact Hebrew expression here—literally, "one who consults in the word of God"—does not occur elsewhere in the Bible. The expression "to consult God" (*šᵓl bēᵓlōhîm*) appears several times,[137] though less often than the expression "to consult the LORD" (*šᵓl bYHWH*),[138] and David is often the subject of the latter.[139] The narrator's side comment is particularly worrisome. Absalom has a courtier whose advice is equivalent to David's direct inquiry of God. At present Absalom is on the roof of the palace having sex with David's concubines, the result of Ahithophel's first bit of advice that fulfilled God's word spoken through Nathan to David. Thus, we know that the counsel that Ahithophel is about to give is reliable and Absalom knows it too. Our question becomes ever more pressing: will God answer David's prayer to foil Ahithophel's oracular advice and if so, when? If an answer does not come soon, David is finished.

4.8.2.4 ABSALOM AND AHITHOPHEL: SECOND COUNSEL (17:1-4)

To keep us focused on the theme of giving advice, the narrator abruptly shifts scenes. Absalom has finished with David's concubines and is again listening to Ahithophel, who tells him to gather his forces immediately and to attack David, who he believes will be tired and discouraged from his defeat and flight. He is right! That is the exact condition in which we left David (16:14). Correctly assessing the military situation, Ahithophel is indeed an advisor who can be likened to someone who consults God (16:23). The surprise attack will terrify a weary David and put his allies to flight, and only David will die in the conflict. Then all the people will come to Absalom as a bride returns to her husband.[140] Once David is dead there will be peace. Absalom is pleased with the advice that foresees his father's assassination, a sharp contrast to David who will bid his commanders to preserve the life of his rebel son (18:5).

Unbeknownst to Ahithophel, his advice contains a prophetic overture of what will befall Absalom and his rebel band. Ahithophel predicts that all the people who are with David will "flee" (17:2: *nws*). In fact, it is Absalom's supporters who flee once their leader is dead (18:17: *nws*).

---

[137] Judges 18:5; 20:18; 1 Samuel 14:37; 1 Chronicles 14:10, 14. In 1 Samuel 22:15, when Ahimelech declares his innocence before Saul, he confesses that he has consulted God for David on other occasions.

[138] See Judges 1:1; 20:23, 27; 1 Samuel 10:22; 22:10.

[139] See 1 Samuel 23:2, 4; 30:8; 2 Samuel 2:1; 5:19, 23.

[140] Most English translations of this verse follow the LXX, which reads, "as a bride returns to her husband. You seek the life of one man." As the NJPS notes, the meaning of the Hebrew is uncertain.

He tells Absalom that he will strike down David (17:2: *nkh*). In fact, it is Absalom who will be struck down (18:15: *nkh*). After David's death, Ahithophel will "bring back" (17:3: *šwb*, hiphil) all the people to Absalom. As it turns out, it is Absalom's supporters who seek to bring back David to Jerusalem (19:10 [MT 19:11]: *šwb*, hiphil). As Ahithophel sees it, the people are the "bride" and Absalom is their "husband" to whom they will return. But, in fact, Jerusalem is the bride (see, for example, Jer 2:2) and David, under this simile, will be her returning husband. And finally, Ahithophel predicts that if Absalom follows his advice there will be peace (*šālôm*). When Ahimaaz outruns the Cushite to reach David with the news of the battle in which Absalom is killed, he will say one word to the king, *šālôm*, translated in the NRSV with "All is well" (18:28). Thus, the "shalom" that Ahithophel predicts for Absalom will come to David (though David, at that point, will only be concerned about Absalom's fate and that news does not bring him "shalom"). But this will happen only if God intervenes since, as the scene concludes, Absalom and the elders of Israel are ready to accept Ahithophel's astute advice.

4.8.2.5 ABSALOM AND HUSHAI (17:5-14A)

Absalom makes the fatal decision of calling Hushai back to court, even though he and his council have already approved Ahithophel's strategy, which, had he followed, would have brought him victory. God has begun to intervene.

STRUCTURE

Introduction: Absalom asks Hushai a question and seeks his counsel (17:5-6)

Hushai's response to Absalom's question (17:7-10)
A. Ahithophel's advice is not good (*lōʾ ṭôbâ*) (17:7)
   a. David is a warrior (17:8a)
      b. Simile: like a bear (17:8b)
         c. David's strategy (17:8c-9a)
         c'. Absalom's defeat (17:9b)
      b'. Simile: like the heart of a lion (17:10a)
   a'. David is a warrior (17:10b)

Hushai's counsel (17:11-13)
   a. What all Israel (numerous like sand) will do (17:11)
      b. What will happen to David (17:12)
   a'. What all Israel will do—not even a pebble of David's hiding place will remain (17:13)
A'. Hushai's counsel is good (*ṭôbâ*) (17:14a)

The Hebrew word "good," *ṭôbâ*, forms an inclusion to this scene: Hushai begins by judging Ahithophel's advice to be "no good," and at the end of the scene Absalom and the people of Israel declare Hushai's advice to be "good" (*ṭôbâ*; rendered correctly with "better" in the NRSV in order to capture the comparative sense of Hebrew *min*). Hushai's speech can be divided into two parts. The first part (17:7-10) answers Absalom's first question: "Should Ahithophel's advice be implemented?" The second part (17:11-13) responds to Absalom's order, "you tell us."

COMMENTARY

Absalom summons Hushai, reports Ahithophel's advice to him, and then solicits his assessment of this advice. If necessary, Hushai can add his own recommendation. Hushai, recognizing that Ahithophel's sound counsel has put David's life in jeopardy, needs to discount it. In Hushai's opening line, the Hebrew root *yʿṣ* ("to give advice") appears twice: "the advice that Ahithophel has advised" (translation mine). This type of cognate accusative (enjoyed in biblical Hebrew but not in English) underscores the advice theme that is at the core of these scenes. Hushai's argument against Ahithophel's recommendation runs seven verses, or twice the length of Ahithophel's speech, which took only three verses (17:1-3). Ahithophel advised a swift attack, while Hushai's lengthier discourse buys the exhausted David time to recoup his strength. His rhetoric, "You know your father . . . ," cajoles Absalom to a naïve, subconscious consent: "Yes, of course, I know that my father is a fierce warrior." By referring to the king as "your father," he underscores the close relationship between the king and his usurper. Hushai then adopts a simile: David and his forces will be like a she-bear in the wild bereaved of her cubs. The frightening image appears in Proverbs 17:12 to express extreme danger: "Better to meet a she-bear robbed of its cubs than to confront a fool immersed in folly." The prophet Hosea envisions divine wrath like a "bear robbed of her cubs" (Hos 13:8). Hushai's hyperbolic warning should give Absalom pause. He has deprived David of his kingdom and therefore David, like a wild bear desperate for her cubs, will be enraged. (This simile also implies that David should not have been deprived of his kingdom any more than a she-bear should be deprived of her cubs.) Hushai reminds Absalom of David's warrior spirit, focusing Absalom's attention on the potential threat that David poses to his rebellion. He needs to slow Absalom down since we know that right now David is more exhausted than enraged.

The second reason, Hushai argues, that Ahithophel's advice is worthless is that David will not pass the night with his militia. Hushai knows this to be false since David is presently with his troops awaiting the news from Absalom's court (15:35-36). But Hushai, whom Absalom recognized as David's friend (16:17), proffers his advice as if he knows David's plans. Then he helps Absalom imagine what will happen if he attacks immediately. He will walk into an ambush, giving David a swift victory against a portion of his forces, the news of which will dishearten the rest of Absalom's troops. To drive his point home, he advances another vivid metaphor: Absalom's lion-hearted warriors will melt before the bereft she-bear David, who is surrounded by fierce fighters. Hushai amplifies his exhortation with a Hebrew infinitive absolute that modifies the verb "to melt" (17:10: *himmēs yimmās*), a construction that, though difficult to capture in English, may be translated, "[his heart] will melt away to nothing." Thus, Absalom should not launch an immediate attack on David. The rebel leader who successfully strategized a rebellion at a Jerusalem gate (15:1-6) is beguiled by Hushai's flourish. God is at work in the background.

Having ruled out Ahithophel's advice, Hushai now offers his own. If his description of David's military prowess was a bit overstated in his preamble, now Hushai exaggerates Absalom's potential, *if he waits* to gather his troops from Dan to Beer-sheba. His opening statement makes use of another Hebrew infinitive absolute to intensify the verb "to gather" (*'sp*) in 17:11, which the NJPS translation, "be called up," captures better than the NRSV's "be gathered." By summoning troops from the whole land, his army will be as numerous as the sand on the seashore.[141] Hushai's advice, because it specifically counsels Absalom to join the battlefront, ensures Absalom's ruin. By contrast, when David informs his troops that he will join them in the battle (18:2-3), his men insist that the king remain safe within the walls of Mahanaim. Hushai's advice sends Absalom to his death.

Hushai continues with hyperbolized similes. But will Absalom fall for this fanfare? The rebel forces will come upon David wherever he may be found (he does not elaborate on how they will find him) and will besiege him like dew that falls on the ground (17:12). The image of "dew" is often associated with God's blessing. In Genesis 27:28, Isaac blesses Jacob, wishing that God might bestow upon him the "dew of heaven." The "heavens dripping dew" is a blessing upon the land of Israel (Deut 33:28). The story of Gideon and the fleece (Judg 6:36-40) teaches that the dew (like the rain, cf. 1 Kgs 17:1) is a gift from God and entirely under God's control. Hushai's dew metaphor holds a double meaning. Can God, who blesses the land with the gift of dewfall, allow Absalom and

---

[141] This metaphor, which expresses an innumerable quantity (Gen 22:17; 32:12; Jer 15:8; 33:22), is also used to exaggerate troop strength (Josh 11:4; 1 Sam 13:5) and wealth (Judg 7:12).

his conspirators to become the dew that murders David, God's chosen king? Hushai fools the usurper into believing as much, promising that neither David nor any of his troops will survive. In fact, it is Absalom who will not survive.

Hushai's speech ends with the roll of kettledrums and a final crash of cymbals that build up Absalom's expectations beyond imagination. If David retreats to a city, all of Israel will bring ropes and drag the city down to the valley so that not even a pebble of it will remain. In fact, Absalom's troops never get close to Mahanaim, where David is holed up. Absalom and his rebels fall for Hushai's theatrics, perhaps already envisioning their victory over David's forces.

4.8.2.6 Third Interruption Regarding Ahithophel: God Has Intervened with Regard to Ahithophel's Advice (17:14b)

In 15:31 we learned of Ahithophel's betrayal of David, and then in 16:23 came the worrying news that Ahithophel's advice was divinely inspired. The narrator interrupts the story for the third time (again with *wĕ X qātal*) to inform us that David's prayer in 15:31 has been answered, though not precisely as David expressed it. He had prayed that God might turn Ahithophel's advice into foolishness. But God allowed Ahithophel to advise Absalom like someone who consulted God, and it was Absalom's perception of that good advice that God turned into foolishness. And so God has frustrated (Hebrew *prr*) that *good* advice, just as David had hoped in 15:34 (using the Hebrew verb *prr*). In this brief aside, we also learn God's opinion of Absalom's rebellion. Translated literally, the last phrase in 17:14 reads "so that the LORD might bring ruin upon Absalom."[142] Now the suspense is reduced; we know how the story of the rebellion will end.

4.8.3 *David Reaches Mahanaim (17:15-29)*

David is about to learn of Absalom's designs on him and will have to continue his flight, reaching Mahanaim, where he receives widespread support. From there, he will send out his troops and wait for news about the battle and about the fate of his son Absalom.

---

[142] When God brings ruin on someone, it normally means that person's untimely end (see 1 Kgs 14:10; 21:21; 2 Kgs 21:12).

4.8.3.1 David Learns about Absalom's Strategy (17:15-22)

STRUCTURE

A. Hushai sends word to David (17:15-16)
   B. Dangers and complications (17:17-20)
A'. Hushai's news reaches David (17:21-22)

The verb "to inform" (Hebrew *ngd*), appears five times in this scene as David learns about what has transpired in Absalom's court. In the A section, Hushai informs Zadok and Abiathar of Ahithophel's counsel. He urges them to go quickly to David and tell him to cross the Jordan with all the people who are with him. In the A' section, Jonathan and Ahimaaz pass the news to David, exhorting him to follow Hushai's counsel, which David obeys. Despite the messengers' haste, at the center of this scene they are forced to suspend their travels momentarily.

COMMENTARY

We leave Absalom's court, traveling with the messengers back to David's camp, and the language of "crossing over" (Hebrew *ʿbr*), characteristic of David's flight from Jerusalem, returns (see section 4.8 above). The narrator presumes that we remember the strategy David orchestrated as he was fleeing Jerusalem. Zadok and Abiathar, along with their sons, Ahimaaz and Jonathan, were ordered back to Jerusalem with instructions to come and inform him of Absalom's strategy. Hushai too was sent back with the task of informing Zadok and Abiathar of the news at court (15:35). That plan now swings into action. Hushai reports to Zadok and Abiathar in summary fashion the counsel that Absalom has received. The action is moving at a fever pitch (the adverb "quickly" [*mĕhērâ*] appears three times in this scene). Hushai, worried that Ahithophel's counsel might be adopted, advises David to continue his flight across the Jordan. We know that such haste is not necessary because Absalom has accepted Hushai's counsel, but apparently Hushai himself is not aware of that. Because Ahimaaz and Jonathan could not appear in Jerusalem, they stayed at En-rogel, which is near Jerusalem, perhaps at the south end of the Kidron Valley where it joins the Hinnom Valley.[143] They had organized for a young slave girl to be their conduit. This scene, which delays the arrival of the news to David (and thus gives Absalom more time to garner his forces), would have us sitting on the edge of our seats

---

[143] When Adonijah usurps the kingship he travels to the stone "Zoheleth," which is near En-rogel (1 Kgs 1:9).

were it not for the fact that we know the outcome of the rebellion. God
has heard David's prayer and so disaster awaits Absalom and his rebel
forces (17:14). But the characters in the story do not know the outcome
and so they hurry the news to David.

Ahimaaz and Jonathan are spotted near Jerusalem and Absalom is
informed. The two messengers, apparently aware that they have been
detected, head toward the home of a resident of Bahurim and hide in
his well. Their forced detour delays the arrival of the news to David.
At Bahurim David met the cursing Shimei (16:5), who represented the
remnants of Saul's house that rejected David's kingship. But this man
and his wife, also residents of Bahurim, are on David's side. The narrator skips over any dialogue between the messengers and the well
owner and his clever wife, who springs into action to provide them
asylum. The narrator has us observe her scheme, and when Absalom's
men arrive and interrogate her, she beguiles them. Not believing her,
they search the premises without result and return to Jerusalem. The
scene provides some comic relief (17:19-20): the woman, with her well
covering and sprinkled grain, outsmarts Absalom's men. Did they not
think to check for a well in the courtyard—an obvious hiding place?
Just as Absalom could not recognize Ahithophel's good advice, so his
two emissaries fail to discover where Ahimaaz and Jonathan are hiding. God has determined the outcome and so David's informants will
not be impeded.

Ahimaaz and Jonathan ascend from the well and hurry to David,
who, learning of Ahithophel's advice, crosses over to the other side of
the Jordan immediately. He presumes, not knowing that God has intervened, that Absalom will follow Ahithophel's strategy. The significance
of this crossing becomes clear once Absalom is dead and David begins
his journey back to Jerusalem (2 Sam 19). The narrator will focus our
attention on the Jordan and on the victorious David's crossing back
toward Jerusalem (19:15, 18, 31, 36, 39, 41). In this scene we learn why
David was forced to exit Israel and cross the Jordan.

4.8.3.2 FOURTH INTERRUPTION REGARDING AHITHOPHEL: AHITHOPHEL DIES (17:23)

We reach the fourth and final interruption (*wě X qātal*) regarding
Ahithophel. The narrator could have simply noted that Ahithophel
hanged himself. Instead, we observe Ahithophel's deliberate actions:
his travel from Jerusalem to his hometown, his preparations for death, his
suicide, and then his burial. Why all this detail? In the Bible, the phrase

"to set one's house in order" signals a person's impending death,[144] and so Ahithophel, who is not fatally ill, reveals his determination to end his life by putting his affairs in order. His suicide is not an act of passion; he has recognized his fatal error in supporting Absalom. (We never learn why he betrayed David, even as he prepares to die.) More important, having recognized that Absalom, so easily duped by Hushai's florid rhetoric, is incompetent, he knows that the rebellion is doomed to failure and that David will eventually return to Jerusalem. Ahithophel joins other biblical characters who opt for suicide: Abimelech (Judg 9:54), Saul and his armor-bearer (1 Sam 31:4-5), and Zimri (1 Kgs 16:18).[145] The lives of these four were at immediate risk and suicide was their only escape. Ahithophel's life is not in imminent danger, but it could be when David reenters Jerusalem, and so he too escapes what he believes is his inevitable humiliation. His death foreshadows Absalom's own demise. Ironically, his suicide offers more good advice to Absalom: the usurper should withdraw his rebels now. Thus, in life and in death Ahithophel gave advice like someone who consulted God. We never learn of Absalom's reaction to the suicide. David's counselor receives proper burial in his ancestral tomb and the narrator makes no comment on the manner of Ahithophel's death.

4.8.3.3 The Movements of the Two Camps (17:24-29)

The narrator updates us on David's movements (background information introduced with *wě X qātal*). He has reached Mahanaim, the town to which Abner brought Ishbaal, Saul's son, for his coronation (2:8-9). We could expect that this town would have remained loyal to Saulide rule. As soon as David entered Saulide territory, Shimei accused him of having the blood of Saul's house on his hands (16:5-8). Do the people of Mahanaim support Shimei's charges? The narrator holds us in suspense, shifting to the simultaneous movements in Absalom's camp. We last saw Absalom in Jerusalem as he foolishly judged Hushai's advice to be better than that of the now-dead Ahithophel. While David has traveled to Mahanaim, Absalom has crossed the Jordan and is now on the same side of the river as David. He has followed Hushai's advice (17:11), joining in the battle. Over his army, Absalom has appointed Amasa, whose family background in the Hebrew text is obscure. Ithra, Amasa's father,

---

[144] Isaiah advises the fatally ill Hezekiah "to set his house in order" since he is to die (2 Kgs 20:1).

[145] Abimelech and Saul were fatally wounded. When Zimri, holed up in Tirzah, saw that Omri had taken the city, he burned down the king's palace over his own head.

is called an Israelite in the Hebrew text, though most English translations follow 1 Chronicles 2:17 and call him an Ishmaelite. His mother is said to be Abigail, sister to Zeruiah, but daughter of Nahash, information that conflicts with 1 Chronicles 2:13-16, which lists Abigail and Zeruiah as David's sisters, the daughters of Jesse. Despite this confusion, it seems that Amasa is Joab's cousin and David's nephew, which explains David's remark to him after the rebellion is crushed: "Are you not my bone and my flesh?" (2 Sam 19:13). These details, though confused, remind us that this national strife is very much a family affair. Absalom's alliance with Amasa also reveals that the usurper has succeeded in co-opting into his rebellion high-ranking members of Jerusalem society. Later, Amasa will play a crucial role in resolving the rebellion (19:14), and David will appoint him as commander over his army, a decision rejected by Joab, who will murder Amasa (20:10). We leave Absalom and his army encamped in Gilead, a region east of the Jordan that includes Mahanaim, David's present location.

Have the citizens of Mahanaim joined the rebellion? What might have been a hostile reception turns out to be a marvelous welcome. Three leaders from different regions of Saul's dominion converge on Mahanaim to assist the fugitive David. Shobi, son of Nahash is from Rabbah. This is the city David besieged (11:1) during his affair with Bathsheba and eventually conquered (12:26-31). How it became such a friendly ally so quickly is not explained. But it has and Shobi, who appears only here in the Bible, comes bearing gifts. Next onstage comes Machir from Lo-debar, who provided refuge for Mephibosheth, Jonathan's son and potential heir to Saul's throne (9:4). As Mephibosheth's protector, he was once loyal to Saul. But his loyalties have changed. (Mephibosheth's loyalty to David is, for the moment, in question.) Though the exact location of Lo-debar is unknown, it was likely part of Saul's realm and near Mahanaim. Finally, Barzillai, being a Gileadite, is also from the region around Mahanaim, but the location of his hometown, Rogelim, is also unknown. Later Barzillai will greet the victorious David as he crosses the Jordan returning to Jerusalem (19:31-40). These three persons, from three different cities, indicate that David enjoys widespread support in the region once under Saul's authority. By contrast, the narrator makes no mention of the welcome or support that Absalom received as he encamped at Gilead. The supplies that accompany Shobi, Machir, and Barzillai, a veritable caravan of furniture, foods, and animals, witness to the fervent support that David enjoys. These allies, concerned about David's weary and hungry troops as they prepare to meet the rebel forces, are firmly committed to David in this rebellion.

4.8.4 The Rebellion Is Crushed and Absalom Is Executed (18:1–19:8c)

David the king sends his troops against the rebels, while David the father worries about his son's fate. He organizes his troops for battle and then gives special instructions regarding Absalom to Joab, Abishai, and Ittai: they are to "deal gently" with his son. As the episode closes, Joab, who never had any intention of following that order, confronts David over his unwarranted affection for his son, whom Joab views as a rebel usurper who had to be eliminated.

STRUCTURE

A. David instructs his troops and his commanders, giving specific orders to Joab regarding Absalom (18:1-5)
  B. The rebels are defeated and Absalom is executed (18:6-18)
  B'. News from the battlefront reaches David (18:19-33)
A'. Joab confronts David regarding Absalom (19:1-8abc)

The center of this episode reports the defeat of the rebels and the news of the victory making its way to David. In the opening scene, David takes up his position at the gate of Mahanaim to await news of his son's fate (18:4). At the end of the episode, David, having grieved his son's death, returns to that position at the gate (19:8).

4.8.4.1 DAVID INSTRUCTS HIS TROOPS AND HIS COMMANDERS (18:1-5)

STRUCTURE

A. Battle narrative (18:1-2ab)
    a. Battle formation (18:1)
      b. Joab, Abishai, and Ittai (18:2ab)
  B. The king and the troops (18:2c-4a)
    c. The king speaks (18:2c)
      d. The troops object (18:3)
    c'. The king speaks (18:4a)

A'. Battle narrative (18:4b-5)
    a'. Battle formation (18:4b)
      b'. Joab, Abishai, and Ittai (18:5a)
  B'. The king and the troops (18:5bc)
    c". The king's speech is overheard by the troops (18:5bc)
      [d'. No one objects]

The structure of this scene underscores the absence of any objection to David's order regarding Absalom. In the first exchange David announces his intention to join the battle, but his troops object and his order is reversed. In the second exchange the king issues a command to Joab, Abishai, and Ittai, who seem, by their silence, to consent, and the troops who overheard the order also remain silent. But will the king's second order also be reversed?

COMMENTARY

The scene opens with David, fully in command, dividing his troops into tactical units as the time for battle approaches. His three generals, Joab, Abishai, and Ittai, are to lead three columns.[146] The king initiates a dialogue with his troops: he will be joining them in the battle (the Hebrew expression—*gam-ʾănî*, "even I"—articulates David's resolve). But the troops vehemently object to his decision, ordering their king to remain in Mahanaim ("you shall not go out") and explaining that the king's life is worth more than the lives of half the troops. Assurance of his security in the city will bolster their morale. Their tactical recommendation recalls Ahithophel's good military advice that Absalom rejected, "I would strike the king alone" (17:2), since the death of the king would scatter the troops.[147] The counsel of David's troops contrasts sharply with Hushai's advice to Absalom (17:11), who, following that advice, marches out to his death.

David positions himself beside the gate, just as Eli, the priest at Shiloh, sat by the gate awaiting news of the battle between the Israelites and the Philistines (1 Sam 4:13, 18). From this location, the king issues a final order: "deal gently for my sake with the young man Absalom." In 2 Samuel 18:2 David spoke to his troops of his intention to join them in battle and they rejected his proposal. Now he gives an order to his three commanders, Joab, Abishai, and Ittai. But unlike the troops, these commanders, and, more specifically, Joab, offer no objection. Only later, when, in his longest speech in the David Narrative (19:5-7), Joab confronts David over his affection for Absalom, do we learn how he would have responded. For now he remains silent, recalling his exit from court after David's alliance with Abner (3:26). Back then Joab intended to kill Abner just as now he intends to kill Absalom if given the opportunity.

[146] As he was fleeing Jerusalem, David questioned Ittai's presence among his commanders, but Ittai swore an oath of loyalty to David (15:19-22).

[147] When the king of Aram prepares for battle against Ahab, king of Israel, and Jehoshaphat, king of Judah, he instructs his forces to focus their attack on King Ahab alone (1 Kgs 22:31).

David refers to Absalom as "the young man," a title that reaches back to 14:21 (see the discussion there), when David, after his encounter with the beguiling Tekoite widow, ordered Joab to bring "the young man," Absalom, back to Jerusalem. An obedient Joab executed the royal order at once. Now David, again referring to his son as "the young man," gives another order to Joab regarding Absalom: he is to bring him back alive. But this time Joab has no intention of following the order. The narrator ensures that we know that *all the troops* heard the command. In that audience is the warrior who will see Absalom caught in an oak tree and will refuse to kill him. When Joab scolds that soldier for failing to act, that soldier will remind Joab of David's original order (18:12). We leave David beside the gate, watching and waiting. At that gate, where he gave the order to protect his son's life, he will learn of his son's death (18:24), and later, in an upper chamber in the gate-house, he will mourn his loss (18:33).

David's final wish for Absalom reprises the leitmotif of the king's misguided affection for his son (see especially 15:7-9) that began when he kissed Absalom, who had returned from his self-imposed exile after he murdered his brother Amnon (14:33). David failed to observe Absalom's fomenting rebellion in Jerusalem (15:1-6), and he naïvely gave him leave to go to Hebron where the rebel organized the insurrection against his father. Now we are allowed a glimpse into the depths of David's affection. His final words to his troops are not an exhortation toward victory but rather an order on how his rebel son should be treated once captured. The king, seemingly oblivious to his son's treason, longs to see him again. When both Ahithophel and Hushai predicted David's death, Absalom expressed no remorse. But David, a tragic hero but for God's intervention, is both a king, who must crush the rebel forces, and a father, worried for his son's safety in the upcoming battle. For Joab, Absalom is a rebel leader who must be eliminated.

4.8.4.2 THE REBELS ARE DEFEATED AND ABSALOM IS EXECUTED (18:6-18)

The narrator's description of the battle is intended to underscore that God is fighting for David. The focus is on Absalom's capture and death and the end of the rebellion. Joab remained silent when David ordered him to deal gently with his son Absalom (18:5). Now we learn how Joab would have responded had he spoken up.

STRUCTURE

A. The battle in the forest (18:6-8)
  B. Joab's speech and Absalom's death (18:9-15)
A'. Absalom is buried in the forest (18:16-18)

4.8.4.2a The Battle in the Forest (18:6-8)

STRUCTURE

A. The forest (18:6)
  B.   The defeat (18:7)
A'. The forest (18:8)

The structure of this passage underscores the role that the forest played in Absalom's defeat.

COMMENTARY

David's forces march out from Mahanaim to meet Absalom's rebels in the forest of Ephraim. While the exact location of this wooded area is unknown, it must be on the east side of the Jordan River across from the region that is normally identified with Ephraim. This discrepancy does not seem to worry the narrator, who is often not concerned that we have a precise grasp of a scene's geography. Specific details about the battle are ignored (similar to the battle accounts in 2 Sam 8 and 10), and the narrator describes it not as a victory for David but as a defeat for the aggressors, drawing our attention to the vast extent of their losses: twenty thousand soldiers dead. Such exaggerated casualty counts remind us that God is fighting for David (see 8:1-14 and 10:18). The normal Hebrew idiom to describe the carnage is that the sword "eats" (*ʾkl*) its victim (see Deut 32:42; 2 Sam 2:26; 11:25; Isa 1:20; 31:8; and elsewhere). In this scene, the narrator reworks that metaphor so that "the forest" becomes the subject of the verb "to eat" (*ʾkl*), the only instance of such in the Bible (the NRSV translates the Hebrew into idiomatic English: "the forest claimed"). This strange language signals that David's forces received help from God, who used the forest to ensure a victory.[148] In Joshua 10:11, hailstones sent by God are more effective than the sword in killing the enemy. God's control over nature guarantees victory for David just as it did for Joshua. That forest, which consumed more than the sword did, is about to consume Absalom when he becomes entangled in a large oak tree, leaving him exposed to attack.

---

[148] In Isaiah 56:9 God summons the wild animals of the forest to "eat" (*ʾkl*) the people.

4.8.4.2b Joab's Speech and Absalom's Death (18:9-15)

The narrator, making short shrift of the battle scene, recounts the execution of the usurping king and, consequently, the end of the rebellion. But the center of this scene is not the rebel's execution but a dialogue between Joab and an anonymous soldier.

STRUCTURE

  A. Absalom is caught in the oak tree (18:9-10)
    B. The man speaks to Joab (18:10)
      C. What Joab promises he would do for the man (18:11)
        D. The king's order regarding Absalom is retold (18:12)
      C'. What the man thinks Joab would really do to him (18:13)
    B'. Joab responds to the man (18:14a)
  A'. Absalom dies in the oak tree (18:14b-15)

As the scene opens, Absalom becomes ensnared in an oak tree, and as it closes, Absalom dies in that same tree. But most of the scene is taken up by the confrontation between Joab and the man who has seen Absalom's predicament (five verses). In the C/C' sections there is a sharp contrast between what Joab promises the man and what the man really believes Joab would do to him were he to kill Absalom. By placing the repetition of David's final order to Joab at the center of the scene, the narrator draws our attention to Joab's determination to kill Absalom despite David's order.

COMMENTARY

Absalom is traveling on his mule, a symbol of his kingship,[149] through the forest of Ephraim that is consuming his forces more than the swords of David's fighters. While riding his royal mule, he encounters David's men. Alone and undefended, it would appear that Absalom turned to flee and his mule carried him under the snarled branches of an oak tree, leaving "his head caught fast in the oak." The reason for the narrator's lengthy description of Absalom's personal barbering in 14:25-26, which seemed quite odd at the time, becomes clear. Absalom cut his hair annu-

---

[149] When the news of Adonijah's usurpation comes to David, he orders Zadok, Nathan, and Benaiah to seat Solomon on his *mule* (1 Kgs 1:33, 38, 44) and to lead him down to the spring of Gihon for his coronation.

ally, weighing the trimmings and then announcing their weight. Now, as he tries to escape David's forces, the hair that he so treasured costs him his life when it entangles him in the jumbled branches of an oak tree, leaving him suspended in midair—an easy target. Had Absalom been less preoccupied with his hair and cut it more often, he would have passed unhindered under that tangle of oak branches. He is doomed by his own obsession. The narrator zeros in on the mule that continues trotting along apparently unaware that it has lost its passenger. The tragic and the comic embrace as we watch the royal mule exit the scene without its royal owner. Just as we laugh at Hamlet's banter with the gravediggers, though they are digging Ophelia's grave,[150] so the exiting mule without its king amuses, though the rebel leader is now ready for execution.

We leave Absalom hanging in the oak tree to attend the dialogue between Joab and an anonymous soldier, who, having reported on Absalom's entrapment, expects Joab to observe David's order to deal gently with Absalom, which, the soldier believes, means Absalom's safe return to his father. With Absalom suspended from the tree branches, Joab can easily accomplish David's will. But when Joab scolds the soldier for not executing the defenseless usurper, we are certain of his intention. Promising the soldier a reward, he tries to lure him to kill Absalom, thus saving him from having to do it himself. The precise value of the reward itself—ten pieces of silver and a belt—is difficult to assess today, but Joab presumes it is sufficient to convince the soldier to act. But the soldier declares that even if Joab were to increase the prize a hundredfold, he would not "raise his hand" against the king's son. This idiom (literally in Hebrew "to stretch out the hand") appears when David impedes Abishai from killing King Saul (1 Sam 26:9) and when he accuses the Amalekite messenger of doing just that (2 Sam 1:14). While not recognizing Absalom's kingship, the soldier does acknowledge that Absalom is a member of the royal family, and he reminds Joab that David's order regarding Absalom was heard by the entire army. (Did Joab need to be reminded?) His reprise is even more specific than David's original words (18:12): Joab should *protect* Absalom, whom he refers to as "the young man," the same designation that David used when he gave his order. This language

---

[150] *Hamlet*: What man dost thou dig it for?

Gravedigger: For no man, sir.

Hamlet: What woman, then?

Gravedigger: For none, neither.

Hamlet: Who is to be buried in't?

Gravedigger: One that was a woman, sir; but, rest her soul, she's dead. (act 5, sc. 1, lines 119–25)

reminds us that the national struggle between king and usurper is also a family struggle between father and son. For David, the rebel leader is his son and the leitmotif of David's misguided affection returns (see 18:1-6). For Joab, Absalom is an insurrectionist whose elimination is a national imperative; the father's affections are irrelevant.

Though the soldier's reiteration of David's order would seem to be sufficient for explaining why he will not be lured by Joab's reward, he adds gratuitous information that provides a critical insight into Joab's character. First, he explicitly labels the murder of Absalom a treasonous act (18:13), the same Hebrew term that the narrator used to describe the rebellion in 15:12. Furthermore, he believes that when the king hears of it, Joab will "stand aloof" from him.[151] The soldier recognizes that Joab would let him take the fall for murdering the king's son, and so he plainly charges his general with duplicity. He deems him a thoroughly ruthless leader. Thus, even though David's affection for his son is a tragic flaw that nearly destroys him, we can imagine that Joab's leadership would be far more brutal (see "Joab" in section 1.4.3 above). Since the soldier is not tempted by the reward, Joab cannot lose more time debating with him the merits of Absalom's execution. The rebel leader may soon free himself from the branches.

The story of Absalom's death comes in two stages. Joab takes three spears to thrust into Absalom's heart. The narrator ensures that we know that Absalom was still alive, and therefore Joab could have complied with the king's order, "deal gently" (David's words in 18:5), taking prisoner the king's helpless son. In the second stage of Absalom's death, Joab's armor-bearers complete the execution. Because of our empathy for David, we watch Absalom's death with a divided heart, knowing that Absalom would have killed his father without remorse, but also aware that David has had his mind on Absalom (see 14:1) for a long time. Joab dismisses David's affections as unwise and, given that we know that Absalom's intentions were to kill his father, he is right. As he murders the king's son, his power in David's court reaches its apex. On his deathbed, David will order Solomon to kill Joab (1 Kgs 2:6: "you should not let his grey hair go down to Sheol in peace") for the murders of Abner (2 Sam 3:27) and Amasa (20:10) done in peacetime. He will make no mention of Joab's murder of the undefended Absalom, perhaps because this death occurred in a military theater. We never learn if David came to know how Absalom died. But the soldier's remark that nothing is hidden from the king (18:13) suggests that he did.

---

[151] The Hebrew phrase, which appears only here in the Bible, is rather cryptic. Translated literally, it means, "you will take your stand from before."

4.8.4.2c Absalom Is Buried in the Forest (18:16-18)

With the leader of the rebellion dead, Joab blows the shofar and his troops immediately leave off the chase.[152] Ahithophel's advice has proven true (17:2-3): "I will strike down only the king, and I will bring all the people back to you," though ironically, the king that is struck down is the usurper, not David. Joab's armor-bearers, who killed Absalom, now take his body and cast it in a pit in the forest of Ephraim where the battle took place. Absalom's disgraceful burial contrasts with Ahithophel's, who, after his suicide, was interred in the tomb of his father (17:23). The Hebrew verb to describe Absalom's burial—*wayyašlîkû*—is derogatory. The NJPS translation, "flung," captures the sense a bit better than the NRSV's, "threw." The expression a "great heap of stones" occurs two other times in the Bible (Josh 7:26 and 8:29) where it also describes disgraceful burials. In Joshua 7 Israel is defeated at Ai because Achan had absconded with objects "devoted" to God (Josh 7:1). When his crime is discovered, Achan and his family are executed and a "great heap of stones" is thrown over Achan's corpse (Josh 7:26). In Joshua 8 the king of Ai is executed, his body is also flung down (*wayyašlîkû*), and a "great heap of stones" (translation mine) is placed over it (Josh 8:29). Thus, the heap of stones that covers Absalom's corpse puts him in the miserable company of the unfaithful Achan and the king of Ai, Joshua's enemy. This is the narrator's final judgment on Absalom and his rebellion.

The predictions of both Hushai and Ahithophel come to pass in a way that Absalom failed to perceive (see section 4.8.2.4 above, on 2 Sam 17:1-4). David was supposed to be the leader killed and all his forces put to flight (so Ahithophel in 17:2). Instead, Absalom is dead and his forces have fled. Hushai envisioned David hiding in a pit (17:9), in Hebrew, a *pahat*, a rare term that from Genesis to 2 Kings occurs only in Hushai's prediction and in this description of Absalom's hasty burial. Thus, in the end, it is not David who hides in a pit but Absalom's corpse that is flung into one. Absalom's story concludes with an aside that contrasts his expected royal burial with the ignominious burial that he received. He had prepared a monumental tomb in the King's Valley (perhaps a reference to the Kidron Valley, east of Jerusalem),[153] but instead, his corpse lies in a pit covered with a heap of stones. Absalom built it because he had no son to carry on his name, a statement that forgets the list of Absalom's children in 14:27. Our narrator is undisturbed by this apparent contradiction, and perhaps we are to suppose that by the time

---

[152] In 2:28 he did the same to call off the pursuit of Abner's men.

[153] McCarter, *II Samuel*, 409.

of Absalom's usurpation his three sons were dead.[154] The monument, the narrator reminds us, is still visible "to this day," the fourth time that this phrase appears in 2 Samuel (see 4:3). Whoever beholds Absalom's monument senses the irony that its owner is not buried inside. He had hoped the monument would preserve his memory, but he need not have worried. His story is enshrined in one of the world's best-known narratives.

4.8.4.3 News from the Battlefront Reaches David (18:19-33)

The news of the victory over the rebel forces gradually reaches the king, who is focused solely on the fate of his son. The first scene treats the question of informing David, the second reports the dialogue between David and the sentinel who has caught sight of the runners, and the third scene reports the news' arrival. This protracted account of how the bulletin traveled to David seems unnecessary; the narrator could have reported it in a single verse. But the leitmotif of David's misguided affection for Absalom, lurking in the background, now comes to center stage.

STRUCTURE

A. Joab, Ahimaaz, and the Cushite (18:19-23)
    B. David and the sentinel (18:24-27)
A'. David, Ahimaaz, and the Cushite (18:28-33)

In the first scene, Ahimaaz wants to run and inform David "that the Lord has delivered him from the power of his enemies" (18:19). In the final scene, the news reaches David when the Cushite informs him: "the Lord has vindicated you this day, delivering you from the power of all who rose up against you" (18:31). These two phrases, which frame these three scenes, do not convey the news that David wants to hear. The middle scene (B) delays the arrival of the report of Absalom's death, heightening the suspense while David's hopes rise. But we know what is coming, and so we watch for David's reaction.

---

[154] Hertzberg, *I and II Samuel*, 334–35.

4.8.4.3a Joab, Ahimaaz, and the Cushite (18:19-23)

STRUCTURE

A. Let me run (18:19)
    B. Joab's objection (18:20)
        C. The Cushite can go (18:21ab)
            D. The Cushite ran (8:21c)

A'. Let me run (18:22a)
    B'. Joab's objection (18:22bc)

A". I will run (18:23a)
    [B".*no objection*]
        C'. Run (18:23b)
            D'. Ahimaaz outran the Cushite (18:23c)

The scene is about "running" (the Hebrew root *rwṣ*, "to run," appears seven times) the "good tidings" (the Hebrew root *bśr*, "good news," appears five times) to David. There are three exchanges, each of which begins with Ahimaaz, who insists that he will "run" the news to David. In the first two exchanges Joab offers objections: (1) the king's son is dead and (2) you will not receive a reward. In the third exchange Joab no longer objects and Ahimaaz departs. The D/D' sections compare the two runners: Ahimaaz outpaces the Cushite.

COMMENTARY

With Absalom dead and the battle in abeyance, our thoughts turn to David, whom we left waiting at the gate of Mahanaim for news of his son's fate. Ahimaaz nominates himself as the one to run the news to David, announcing to Joab the contents of his message: the Lord has delivered David from his enemies. The Hebrew expression, "to deliver, to vindicate" (*špṭ* + *miyyad*), occurs three times in the Bible and two of them appear in this episode (18:19, 31). The third instance appears when David prays that the Lord vindicate him against Saul (1 Sam 24:15), after he absconds with a piece of Saul's cloak without exploiting the opportunity to kill him. Ahimaaz' words to Joab recall David's earlier prayer and suggest that just as God "vindicated him against" Saul, so God has "vindicated him against" Absalom and his rebel forces. But David does not see it this way.

The Hebrew root *bśr* (translated in the NRSV with "carry tidings") almost always denotes bringing *good* news. This word choice celebrates the victory over the rebels while, at the same time, it forgets that David's primary concern was for his son (2 Sam 18:5). So Joab reminds Ahimaaz that he cannot present himself to David as a herald of "good news" (*bĕśōrâ*) because the king's son is dead. In the next scene David will express his hope *three times* that the runners, sighted by the sentinel, bear "good news" (*bĕśōrâ*). The word *bĕśōrâ* draws our attention to the different interpretations of Absalom's defeat. For Joab, Ahimaaz, and the troops, their victory is good news, but for David, it is a calamity (the leitmotif). Joab has been closely monitoring the king's sentiments toward Absalom since Absalom's exile (14:1), and so he knows—and we know—how the king will react. Hence, when Joab appoints the Cushite as herald, instead of using the Hebrew root *bśr*, "to bring good tidings," he simply orders him to "inform" (*haggēd*) the king of his news.

But why is Ahimaaz so determined to run to David?[155] His unexplained motivations are not the main issue for the narrator, who instead focuses our attention on Joab's choice for a Cushite to run the news. We know that Ahimaaz, son of Zadok, is one of David's most loyal subjects. He risked his life, hiding in a well in Bahurim (17:18), to bring the intelligence of Absalom's military plans to David. Moreover, Ahimaaz, like the anonymous soldier whom Joab tried to entice to kill Absalom (18:11), must have heard David's final order to Joab since the narrator insists that *everyone* heard it (18:5). So perhaps Joab deters the enthusiastic Ahimaaz, because he is suspicious of how David's loyal messenger will report Absalom's death. Will he tell David that Joab disobeyed the royal order? In fact, when Ahimaaz reaches David he pretends not to know Absalom's fate. But the Cushite, a foreigner, seems to know nothing of David's original order in 18:5 regarding Absalom, and so when he reaches David, he enthusiastically announces (18:32), "May the enemies of my lord the king . . . be like that young man [Absalom]."

Once the Cushite has departed, Ahimaaz again announces his intention to run after the Cushite, without any mention of bringing "good news" to David. Joab questions Ahimaaz' motives, wondering why he is so eager when he can expect no reward (this reasoning reveals more about Joab's character: no reward, no need to run the news). The reader is equally confused about Ahimaaz' motives, though not as suspicious as Joab. In the end Ahimaaz insists and Joab consents, figuring that the Cushite will anticipate Ahimaaz' arrival. But the narrator reports that Ahimaaz took another path and outran the Cushite. He will be the first to reach David. What will he report about Absalom's death?

---

[155] His resolve increases as the scene unfolds: the cohortative + *nāʾ* in 18:19 becomes a *yiqtol* (*ʾārûṣ*) in 18:23.

4.8.4.3b David and the Sentinel (18:24-27)

The narrator teases us by delaying the arrival of the news with this account of the approaching messengers. When, in *Macbeth*, Macduff's wife and children are killed, the bard shifts to a scene with a prolonged dialogue between Malcolm and Macduff. We hang on Macduff's every word, knowing that the news of his family's execution is making its way toward him. When the messenger Ross comes on stage, Shakespeare has us wait still longer, raising the tension to an unbearable pitch until Macduff cries out: "Keep it not from me" (act 4, sc. 3, line 201). These words could well be on David's lips now.

STRUCTURE

Background: David is at the gate, where we left him (18:24a)

A. First sighting of a messenger (18:24b)
   B. The information is passed to the king (18:25a)
      C. The king reacts: it is good news (18:25b)

A'. Second sighting of a messenger (18:26a)
   B'. The information is passed to the gatekeeper (18:26b)
      C'. The king reacts: it is good news (18:26c)

A". Third sighting: the first messenger is Ahimaaz (18:27a)
      C". The king reacts: it is good news (18:27b)

This structure reveals the scene's repetitive nature that delays the arrival of the news while heightening David's hope for a positive report. A first messenger is spotted, and, because he is alone, he brings good news. A second messenger is spotted and he too is alone, so he too brings good news. When the first messenger, Ahimaaz, is recognized, David declares him "a good man," and thus he brings good news. The king expects to receive the good news about his son, and we are ready to observe his reaction.

COMMENTARY

The narrator opens the scene with background information that is contemporaneous (*wĕ X qātēl*) to the preceding events—the battle, Absalom's death, and Joab's decision regarding who should bring the news to David. During these scenes, David has not moved from his position at the gate whence he dispatched his troops with the special order regarding Absalom (18:5). We go up over the gate with the sentinel and look out with him toward the battle area (the forest of Ephraim). From our vantage point we can also see David below, awaiting the sentinel's word.

The narrator slows the action as we watch the sentinel raise his eyes and look out. The Hebrew expression in 18:24 (literally) "to lift up one's eyes and see and behold" focuses our attention on the object coming into view,[156] so that, with the sentinel, we too catch sight of a man running alone. The news is passed to David who notes that, since the runner is alone, he bears good news (the NRSV translates *běśôrâ* with "tidings"). Several soldiers fleeing toward Mahanaim could signal their escape from defeat. David's confidence that the news is good only heightens the tension in us. The narrator has us view the first runner drawing closer. A second runner is spotted and the sentinel passes the information to the gatekeeper. It is time to open the gate. David again trusts that it is good news. Noting the runner's gait, the sentinel believes the first runner to be Ahimaaz. David knows him to be a good man; he brought the news of Absalom's military plans to him (17:17-22). Thus the approaching news must be good. Our hearts are with David who is in for a shock.

4.8.4.3c David, Ahimaaz, and the Cushite (18:28-33)

STRUCTURE

A. The good news (18:28)
    B. David asks about Absalom's "shalom" (18:29a)
        C. The response (18:29b)
            D. The king's reaction (18:30)

A'. The good news (18:31)
    B'. David asks about Absalom's "shalom" (18:32a)
        C'. The response (18:32b)
            D'. The king's reaction (18:33)

The runners, who are bringing the "good news" to the king about the victory, are about to meet a father who only wants information about his son. The arrival of Ahimaaz, the first messenger, only delays the news of Absalom's fate, increasing our anxiety for the overdue arrival of the second messenger.

COMMENTARY

Ahimaaz outran the Cushite and so realized his original wish to bring the news to David. Greeting the king with obeisance, his first word,

---

[156] This expression appears for the first time in the Bible in Genesis 18:2 when Abraham raises his eyes and sees the three men who will announce to him the birth of Isaac.

"shalom" (*šālôm*), is patient of a few interpretations. It can be taken as an initial greeting, as reflected by the NAB and the NJB, or as an initial report of the victory, as in the NJPS, NRSV, and REB—"All is well!" The latter translation is more appropriate given that Ahimaaz' opening word recalls Ahithophel's wise advice to Absalom in 17:3: "You [Absalom] seek the life of only one man [David], and all the people will be at peace [*šālôm*]." Ahithophel's advice has proved true, though the shalom has come to David and not to Absalom as Ahithophel had intended. But the victory is not the shalom that most interests David, who immediately turns to the question of the shalom of his son (18:29): "Is it well [*šālôm*] with the young man Absalom?"

Ahimaaz then elaborates on the shalom that he has announced: God has won the battle for David, who now learns what we have known for some time: God heard David's prayer (15:31) and frustrated Absalom's capacity to discern between the counsel of Ahithophel and Hushai (17:14). The Hebrew expression that Ahimaaz borrows to announce the victory—God has "closed" (*sgr*, *piel*) David's enemies (NRSV: "[God] has delivered up the men")—appears on three occasions in the David Narrative. When Goliath laughs at the youthful David who comes to confront him, David expresses his confidence that God will "close" (*sgr*, *piel*) Goliath in his hand (1 Sam 17:46). In 1 Samuel 24:18 (MT 24:19), Saul, now aware that David just spared his life, admits that God "closed" (*sgr*) him in David's hand. Finally, in 1 Samuel 26:8, Abishai, seeing David's opportunity to assassinate Saul, tells him, "Today God has closed [*sgr*] your enemy in your hand" (translation mine). This phrase, which has traced God's fidelity to David, is now found on the lips of Ahimaaz. But David will have none of it. He wants to know about Absalom: "Is it well [*šālôm*] with the young man Absalom?" If "all is well," then, in David's mind, Absalom too must be well. He has completely forgotten that Absalom is the usurper who sought his life! Ahimaaz sidesteps the question, speaking about a mysterious "great tumult," perhaps a reference to the sound of the troops celebrating Absalom's murder. We assume that he knows Absalom's fate and opts not to reveal it, aware that David's final order to Joab, Abishai, and Ittai was ignored. The Cushite, a foreigner, can break that news. So we wait for him to arrive.

The leitmotif of David's misguided affections for Absalom is now at center stage. No word of thanks to God, no joy, no celebration is found on David's lips, even though he has learned that his prayer regarding Ahithophel's advice was fulfilled by God. Such fitting expressions of gratitude are supplanted by the father's fear for his son's fortunes in battle. When his interrogation of Ahimaaz proves fruitless, he tells him to stand aside as the Cushite comes onstage. The Cushite's first words announce the victory (again the Hebrew root *bśr* appears), and then he repeats Ahimaaz' words to Joab in 18:19 (*špṭ* + *miyyad*): "The LORD has vindicated you today from the hand of all those who rose against you" (translation mine). The news that should delight a king comes to a father who is worried only about his son. Thus, as soon as the Cushite has finished his announcement, he inquires again about the shalom of "the young man" Absalom. The Cushite, knowing nothing of David's order to his generals, an order heard by "everyone" but him, naïvely exclaims: "May the enemies of my lord the king . . . be like that young man."

Now the stage goes dark with a single spotlight shining on David as Ahimaaz and the Cushite fade into the shadows. The king who remained at the gate waiting for news of the battle was really more a father waiting to learn about his son's fate. Now he knows. The narrator chooses the Hebrew verb *rgz* to capture his anguish. This verb describes the "quaking" of the earth and the heavens (1 Sam 14:15; 2 Sam 22:8; Isa 5:25; Joel 2:10), and it refers to peoples trembling with fear (Isa 32:11; 64:2; Joel 2:1) and panic (Exod 15:14). Thus David, trembling, panicking, and quaking, ascends the gate as he weeps and calls out "my son" five times. He utters the universal prayer of parents who have lost a child: "Would that I had died instead of you." As a king, he strategized the defeat of his rebel son. As a father, he mourns his death. This fleeting glimpse into David's soul unmasks the inadequacy of language in such intense moments of human suffering. William Faulkner, in *Absalom, Absalom!*, bemoans language as a "meager and fragile thread . . . by which the little surface corners and edges of men's secret and solitary lives may be joined for an instant now and then before sinking back into the darkness where the spirit cried for the first time and was not heard and will cry for the last time and will not be heard then either."[157] For a passing moment we hear the cry of David's spirit as his secret and solitary life bubbles up to the surface. But Joab will soon arrive and the distraught father will sink back into his unspeakable solitude as his role as king reemerges.

4.8.4.4 JOAB CONFRONTS DAVID REGARDING ABSALOM (19:1-8ABC)

As the scene opens, the king-father remains above the gate bewailing his dead son. As it concludes, the king (the father in him now suppressed) descends from the gate to greet his troops.

---

[157] William Faulkner, *Absalom, Absalom!* (New York: Modern Library College Editions, 1936), 251.

STRUCTURE

A. Joab is informed (*ngd*; MT 19:2) that the king has not received
his troops (19:1-4)
   a. The king mourns his son (19:1)
       b. The victory becomes mourning (19:2a)
   a'. The king mourns his son (19:2b)
        b'. The victory becomes a defeat (19:3)
   a". The king mourns his son (19:4)

B. Joab's speech (19:5-7)
   Preamble: three accusations (19:5-6)
   c. Today David's loyalties are backward (19:5-6a)
       d. Today David has made clear (*ngd*; MT 19:7) his dis-
           loyalty to his troops (19:6b)
   c'. Today David's loyalties are backward (19:6c)
   Three imperatives: arise, go out, and speak (19:7a)
   Threat: if you do not obey, you will suffer disaster (19:7b)

A'. The troops are informed (*ngd*; MT 19:9) that David will receive them (19:8abc)

Joab, returning from the battle, is informed (*ngd*) of David's grief and
sees his troops (19:2 [MT 19:3]: *kol hāʿām*) reentering the city as if they
had been defeated. As the scene closes, David has ceased his mourning
and the troops (19:8 [MT 19:9]: *kol hāʿām*), informed (*ngd*) that David has
retaken his position at the gate, come to greet their king. Joab's speech
at the center of the scene changes David's disposition. He makes three
accusations, issues three imperatives, and then threatens David with
calamity. At the center of his accusations, Joab charges that David has
made clear (*ngd*) his disloyalty to his troops.

COMMENTARY

In this scene we hear the speech that Joab should have given when
David ordered him to be gentle with "the young man Absalom" (18:5).
Back then Joab made a strategic decision to remain silent, though he fully
intended to eliminate the rebel Absalom. Now the narrator brings us
into the chamber over the gate to attend the confrontation between the
victorious commander and his king, who, for the moment, is the father
of a dead son rather than the commander in chief. As the scene opens,
David is still above the gate crying out for Absalom, and Joab, returning
victoriously to Mahanaim and thus assuring David's safe return to Jerusalem, is informed of David's reaction (the Hebrew particle *hinnēh* [19:1;

MT 19:2], "behold," left untranslated in the NRSV, focuses our attention squarely on David in mourning). Joab recognizes that the king's grief has turned the victory celebration for the troops into a mourning ceremony. These same troops insisted that, for his protection, David remain safely in the city (18:3). Their triumphant return is nullified by the father's emotional state and so they steal into the city like thieves or defeated fugitives. The whole city can hear him crying out for his son Absalom, whom the victorious troops considered a notorious usurper.

Joab ascends to the room over the gate to make his longest speech in the David Narrative, and the relationship between these two main characters comes to a climax. Aware of David's attachment to Absalom (beginning in 14:1), Joab knew that David would not receive the full report from the battlefront—the victory plus Absalom's death—as good news. His response to Ahimaaz anticipated David's anguish (18:20: "You are not to carry tidings today . . . because the king's son is dead"). Entering the room over the gate, Joab meets Absalom's father who at the moment has little interest in the military victory, which for him is a personal tragedy. The general does not prostrate before the king in obeisance, as he did in 14:22, but immediately launches into his attack. The humiliation that the troops feel is the king's fault. They saved his life and the lives of his household (Joab lists the components of David's household, repeating the term "life" five times). The king loves those who hate him (Absalom and the rebels) and hates those who love him (Joab and the troops). (We know that Absalom would have killed David [17:1-4]). In Joab's mind, the king mourns a rebel usurper. Joab repeats the term "today" five times, insisting that the victory has come to the king *this very day* when the king can only cry about his dead son. He accuses David of wishing that Absalom were alive and his own troops were dead. Not quite true. David, as a father, only wishes that he were dead and his son Absalom were alive (18:33). He never prayed for a rebel victory. Joab exaggerates, rejecting the king's behavior for the sake of his troops.

Joab issues three imperatives to the king (get up, go out, and speak kindly), ordering the king about like one of his soldiers. He did the same after David's affair with Bathsheba and the murder of Uriah when he commanded David to muster the troops and conquer Rabbah (see the discussion of 12:26-31 in section 4.4.11 above). Joab insists that David repair the damage that all his weeping and howling have caused among the troops, threatening him with an oath before God! If he does not greet his troops, they will abandon him and a calamity will befall him worse than anything that has happened since his youth. Such a threat recalls several disasters that befell the youthful David, including Saul's murderous spear-throwing (1 Sam 18:11 and 19:10). The general is at the apex of his power (from which David will shortly remove him). Interestingly, he makes no mention of how Absalom died. In his present state, David does not need to know that Absalom could easily have been captured alive.

The mourning father offers Joab no response. He obeys, reassuming his role as king and descending to the gate whence he sent the troops into battle. The troops, who at the beginning of the scene were informed (Hebrew *ngd*) of the king's grief, now are informed (*ngd*) that the king has retaken his place at the gate. They come before him, but the scene is hardly one of victorious jubilation. This event concludes the leitmotif of David's misguided affections for Absalom. Despite Joab's scolding, we are left with the impression that David merely suppressed his fatherly affection for his beloved Absalom, the usurper who would have killed him.

4.8.5 David's Reentry into Jerusalem (19:8d–20:3)

The story of David's flight from Jerusalem to Mahanaim is now told in reverse as David "crosses over" the Jordan back to Jerusalem. The rebellion is gradually undone. The Hebrew verb *šwb*, "to return" (*qal*) and "to bring back" (*hiphil*), dominates this account.

4.8.5.1 DAVID AND THE REMNANTS OF THE REBELLION (19:8D-14)

The rebel leader is dead. But is the rebellion over? How will Absalom's forces and his allies in Jerusalem react to his death? After Saul's death, Abner crowned Ishbaal as Saul's successor, despite David's overtures to the people of Jabesh-gilead that they accept him as king (2:5-10). Will the Absalom faction in Jerusalem find a successor among their ranks? The narrator brings us back to the battlefield where Absalom's forces, apparently aware that their leader is dead, are fleeing to their homes. We might expect David's forces to be in hot pursuit of the enemy, just as they pursued and slaughtered the Philistines after David slew Goliath (1 Sam 17:51-53). Instead, the rebels seek a path of reconciliation.

4.8.5.1a The Discussion among the Rebels (19:8d-10)

STRUCTURE

The tribes of Israel flee to their homes (19:8d)

The people are quarrelling among themselves (19:9ab)
    Two arguments (19:9cd)

1. The king delivered us from our enemies
2. The king delivered us from the Philistines

The current situation (*wĕʿattâ*) (19:9e-10a)
1. David has fled the land
2. Absalom is dead

They resolve to bring the king back (19:10b)

COMMENTARY

The narrator interrupted the battle scene to report on how the news of Absalom's death reached David, the reception of that news, and the subsequent confrontation between the king and his commander. Now we return to the field where the rebel forces are in chaos. The news of their flight fulfills Ahithophel's prediction in 17:2, though it is Absalom's rebels who flee and not David's troops. What will these defeated fugitives decide about their rebellion? Will they regroup? We listen in as they wrangle among themselves. This is the first reference to the "tribes of Israel" since 15:10, when Absalom sowed the seeds of his revolt among them. Their deliberations, which reference how David saved them from their enemies and from the Philistines, reprise Abner's announcement to the "elders of Israel" years ago:

> Abner sent word to the elders of Israel, saying, "For some time past you have been seeking David as king over you. Now then bring it about; for the LORD has promised David: Through my servant David I will save[158] my people Israel from the hand of the Philistines, and from all their enemies." (3:17-18)

These rebels, once loyal to Absalom, now inadvertently bear witness to the fulfillment of the promise made to David that was announced by Abner when David assumed dominion over their territory that was once ruled by Saul.

The squabbling Israelites note that the king has fled "from the land" because of Absalom. David needs to *return* to the land, namely, to Jerusalem, and thus the leitmotif for the remainder of the story of Absalom's rebellion is introduced: "the king's return," or "the bringing back of the king" to Jerusalem. They acknowledge their crime: they anointed Absalom as king over themselves, implying that God, who chose Saul and David and had them anointed, was not consulted when they chose

---

[158] *BHS* reads, "he has saved," but many Hebrew manuscripts and versions read, "I will save."

Absalom. They mention Absalom's death in battle without any further details and conclude (*wĕ'attâ*) with a self-incriminating question, "Why do you say nothing about bringing the king back?" which reflects the internal debate within the "tribes of Israel," on whom we are eavesdropping. The question is not so much seeking information as it is rhetorical: "You should not be so silent about the king's reentry into the land." The scene ends abruptly, but we know that the rebel forces are once again loyal to David.

4.8.5.1b David Confronts the Elders of Judah (19:11-14)

STRUCTURE

   A. The king sends (*šlḥ*) word to the elders of Judah (19:11a)
      B. The message to the elders (19:11b-12)
         Question: Why should you . . . ?
         Arguments
            1. Word of Israel's loyalty has reached the king
            2. You are my bone and flesh
         Question: Why should you . . . ? (19:12b)

      B'. The message to Amasa (19:13)
         Argument: a rhetorical question: Are you not my bone
            and my flesh?
         Decree: an oath formula
   A'. Amasa sends (*šlḥ*) word back to the king (19:14)

The scene (A) begins with David sending word to his two allies in Jerusalem, Zadok and Abiathar. It concludes (A') with word coming back to David from Jerusalem from his new ally, Amasa. The center of the scene reports David's messages that succeed in winning over the elders of Judah.

COMMENTARY

The Hebrew construction *wĕ X qātal* that opens this scene allows the narrator to maintain two stages for the action, one on which the fleeing Israelites debate their allegiance to David (19:9-10) and the other on which David confronts the leadership in Jerusalem. Now that Absalom is dead, what do the elders of Judah in Jerusalem intend to do? Will David have to assail the city to reconquer it from the forces loyal to Absalom that are governing the city at present? David, who is still in Mahanaim, has two agents in Jerusalem, the priests Zadok and Abiathar, whom he ordered to return the ark of the covenant to the city with this prayer: "If I find favor in the eyes of the LORD, he will bring me back and let me see both it [the ark] and the place where it stays" (15:25). As David orchestrates his reentry, he knows that God has responded favorably to his plea.

During Absalom's usurpation, Zadok and Abiathar worked undercover in Jerusalem, gathering intelligence for David (15:27-28). With Absalom dead, they make themselves known to the Jerusalemite leadership (the "elders of Judah"), that is, to Absalom's allies in the city. David orders Zadok and Abiathar to question them: "Why should you be the *last* to return the king to his palace?" The operative word here is "last," as it subtly informs Absalom's Jerusalem/Judah faction that everyone else is already back with David. Though it can be read as a veiled threat, it seems that David's message intends to build an alliance rather than to intimidate. He reminds them: "you are my kin, you are my bone and flesh" (repeating the pronoun "you" [ʾattem] so as to underscore his relationship with these leaders once loyal to Absalom). This formula appeared in 5:1 when, upon Ishbaal's assassination, "all the tribes of Israel"—those once loyal to Saul—came to David to establish a pact with him, saying to him, "We are your bone and your flesh." Now David replays this conciliatory formula to establish a truce with those who abandoned him for Absalom. The victorious king seeks to reestablish his rule in Jerusalem without a military assault. Thus he invites (with some insistence) the elders of Judah to prepare for his return. He issues a second order to Zadok and Abiathar. They are to greet Amasa with the same conciliatory formula: "Are you not my bone and my flesh?" David is resolved to establish a truce with him, swearing an oath before God that Amasa will replace Joab as his military commander.

David's negotiations with the leadership that went over to Absalom's side are the first in a series of politically expedient decisions that he makes as he returns to Jerusalem. What better way to regain his authority in the city than to appeal to Absalom's supporters with a conciliatory offer of amnesty if they assist in his peaceful return to the city. High-ranking members of Jerusalem society, such as Amasa, participated in the rebellion (see 17:25) and so David's throne is still vulnerable. In fact, even before he reaches Jerusalem, Sheba son of Bichri will initiate another revolt against him (20:1). So the victorious king opts for reconciliation with his rivals, including Absalom's commander, Amasa, who is to replace Joab. The narrator is silent on David's motives for ousting Joab, but we can hardly help jumping to the conclusion that David knows how Absalom died. And if the rebels too know how Joab executed their defenseless leader, then his exclusion from David's court will further appease them. We learn later what Joab thinks of his ouster when he murders Amasa (20:10), but David will have the last word on that (1 Kgs

2:5-6). For now, Amasa brings the people of Judah, who had sided with Absalom, back over to David.

We shift from David at Mahanaim to inside the walls of Jerusalem where David's conciliatory missives meet with instant success. Amasa persuades the people of Judah to a unanimous support of David, and they send word to the king inviting him back to the city. Thus, the king will return to Jerusalem to see the ark of the covenant and its abode. His prayer as he fled the city (15:25-26) has been answered.

4.8.5.2 THE KING CROSSES BACK OVER THE JORDAN (19:15-40)

With Absalom's troops and the elders of Judah on his side, David starts back to Jerusalem. It was a dramatic moment during his flight when, having received word from Ahimaaz and Jonathan, David crossed the Jordan (17:22). Now, after much discussion about bringing the king back (*šwb, hiphil*) to Jerusalem, finally in 19:15 the king himself is the subject of the Hebrew verb "to return" (*šwb*); his reentry is underway. When David fled Jerusalem, Hushai (15:32) and Ziba (16:1) came to meet him (see the discussion of *liqraʾt*, "to meet," in section 4.8.1.2a above). Now the people of Judah (19:15), Shimei (19:16, 20), and Mephibosheth (19:24, 26) come to meet David (*liqraʾt* appears five times in 19:15-25) to assist with his return. This episode opens when David arrives at the Jordan River across from Gilgal (19:15), and it closes when, having crossed the Jordan, David reaches Gilgal (19:40).

4.8.5.2.1 The King Reaches the Jordan River across from Gilgal (19:15)

As the king reaches the east side of the Jordan River, the people of Judah come to Gilgal, a place along the west side of the Jordan River near Jericho, whither the Israelites arrived when, under Joshua's leadership, they crossed the Jordan River for the first time. During that crossing, Joshua, following God's order, took twelve stones from the middle of the river and built a monument to God's fidelity:

> Those twelve stones, which they had taken out of the Jordan, Joshua set up in Gilgal, saying to the Israelites, "When your children ask their parents in time to come, 'What do these stones mean?' then you shall let your children know, 'Israel crossed over the Jordan here on dry ground.'" (Josh 4:20-22)

Now the people of Judah rush to this sacred place to greet their returning king and to accompany him across the Jordan. David's arrival at Gilgal, like Joshua's arrival, marks God's fidelity to him.

4.8.5.2.2 The King Meets Individuals on His Way Back to Jerusalem (19:16-40)

The narrator opens up three stages: as David arrives at the Jordan (1) Shimei and Ziba hurry down to meet him (19:16-17); (2) at the same time Mephibosheth is coming down to explain himself (19:24); and (3) we also see Barzillai the Gileadite from Rogelim descending toward the Jordan to support David (19:31). Shimei (16:5-13) and Barzillai (17:27) met David as he was fleeing from Jerusalem; Mephibosheth was the subject of David's earlier conversation with Ziba (16:1-4). All three are now heading to meet the victorious king. Shimei, who symbolizes the most extreme faction of rebels, arrives first, and David, by granting him clemency, continues his conciliatory handling of Absalom's supporters as he reenters Jerusalem. In his decision regarding Mephibosheth, David maintains both his alliance with Ziba, once a member of Saul's household, and his agreement that Mephibosheth shall enjoy a pension in the royal palace. Finally, the reception of Barzillai the Gileadite, who aided David in his hour of need, signals the king's desire to reward those who sided with him during the rebellion.

4.8.5.2.2a Shimei, the People of Judah, and Ziba Rush to Meet David (19:16-18a)

At the beginning of the rebellion David ordered his courtiers to hurry out of Jerusalem (15:14). Now the roles are reversed as Shimei hurries to meet the victorious king, whom he earlier accused of having murdered members of Saul's household (16:7-8). How will David treat him? He is traveling with a large contingent from Judah and Benjamin, perhaps the faction that sided with him and Absalom against David. With them is Ziba, another person once loyal to Saul, along with his retinue of fifteen sons and twenty servants, whom we last met in 9:10 when David ordered them to work Saul's lands for Mephibosheth's benefit. From those lands Ziba had provided generous provisions to the then fugitive king (16:1). When David inquired about Mephibosheth's absence, Ziba concocted the unlikely tale that Mephibosheth, Saul's grandson, was hoping to succeed to Saul's throne. When Mephibosheth tells his side of the story to David, Ziba, who we suppose is present, offers no rebuttal. The narrator closes this reintroduction of Shimei and Ziba by focusing on their motivations: they are hurrying to the Jordan to be of assistance to the king. Translating the Hebrew literally: they want to do "the good" (in Hebrew *haṭṭôb*) in the king's eyes. This comment recalls the prayer David uttered as Shimei pelted him with stones when he beseeched God to return to him "good" (*ṭôbâ*; 16:12) instead of Shimei's cursing. This "good" is now coming to David and, ironically, it is Shimei himself who is bringing it! There is a marvelous alliteration in 19:18 (MT 19:19) that highlights the significance of David's "crossing over" the Jordan: *wĕʿăbĕrâ hāʿăbārâ laʿăbîr*. Translated literally, it reads: "the crossing was crossing over to make cross over [the king's household]." Though the Hebrew text of this verse has been recognized as problematic, it appears to underscore the leitmotif of David's crossing out of the land and his reentry (see section 4.8 above).

4.8.5.2.2b David and Shimei (19:18b-23)

STRUCTURE

  A. Shimei comes onstage (19:18b)
    B. Shimei's plea (19:19-20a)
      C. Shimei confesses that David is king *this day* (19:20bc)
        D. Abishai addresses David (19:21)
        D'. David responds to Abishai (19:22a)
      C'. David asserts that he is king *this day* (19:22b)
    B'. The king's decree to Shimei (19:23)
  A'. [No response from or exit for Shimei]

This structure follows closely that of David's first encounter with Shimei in 16:5-13: Shimei cursed, Abishai condemned him, but David prevented Abishai from executing Shimei. This time Shimei pleads for forgiveness, Abishai again condemns him, and again David prevents Abishai from killing him.

COMMENTARY

Just as David is about to cross the Jordan, Shimei prostrates before him in sharp contrast with his previous stone throwing and reviling. In their first meeting he had scorned David as a murderer and labeled him a scoundrel. Now he honors him with the titles "my lord the king" (twice), the very title with which Abishai addressed David when Shimei reviled him (16:9: "Why should this dead dog curse my lord the king?"). Shimei beseeches the victorious king with two imperatives: don't hold me guilty and don't remember what I did. His survival depends on the king's readiness to forgive him, and so he confesses his sin (19:20) and, in his bid for clemency, points out that he is the first of the house of Joseph (a reference to the territories of Ephraim and Manasseh, a region once governed by Saul) to meet the king.

Before the king can rule on Shimei's plea, Abishai intervenes just as he did when Shimei confronted David the last time (16:9). He charges Shimei with treason because he has reviled the Lord's anointed. But, just as David rejected Abishai's advice to kill the reviling Shimei (16:10-11), so now he rejects Abishai's advice to kill the penitent Shimei, responding as he did in 16:10: "What have I to do with you, you sons of Zeruiah?" On this occasion, however, he adds, "that you should today become an adversary to me." David recognizes that Abishai's advice would further destabilize his fragile rule. The rebellion won over key members of David's court (Ahithophel) and family (Amasa), and, though Absalom was defeated, David's reemerging reign is hardly secure (even before he reaches his palace in Jerusalem he will have another rebellion on his hands [20:1-2]). As he travels home, he must solidify his power, and avenging himself against his opponents hardly serves that goal.

His rebuke of Abishai (at the center of this scene) and his earlier ousting of Joab (19:13) signal that David has jettisoned the sons of Zeruiah from his inner council and has rejected their politics of revenge that has already led to the death of Absalom. He asserts his authority over Israel, namely, over those factions in the "tribes of Israel" that supported Absalom (see 15:10 and 19:9). His oath to Shimei that he shall not die for his participation in the revolt against the crown informs all of Absalom's allies, among whom Shimei was the most ardent, that they will receive clemency, not vengeance. The narrator closes the scene without a word from Shimei, shifting abruptly to Mephibosheth's arrival.

But this is not the last we hear of Shimei. As he lay dying, David remembers Shimei's insults, forgets Shimei's plea for mercy, and rewrites the oath he swore to him in this scene:

> There is also with you Shimei son of Gera, the Benjaminite from Bahurim, who cursed me with a terrible curse on the day when I went to Mahanaim; but when he came down to meet me at the Jordan, I swore to him by the LORD, "I will not put you to death with the sword." (1 Kgs 2:8)

He then recommends that Solomon not allow Shimei to die a natural death. By 1 Kings 2 David's reign (and Solomon's) is secure and thus the reasons for which David granted Shimei clemency no longer exist. So Solomon places Shimei under house arrest on pain of death (1 Kgs 2:36). When Shimei violates his house arrest by pursuing his escaped slaves to Gath, Solomon orders him executed. His final words to Shimei (1 Kgs 2:45) reprise God's promise to David in 2 Samuel 7:13: "the throne of David shall be established before the LORD forever." This is the very promise that Shimei denied when he reviled David.

4.8.5.2.2c David Meets Mephibosheth (19:24-30)

As Ziba and Shimei are rushing to meet (*liqra᾽t*) David (19:16-18), Mephibosheth is descending from Jerusalem to the Jordan. The Hebrew construction *wĕ X qātal* raises the curtain on this second stage of near simultaneous action.

STRUCTURE

A. Mephibosheth's loyalty to David (19:24)
  B. The king's question (19:25)
    C. Mephibosheth's explanation
      1. What Ziba did to him (19:26-27a)
      2. What David did for him (19:27b-28)
  B'. The king's decision (19:29)
A'. Mephibosheth's loyal response (19:30)

The scene opens with signs of Mephibosheth's fidelity to David (his unkempt appearance) that confute Ziba's accusation in 16:3. It concludes with Mephibosheth declaring that his loyalty to David never wavered (his only concern was the king's safe return). The B/B' sections present the king's question and his final decision. At the center of the passage is Mephibosheth's speech that comes in two parts. In the first part he responds to Ziba's accusations and in the second part he commends David for his kindness to him that began in 2 Samuel 9.

COMMENTARY

While fleeing Jerusalem, David met Ziba (16:1-4), who claimed that Mephibosheth, Jonathan's son, had refused to join the king's exodus from Jerusalem because he supposed that Absalom would return Saul's kingdom to him. At the time, Ziba's story seemed difficult to swallow. Would David's usurping son want to release part of his realm to Saul's descendant? But the fugitive David, needing allies in that hour, believed Ziba and transferred all of Mephibosheth's land into Ziba's hands. At that time, the fugitive king's decision remained without effect. But now that the victorious king is returning to Jerusalem, Ziba can assert his ownership over all of Mephibosheth's property. The narrator never pronounces on the veracity of Ziba's accusations, but several details suggest that Ziba was lying.

The scene opens by focusing our attention on Mephibosheth's personal grooming since David fled Jerusalem. He has not taken care of his feet, trimmed his beard, or washed his clothes the entire period of David's exile. While fleeing Jerusalem, David and his supporters expressed their humiliation with gestures of public lament (see the discussions in sections 4.8.1.1d and 4.8.1.1f above). The king went along weeping and walking barefoot with his head covered (15:30). Hushai, a strong ally of

David, appeared before him with his clothes torn (15:32)—an expression of solidarity with his humiliated sovereign. Now the narrator pauses to describe Mephibosheth's appearance and we learn that he too has participated in the humiliation of his liege, even though he remained in Jerusalem.[159] Mephibosheth's unwashed clothes may also express his penance for his failure to accompany David. Now, as the victorious king returns, he wants him to see his repentant gestures and to hear his version of events. The narrator's description of Mephibosheth's penance is the first piece of evidence against Ziba's accusations.

When David met Ziba he questioned him about Mephibosheth's whereabouts (16:3). David now poses that question directly to Mephibosheth, who seems to be aware of Ziba's version of events. (Had Ziba informed Mephibosheth that David had transferred all his property to him?) In a short speech Mephibosheth contrasts Ziba's lies with David's generosity toward him. It was indeed his intention to escape Jerusalem with the king, but Ziba tricked him. He reminds David that, because of his disability, he needed Ziba's help to mount his donkey after he ordered it saddled. Suddenly, those donkeys that Ziba gifted to the fleeing David come to mind (16:1-2). Should Mephibosheth have been riding on one of them? Did Ziba accord David the very donkey upon which Mephibosheth was intending to flee Jerusalem? Four times Mephibosheth venerates David with the title "my lord my king," perhaps worried that David will still side with Ziba and he will be executed as a traitor. We stand alongside David trying to decide between Ziba's accusation and Mephibosheth's defense. Did Mephibosheth really hope that the rebel Absalom would return Saul's kingdom to him?

In the second half of his speech, Mephibosheth extols David's treatment of him. David is "like an angel of God." This is the third and final time that this simile is applied to David. In 1 Samuel 29:9, Achish, king of Gath, used it to describe David's innocence and honesty before him. The wise woman of Tekoa complimented his acumen with this simile (2 Sam 14:17) and went on to say that David had wisdom like that of an angel of God (14:20), though, because she had just beguiled him, her words betrayed a flattering tone. Now Mephibosheth employs this image to describe David's kindness to him as he recommends that the king do to him whatever he thinks is best, reminding David of the clemency he granted to him when he brought him into the royal household (2 Sam 9). He concludes by asking an obvious, rhetorical question: "What right do I still have to plead to the king?"

---

[159] Not caring for one's physical appearance expresses lament and humiliation. The humiliated "Lady Jerusalem" is portrayed as sitting in filthy clothes (Lam 1:9).

David interrupts Mephibosheth's speech to announce his decision. He and Ziba will divide the land. It is a rather strange verdict given that the evidence points to a mendacious Ziba. But the decision should be interpreted as another sign of the king's attempt to reestablish his shaky reign. Ziba was an important Saulide courtier, someone whom David cannot afford to alienate now. So, even if we suspect Ziba of treachery, political expediency requires that he will retain a portion of Mephibosheth's land. Mephibosheth responds by declaring that he no longer has any interest in his grandfather's lands since the king has returned home. He was rushing to greet the king in order to clear his slandered name, not to reverse the royal decree about his lands. We never hear David's reaction to Mephibosheth's statement of fealty. More important, we never hear from Ziba, though he too was rushing to greet the returning king (19:17). His silence convicts him of duplicity.

4.8.5.2.2d David and Barzillai; David Crosses the Jordan (19:31-39)

STRUCTURE

A. Barzillai comes to cross the Jordan with the king (19:31)
  B. What Barzillai did for David (19:32)
    C. The king's request to Barzillai: "Come over with me . . ." (19:33)
      D. Barzillai declines: six rhetorical questions (19:34-36)
    C'. Barzillai's requests for the king (19:37)
  B'. What the king will do for Barzillai (19:38)
A'. The king crosses the Jordan with Chimham and Barzillai (19:39)

As the scene opens Barzillai intends to cross the Jordan with King David. As it closes David has crossed the Jordan with Barzillai (he conceded to go that far with the king in 19:36a) and Chimham. The B/B' sections compare what Barzillai did for the fugitive David to what the victorious David will do for Barzillai. The C/C' sections compare David's request to Barzillai with Barzillai's request to David. The center of the text is a series of rhetorical questions that underscore Barzillai's age and ask why the king should be so generous to him. These questions reveal the purpose of this scene: the king will reward those who remained loyal to him during the rebellion.

COMMENTARY

Barzillai comes on the scene with the intention of escorting the king across the Jordan River. The Hebrew construction *wĕ X qātal* (19:31; MT

19:32) allows the narrator to present Barzillai's journey to David as simultaneous with the travels of Shimei and Mephibosheth. We are meant to feel the rush of people coming to greet the victorious king. Barzillai, a wealthy, old Gileadite, is on the west side of the Jordan with David. He, Shobi son of Nahash, and Machir son of Ammiel were David's most generous benefactors, providing food and furniture to the fugitive king upon his arrival in Mahanaim (17:27-29). Immediately, David invites this faithful ally to join him in crossing the Jordan and then to travel on with him to Jerusalem. The narrator plays on the Hebrew root *kll* ("to provide for"): Barzillai *provided for* (19:32; MT 19:33) David during his flight, so now David will *provide for* (19:33; MT 19:34) Barzillai as an expression of his gratitude. This wordplay captures the purpose of this scene: David is loyal to those who supported him during his flight from Absalom.

With a series of rhetorical questions, the octogenarian discreetly declines the king's largess. He would be a dreadful royal counselor as his discernment skills have become dull in his old age. Moreover, his age prevents him from enjoying life in David's court—the king's table and court entertainment. His fifth question functions as the response to the previous three: he would only be a burden to the king. He consents to travel with David a short distance across the Jordan. His final rhetorical question reveals why the narrator wants us to hear his speech. Translated literally it reads: "Why should the king reward me that reward?" The cognate accusative here underscores the king's intention to reward those who assisted him during Absalom's rebellion. David would even reward someone who, by his own admission, cannot be a valuable asset at court. But this is another strategic move by David to strengthen the reestablishment of his rule. As he granted clemency to his enemies, so he will compensate his allies. Barzillai requests permission from David to live out the rest of his life in his hometown and suggests that David pass his reward to Chimham, who appears only here in the Bible. Barzillai bids the king: "Do for him [Chimham] whatever *you* [David] think best." David betters Barzillai's request, adding, "all that you desire of me [literally: choose for me], I will do for you" (19:38). David's bountiful response to Barzillai, beyond what was asked, signals that the returning king plans to reward his allies. As the scene concludes, David kisses and blesses Barzillai (an expression of their alliance), who returns home.

4.8.5.2.3 David Crosses over the Jordan to Gilgal (19:40)

David has been ready to cross the Jordan since 19:15, but his travels were interrupted by his encounters with Shimei, Mephibosheth, and Barzillai. The significance of his Jordan crossing and arrival at Gilgal recalls the first crossing of the Jordan by Joshua and the Israelites (Josh 3). Just as God maintained his promise to those first Israelites by bringing them into the Promised Land at Gilgal, so God has maintained the promise announced to David in 2 Samuel 7:16 ("Your house and your kingdom shall be made sure forever before me; your throne shall be established forever") by bringing him across the Jordan to Gilgal. During the crossing the people of Judah and Israel come back on stage (see section 4.8.5.2 above). While *all* the people of Judah are with David, only *half* the people of Israel facilitate the king's crossing. The narrator's observation leaps off the page. Why is Israel not unanimously present? This detail bridges us to the next scene.

4.8.5.3 Israel and Judah Quarrel; David Returns to Jerusalem with Another Rebellion Underway (19:41–20:2)

Before the story of Absalom's rebellion comes to a conclusion (David has not yet reentered Jerusalem), a new crisis arises: Israel secedes from Davidic rule. This scene lays the foundation for a short-lived rebellion that foreshadows the permanent division of David's kingdom in 1 Kings 12.

STRUCTURE

A. Israel and Judah (19:41-42)
    B. Israel has ten shares in David (19:43abc)
        C. The narrator's aside: Judah's harshness leads to secession (19:43d)
    B'. Israel has no portion in David (20:1)
A'. Israel and Judah (20:2)

This scene opens with a dispute between Israel and Judah over their affiliation with David (A section). As it closes, Israel and Judah are no longer united under Davidic rule (A' section). In the B section, the people of Israel claim their "ten shares" in the king. In the B' section, those ten shares abandon the king. At the center of the text the narrator comments on a critical question in the history of Israel and Judah: what led to the secession of Israel? He appears to cast the blame on the people of Judah.

COMMENTARY

Before David reaches Jerusalem, his shaky reign is beset by another, albeit short-lived, rebellion. When he began his journey back to Jerusalem, the "tribes of Israel" decided to come back under his sway (19:9-10). At the same time, David's missives to the rebels in Jerusalem, the Judah faction, were well received. Now these two blocs, Israel and Judah, confront one another. The *hinnēh* clause (19:41; MT 19:42) at the beginning of this scene focuses our attention on "all the people of Israel" (not just the *half* that accompanied him across the Jordan in 19:40), who approach the king with their question: "Why have our kindred the people of Judah stolen you away, and brought the king and his household over the Jordan?" The use of this Hebrew verb *gnb*, translated in the NRSV with "stolen," suggests that David's flight from Jerusalem was more like a kidnapping.[160] Are the "people of Israel" trying to rewrite history?

Before the king can answer the charge, the people of Judah intervene. Ignoring Israel's strange accusation, they justify their actions: the king is their kin, though they have not exploited their relationship to him. Their turn of phrase—"Have we eaten at all at the king's expense?"—appears in 9:10 when David assured Mephibosheth of a place at the king's table (9:7), meaning that his expenses would be covered by the palace. Judah denies that they have helped themselves to the king's largess. The people of Israel counter Judah's claim on David by affirming that they have ten shares (in Hebrew: "ten hands") in the king (Judah has only one). For the first time "Israel" is associated with the "ten tribes" that will eventually comprise the "northern kingdom." In 1 Kings 11:29-36, after the narrator reviews Solomon's transgressions (1 Kgs 11:6: "Solomon did what was evil in the sight of the LORD"), the prophet Ahijah meets Jeroboam, the future king of the northern kingdom and, tearing his new cloak into twelve pieces, orders Jeroboam to pick up ten of them. The garment symbolizes David's kingdom, and the ten pieces that Jeroboam collects represent the ten tribes that will comprise his dominion (see 1 Kgs 12:16).

The antagonism intensifies when the people of Israel claim that Judah has despised them (2 Sam 19:43; MT 19:44), employing the same Hebrew verb (*qll*) that described Shimei's abuse of David in 16:5-13. Israel reminds Judah that they were the first to want to bring the king back (19:9-10). The narrator now intervenes with a critical observation at the center of this scene: the words of Judah were "harsher" (*qšh*) than the words of Israel. This language foreshadows the permanent secession of these ten tribes (the northern kingdom) from Judah (the southern kingdom). In 1 Kings 12, Israel, under the leadership of Jeroboam, complains to Rehoboam, Solomon's successor, of their harsh (1 Kgs 12:4: *qšh*) treatment under Solomon and seeks to negotiate new terms of their service. When Rehoboam (the future king of Judah) rejects their complaint, the

---

[160] This Hebrew verb, *gnb*, "to kidnap," appears in Exod 21:16: "Whoever kidnaps [*gnb*] a person, whether that person has been sold or is still held in possession, shall be put to death."

ten tribes secede. In the conflict between Israel and Judah in this scene, Judah's harsh words (19:43d) will incite the ten tribes of Israel to an unsuccessful attempt at secession. Later, Solomon's harsh treatment of them will lead to a permanent division of the Davidic kingdom. This nascent conflict may also explain why, in 19:40, only *half* the people of Israel are present for the king's reentry. David has not regained the trust of all Israel.

The narrator, employing the Hebrew construction *wĕ X qātēl* (20:1), introduces a contemporaneous event: Sheba son of Bichri observes this exchange between Israel and Judah. Even though Judah provoked Israel with harsh words, Sheba is a scoundrel for fomenting rebellion among Israel. He is also a Benjaminite, from the same tribe as Shimei son of Gera (and King Saul), who reviled David during the flight from Jerusalem (16:11). Israel had just insisted that it had ten shares in David's kingdom to Judah's one when Sheba the secessionist declared that they have no interest at all in Davidic rule. With a blast of the trumpet, Sheba signals that Israel's troops must depart. His speech is nearly identical to the Israelites' future speech of secession to King Rehoboam (1 Kgs 12:16): "What share do we have in David? We have no inheritance in the son of Jesse. To your tents, O Israel!" Sheba's rebellion is different from Absalom's, who garnered support among the "tribes of Israel" (2 Sam 15:10) but also enjoyed support among some Judahites (Ahithophel came from Giloh, a town in Judah). This rebellion of the ten tribes of Israel signals an uncertain future for a unified Davidic kingdom.

4.8.5.4 ABSALOM'S REBELLION IS OVER (20:3)

Upon his return to the palace, David deals with the lingering question of his ten concubines, whose sequestering in this brief scene signals the end of Absalom's insurrection. Their story began in 15:16 when David, abandoning his palace to the rebels, left these ten women to manage the royal household. To solidify his usurpation, Absalom had sexual relations with them in a tent on the palace roof (see 16:22). They symbolize Absalom's short-lived reign and David's temporary defeat. The returning king places them under guard and does not have sexual relationships with them (nor will anyone else) so that there will be no question as to the paternity of any offspring, if one of them has become pregnant by Absalom. When, in 1 Kings 2:13-25 Adonijah seeks David's concubine Abishag for a wife, Solomon orders his execution (see also Ishbaal's accusation against Abner in 2 Sam 3:7). Thus David does not dismiss them from his court nor leave them free to marry. Their house arrest is mitigated by David's care for them (the Hebrew verb *kll* is the same verb used to describe how Barzillai provided for David and David offered to provide for Barzillai in 19:32-33; MT 19:33-34). As the ten concubines are relocated to their new quarters, the curtain drops on Absalom's rebellion.

4.9 Sheba's Rebellion and Joab's Return to Power (20:4-22)

While making his way back to Jerusalem, David dismissed Joab as his chief military officer (19:13), replacing him with Amasa. But when the narrator lists David's courtiers, immediately after this episode, Joab is back in his position (20:23), though David is never said to have made this reappointment. Absent as this episode opens, Joab reappears onstage without comment from the narrator and effects his own reappointment. As the episode concludes, it is Joab, not Abishai, who sounds the trumpet to break off the assault against Abel of Beth-maacah. The story of Sheba's rebellion recounts how Joab returned to power.

STRUCTURE

    A. Amasa leaves Jerusalem (20:4-5)
        B. The pursuit of Sheba begins (20:6-7)
            C. The execution of Amasa (20:8-10a)
        B'. The pursuit of Sheba continues (20:10b)
    A'. Joab replaces Amasa (20:11-12)
        B". The pursuit of Sheba continues (20:13)
            C'. The execution of Sheba (20:14-22a)
        B'''. The pursuit of Sheba ends (20:22b)
    A". Joab returns to Jerusalem (20:22c)

The inclusion (A/A") underscores the key development in this episode: Amasa sets out from Jerusalem but Joab returns. This development is punctuated by the ongoing pursuit of Sheba (B sections). Two turning points (C/C') report two executions. The first allows Joab to return to power while the second allows him to return victorious to Jerusalem.

4.9.1 Amasa Leaves Jerusalem and the Pursuit of Sheba Begins (20:4-7)

Having just settled the final detail of Absalom's rebellion (sequestering the ten concubines), David confronts a new insurrection. Ten tribes of Israel have seceded under Sheba's leadership. David summons his commander, Amasa, whom he recently appointed to replace Joab (19:13). Once loyal to Absalom, Amasa is now ready to do the king's bidding. He is to muster conscripts in Judah and return to Jerusalem within three days. The general heads off to execute the royal order, but the third day passes without his return. Should we be suspicious of Amasa, who was among the rebels seeking David's life? The narrator teases us by withholding any comment on Amasa's tardiness, though David does not seem to suspect that Amasa's delay bodes sedition. But he cannot wait as the delay only provides Sheba time to solidify his insurrection. Were Sheba to capture "fortified cities," as David fears, he would have a strategic base from which to govern and wage war. At the end of the Bathsheba affair, Joab threatened to take Rabbah, a fortified city, and put his own name on it if David did not join the battle (12:28). Amasa's delay now poses a similar threat: if Sheba establishes his authority in several Israelite cities, his rebellion will be difficult to defeat.

So David rouses Abishai, Joab's brother. He can hardly appeal to Joab, whom he just dismissed from his court. On several occasions the king has distanced himself from the violence of these two brothers, the "sons of Zeruiah" (see 3:39; 16:10; and 19:22). But now he desperately needs the military skills of one of them as he worries that Sheba may prove to be a greater threat than Absalom. Aware of Israel's history through to the end of 2 Kings, we can hear a tragic irony in his words. Sheba's rebellion is markedly different from Absalom's, since Absalom had garnered support among various factions inside and outside of David's court. But Sheba's revolt involves the "ten tribes of Israel" against the tribe of Judah. While this secession from Davidic rule will be short-lived (soon the wise woman from Abel of Beth-maacah will be tossing Sheba's head over the wall of her city), Sheba's insurrection foreshadows the future rebellion under Jeroboam (1 Kgs 11:26-40; 12:12-19), which will, as David now speculates in regard to Sheba's rebellion, prove far worse for the Davidic line than Absalom's rebellion. It will leave his dominion permanently sundered.

David tells Abishai to take his "lord's" men (2 Sam 20:6), which we assume is a reference to David's men, but in 20:7 we learn that the men under Abishai's command are in fact "Joab's men." This striking shift foreshadows what is to come: Joab, without the king's permission, intends to retake command of the troops that the narrator appears to have already given back to him. Only in the next verse (20:8), as the pursuit of Sheba begins, do we learn that Joab is now with his troops. The Cherethites and the Pelethites (see the discussion in section 3.8 above), who accompanied David on his flight from Jerusalem (15:18), also join in the pursuit.

4.9.2 Joab Murders Amasa and Reassumes His Rank as General (20:8-13)

The scene shifts not to the pursuit of Sheba, as we expect, but to the account of Amasa's murder and Joab's reemergence as David's general. Abishai's troops have traveled about ten kilometers (six miles) northwest of Jerusalem to Gibeon and are in Benjaminite territory, an area once ruled by Saul and now part of the territory of the "ten tribes" that Sheba has led into rebellion. As David's troops approach the great stone at Gibeon, Amasa is coming to greet them, having remained loyal to David. Had he betrayed the king and joined Sheba's insurrection he would hardly have approached David's forces undefended. We await an explanation for his tardiness, but Joab prevents us from hearing it. He is only interested in Amasa's elimination and allowing his rival to speak would only complicate matters. As Joab and Amasa approach one another, the narrator slows down the action so that we focus on the sword fastened to Joab's waist. The attention the narrator gives to Joab's weapon recalls the assassination of Eglon, king of Moab (Judg 3:15-23). In Judges 3:16 the narrator describes the left-handed Ehud fastening his sword on his right hip under his garments. Thus, the entire time that Ehud meets with Eglon, we are observing the sword and awaiting its revelation. In this scene, as Joab comes into view, the narrator notes the position of the sword as in a thriller movie when the camera focuses on the murder weapon. So, with one eye on that sword, we nervously observe Joab's fake salutation, "Are you well, my brother?" followed by a kiss as Joab's right hand rises to grasp Amasa's beard.

Unfortunately, the Hebrew text leaves us perplexed as to the precise sequence of the events that follow. The NRSV in 20:8 (together with most English translations) follows the Hebrew: "As he [Joab] went forward it [the sword] fell out." The problem is that if the sword, on its own accord, fell out of its sheath, how could Amasa have failed to notice it crashing to the ground? And, if Joab's sword has fallen to the ground, how does it find its way back into his hand in 20:10 for Amasa's murder? Ancient interpreters were equally confused by the Hebrew text. Josephus offers an explanation:

> When Amasa approached to greet him, Joab caused the sword to fall, of itself, out of its sheath, and then lifted it up from the ground.[161]

The author of the Syriac (Peshitta) version, who probably had a Hebrew text similar to what we find in the Masoretic Text, rendered 2 Samuel 20:8 as follows:

---

[161] *Ant.VII.11.7.* This translation is taken from Christopher Begg, *Judean Antiquities Book 5–7: Translation and Commentary*, ed. S. Mason, Flavius Josephus: Translation and Commentary 4 (Leiden: Brill, 2005), 282.

> They came to the great rock in Gibeon and Amasa came in front of them.
> Joab was girt with his armor, and his sword was fastened and set on his
> hips like a dagger. As he went forth, his hand fell on his sword.

Though the Syriac version is normally faithful to its Hebrew original,
the translator could not present the Hebrew text to his audience without
some adjustment. Accordingly, he has Joab's hand "fall" onto his sword
and the description of the sword "falling" to the ground is eliminated.
But these textual quandaries do not obfuscate the main event: Joab speedily dispatched his rival.

Amasa's murder echoes that of Abner's (3:27). Both soldiers are victims
of Joab, both are stabbed in the stomach, and in both cases Joab draws his
unsuspecting victim close to himself for the murder. Both men were allied
with David, and Joab's action disrupts David's maneuvers to secure his
regime in a time of instability. In Abner's case, we can guess Joab's intention after his confrontation with David (3:23-25). In Amasa's case, we only
learn of Joab's scheme as he stabs Amasa, though the narrator's ominous
attention to Joab's sword warned of the violence. In an instant, Amasa is
murdered, a victim of Joab's duplicity. The slow-motion narration and the
fact that Joab does not allow Amasa to explain his delayed return to David
confirm that the murder was unjustified. Joab simply wanted to return to
power, and we would expect nothing less from him (recall Joab's maneuver
to entice one of his soldiers to kill Absalom in 18:9-15). David had been
trying to gain the loyalty of Absalom's rebels by appointing Amasa as
commander of the military, a strategy that Joab has just ruined. Joab is now
back in David's court, but David does not know it. The narrator is silent
on whether Abishai played a role in bringing his brother back on board.

With Amasa wallowing in his blood, Joab and his brother Abishai continue their pursuit after Sheba. But will the troops follow Joab? David's
forces have just witnessed an act of treason—the assassination of the king's
choice to lead his army. Will they abandon their pursuit of Sheba and return
to David to denounce Amasa's murder? Immediately, one of Joab's back-
ers, apparently someone who would have supported Amasa's execution,
takes his stand beside the corpse (so the NJPS translation) and challenges
the troops. The narrator presents three simultaneously occurring events:

20:10b: Joab and Abishai went after Sheba (*wĕ X qātal*)
20:11:   But a man stood beside Amasa's corpse (*wĕ X qātal*)
20:12:   Meanwhile Amasa was wallowing in his blood (*wĕ X qātēl*)

We imagine Joab and Abishai already offstage in hot pursuit while the
troops remain onstage beside their leader who lies in a pool of blood. Then
"one of Joab's men" (the NJPS's translation of Hebrew *naʿar* in 20:11 with

"henchmen" gets to the heart of the matter) speaks to the troops: "Whoever favors Joab, and whoever is for David, let him follow Joab." If the troops are loyal to David, then they should be for Joab. But the corpse of David's nominee for chief military officer is still lying on the road that the troops must travel and its presence brings them to a halt. So Joab's henchman transfers Amasa's remains to a field and covers them.[162] Now the troops, no longer seeing the corpse, follow Joab and the pursuit of Sheba continues.

4.9.3 Sheba Dies and Joab Returns to Jerusalem (20:14-22)

Sheba son of Bichri passes through "all the tribes of Israel," the territory of his new dominion, seeking refuge. He garners the support of the Beerites, often emended to Bichrites (so most English versions), referring to Sheba's own clan members. When Sheba reaches the town of Abel Beth-maacah, David's fears (20:6) come true: Sheba has found protection in a fortified city. Abel Beth-maacah is a northern city, perhaps near Dan, and is part of the territory that Sheba intends to govern. It seems that the city, for the moment, has accepted the rebels or has been overwhelmed by them. But this is the last we hear of Sheba; no last word is afforded him before the wise woman executes him. The narrator is far more interested in what happens along the wall since this episode is about Joab, not about Sheba. Arriving at Abel Beth-maacah, Joab's troops lay siege to the city, constructing a rampart against its walls. The people of Abel Beth-maacah do not seem to defend their city, and the wise woman's questions suggest that they know nothing of Sheba's rebellion against David. Joab treats the city as he did Amasa: just as he summarily eliminated Amasa, so he will destroy this city. The brutal killer is about to meet his foil.

Once Joab has constructed the siege ramp (20:15), we await the breach of the wall and the fall of the city. Instead, we hear the voice of a woman from within. We know precious little about her, not even her name, but we know she is wise. Her character recalls the wise Tekoite in 14:2. Both are clever women who intervene in the lives of men more powerful than themselves to alter the course of events. The wise Tekoite woman manipulates the king into swearing an oath (14:11) and then confronts him regarding the status of his exiled son Absalom (14:13). The wise woman

---

[162] The ancient narrator does not explain the problem (a taboo?) of Amasa's corpse on the road for the modern reader. The scene recalls how the spot where Asahel (a commander) was murdered also brought people to a halt (2:23). Now, the body of their commander, Amasa, lies on the road, and it has the same impact on "all the people" (that is, the troops).

of Abel Beth-maacah confronts the king's chief military commander as to the purpose of his siege, ordering him to appear before her. Surprisingly, Joab complies. In a rather comic exchange, the commanding woman refers to herself as "your maidservant" (20:17) as she addresses the general whom she has just summoned to appear before her. This staging increases our anticipation for her speech. The Hebrew verb *šmˁ*, "to listen," appears four times (20:16-17). Twice the wise woman calls on Joab's army to listen. When Joab arrives, she tells him to listen too, and Joab responds that he is. Listening is not one of Joab's strengths, and the wise woman does well to counsel him.

The wise woman's intervention has already delayed the city's destruction. Now the rampart building ceases as the troops listen to the dialogue between their general and the sage. She reminds Joab how it was once said that people would make inquiry in Abel (Beth-maacah) in order to settle disputes. Her city is a city of peacemakers among whom she is the leading citizen (20:19). This city was "listened to" in the past as it will be now as she announces the agreement: Joab gets Sheba's head and Abel Beth-maacah is spared. She closes with a highly charged accusation: "Why are you trying to swallow up the inheritance of the LORD?" It is not any old city that Joab is besieging; he has attacked the Lord's inheritance, a designation that Joab does not dispute. The expression "inheritance" (*naḥălâ*) in reference to the land of Israel occurs in the song of Moses and Miriam (Exod 15:1-21): God brought the people into the land and planted them on his own inheritance (Exod 15:17: *naḥălâ*). The term appears often in the Bible to refer to the land given by God to the Israelites (Deut 4:21). Deuteronomy 15:4 reminds Israel of this special relationship: "There will, however, be no one in need among you, because the LORD is sure to bless you in the land that the LORD your God is giving you as a possession [*naḥălâ*] to occupy." (Israel only has tenure of the land—not ownership.) By appealing to this charged language, the wise woman stops Joab cold. The reckless general is not merely launching an attack against a northern city in Israel. He is trying to destroy God's inheritance. Joab denies her charge, swearing an oath that such was not his intention: "Far be it from me, far be it, that I should swallow up or destroy!" (2 Sam 20:20). But he is lying. The narrator in 20:15 employs the Hebrew word "destroy" to describe Joab's attack (literally): "the entire army that was with Joab was *destroying* by bringing down the wall" (translation mine). The wise woman is no fool—she has correctly assessed Joab's intention, and her wisdom has successfully halted his assault and saved her city.

The general presents his case before the woman who is really in charge. She should know that Sheba raised his hand against the king, he explains, and he only seeks the rebel's life. She agrees to throw Sheba's head to Joab from the wall—the very wall that Joab sought to destroy, and the matter is speedily settled. With the leader of the insurrection dead, Joab sounds the retreat and the troops disperse while Joab returns to Jerusalem. This is the third time in the David Narrative that Joab sounds the trumpet to signal the end of a battle (see 2:28 and 18:16). He is back in charge. The episode concludes despite a major loose end: what was David's reaction to Joab's reentry into Jerusalem with Sheba's head in hand? David was expecting Abishai and Amasa (where is Abishai?). He certainly did not expect Joab. How did he react to the report that his strategic choice to lead his army after Absalom's rebellion had been executed by the deposed general? When David says nothing we recall his words after Joab eliminated Abner: "Today I am powerless, even though anointed king; these men, the sons of Zeruiah [a reference to Joab], are too violent for me" (3:39). Only as he lies dying will we learn of his reaction to Amasa's murder when, in his final instruction to his successor, Solomon, he urges Joab's execution:

> Moreover you know also what Joab son of Zeruiah did to me, how he dealt with the two commanders of the armies of Israel, Abner son of Ner, and Amasa son of Jether, whom he murdered, retaliating in time of peace for blood that had been shed in war, and putting the blood of war on the belt around his waist, and on the sandals on his feet. Act therefore according to your wisdom, but do not let his gray head go down to Sheol in peace. (1 Kgs 2:5-6)

David cites the murders of Abner and Amasa as the reason for Joab's elimination since Joab murdered in "peacetime." He could have also admitted that on both occasions these murders harmed his strategy to secure his throne. Joab was also responsible for the death of David's beloved Absalom (2 Sam 18:14), but the narrator is silent as to how much David knows about that execution, leaving us to speculate on David's hidden motives. David bequeaths the Joab problem to his successor because, as he confessed in 3:39, he lacked the power to handle it himself, having been significantly weakened by two rebellions, both of which required Joab's military skill to keep him on his throne. But his dying wish in 1 Kings 2:5-6 suggests that had he been able to, he would have executed Joab. For now, David has no choice but to accept Joab as his general.

4.10 David's Court: A Second List (20:23-26)

This is the second time the narrator pauses the storyline to name David's courtiers. This list should be read in conjunction with the previous one in 8:15-18 where the function of these lists within the David

Narrative was discussed (section 3.8, above). The first list appeared after David had established his capital in Jerusalem, had relocated the ark of the covenant to his city, and had subdued the surrounding threats to his rule. His reign was sufficiently secure to establish a government. This second list of courtiers has a similar function. David has just survived two rebellions and this list of appointments to David's post-rebellion court signals that his rule is once again secure.

Most of the characters in this list were mentioned in the previous one. Joab, commander of the army, heads the list as he has just regained his post (without David's permission). He is by far the most powerful member of the court, rivaling even David's authority. Benaiah, who will later replace Joab (see 1 Kgs 2:34-35), is still captain of the Cherethites and the Pelethites, the troops that remained loyal to David through Absalom's rebellion (15:18). Jehoshaphat is still the royal recorder. The priests in this list are Zadok and Abiathar, the same names that should be read in 8:17. Ira the Jairite is not mentioned in the earlier list and does not appear again in the David Narrative.[163] Sheva, David's secretary, was called Seraiah in 8:17. We have either a different person or a variation on the spelling of the same person's name (the two names are much more alike in Hebrew than in English). The narrator makes no comment on this minor incongruence. What is important is that David has reestablished his court.

Adoram, the chief of "forced labor," was not mentioned in the first list. The idea of "forced labor" appears in Exodus 1:11 immediately after the Pharaoh "who knew not Joseph" ascends to the Egyptian throne. He appoints bosses of "forced labor" over the Israelites to oppress them. With his reign securely reestablished, David is able to exploit forced laborers and Adoram is to be their boss. Adoram's appointment lasts through to 1 Kings 12:18 when King Rehoboam sends him to negotiate with the recently seceded northern tribes. But the northern rebels kill Adoram, making him the first victim of the periodic wars between the northern and southern kingdoms. Adoram's inclusion in this list, like Sheba's words of rebellion in 2 Samuel 20:1, foreshadows the catastrophe that looms in the not-too-distant future. After quashing this first attempt at secession, David appoints the person whose eventual murder will signal the permanent division of his kingdom.

---

[163] Ira the Jairite is sometimes thought to be the same person as Ira the Ithrite in 23:38 (Jairite and Ithrite could be confused in Hebrew). But it is unlikely that Ira, the priest, is also Ira, the warrior, who was a member of the "Thirty" (23:24-39).

Chapter 5

ACT 5: DAVID'S PUBLIC LIFE DRAWS TO A CLOSE
2 SAMUEL 21–24

5.1 Introduction

The final four chapters of 2 Samuel seem to lack cohesiveness, and, because they stand apart from the preceding episodes, they are sometimes labeled an "appendix."[1] No other section of the David Narrative demands more collaboration from the reader in the quest for a meaningful interpretation. Some of the events recounted in these chapters seem to be more closely related to the consolidation of Davidic rule in Jerusalem (2 Sam 5). Shimei's charges against David (16:8: "the LORD has avenged on all of you the blood of the house of Saul, in whose place you have reigned") and David's question in 9:1 ("Is there still anyone left of the house of Saul?") seem to presuppose that Saul's sons had already been executed under David's order, an event that is recounted in these chapters (21:1-14).[2] But the David Narrative is not a chronicle of events. It is a portrait of a king and his reign. Thus, though some of these final episodes may be out of chronological order, as many scholars argue,

---

[1] They have been called an "appendix" since they do not belong to what Leonhard Rost identified as the original narratives (The History of David's Rise [1 Sam 16:14–2 Sam 5:25] and The Succession Narrative [2 Samuel 9–20; 1 Kings 1–2]); see Leonhard Rost, *Die Überlieferung von der Thronnachfolge Davids*, Beiträge zur Wissenschaft vom Alten und Neuen Testament 42 (Stuttgart: Kohlhammer, 1926). McCarter labeled them a "miscellany, a repository of diverse materials pertinent to the reign of David"; see P. Kyle McCarter, *II Samuel*, Anchor Bible 9 (Garden City, NY: Doubleday, 1984), 16.

[2] Hans W. Hertzberg, *I and II Samuel*, trans. J. S. Bowden (Philadelphia: Westminster Press, 1960), 381.

their location near the end of the David Narrative serves to complete the narrator's depiction of his protagonist, and that objective prevails over the chronological discrepancies that we notice while reading act 5.

Scholars have long been in agreement that these episodes, despite their apparent disaggregation, are carefully crafted into a concentric, three-tiered structure:[3]

> A. National crisis (21:1-14)
>   B. Lists of David's warriors and accounts of heroic deeds
>   (21:15-22)
>   C. Poem (22:1-51)
>   C'. Poem (23:1-7)
>   B'. Lists of David's warriors and accounts of heroic deeds
>   (23:8-39)
> A'. National crisis (24:1-25)

The purpose of these chapters within the David Narrative is made explicit at the center of this concentric structure in the incipit to David's second poem (23:1): "These are the last words of David." This notice, coming from a laconic narrator who has given no indication of David's age in the previous episodes, informs us that the David Narrative is drawing to a close. Our hero still has two significant deeds to accomplish in his life, and they are woven around his penultimate (22:1-51) and ultimate (23:1-7) testaments given in two poems. Thus, these chapters should not be reduced to an "appendix," which the *Oxford English Dictionary* defines as "not essential to a text's completeness."[4] Rather, they represent the first of the narrator's final brush strokes to his masterwork:

> A. David's penultimate public act (21:1-14)
>   B. David's decline and his exit from military affairs (21:15-22)
>   C. A penultimate testament: David sings a song (22:1-51)
>   C'. David's ultimate testament (23:1-7)
>   B'. David's decline and his exit from military affairs (23:8-39)
> A'. David's final public act (24:1-25)

After these episodes all that remains for the narrator to tell is the story of King Solomon's succession. Then King David can die (1 Kgs 1–2).

---

[3] André Caquot and Philippe de Robert, *Les Livres de Samuel*, Commentaire de l'Ancien Testament 6 (Genève: Labor et Fides, 1994), 578–79; McCarter, *II Samuel*, 18–19; Hertzberg, *I and II Samuel*, 415.

[4] *Oxford English Dictionary* (Oxford: Oxford University Press, 2004), *s.v.* "appendix."

5.2 David's Penultimate Public Act: A Final Contrast between David and Saul (21:1-14)

This episode, which initiates the narrator's closing portrait of David, reprises several events from 1 and 2 Samuel. It reaches back to Saul's rise to power and his rescue of the people of Jabesh-gilead (1 Sam 9–11). It also looks back to David's pact with Jonathan (1 Sam 20:12-17; 20:42), and it recalls Saul's death and his stealthy burial by the people of Jabesh-gilead (1 Sam 31). David, who long ago lamented his fallen predecessor's demise (2 Sam 1:17-27), now provides him with a proper burial—a final illustration of his enduring loyalty to the king he succeeded. This episode replays the contrast between David and Saul with respect to their fidelity to their oaths, a theme that was signaled by the first allusions to David in 1 Samuel 13:14 ("the LORD has sought out a man after his own heart") and 15:28 ("The LORD has torn the kingdom of Israel from you this very day, and has given it to a neighbor of yours, who is better than you"). Various events in the David Narrative have illustrated how David proved to be a king more faithful to God than Saul. This episode offers a final example: Saul tried to kill the Gibeonites, violating an oath that Israel had sworn to them (2 Sam 21:2), but David preserved Mephibosheth alive (21:7), according to the oath he had sworn to Jonathan. In both cases, the narrator digresses to remind us of these two oaths, one broken and one observed. Now David, as one of his final acts, has to resolve the trouble that Saul's infidelity left behind.

STRUCTURE

    A. God is angry (21:1)
        B. David seeks to resolve Saul's crime (flashback) (21:2-4)
            C. The Gibeonites' demand (21:5-6)
                D. David is faithful to his oath to Jonathan (21:7)
            C'. The Gibeonites' demand is met (21:8-9)
        B'. David accords Saul proper burial (flashback) (21:10-14c)
    A'. God is no longer angry (21:14d)

The episode's concentric structure puts David's fidelity to his oath to Jonathan at the center. By contrast, Saul violated the oath made to the Gibeonites. God's initial anger over the bloodguilt and its resolution form the inclusion (A/A'). The episode is balanced by two flashbacks (B/B'). The first flashback recounts Saul's violation of the oath that the Israelites had sworn to the Gibeonites. The second recounts his death and humiliation—the price he paid for his infidelity to God's command.

COMMENTARY

The opening phrase of this episode, "Now in the days of David," indicates a break in the narrative, though no notice of David's regnal year is given. Since the drought is in its third year, at least three years have passed since Sheba's rebellion. Biblical droughts signal divine discontent since precipitation is within God's providence, as the flood story so clearly teaches (Gen 7:4). The psalmist often sings of God who provides the rain (Pss 68:9; 135:7; 147:8), and in Deuteronomy 11:13-17 obedience to God's commandments means rain and, consequently, a good harvest. Worshiping other gods means drought and death:

> Take care, or you will be seduced into turning away, serving other gods and worshiping them, for then the anger of the LORD will be kindled against you and he will shut up the heavens, so that there will be no rain and the land will yield no fruit; then you will perish quickly off the good land that the LORD is giving you. (Deut 11:16-17)

When Elijah appears in 1 Kings 17:1, King Ahab has been up to no good, building an altar to Baal and erecting a sacred pole (1 Kgs 16:31-34). Elijah conveys the divine reaction: there shall be no rain until Elijah, who stands in God's presence, says so. In 1 Kings 17–18 the drought's effects are narrated: a Zarephath widow prepares to kill herself and her son (1 Kgs 17:12), and Ahab and Obadiah search for water for their languishing animals (1 Kgs 18:5).

Since God has shut up the heavens, David needs to know why, and so he "seeks the face of the LORD" (a literal translation of the Hebrew). This Hebrew expression appears in Hosea 5:15 when God warns the Israelites that, once they acknowledge their guilt, they will seek his face. Thus, David is doing more than merely inquiring of God as he has done in the past for help with battle strategies. He is seeking forgiveness, but he needs God to point out his fault. God immediately discloses the reason for the drought: there is a bloodguilt on Saul's house. Even though David is not the guilty party, he has to make atonement to resolve the crisis. The question of "bloodguilt" responsibility has been a regular feature in 2 Samuel. When David ordered the execution of the Amalekite messenger who brought the news of Saul's death (2 Sam 1:16), he declared himself innocent of that blood. After Joab murdered Abner, again David declared himself innocent (see the discussion in section 2.7 above). The shedding of innocent blood gives the "avenger of blood" the right to take the life of the murderer:

> But if someone at enmity with another lies in wait and attacks and takes the life of that person, and flees into one of these cities [cities of refuge], then the elders of the killer's city shall send to have the culprit taken from there and handed over to the avenger of blood to be put to death. (Deut 19:11-12)

God now informs David that the Gibeonites have this right.

Though Saul was already dead before 2 Samuel began, his memory has cast its shadow over David's reign. Michal, Saul's daughter, upbraided David for his behavior during the ceremonies that transferred the ark to Jerusalem. She recognized the ark's relocation to David's royal city (6:16, 20-23) as a consolidation of David's power over against her father's descendants. David brought Mephibosheth, Saul's grandson (Jonathan's son) into his court (2 Sam 9). And during Absalom's rebellion, Shimei upbraided David with the residual resentments of those who had remained loyal to Saul (16:8). The story of this drought represents the penultimate time that Saul's reign is recalled. (The very last mention of Saul in the historical books comes in 22:1.) Once his bones are laid to rest in his ancestral tomb, the shadow of his memory fades away.

Since we have no idea as to Saul's crime against the Gibeonites that incurred this bloodguilt, the narrator provides a flashback. The association of the Gibeonites with the Amorites provides little light on the matter as Saul is not said to have attacked either group. The Gibeonites appeared for the first time in Joshua 9–10. Having learned of the defeat of Jericho and Ai, they tricked Joshua into thinking that they were not a local people (hence not subject to extermination from the land [Josh 1:1-5]). Joshua engaged them in a treaty (his first after crossing into the land), and the Israelite leaders swore an oath to preserve them alive (Josh 9:15). Thus, even without knowing the specifics of Saul's assault on the Gibeonites, his attack against them directly violated this treaty and the oath sworn in the first days of the Israelites' presence in the land. Its violation must be atoned for, and since Saul is dead, the culpability falls on his descendants.

That the Gibeonites are a remnant of the Amorites is entirely new information in the Bible.[5] Whatever their roots, what is at stake is that their presence in the land of Israel was guaranteed by an oath. Saul violated this oath by seeking to eliminate them, and the residual effect of this violation is the drought. (This flashback offers further evidence to justify God's choice for David over Saul.) The narrator's explanation for Saul's actions—that they were due to his "zeal" (*bĕqannō'tô*[6]) for Israel and Judah—suggests a mitigating circumstance that lessens the gravity of Saul's crime.

---

[5] In the book of Joshua, the Gibeonites seek protection from the Amorites (Josh 10:6) and Joshua obliges them.

[6] Hebrew *qn'* can range in meaning from a positive nuance ("zeal") to a negative one ("jealousy," as in Gen 37:11). Here, since Saul's motivation is to fulfill a divine command, translators regularly and rightly highlight the positive connotation.

David moves to resolve the bloodguilt and thus end the three-year drought. His question to the Gibeonites is not "What do *you* want?" but "What can *I* do for you? How can *I* atone?" The problem is his. He needs to act so that the Gibeonites will "bless the heritage of the LORD." The term "heritage" (*naḥălâ*) hearkens back to the Deuteronomic covenant: God created the people of Israel for himself as a possession (*naḥălâ*; Deut 4:20) and bestowed the land upon them. Saul's violation of the Gibeonites has led to a drought so that the land, the Lord's heritage, is no longer fruitful. The divine promise is out of joint, and David has to set it right: the Gibeonites must bless the Lord's heritage. The Gibeonites respond that it is not a matter of money; nor do they want to attack and kill in Israel. In effect, they are telling David, "It is not up to us to resolve your drought." They did not come to David with a claim for vengeance and thus they refuse to extract the blood vengeance themselves. David gets the point and repeats his initial question: "What do you want *me* to do for you?" He needs to expiate before God Saul's crime against the Gibeonites. The Gibeonites remind David of the charge against Saul, that he tried to exterminate them from the borders of Israel, and then they demand seven of Saul's descendants, sons or grandsons will do, as an atonement for the bloodguilt. What they intend to do, namely, the precise torture implied in the verb *yqʿ*, is not clear ("impale" in most English translations). Driver suggests that it may refer to a form of hanging.[7] This verb appears in Numbers 25:4 in a passage that parallels some aspects of 2 Samuel 21:1-14. In Numbers 25:1-5 God declares that the leaders who have worshiped Baal are to be "impaled before the LORD" (the expression "before the LORD" also appears in 2 Sam 21:6). In Numbers 25:1-5, the issue is apostasy; in 2 Samuel 21:1-14 it is oath violation. In both scenes God is directly involved and the executions are acts of propitiation.

David, without objection, proceeds with the selection of Saul's descendants to be transferred to the Gibeonites. When David spares Jonathan's son Mephibosheth, the narrator flashes back to the oath between David and Jonathan so that we might take note of David's fidelity to that oath (21:7). This digression, which could have been entirely omitted, underscores the contrast between Saul and David: Saul violated Israel's oath but David was faithful to his oath (note the repetition of the term "oath" [*šĕbûʿâ*] from 21:2 [*šbʿ*]) that he swore to Jonathan long ago:

> Then Jonathan said to David, "Go in peace, since both of us have sworn [*šbʿ*] in the name of the LORD, saying, 'The LORD shall be between me and you, and between my descendants and your descendants, forever.'" He got up and left; and Jonathan went into the city. (1 Sam 20:42)

---

[7] Samuel R. Driver, *Notes on the Hebrew Text and the Topography of the Books of Samuel* (Oxford: Clarendon, 1913), 351.

David surrenders Rizpah's two sons to the Gibeonites. Rizpah was last mentioned in 2 Samuel 3:7 when Ishbaal accused Abner of having sexual relations with her, a charge never verified. Now we learn that she bore Saul two sons. David also takes the five sons of Merab,[8] the woman who was to be his wife until Saul reneged on his promise (yet another of Saul's infidelities, see 1 Sam 18:17-19). Her sons should have been David's offspring, but instead they are the offspring of Adriel, son of Barzillai the Meholathite. Now David hands those sons over to atone for the bloodguilt Saul brought on his family. Certainly their elimination only solidifies David's power over the remnants of the Saulide regime, but the narrator makes no allusion to this collateral benefit for David.

No description of the actual "impaling" or "hanging" is provided. Instead, the narrator focuses on the season of their execution. Rizpah, mother of two of the victims, protects the corpses from the birds of the air and the beasts of the field. Her worry about what animals might do to these corpses recalls Goliath's threat to the young David (1 Sam 17:44): "Come to me, and I will give your flesh to the birds of the air and to the wild animals of the field." The ultimate retribution against an enemy is the desecration of his corpse by savage animals (recall Jezebel's fate [2 Kgs 9:36]).[9] Since the corpses remain exposed until the rains come, Rizpah guards them from this sacrilege. Does a primitive ritual of propitiation during a time of drought underlie the scene? Probably so, but the narrator is not interested in these earlier traditions. The event has been recast into a question of atonement for a bloodguilt, which the narrator exploits as a final chance to contrast David and Saul.

Rizpah's action reminds David of the current burial state of Saul's remains. He will imitate her reverence for the bodies of Saul's descendants by retrieving Saul's bones. Like the story of Saul's oath violation, the narrator provides a flashback to remind the audience of Saul's burial, but, unlike the previous flashback (21:2), these events are known to the reader. In 1 Samuel 31 Saul lost his battle with the Philistines, and he and his three sons, Jonathan, Abinadab, and Malchishua, died in the battle. Now David retrieves their remains from the people of Jabesh-gilead (about eighty kilometers [fifty miles] northeast of Jerusalem), who had buried them under "the tamarisk tree" in their territory (1 Sam 31:13).[10]

---

[8] The MT reads "Michal" instead of "Merab," but the ancient translations are correct in reading "Merab," since she and not Michal was the wife of Adriel (see 1 Sam 18:17-19).

[9] One of the curses prescribed in Deuteronomy 28:26 is that the corpses of those who fail to observe the covenant will be exposed to scavenging animals.

[10] The narrator, focusing on the bones of Saul and Jonathan, forgets that Saul's other two sons, Abinadab and Malchishua, were killed as well (1 Sam 31:2).

The people of Jabesh-gilead (also known as Jabesh) have figured prominently in Saul's life and now, as final respects are paid to him, they are back onstage. At the beginning of Saul's rise to power (1 Sam 11), it was the people of Jabesh whom Saul rescued from the clutches of Nahash. They remained loyal to Saul as demonstrated by the risk they took to retrieve his corpse from its disgraceful exposure on the walls of Beth-shan. Their influence in Saul's court becomes clear in 2 Samuel 2:4b-7 when David seeks an alliance with them after Saul's death. Now, as Saul is mentioned in the historical books for the penultimate time, the narrator remembers the people of Jabesh-gilead. They function as a grand inclusion to the Saul-David Narrative: the people whom Saul rescued at the beginning of his reign now hand over his remains to his successor who is nearing the end of his reign.

David collects these bones (no objection from the people of Jabesh-gilead) and gathers them together with the seven descendants of Saul that were recently impaled. Thus, the remains of Saul and his family are reunited in burial at Zela, in the tomb of their father Kish. The location of Zela is unknown, but it is one of the towns of Benjamin (Josh 18:28), Saul's tribe of origin. Thus, the story of Saul's life has come to a proper conclusion with his royal burial in the family tomb. The last phrase, "They did all that the king commanded," reminds us that David is behind this decorous burial—a final testimony to his unwavering loyalty toward Saul. The narrator has calmed any remaining suspicion on our part that David wanted Saul's heirs eliminated (recall Shimei's accusations in 16:8). The episode concludes with the good news that God is appeased.

5.3 David's Decline and His Exit from Military Affairs (21:15-22)

The previous scene brought to a conclusion the contorted relationship between David and Saul. This episode lowers the curtain on David's career as a warrior. For the first time, our hero becomes weary and needs assistance to win. These four scenes read like a précis of past battles with one sharp contrast: the once victorious David is supplanted by his victorious soldiers. Each scene is infuriatingly cryptic and passes in a flash. We have no idea how much time has passed since the drought ended; nor do we know how old David is or what regnal year he is in. Not even a location is given for the first battle. But one thing is clear: David goes into retirement. The scene forms an inclusion with David's victory over the Philistine in 1 Samuel 17.

STRUCTURE

A. David and his men go out for battle with the Philistines (21:15)
   B. Scene 1: Abishai kills Ishbi-benob (21:16-17)
      a. The enemy's ferocity is depicted
      b. The enemy is defeated
     C. Scene 2: a battle with the Philistines in Gob: Sibbecai kills Saph in Gob (21:18)
     C'. Scene 3: another battle with the Philistines in Gob: Elhanan kills Goliath in Gob (21:19)
   B'. Scene 4: Jonathan kills an unnamed warrior (21:20-21)
      a'. The enemy's ferocity is depicted
      b'. The enemy is defeated
A'. Conclusion: David and his men killed the four descendants of the giants (21:22)

These four scenes are bound together by the inclusion *"David and his men* descended" (21:15) and "they [the four Philistines] fell by the hands of *David and his men"* (21:22; translation mine). Scenes 1 and 4 have the same structure: the adversary appears, his military strength is described, and he is defeated by an Israelite warrior. Scenes 2 and 3 are alike in that an Israelite warrior defeats a Philistine warrior. The language of the scenes is repetitive: each begins with "again there was a battle" (21:18 prefixes "afterwards"); three of four foes are said to be "descendants of the giants" (the summary of the scenes notes that all of them were, in fact, "descendants of the giants" [21:22]); and the Hebrew verb *nkh,* "to strike" (NRSV usually translates it with "to kill"), repeatedly describes the defeat of each Philistine.

5.3.1 David and His Men Go out for Battle with the Philistines (21:15)

The Hebrew expression that opens this episode, "the Philistines had a battle with Israel" (translated literally), appears only here in the Bible and may identify the Philistines as the aggressors. The NRSV suggests as much, "The Philistines went to war again with Israel," but the NJPS does not, "Again war broke out between the Philistines and Israel." In the David Narrative the Philistines are usually the aggressors, as in 1 Samuel 17:1, the first time they appear in David's life. After David conquers Jerusalem, they attack twice (2 Sam 5:17, 22). This time, David and his men are quick to respond to their renewed incursion, but as the battle ensues, David becomes weary. For the first time our champion is losing to the Philistines![11] He is old.

5.3.2 Scene 1: Abishai Kills Ishbi-benob (21:16-17)

As the first scene begins, David's opponent comes onstage. Ishbi-benob is from the descendants of "the giants" (so translated in the NRSV[12]), in Hebrew *hārāpâ*, who are described in Deuteronomy 2:21 as "a strong and numerous people, as tall as the Anakim." Goliath, the Philistine in 1 Samuel 17, is not said to be a descendant of the *hārāpâ*, though the narrator notes his extraordinary height (1 Sam 17:4). The description of Ishbi-benob's spear echoes the extended description of Goliath's weaponry (1 Sam 17:5-7). Goliath's spear weighed some five thousand shekels of bronze, whereas Ishbi-benob's spear weighs only some three hundred shekels of bronze.[13] The weight, "shekels of bronze," appears only here and in 1 Samuel 17:5, underscoring the connection between the presentation of Ishbi-benob and Goliath. While scholars suggest modern weight equivalents, these are at best approximations, if not, as in the case of these two instances of bronze shekels, downright guesses.[14] But we do not need to know the exact weight of Ishbi-benob's weapon to grasp the narrator's purpose: Ishbi-benob, like Goliath, is a formidable warrior who could throw a heavy spear. And like Goliath, Ishbi-benob's intention is to kill David.

Abishai, son of Zeruiah, brother to the powerful Joab and the deceased Asahel (2 Sam 2:23), arrives to assist the weary David. His military prowess was confirmed in 10:14 when the Ammonites fled before him. When David sought an associate in his second stealthy attack against Saul, Abishai volunteered (1 Sam 26:6). He would have killed Saul, but David prevented him (1 Sam 26:8-9). He would have killed the cursing Shimei as David fled Absalom (2 Sam 16:9) and the penitent Shimei as David returned to Jerusalem (19:21), but both times David intervened.

---

[11] The only other time David is said to be weary is in 16:14 as he flees from Absalom, and there too he appears to be losing.

[12] The majority of English translations, including the NJPS, opt for a transliteration: "he was a descendant of the Raphah."

[13] These units of weight are normally associated with a metal, most often silver, but also bronze and iron.

[14] See Yigal Ronen, "The Enigma of the Shekel Weights of the Judean Kingdom," *Biblical Archaeologist* 59 (1996): 122–25. He notes that the system of weights in the Judean kingdom was based on pieces of silver.

Now David, who in the past has prevented Abishai from killing, needs him to slay the ferocious Ishbi-benob. Where is the mighty David who slew Goliath singlehandedly?

The first scene concludes with an oath by David's men: the king is not to go into battle again, lest he quench the lamp in Israel. This oath echoes the troops' response to David in 18:3 when they impeded him from assisting in the battle against Absalom's rebels. They reminded him of his importance as their king: "You are worth ten thousand of us." Back then, the troops merely stopped David from joining in a particular battle. Now they *swear an oath* that David is not to go out with them in any battle in the future. David has become a warrior emeritus. The troops explain that they cannot allow David to "quench the lamp of Israel." This metaphor (lamp) is developed in 1 Kings 11:36 where it refers to the Davidic line that will rule in Jerusalem:

> Yet to his son [Solomon] I will give one tribe, so that my servant David may always have a lamp before me in Jerusalem, the city where I have chosen to put my name.[15]

5.3.3 Scenes 2 and 3: Battles with the Philistines (21:18-19)

The second scene has the same introduction as the first (21:15) with the exception that the place where the battle occurred, Gob, is named, though its location is unknown. The protagonist, Sibbecai, appears in a parallel passage in 1 Chronicles 20:4. In 1 Chronicles 11:29 and 27:11 he is listed as one of Israel's elite military leaders. Otherwise little is known about him and the Hushathites, though Mebunnai the Hushathite is a member of David's military elite, the Thirty (2 Sam 23:27), suggesting that the Hushathite clan was closely allied with David. Sibbecai kills Saph, another giant (or *hārāpâ*), who is mentioned only here in the Bible. The weary David is entirely out of the picture—the oath that retired him, sworn in 21:17, is observed.

The next battle is also in Gob and also with the Philistines. Elhanan, a member of the Thirty (23:24), is second in the list, right after Asahel. Two passages give him different fathers:

Elhanan son of Jaare-oregim, the Bethlehemite (21:19)
Elhanan son of Dodo of Bethlehem (23:24)

---

[15] The allusion to David's descendants on the throne in Jerusalem as a "lamp" bestowed upon David by God appears again in 1 Kings 15:4.

These two verses probably refer to the same person and they represent yet another minor inconsistency in the David Narrative about which the narrator makes no comment.[16] More problematic is the news that Elhanan killed Goliath the Gittite. This incongruity is not easily dismissed since the death of Goliath at the hands of David is central to David's rise to prominence. The phrase, "the shaft of his spear was like a weaver's beam," because it is identical to the phrase in 1 Samuel 17:7 (reading the *qere*), suggests that we have the same person. Who then killed Goliath, David or Elhanan? The Chronicler, the first interpreter of the David Narrative, spotted the problem and offered a solution: "Elhanan son of Jair [*qere*] killed Lahmi the brother of Goliath the Gittite" (1 Chr 20:5). Thus, David defeated Goliath and Elhanan defeated Goliath's brother. Many scholars regard 2 Samuel 21:19 as an early tradition about Goliath's defeat that was later transferred to David and embellished. Hertzberg's sober suggestion that "Goliath" indicates a "type," namely, a fierce warrior, may be correct.[17] In any case, either the narrator did not see the incongruity between the two passages (1 Sam 17 and 2 Sam 21:19), or he did not consider it a problem for reasons we may never know.

5.3.4 Scene 4: Jonathan Kills an Unnamed Warrior (21:20-21)

The fourth scene starts out like the others: "there was again war at Gath," one of the five principal Philistine cities. The narrator focuses our eyes on the unnamed foe's hands and feet. He has six fingers on each hand and six toes on each foot. He, like Ishbi-benob, receives a description that hearkens back to that of Goliath in 1 Samuel 17:4-7. This super-digited fighter "taunts" (*ḥrp*) Israel, borrowing a word from Goliath's playbook (in 1 Sam 17 *ḥrp* appears five times: 17:10, 25, 26, 36, 45). He also shares Goliath's fate when he is defeated by Jonathan, the son of David's brother Shimei.

---

[16] In the lists of David's courtiers, 8:15-18 and 20:23-26, the name of David's secretary has diverse spellings and the names of David's priests are confused. A more egregious confusion of names appears in the previous episode where the Hebrew text reports that Michal, not Merab (as in most English translations) had five sons (21:8). But Michal was pronounced childless in 6:23. The narrator remains undisturbed by these inconsistencies that annoy modern exegetes. So perhaps Elhanan son of Jaare-oregim is the same warrior as Elhanan son of Dodo, member of the Thirty.

[17] Hertzberg, *I and II Samuel*, 387.

5.3.5 Conclusion (21:22)

This verse serves as the conclusion to all four scenes: "they [the four Philistine opponents] fell at the hands of David and at the hands of his servants." The narrator gives David a role in these victories, but, in fact, David was tired out before any of these four Philistines were defeated. These scenes drop the curtain on David's days as a warrior and form an inclusion with David's first heroic act, his victory over Goliath (1 Sam 17). Now our hero is weary. His final testaments are just ahead.

5.4 A Penultimate Testament: David Sings a Song (22:1-51)

David has buried his predecessor and one-time foe with appropriate funerary rites (21:11-14), and his own military prowess has begun to wane (21:15). Now there is a pause in the action as we listen to the longest speech in the David Narrative. Our hero is about to sing a song. Poetry, by its very nature, lends itself to "rereading" in different settings. Prince Hal's departing words to the dying Hotspur, his rival and literary foil, easily leap from their original context into present-day elegies:

> Adieu, and take thy praise with thee to heaven,
> Thy ignominy sleep with thee in the grave,
> But not remembered in thy epitaph. (*Henry IV, Part 1*, act 5, sc. 4, lines 98–100)

So too, some of Israel's poems, whose original setting was in preexilic Israel, were *reread* (i.e., adapted) during Israel's exilic and postexilic experience. The last two verses of Psalm 51 (vv. 18-19), for example, appear to be an addition for later readers who hoped for the restoration of Israel. It is precisely because the psalms lend themselves to "rereading" that they are still enjoyed today. Scholars generally agree that the poem in 2 Samuel 22 (= Psalm 18) is an independent piece inserted here.[18] The incipit (or superscription) bridges the poem to its narrative setting:

---

[18] See Walter Brueggemann, "2 Samuel 21–24: An Appendix of Deconstruction," *CBQ* 50 (1988): 387; Arnold A. Anderson, *2 Samuel*, WBC 11 (Waco TX: Word Books, 1989), 262; and Caquot and de Robert, *Les Livres de Samuel*, 596. The mention of the Temple in 22:7, which is not yet built, and David's reference to himself in the third person in 22:51 are further indications that this song is an insertion.

> David sang the words of this song to the Lord on the day the Lord de-
> livered him from the hands of all his enemies and from the hands of Saul.
> (2 Sam 22:1; translation mine)

This incipit does not disclose the psalm's original *Sitz im Leben*. Rather,
it *rereads* this psalm (an individual psalm of thanksgiving) in its new
context. God has delivered David from *all his enemies*, and now David's
life is drawing to an end.[19] How should the reader interpret the story of
David's life? And how should David be remembered? This song holds
the clues.

David's song celebrates God's rescue of the just one. Read in its new
context, it brings into sharp relief the central theme of the David Narrative: God was always on David's side, choosing him, protecting him,
advising him, forgiving him, and winning for him (see section 1.3 above,
"The Theme of the David Narrative"). Divine intervention determined
David's election as king (1 Sam 16:1 and 2 Sam 5:2). Samuel, summoned
by the medium at Endor, reminded Saul of that election (1 Sam 28:17).
Twice (1 Sam 18:14 and 2 Sam 5:10) the narrator told us that God was
with David. When Jonathan argued with his father about David, he asserted that it was "the Lord" who had given David victory over Goliath
(1 Sam 19:5). Abigail, speaking to David, made the same declaration
(1 Sam 25:26-31). David too proclaimed his trust in God as he went out
against Goliath (1 Sam 17:37), and when his life was at risk because of the
destruction of Ziklag, he "strengthened himself in the Lord" (1 Sam 30:6).

Over and over the narrator has reminded us that God wins for David.
After David defeated the Arameans and Edomites, the narrator inter-
jected that God gave David victory wherever he went (2 Sam 8:6, 14). In
1 Samuel 24:4 and 1 Samuel 26:8 David's men (Abishai in 1 Sam 26:8),
having sneaked up on Saul, recognized that it was God who delivered
Saul into David's power. When Abner spoke to the elders of Israel, he
enunciated the Davidic credo: God, through David, would defeat Israel's
enemies (2 Sam 3:18). In 2 Samuel 7 God announced David's place in
Israelite history: God would remain faithful to David and his descendants forever. Now, at the end of his life, David celebrates his unique
relationship with God in this song.

At the center of the song David explains why God delivered him (22:21-
25). He speaks of his righteousness, his "cleanness of hands," and his
blamelessness before God. Such language hardly squares with his life.
Would he whitewash his past? Perhaps. But when this poem is read as a
bridge to the narrative that lies ahead, these verses introduce the qualities

---

[19] Other incipits link particular psalms to events in David's life: see Psalms 3, 30,
34, 51, 52, 54, 56, 57, 59, and 60.

for which David will be remembered. Future kings will have to measure up to the memory of his righteousness or risk condemnation. The interpretation that follows reads this poem not as an extraneous insertion (another element of the so-called appendix) but as an essential component of the narrator's portrait of David and his reign. We are to imagine David singing this song after his valiant strength has faded and just before he utters his "last words" (23:1) and retires to his deathbed (1 Kgs 1–2).

STRUCTURE

The incipit: God delivered David (22:1)
A. Introduction: David invokes God, his savior (22:2-4)
  B. David recalls that God heard his cry (22:5-7)
    C. Weather theophanies: God won David's battles (22:8-16)
      D. David sings of his deliverance by God (22:17-20)
        E. David's legacy: his righteousness (22:21-25)
        E'. God delivers all the righteous (22:26-28)
      D'. David sings of the victories God gave him (22:29-31)
    C'. David was victorious with God's help (22:32-43)
  B'. What God did for David (22:44-46)
A'. Conclusion: David praises God for his steadfast love (22:47-51)

The inclusion to this song (A/A' sections) is signaled by the titles for God such as "my rock" (22:3 and 22:47). The B/B' sections balance David's cry with God's response: David called out (22:7) and God rescued (22:44). The C/C' sections describe divine theophanies (22:11: "he was seen upon the wings of the wind") and what David accomplished with that divine support (22:38: "I pursued my enemies and I destroyed them"). The D/D' sections parallel how God rescued David (22:18: "He delivered me from my strong enemy") with how God prepared David as his warrior (22:35: "he trains my hands for war"). The center of this song (E/E' sections) introduces the themes that will shape the memory of David for future generations.

5.4.1 The Incipit: God Delivered David (22:1)

The incipit informs the reader that this poem flows naturally from the story of David's life.[20] David's various adversaries are lumped together

---

[20] The Hebrew text labels this psalm a "song"; several psalms in the Psalter are referred to as "songs" (see, for example, Pss 30, 46, and 68).

under the category "enemies," while Saul receives special mention, since a third of the David Narrative was taken up with his deadly pursuit of David. The key word in this incipit is "delivered" (*nṣl*): God *delivered* David from his enemies. Appearing twice in the song itself (vv. 18, 49), it focuses the reader's attention on this central theme of the David Narrative (see section 1.3 above), which was introduced in David's first speech before an incredulous Saul.[21] The narrator withheld the microphone from David all through 1 Samuel 16. Did David have nothing to say after Samuel anointed him king (1 Sam 16:13)? What did he think about his transfer to Saul's court (1 Sam 16:19-22)? This delay builds up the reader's expectation for the hero's first speech, which comes when David stands before Saul:

> Saul said to David, "You are not able to go against this Philistine to fight with him. You are a boy while he has been a warrior from his youth." But David answered Saul, "Your servant was a shepherd for his father's flocks. Whenever a lion or bear would come and carry off a lamb from the flock, I would go out after it, strike it and deliver [*nṣl*] the lamb from its mouth. If it rose against me, I would grab it by the beard, strike it down and kill it. Your servant struck both lions and bears. So this Philistine, this uncircumcised, will be like one of them because he has reproached the ranks of the living God." Then David said, "The LORD who delivered [*nṣl*] me from the power of the lion and from the power of the bear will deliver [*nṣl*] me from the power of this Philistine." (1 Sam 17:33-37a; translation mine)

As David stepped onto the stage of history, his speech introduced the central theme of the David Narrative: his victories were God's doing. Now, as his life draws to a close, David sings a song to express his thanks to God, who has fulfilled the speech that he made before Saul long ago.

5.4.2 Introduction: David Invokes God, His Savior (22:2-4)

The song opens with a series of divine titles. The first-person pronominal suffix in Hebrew, "my" (appearing ten times in these three verses), underscores the intensity of David's relationship with God. These images for God share a common theme: God is David's "savior." God as a "stronghold" (*mĕṣūdātî*) recalls David's withdrawal to a stronghold as he fled from Saul (*mĕṣûdâ* in 1 Sam 22:4 and 24:22 [MT 24:23]). Now we learn that during those moments of retreat, he was under divine protection—God was his "stronghold." The divine title "one who

---

[21] David's first utterances come when he asks about the reward for dispatching the Philistine (1 Sam 17:26) and in response to his older brother's accusation (1 Sam 17:29).

gives me escape" (2 Sam 22:2, translation mine; NRSV: "my deliverer") reprises David's narrow escapes during his life:[22] when Saul hurled his spear, David got away (1 Sam 19:10); Michal helped David escape Saul's clutches (1 Sam 19:11-12, 17, 18); David fled to the cave of Adullam to "escape" Saul (1 Sam 22:1); and he "escaped" to the Philistines in the hope that Saul would give up his hunt for him (1 Sam 27:1). David's song now informs us that at the time of each escape God was protecting him.

The divine titles continue in 22:3. God is referred to as "savior" three times: "horn of my salvation" (*qeren yišî*); "my savior" (*mōšîî*); and "you save me" (*tōšîʿēnî*). God as "savior" is often implicit and sometimes explicit in the David Narrative. The Hebrew root *yšʿ*, "to save," which appears eight times in this poem, appeared for the first time in the David Narrative in 1 Samuel 17:47 when, in response to Goliath's taunts, the armorless David trusted that God would deliver his adversary into his hands, since God does not save (*yšʿ*) with sword and spear. In 2 Samuel 8:6 and 8:14 the narrator made the theme explicit: "The LORD saved [*wayyôšaʿ*] David wherever he went."

In 22:4 David appeals to God and announces the theme of his song: God has saved him from his enemies (a repetition of the incipit). The expression "from my enemies" echoes language from David's life. Abigail declares that the Lord will fling out David's enemies (1 Sam 25:29). When the opportunity comes to eliminate Saul, David's men refer to Saul not as "king" but as David's "enemy": "The men of David said to him, 'Here is the day of which the LORD said to you, "I will give your enemy into your hand"'" (1 Sam 24:4, see also 26:8). David acknowledges that God rescues him from his enemies after he defeats the Philistines (2 Sam 5:20): "The LORD has burst forth against my enemies before me." This theme appears again in 7:1, "The LORD had given him rest from all his enemies around him," and in 7:9, "I [God] . . . have cut off all your enemies from before you." Now David sings of the divine rescue that he so often enjoyed during his lifetime.

5.4.3 David Recalls That God Heard His Cry (22:5-7)

David appeals to the images of waves, torrents, the snares of death, and the cords of Sheol to describe the travails he endured. Often his life was at risk, beginning with his flight from Saul to his flight from his own son Absalom (16:11: "My own son seeks my life"). For much of the

---

[22] The song uses the Hebrew verb *plṭ*, whereas the narrative always has *mlṭ*. These two verbs are parallel in Ps 22:4-5 (MT 22:5-6).

narrative he lived on the edge, and now he sings that while on the edge he invoked the Lord: "In my distress I called upon the LORD; to my God I called" (22:7a). In fact, whenever David inquired of God, the divine response came quickly (1 Sam 23:2, 4, 10-12; 30:8; 2 Sam 2:1; 5:19, 23; 21:1). God's receptivity to David contrasts with the deaf ear that Saul received (1 Sam 28:6). The phrase "in my distress" (2 Sam 22:7) recalls 1 Samuel 30:6 when David was in "great distress" (translated "great danger" in the NRSV) because his people, seeing the destruction of their town Ziklag, would have stoned him. David "strengthened himself in the LORD," inquired of the Lord, and the Lord heard his plea (1 Sam 30:8). David himself testifies to this divine support in 2 Samuel 4:9: "As the LORD lives, who has redeemed my life from every distress" (translation mine). When the fugitive David begged God to render Ahithophel's counsel foolish (15:31), God heard his cry (17:14). Had God not received David's prayer, Absalom would have killed him. Now David gives thanks to God who heard his plea.

5.4.4 Weather Theophanies: God Won David's Battles (22:8-16)

Images of thunder, lightning, dark clouds, and wind (a storm theophany) celebrate God's rescue during David's military campaigns. Though much of this dramatic weather imagery does not appear in the David Narrative, God was always intimately involved with David's military campaigns, not only giving permission (1 Sam 23:2 and 30:8) and indicating targets (Hebron in 2 Sam 2:1), but also advising a military strategy (5:22-25). In the latter scene, God told David to listen for the sound of his marching on the tops of the trees (cf. God riding on the wind in 22:11). But this divine theophany is nowhere near as spectacular as the smoke and glowing coals emanating forth from God about which David now sings.

5.4.5 David Sings of His Deliverance by God (22:17-20)

These verses continue to celebrate God's deliverance of David, reprising the main theme of this psalm announced in the incipit. That David's adversaries were stronger than he echoes the contest with Goliath (22:18c). That God was David's support (22:19) recalls the interjections by the narrator that the Lord was with David during his lifetime (1 Sam 18:14 and 2 Sam 5:10). Now we learn the reason why God did all this for David: God "delighted" in him (22:20). Nowhere else in the David

Narrative is this said so explicitly, but God's preference for David over his older brothers (1 Sam 16:6-13) and the promise to establish David's house forever (2 Sam 7) testified to God's "delight" in him.

5.4.6 David's Legacy: His Righteousness (22:21-28)

David sings of the reward (22:25: *wayyāšeb*) that God conferred on him because of his righteousness (22:25: *kĕṣidqātî*). This phrase echoes David's words after he spared Saul's life: "The LORD rewards [*yāšîb*] everyone for his righteousness [*ṣidqātô*]" (1 Sam 26:23). David's own righteousness was extolled in 2 Samuel 8, when, before introducing the members of David's court (8:16-18), the narrator remarked: "David administered justice and equity [*ṣĕdāqâ*: 'righteousness'] to all his people" (8:15). But some of the lauds in this section of the psalm are at variance with events in David's life. We know that our hero's past is not an unassailable record of faithful observance of God's law, but his song looks forward to the commendations he will receive after his death. Solomon, in his first speech after his father's passing (when he begs for a "listening heart"), reminds God that David walked "in faithfulness, in righteousness, and in uprightness of heart" (1 Kgs 3:6). When the prophet Ahijah confronts Jeroboam with the news that he will be the king over what will become the northern kingdom, he orders him to walk in God's commandments, just as David did (1 Kgs 11:38). David's fidelity becomes a refrain in 1 and 2 Kings—a measuring stick by which those who occupy his throne are judged.

When David sings of how he has observed (*šmr*) the ways of the Lord (22:22), he is writing his epitaph. Later, God will warn Solomon to observe (*šmr*) the divine ordinances just as "David your father" did (1 Kgs 3:14). David's faithful "observance" is mentioned again in 1 Kings 6:12. David also sings of his "blamelessness" (*tāmîm*), another aspect of his legacy. In a second appearance to Solomon, God warns the king to walk like David his father with "blamelessness of heart" (*bĕtom lēbāb*; 1 Kgs 9:4, rendered in the NRSV with "integrity of heart"). Of course, we cannot help but wonder how the murder of Uriah squares with David's claim to righteousness, fidelity, and, especially, blamelessness. He even claims to have never turned aside (*swr*) from God's statutes (22:23). Are we to forget about the Bathsheba affair as the Chronicler does (1 Chr 20:1-3)? Even the narrator, who readily cooperates with David's self-appraisal, will on a later occasion interrupt this cheery tune with a reminder that on one occasion David did indeed "turn aside" from the Lord's command:

> Because David did what was right in the sight of the LORD, and did not turn aside [*swr*] from anything that he commanded him all the days of his life, except in the matter of Uriah the Hittite. (1 Kgs 15:5)

In 1 Kings, the narrator will distance himself from such a panegyric with an unhappy recollection of the facts. Here, David does not. But we know that David's song and David's life are not in perfect congruence.

God requites the "loyal one" (22:26: *ḥāsîd*), recalling David's loyalty to Jonathan (the term *ḥesed* appears in 9:1, 3, 7) that brought Mephibosheth, Jonathan's son, into the royal palace (2 Sam 9). God "saves" (*yšʿ*) the "humble" and casts his eye against the "haughty" (22:28), alluding to David's contest with the haughty Philistine. David's legacy will reach beyond 2 Kings. Jeremiah will look for a "righteous branch" to spring up for David (Jer 23:5 and 33:15), and Mattathias, father of Judas Maccabeus, in his farewell address, will remember David as a merciful king (1 Macc 2:57). David's memory stretches into the New Testament when the angel Gabriel announces to Mary that God will give David's throne to Jesus (Luke 1:32). His legacy begins in the verses of this song.

5.4.7 David Sings of the Victories God Gave Him (22:29-31)

As a young warrior, David warned Goliath: "the battle is the LORD's" (1 Sam 17:47). Now he sings of how the Lord assisted him in battle. God, like a lamp, illuminated his path so that he could leap walls and crush his enemies. This imagery evokes David's military victories over the Jebusites (2 Sam 5:6-8), the Philistines (5:17-25), the surrounding kingdoms (8:1-14), and the Ammonites (12:29-31). The military language continues: God is a "shield for all who take refuge in him" (22:31), which recalls David's testimony before Saul that God would save him from Goliath (1 Sam 17:37). Goliath's stature and weaponry (1 Sam 17:4-7), which the narrator described in detail, were no threat to David, who tried on Saul's armor and then removed it (1 Sam 17:38-39). Goliath came forth with his "shield-bearer," but David confronted him with the "shield of salvation" (2 Sam 22:36) that the Lord had bestowed on him.[23] That shield has brought him victory throughout his life.

---

[23] In 1 Samuel 17:41 the term for shield is *ṣinnâ* and not *māgēn* as in 2 Sam 22:31, 36.

5.4.8 David Was Victorious with God's Help (22:32-43)

The song shifts from what God has done for David to what David accomplished with God's help. Trained by God for battle, David sings about how he "pursued" (*rdp*) his enemies, recalling how, after he dispatched Goliath, the Israelites "pursued" (*rdp*) the Philistines (1 Sam 17:51-52). When David returned from his sojourn with the Philistine ruler Achish and found his city, Ziklag, destroyed by the Amalekites and his wives taken captive (1 Sam 30), he inquired of the Lord: "Should I pursue [*rdp*] this band?" God quickly responded, "pursue" (*rdp*), and David obeyed (1 Sam 30:8), vanquishing the Amalekite raiders (1 Sam 30:17). He sings that he "consumed" (*klh*) his enemies (2 Sam 22:38-39), though even when he slaughtered the Amalekites in 1 Samuel 30, four hundred of them managed to escape. He defeated the Arameans, the Edomites, and the Philistines (though the verb *klh* was not used). The appearance of *klh* (piel), "to consume," in this poem echoes Saul's disobedience—his failure "to consume" the Amalekites that resulted in his dethronement and in the election of David, to whom God alluded just after that event (1 Sam 15:28). God had ordered Saul to go and destroy the Amalekites (1 Sam 15:3). When Saul failed to accomplish this edict, Samuel repeated the divine order: "And the LORD sent you on a mission, and said, 'Go, utterly destroy the sinners, the Amalekites, and fight against them until they are consumed [*klh*]'" (1 Sam 15:18). This poem (2 Sam 22:38-39) now alludes to the contrast between David and Saul: Saul failed "to consume," but David succeeded.

In 2 Samuel 22:42 the poet shifts to the enemies' point of view. They look for rescue but there is none. God does not answer them—a reminder of Saul's fate. When Saul saw the Philistines amassing for the battle in which he would die, he inquired of a taciturn God (1 Sam 28:6 has the same Hebrew expression as in 2 Sam 22:42). But God always answered David's supplications and delivered him.

5.4.9 What God Did for David (22:44-46)

The theme of God's graciousness returns as David sings, "You gave me escape [*plṭ*] from the strife [*rîb*] of *my* people"[24] (22:44; translation mine), reprising the theme of escape from 22:2 (see the discussion there).

---

[24] The Hebrew word *rîb* refers to the legal complaint or cause that a plaintiff brings before a judge. It can also refer to the suffering and strife that a plaintiff has endured during the quarrel with his adversary.

The Hebrew text of 2 Samuel 22:44 reads *ʿammî*, "my people," whereas Psalm 18:43 (MT 18:44) reads *ʿam*, "people." (The NRSV in 2 Sam 22:44 and Ps 18:43 has "peoples.") The reading *ʿammî*, "my people," in the Hebrew text of 2 Samuel 22:44, recalls how God saved David when his own people would have stoned him after the destruction of Ziklag (1 Sam 30:6). In 1 Samuel 24:5 David manages to stealthily cut off a piece of Saul's cloak and in the dialogue that ensues between David and Saul, David prays that God might defend his cause (*rîb* in 1 Sam 24:15; MT 24:16). In 1 Samuel 25:39 David, having learned of Nabal's death, gives thanks to God who defended his cause (*rîb*) against Nabal. Now David, at the end of his career, praises God who heard his cause and saved him during times of strife. While the meaning of 22:45-46 is uncertain, what can be deciphered is that foreigners are obedient to David; they are powerless before him. These "cringing foreigners" recall the peoples defeated by David, such as the Arameans (8:6-8) and King Toi of Hamath (8:9-10), who sent tribute to David. David now sings that God established him as "the head of the nations" (22:44).

5.4.10 Conclusion: David Praises God for His Steadfast Love (22:47-51)

David concludes his song with more divine titles, "my rock" and "the rock of my salvation," which create an inclusion with the series of divine titles that opened the song (22:3) and reprise the song's central theme: God is David's savior, the one who delivered him (*nṣl*) from his enemies. This experience has spurred David to sing: "I will extol you, O LORD, among the nations and sing praises to your name" (22:50). That God gave David "vengeance" (22:48; *nĕqāmôt*) recalls the moment when David, having relinquished his opportunity to kill Saul (1 Sam 24:4-5), produced the evidence of their encounter in a piece of Saul's cloak (1 Sam 24:11). Then he prayed, "May the LORD avenge [*nqm*] me on you" (1 Sam 24:12), a prayer that God heard on David's behalf. The language of the final verse (2 Sam 22:51) celebrates God's "steadfast love" (*ḥesed*) that is promised to David and to his descendants "forever" (*ʿad ʿôlām*). The terms "steadfast love" and "forever" hearken back to Nathan's oracle that established David's place in the history of Israel (2 Sam 7). David had intended to build a house for God, but instead, God promised to build a house for David. At the end of Nathan's oracle, God pledged never to take his "steadfast love" (*ḥesed*) from David as he did from Saul (7:15). And, God insisted, David's house would be established "forever" (*ʿad ʿôlām*; 7:16). David concludes his song by recalling this pivotal moment in his life.

5.5 David's Ultimate Testament (23:1-7)

The incipit to David's second poem, "These are the last words of David," signals that the David Narrative draws closer to its conclusion. After this poem, there remain two tasks for David to accomplish: he will build the first altar in Jerusalem (2 Sam 24), foreshadowing the construction of the Temple, and then confer his throne on Solomon (1 Kgs 1–2).[25] In great compositions, the protagonist's last words offer a closing reflection on his or her life. Hamlet's final line, "The rest is silence" (act 5, sc. 2, line 300), stills the noise of his tormented self-reflections and is a fitting coda to his life. David's final testament in this poem offers a fitting coda to his life as well. He puts forward two achievements for which he wants to be remembered: that he ruled with justice and that God established with him an eternal covenant. As with 2 Samuel 22, we join the narrator in imagining David uttering this oracle at the end of his life.

STRUCTURE

Incipit (23:1a)
Formal introduction (23:1b)
A. David introduces the divine speech (23:2-3a)
    B. The divine speech: the righteous ruler (23:3b-4)
A'. David comments on the divine speech (23:5)
    B'. The divine speech continues: the wicked ruler (26:6-7)

The B/B' sections contrast two kinds of leadership: the rule of a God-fearer like David over against the rule of the godless. In the A/A' sections, David introduces the divine oracle and then explains how the oracle applies to his kingship.

COMMENTARY

David joins other imposing figures in biblical history who are awarded a final public speech. In Deuteronomy 31:14 God tells Moses that his life is coming to an end and so Moses pronounces a final benediction over Israel (Deut 33). When Joshua announces that he is about to go "the way of all earth" (Josh 23:14), we know we are listening to his final discourse. Not everyone is given such a solemn opportunity: Saul, the first king of Israel, falls on his sword without a final discourse

---

[25] David's very last words are given privately to Solomon in 1 Kings 2:1-9.

(1 Sam 31:4). Now, King David, the greatest king in Israelite history, has arrived at his final oration.

The incipit of 2 Samuel 22 labeled David's words a "song," whereas this speech is called an "oracle" (*nĕʾum*), a genre most often associated with the prophetic transmission of God's word. Of the 376 times that *nĕʾum* appears in the Bible, 365 times it appears in the formula "oracle of the LORD" or the like.[26] Only on a few occasions is the word "oracle" followed by a person's name, as in Numbers 24:3, 15 ("the oracle of Balaam"), in Proverbs 30:1 ("The words of Agur son of Jakeh. An oracle."), and here in 2 Samuel 23:1 ("the oracle of David"). The introduction to Balaam's oracle in Numbers 24:3 ("the oracle of Balaam son of Beor, the oracle of the man [*haggeber*]") is quite similar to the introduction to David's oracle ("the oracle of David son of Jesse, the oracle of the man [*haggeber*]"). More important, both speakers agree that an oracle conveys God's word: Balaam's oracle comes from someone "who hears the words of God" (Num 24:16), and David utters his oracle because "the spirit of God" spoke through him (2 Sam 23:2).

The rare use of David's full name ("David, son of Jesse") forms an inclusion with the beginning of his public life. It appeared in 1 Samuel 17:12 when he was introduced ("David was the son of an Ephrathite of Bethlehem in Judah, named Jesse") and again after his victory over Goliath ("I am the son of your servant Jesse the Bethlehemite," 1 Sam 17:58). Its appearance now, when David, a retired warrior, is about to make his final speech, recalls that young warrior who stood before Saul long ago. The incipit contains three titles for David. He was (1) the one who was exalted, (2) the anointed, and (3) the favorite of the songs of Israel (a possible reading of the Hebrew where the NRSV reads "Strong One"; see below). That David has been "exalted" (*qwm*) recalls his triumphs, with God's help, over his enemies and God's promise to establish (*qwm*) David's house forever (2 Sam 7:12, 25). He calls himself God's "anointed," a reference to his anointing in 1 Samuel 16:13, an event to which Nathan the prophet also referred in 2 Samuel 12:7. This title also bridges this poem back to the closing lines of the previous poem (22:51): "[God] shows steadfast love to his anointed." Thus David, anointed by God at the beginning of his public life, now claims that title in his final testament.

The divine title "God of Jacob" appears for the first time in the David Narrative. In biblical narrative, this title always appears within the longer title: "the God of Abraham, the God of Isaac, and the God of Jacob" (Exod 3:6, 15; 4:5), while the title "God of Jacob" alone is typical of the

---

[26] *TLOT*, 2:693.

psalms (Pss 20:1; 24:6; 46:7, 11; 75:9; 76:6; 81:1, 4; 94:7; 114:7; 146:5). Its unique appearance in the David Narrative suggests that this poem, like 2 Samuel 22, is an insertion in the narrative. Removed from its original *Sitz im Leben*, it has been pressed into service as David's final testament. The Hebrew word *zĕmīrôt* in 23:1 is patient of two interpretations. It usually means "songs," but in some passages it functions as a divine title (see, for example, Exod 15:2 and Isa 12:2). The translation "Strong One" (NRSV and NAB) for *zĕmīrôt* maintains the parallelism with "God of Jacob" in the preceding line, while the translation "songs" (NJB, REB, NJPS) celebrates the tradition that David was a poet and musician. The phrase "spirit of the LORD" (2 Sam 23:2), which now speaks through David, returns us to the day that Samuel anointed David and the "spirit of the LORD" came upon him (1 Sam 16:13). This is the only time in the David Narrative that the "spirit of the LORD" is said to be upon David, and thus it too contributes to the function of this "oracle" as an inclusion to the entire David Narrative.

After this solemn introduction that engenders anticipation in the reader, David transmits the divine message: the one who rules over people justly (*ṣaddîq*) is like the morning light, the rising sun, the cloudless morn, and the sparkling, rain-drenched grass (2 Sam 23:3b-4). (These metaphors are not easily interpreted and English Bibles show a variety and, in some cases, a striking elegance in their translations.) We instinctively relate this oracle to the story of David's reign, which on one occasion, the narrator noted was marked by "justice and equity [*ṣĕdāqâ*] to all his people" (8:15). Like 22:21-25, this verse also wants to establish the trajectory of David's legacy as a righteous and faithful king.

The righteous king rules in the "fear of God" (23:3),[27] an expression that has not appeared in the David Narrative. It looks back to Samuel's farewell discourse in 1 Samuel 12 in which the prophet reminds the people and their king to "fear the LORD" (1 Sam 12:14, 24). Failure to do so means ruin:

> If you will fear the LORD and serve him and heed his voice and not rebel against the commandment of the LORD, and if both you and the king who reigns over you will follow the LORD your God, it will be well; but if you will not heed the voice of the LORD, but rebel against the commandment of the LORD, then the hand of the LORD will be against you and your king.[28]
> (1 Sam 12:14-15)

---

[27] "Fear of the LORD" is a central tenet of wisdom literature (see, for example, Prov 9:10, "The fear of the LORD is the beginning of wisdom," and Sir 19:20, "The whole of wisdom is the fear of the LORD").

[28] The translation "and your king" follows the LXX. The MT reading, "against you and against your ancestors," makes little sense in this context.

Now, at the end of his life, David sings that he has followed the counsel of Samuel who long ago anointed him king. David then shifts the focus onto his own house, which is like "the light of morning," "the sun rising on a cloudless morning," and the "gleaming from the rain on the grassy land," because he has ruled in justice and fear of the Lord. For this reason, God has established with him an "eternal covenant" (2 Sam 23:5, *běrît ʿôlām*, the title of this series of commentaries), reprising God's promise to build an eternal house for him (7:16). Though the term "covenant" was not used in 2 Samuel 7 (see the discussion in 7:18-24), now David employs this sacred term to characterize God's promise to him.

The oracle closes by contrasting the righteous ruler with the godless ruler.[29] The latter is to the former as thorns are to lush grass. A rain-drenched lawn resists fire and is supple and a pleasure to walk on, whereas thorns are quickly consumed, are hard, painful, and demand careful handling to avoid injury. So the righteous ruler brings prosperity to his subjects, while the wicked ruler brings suffering. This imagery echoes the wisdom of Psalm 1: the person who delights in the law of the Lord is like a tree planted by water, while the wicked are like chaff in the wind. Perhaps David can be accused of being a revisionist as he writes his final testament, which forgets some of his crimes and missteps.

5.6 David's Decline and His Exit from Military Affairs (23:8-39)

This episode lists David's commandos and reports their exploits. Our hero is onstage only briefly and, when he does appear, is not even capable of securing the well in his hometown, Bethlehem, which is currently under Philistine control. He continues to be the emeritus warrior who earlier could not defend himself (21:15-22). This list of warriors, collocated near the end of the David Narrative (23:24-39), has a function similar to the two lists of courtiers that appeared earlier. The first one, appearing in 8:15-18 after David's military successes against the Philistines, the Moabites, the Arameans, and the Edomites, and the second, appearing just after he had crushed two rebellions (20:23-26), signaled that David had sufficiently secured his dominion to establish/reestablish his court. This roster of military leaders informs us that David has left behind an extensive military caste to defend his kingdom as he declines and his successor assumes his throne. The Hebrew text of these verses

---

[29] The Hebrew text is extremely difficult to interpret and English translations reflect various possibilities.

is problematic as indicated by the extensive textual notes in any good English translation.

5.6.1 Three of David's Warriors (23:8-12)

STRUCTURE

Title (23:8a)
A. Presentation of the warrior: Josheb-basshebeth (23:8b)
    What he did (23:8c)

A'. Presentation of the warrior: Eleazar (23:9a)
    a. The Philistines gathered (*'sp*) for war (23:9b)
    b. The Israelites withdrew (23:9c)
    c. Eleazar was victorious by himself (23:10a)
    d. God brought about a great victory (*těšûʿâ gĕdôlâ*) (23:10b)

A". Presentation of the warrior: Shammah (23:11a)
    a'. The Philistines gathered (*'sp*) for war (23:11b)
    b'. The Israelites fled (23:11c)
    c'. Shammah was victorious by himself (23:12a)
    d'. God brought about a great victory (*těšûʿâ gĕdôlâ*) (23:12b)

COMMENTARY

These three military contests (especially the second and the third) are markedly similar to the story of David and Goliath in 1 Samuel 17. In 1 Samuel 17:1 the Philistines *gathered* (*'sp*) for war as they do now (2 Sam 23:9, 11). Just as the Israelites fled (*nws*) from Goliath (1 Sam 17:24), they flee (*nws*) from the Philistines in 2 Samuel 23:11 (in 23:9 they "retreat," *ʿlh*). David fought singlehandedly against Goliath and *struck* (*nkh*) him (1 Sam 17:49) as do both Eleazar and Shammah against their respective foes (*nkh* in 2 Sam 23:10, 12). In the Goliath episode, the affirmation that the Lord accomplished a *great victory* (*těšûʿâ gĕdôlâ*) is delayed until the scene when Jonathan, speaking in David's defense, reminds Saul of David's victory and how "the LORD brought about a great victory for all Israel" (1 Sam 19:5). Thus, like other scenes in 2 Samuel 21–24, elements of this episode function as an inclusion with the beginning of the David Narrative. But there is one major difference. Our hero is now entirely eclipsed; his soldiers must fight for him.

The first warrior onstage is Josheb-basshebeth, a Tahchemonite. He is "chief of the Three." His name and patronymic reference, which do not appear elsewhere in the Bible, are judged to be errors in the Hebrew text. Most scholars read with 1 Chronicles 11:11, which parallels this verse, in which Jashobeam, son of Hachmoni,[30] is named "chief of the Three."[31] The relationship of "the Three" (a group hitherto unknown) to Joab, who has regained his command over the army (2 Sam 20:23), is not explained. According to the Hebrew text, Josheb-basshebeth is also known as "Adino the Eznite." Most English translations emend this second appellation to read with 1 Chronicles 11:11: "He wielded his spear." But the cryptic nature of the Hebrew text does not obfuscate the function of this scene: Josheb-basshebeth was able to kill eight hundred persons by himself. He, like his two companions that follow, is a mighty warrior.

Eleazar son of Dodo is second in command. He appears only here, and again the narrator is short on details. Where and when did the battle take place? Whither did Israel withdraw and why? From what little information the narrator does provide, it seems that David withdrew with the rest of his army, which squares with the image of the weary David, who was no longer able to enter into combat. But Eleazar singlehandedly defeated the Philistines, and, despite his weary arm, he held his sword while the army returned only to plunder the slain bodies. The next warrior on stage is Shammah who is known only here and perhaps in 23:33 (reading the Hebrew and not the correction in the NRSV). The Philistines gather at Lehi (its precise location is unknown), the place where Samson once defeated them with the jawbone of a donkey (Judg 15:14-17). Once again the Israelites withdraw, leaving the champion to defend a lentil field singlehandedly. He wins, and the narrator concludes with the refrain: "the LORD brought about a great victory." That the victory belongs to God is about to be amply illustrated in the next scene. These three accomplish feats that the weary David is no longer able to do.

5.6.2 Saving David (23:13-17)

The laconic narration continues. The "three"[32] unnamed protagonists in this scene are members of the "Thirty," a group mentioned for the first time and whose membership roster is just ahead (23:24-39).[33]

---

[30] The unique gentilic, Tahchemonite, is probably a corruption of the slightly more common name, Hachmoni; see Driver, *Notes*, 364. The patronymic reference is mentioned again in 1 Chronicles 27:32.

[31] The MT in this verse, which reads "the Thirty," is usually harmonized with 2 Samuel 23:8 in English translations.

[32] Reading the *qere* in the MT.

[33] These three are not the three warriors just mentioned in 23:8-12.

They come down to David who is in the cave of Adullam, about twenty kilometers (twelve miles) southeast of Jerusalem. Whence they come is not revealed, and the narrator does not explain what David is doing in the place where he once found refuge from Saul as he fled for his life (1 Sam 22:1). Now, the warrior emeritus finds himself again in this cave. Is he so weak that his only option is to take refuge from the enemy that he once conquered with ease?

Details of this scene echo the battles with the Philistines in 2 Samuel 5:17-25. Then, as now, the Philistines took up their position in the valley of Rephaim (see the discussion in section 3.3 above). In those battles, David, with God's help, easily defeated them. In 23:14 David has moved to the "stronghold," the same position he held when the Philistines mounted their attack in 5:17. The Philistine garrison has taken up residence in Bethlehem and no explanation is given as to how or when they began to occupy David's hometown. Instead, the narrator focuses on David who longs for a drink of water, but he wants it from a particular well—the well at the gate of Bethlehem.[34] David continues to be a warrior emeritus: he cannot obtain that "drink" for himself or even participate in the mission that will require an assault on the Philistine position. If the "three" can secure the well for David, the Philistine occupation of Bethlehem will be broken. Thus David's question, "Who will get me a drink from the well of Bethlehem?" probably means, "Who will attack the Philistines in Bethlehem?" The question can be addressed to God, as a prayer, and to his troops, as a veiled command.

To gain access to the well, the three warriors must breach the Philistine camp. The verb, "to make a breach" (bq^c), which recalls 5:20 ("and he [David] said, 'the LORD has made a breach [$prṣ$] against my enemies'"; translation mine), links this scene to David's earlier victories over the Philistines (when David was still an active warrior) in 5:17-25. The three then draw the water from the well by the gate, suggesting that they have captured the water source and defeated the Philistine garrison, though the narrator does not say as much. Instead, we immediately pass back to David, who pours the water out "before the LORD." In 1 Samuel 7:6 the people of Israel gather at Mizpah to draw water and pour it out on the ground as they confess their sin before God. David's ritual action before God is not a confession of sin but rather functions as a response to his original question: "Who will provide me with a drink of water from the well of Bethlehem?" In David's world, the answer is God, and though

---

[34] The construction of "Warren's Shaft" witnesses to the strategic importance of water for the defense of a city. See Yigal Shiloh, "Jerusalem's Water Supply during Siege: The Rediscovery of Warren's Shaft," *Biblical Archaeology Review* 7, no. 4 (1981): 24–39.

God's involvement in securing the well in Bethlehem is not explicit,
God is never absent from David's victories. This gesture and the oath
that follows ("the LORD forbid") acknowledge that the victory belongs
to God (David announced this theme just before he dispatched Goliath
[1 Sam 17:47]), and he declares the victorious draught of water to be
the blood of those who risked their lives. So, following Deuteronomy's
prescription (Deut 12:16), he pours it out on the ground.

The scene concludes with the narrator's interjection: "These were
the exploits of the three warriors." This conclusion reminds us why this
scene appears here: David now leaves the fighting to his commandos,
who enforce the oath they made in 2 Samuel 21:17: "You shall not go out
with us to battle any longer." David's role is limited to confessing that
God has brought about yet another victory for him.

5.6.3 Two More Warriors (23:18-23)

STRUCTURE

A. Abishai son of Zeruiah
   a. Presentation of the warrior (23:18a)
   b. His heroic feats (23:18b)
   c. He was important among the Thirty (23:19a)
   d. But he did not attain to the Three (23:19b)

A'. Benaiah son of Jehoiada
   a'. Presentation of the warrior (23:20a)
   b'. His heroic feats (23:20b-22)
   c'. He was important among the Thirty (23:23a)
   d'. But he did not attain to the Three (23:23b)

Like the three scenes in 23:8-12, these two scenes have similar structures.

COMMENTARY

Unlike the three warriors presented in 23:8-12, these two soldiers
are well known in the David Narrative. Abishai has enjoyed a long history with David, beginning in 1 Samuel 26:6-7 when he accompanied
David to Saul's camp and David refused his counsel to kill Saul. Later
Abishai would have killed Shimei but for David's veto (2 Sam 16:9-11
and 19:21-23). Most recently, he rescued David from the spear of Ishbi-
benob (21:17). To his already numerous accomplishments is added the
fact that he killed three hundred men (probably singlehandedly, though

the narrator does not make this explicit). He is now chief of the "Thirty,"[35] though, despite his extraordinary achievements, he did not acquire a place among the Three, with Josheb-basshebeth, Eleazar, and Shammah. Similarly Benaiah, despite his fantastic exploits, did not achieve membership in the Three. Benaiah's role at court stretches from David's reign to Solomon's, and his greatest exploits still lie ahead of him. He is mentioned for the first time in 8:18 as a member of David's court (in charge of the Cherethites and the Pelethites). He retains that position in David's second court (20:23). But his most important role comes when Adonijah attempts to claim his father's throne. Joab and Abiathar join Adonijah, but Zadok, Benaiah, and Nathan remain loyal to David and ensure Solomon's succession (1 Kgs 1:8). David's final instructions to Solomon regarding the fates of Joab (1 Kgs 2:6) and Shimei (1 Kgs 2:9) are carried out by Benaiah (1 Kgs 2:34 and 2:46), who assumes Joab's post as chief military commander (1 Kgs 2:35). Benaiah also executes Adonijah under Solomon's order. Right after Benaiah kills Shimei, the narrator comments (1 Kgs 2:46b): "So the kingdom was established in the hand of Solomon." Solomon's security is partly achieved by Benaiah's loyalty. His exploit against a lion recounted in these verses recalls a younger David's report of his victory over a lion (or bear) at the beginning of his career as a warrior (1 Sam 17:34-36).

The Hebrew text of 2 Samuel 23:22-23 has confused the numbers three and thirty with the result that the NRSV, which follows the Hebrew text, can baffle the reader. Benaiah wins a name "beside" the "three" warriors (23:22), but did not attain to the "Three" (23:23). Other English translations (REB, NAB, NJB) read "Thirty" in 2 Samuel 23:22 (NJB: "winning him a name among the thirty champions"), which coordinates better with 23:23: "He was renowned among the Thirty." Whatever Benaiah's final position among the warriors, the scene concludes with David appointing him over "his bodyguard." The Hebrew term for this troop, *mišmaʿat*, conveys the idea of "obedience." Ahimelech used the term when he defended David before Saul, reminding Saul that David had acted in obedience (*mišmaʿat*); David was one of Saul's trusted aides (1 Sam 22:14). Thus the NRSV's translation of "bodyguard" expresses Benaiah's readiness to protect David.

---

[35] The Hebrew text in 23:18-19 is problematic. Second Samuel 23:18 declares Abishai to be head of the "Three," but 23:19 reads that he did not achieve membership in the "Three." Most English translations read "Thirty" in 23:18 with the Peshitta version, but the Syriac translator, who most likely had the same Hebrew text that we have, corrected this inconsistency, thereby providing modern English translators with a solution.

5.6.4 The Thirty (23:24-39)

The narrator lists the names of the warriors who were members of "the Thirty," a title that seems to refer to a military rank and not to a specific number since the narrator concludes the list by noting that there were thirty-seven members. Moreover, the exact number of names in this list cannot be determined with certainty because the Hebrew text in 23:32-33 is corrupt. If Jonathan is considered the son of Shammah the Hararite (thus many English translations; but the NJPS reads "sons of Jashen, Jonathan, Shammah the Ararite" and notes that the meaning of the Hebrew is uncertain), then the number of warriors comes to thirty-one. Scholars offer various solutions to attain the narrator's count of thirty-seven, such as adding Joab and "The Three" to the list. It is still difficult to reach thirty-seven, and Hertzberg's insight may be correct: "The institution of the thirty was something alive"[36] and could be extended when necessary. The function of this list was noted above (see the discussion of 20:23-26 in section 4.10 above): David has secured his reign and now his warriors surround him as his prowess wanes and he can no longer defend himself in battle.

5.7 David's Final Public Act (24:1-25)

The story of David's census and its consequences appears to be out of chronological order (see section 5.1 above), since it introduces an entirely new event immediately after David's final words (23:1). Suddenly our hero is back in the lead, giving orders to Joab, though he does not come out of his retirement as a warrior. Rather than another disparate element of an appendix, however, this episode, which ends with the construction of the first altar in Jerusalem, serves as a fitting conclusion to David's public life and the narrator's portrait of his reign. As far back as Karl Budde, this event was considered among the most important in the Old Testament.[37] As we have seen in 2 Samuel 21–23, these closing scenes reprise events from the David Narrative (especially from the beginning of the David Narrative) and look forward to David's legacy. The building of an altar and God's benign acceptance of David's sacrifice look forward to Solomon's speech (1 Kgs 8) before the new Temple that David would

---

[36] Hertzberg, *I and II Samuel*, 407.

[37] Karl F. R. Budde, *Die Bücher Samuel*, KHAT 8 (Tübingen-Leipzig: J.C.B. Mohr [Paul Siebeck], 1902), 326. He writes, "so muss man unser Stück als eines der wichtigsten des ganzen Alten Testaments bezeichnen."

have built but for God's dissent. This episode comes to a climax when the angel readies to destroy Jerusalem. This time God relents, but there will come a time when God will not relent and the consequences for Jerusalem will be calamitous. When that happens, the narrator's story will have reached its conclusion.

STRUCTURE

A. The Lord's anger (24:1)
>   B. David's order, Joab's obedience (24:2-9)
>>   C. David acknowledges his sin (24:10)
>>>   D. The penalty (24:11-13)
>>>>   E. David's choice (24:14)
>>>   D'. The penalty exacted (24:15-16)
>>   C'. David acknowledges his sin (24:17)
>   B'. Gad's order, David's obedience (24:18-25a)
A'. The Lord's anger is appeased (24:25b)

At the center of this episode David chooses his punishment as he acknowledges God's mercy. This is framed by the punishment choices and the punishment exacted (D/D' sections). David's double confession appears in the C/C' sections. His order and Joab's obedience (B section) parallels Gad's order and David's obedience (B' section). The inclusion to the scene is God's anger (A/A' sections) that rages at the beginning and is appeased at the end.

5.7.1 David Orders a Census (24:1-9)

The opening of this episode, "Again the anger of the LORD was kindled against Israel," is surprising since the word "again" suggests a previous occasion of divine wrath. But when? Perhaps the reference is to the drought brought on by the bloodguilt on Saul's house (21:1-14), though God's wrath was not explicitly noted in that scene. David quickly resolved the problem at no cost to himself or his people (except for seven of Saul's descendants), and God was placated (21:14). But why is God angry now? This formulaic expression of divine wrath occurs most often in Deuteronomy to describe the expected divine reaction to human disobedience (see Deut 6:15; 7:4; 11:17; 29:27; 31:17). But what disobedience has led to this reaction in 2 Samuel 24? In Joshua 7:1 the anger of the Lord flares up against Israel only *after* Achan helps himself to some of the spoils of the battle that were devoted to the Lord. The

Lord becomes angry in the book of Judges (Judg 2:14, 20; 3:8; 10:7), but only *after* Israel is accused of apostasy. The case of 2 Samuel 24:1 is the only example where God's anger rages without an explicit crime on Israel's part. Perhaps the formula alone—"the LORD became angry with Israel"—is meant to persuade us that Israel committed an unmentioned infraction. Otherwise, God's anger seems capricious.

To further complicate matters, God incites David to take a census, an action that David later confesses as his own sin. The Chronicler's interpretation of this verse exposes the theological problem (1 Chr 21:1 parallels 2 Sam 24:1): "Satan stood up against Israel, and incited David to count the people of Israel." If Satan is the instigator, then David's sin lies in the fact that he should have resisted, but in 2 Samuel 24:1 God incites David. Within the logic of the narrative, only we know that God has incited him; David is unaware. The meaning of the Hebrew verb *swt*, translated with "to incite" in the NJPS and the NRSV (the REB has "instructed" and the NAB reads "by prompting"), is illuminated by 1 Samuel 26:19, where again God "incites," the only other time in the historical books that God is the subject of *swt*. In all other instances *swt* has as its subject a human being such as Jezebel, whom the narrator accuses of inciting Ahab to sin.[38] In 1 Samuel 26:19 David, having absconded with Saul's spear, wants to know why Saul is pursuing him: "If the LORD has incited [*swt*] you against me, may he accept an offering" (translation mine). David's charge intends to bring to Saul's awareness the possibility that God is behind his actions (but we know that God has not incited Saul to persecute David, his anointed). If so, David is ready to make a propitiatory offering, even though he does not see himself as guilty of any crime (nor do we). In both cases, though the person who is the object of God's incitement (*swt*) is unaware of it, the person is still responsible for the crime committed, and God must be propitiated. Thus, in 2 Samuel 24:1, even though God has been the instigator, David is responsible for his error and is obliged to make an offering (building the altar and so forth) to set things right. The logic may not be apparent to us, but our ancient narrator does not raise an objection.[39]

David orders Joab to take a census of his entire realm, from the northern border of Dan to the southern border of Beer-sheba, the same territory that later will suffer a punishing pestilence (24:15). Joab objects to the plan, hinting that the royal decree is out of line and praying that God might allow David to see his subjects increase a hundredfold. Joab's unexpected piety further illuminates the meaning of Hebrew *swt*, "to

---

[38] 1 Kings 21:25: "Indeed, there was no one like Ahab, who sold himself to do what was evil in the sight of the LORD, urged on [*swt*] by his wife Jezebel."

[39] See the discussion of "The Narrator" in section 1.4.2 above.

incite." Just as David tried to make Saul realize that perhaps God had incited him to his murderous pursuit, so now Joab encourages David to reflect further on his order. Had God given David a direct order, he could pass it along to Joab. But God has not, and Joab perceives the potential error in David's command.

Modern exegetes wonder how a census taking, which was necessary for taxation and military conscription, offends God.[40] What is David's sin? McCarter argues that the men once conscripted were bound by "a complex set of laws of purity," and their failure to conform brought on the plague.[41] But a simpler explanation lies in Old Testament "battle theology," which has been replayed in 2 Samuel 21–24 and is exemplified in the story of Gideon: "The LORD said to Gideon, 'The troops with you are too many for me to give the Midianites into their hand. Israel would only take the credit away from me, saying, "My own hand has delivered me"'" (Judg 7:2). God's problem is that Gideon's immense army could allow the people to think that they were responsible for the coming victory. Thus God orders a laughable method of troop selection that weeds out all but three hundred soldiers who drink water like dogs (Judg 7:5-7). When, with this crude gang, Gideon defeats the Midianites, we learn that the battle belongs to the Lord, whose interest even extends to the question of troop strength.[42] Thus, were Gideon a member of David's court, he would have reminded his liege that 1.3 million troops (Joab's eventual total) do not guarantee victory. But, by enumerating conscripts, David, who has *always* consulted the Lord before making a military decision, now acts as if such consultation is optional. With his huge army he can defeat his enemies—God is sidelined. We are stunned when the king plows over Joab's objection. For now "the word of the king" (2 Sam 24:4: *děbar hammelek*) prevails. But in the end "the word of the LORD" (24:11: *děbar YHWH*) will prevail.

Joab begins the census in the city of Aroer (see Deut 3:12), on the other side of the Jordan valley (about sixty-five kilometers [forty miles] southeast of Jerusalem). From there he heads north into the territory of Gad and then on to the city of Jazer, which is part of Gadite territory (Josh 21:38-39), though its precise location is unknown. The Hebrew

---

[40] See John Bright, "The Organization and Administration of the Israelite Empire," in *Magnalia Dei: The Mighty Acts of God; Essays on the Bible and Archaeology in Memory of G. Ernest Wright*, ed. Frank Moore Cross, Werner E. Lemke, and Patrick D. Miller (New York: Doubleday, 1976), 198.

[41] McCarter, *II Samuel*, 514.

[42] The story of Gideon's victory over the Midianites became part of Israel's lore. The prophet Isaiah also appeals to it (Isa 10:26): "The LORD of hosts will wield a whip against them, as when he struck Midian at the rock of Oreb."

text of 2 Samuel 24:6 is difficult. The land of *taḥtîm-ḥodšî* is unknown
(the NRSV reads "to Kadesh in the land of the Hittites"). Despite these
vagaries, it is clear that Joab is traveling along the eastern bank of the
Jordan River toward Dan, Israel's most northern territory. (He is tracing
the borders of David's dominion.) Then he crosses over toward the coast
to Sidon, and begins heading south to Tyre, which is thirty-six kilometers
(twenty-two miles) south of Sidon. Hiram, the king of Tyre, formed an
alliance with David immediately after the conquest of Jerusalem (5:11).
From Tyre Joab continues south through the land of the Hivites and the
Canaanites, two indigenous peoples whose land God promised to the
Israelites (Exod 3:17). In Joshua 9, the Hivites duped the Israelites into
making a treaty that allowed them to remain in the land. They lived
near the city of Gibeon (Josh 9:17), which is about ten kilometers (six
miles) north of Jerusalem. Joab, continuing south, reaches Beer-sheba,
the southernmost city of the realm.

The lengthy account of Joab's circuit seems unnecessary. The narrator could simply have reported that Joab accomplished the royal decree
and provided the official tally. But Joab's detailed itinerary provides a
bird's-eye view of the realm so that as David's public life draws to a
close, we appreciate the extent of his dominion. The time required for
the census (almost ten months) underscores the huge number that Joab
enumerated—1.3 million men of military age. The count is exaggerated;
archaeologists suppose that the population of Jerusalem at this period
was between 4,000 and 6,400 people.[43] But exactitude is not the point.
With such a massive army David no longer needs to consult the Lord on
military questions. Or at least so he thinks.

5.7.2 David Acknowledges His Sin (24:10-14)

The tone changes quickly. The king who insisted on the census immediately recognizes his transgression and is sick at heart. His military
calculation lacked divine consultation. Without compulsion from God
or a prophet, he seeks forgiveness:

> But afterward, David was stricken to the heart because he had numbered
> the people. David said to the LORD, "I have sinned greatly in what I have
> done. But now, O LORD, I pray you, take away the guilt of your servant;
> for I have done very foolishly." (24:10)

---

[43] David Tarler and Jane M. Cahill, "David, City of" in *ABD*, 2:65.

David's confession *prior* to the arrival of the prophet should not go unnoticed. Each of the three prophets of the books of Samuel (Samuel, Nathan, and Gad) receive the "word of the LORD" only once. In 1 Samuel 15:10 the "word of the LORD" comes to Samuel, in 2 Samuel 7:4 it comes to Nathan, and in 24:11 it comes to Gad. In 1 Samuel 15:10 and 2 Samuel 24:11 it is occasioned by a royal transgression. In 1 Samuel 15:10 Saul acknowledges his transgression only *after* he is confronted by the "word of the LORD" through Samuel. Saul would have duped Samuel (1 Sam 15:13) had he been able to. David behaved similarly in 2 Samuel 12:5-6, when he, like Saul, feigned innocence before Nathan who had been sent by the Lord. But in 24:10 David confesses his sin *before* the "word of the LORD" comes to the prophet. This contrite David, waiting to learn his punishment, leaves behind a far more splendid image at the end of his life than the beguiling David we met in 12:5-6.

The scene shifts to Gad, who made a brief appearance in 1 Samuel 22:5 when he ordered David to abandon the "stronghold," his refuge from Saul's deadly intentions, and to head toward Judah. (In that scene his divine mandate was implied.) David obeyed him without question and Gad has remained offstage until now, when God sends him to David with three choices for a punishment. In 1 Samuel 15 and 2 Samuel 12 the prophet imposed the sanction without discussion: Saul lost his kingdom (1 Sam 15:26) and David's son died (2 Sam 12:14, 18). The process of choosing his punishment offers David the opportunity to express, for a final time, his trust in God (the center of the episode, see the structure above). Had he been mindful of that trust at the beginning of the episode he would never have ordered a census in the first place and his current dilemma could have been avoided.

The first two choices, those not chosen (though David's response could permit either the first or the third option), recall previous incidents in David's life. A seven-year famine recalls the three-year famine in 21:1.[44] The second choice (flight from adversaries) recalls David's flight from Saul, which occupied a third of the David Narrative (1 Sam 18:10–31:7), and his flight from Absalom (2 Sam 15:13–16:14). The third choice, a plague on the land for three days, has never befallen him. Upon hearing these choices, David cries out, "I am in great distress," echoing Saul's reaction (1 Sam 28:15) as the Philistines mounted their attack. When Saul was in distress, God refused him a hearing; he would die in battle

---

[44] The NRSV in 24:13 reads, "Shall three years of famine," with 1 Chronicles 21:12 and against the Hebrew text. This reading coordinates with 2 Samuel 21:1 and the two other threats (*three* months and *three* days). But it is the *lectio facilior* and therefore "seven" is to be preferred.

the next day. But David will be forgiven by God once the punishment is exacted. He will not share Saul's fate.

5.7.3 The Plague and David's Confession (24:15-17)

The dreaded plague begins immediately. Though the seventy thousand killed would not make much of a dent in the 1.3 million enumerated, the fact is that David, who called the census, now watches God trim his population with a plague in the very territory ("from Dan to Beer-sheba") that David ordered enumerated. The narrator draws our attention to Jerusalem and to the destroying angel,[45] who is prepared to devastate David's city. What will become of God's promise to David that his house, kingdom, and throne shall be established forever (2 Sam 7) if the angel continues the assault unimpeded? In this scene God has a change of heart and the city is saved. But the threatened devastation of Jerusalem foreshadows the catastrophe that lies ahead when God will not relent and David's beloved city will be destroyed (2 Kgs 25:8-12).

It is not often that God changes his mind (*nḥm, niphal*). When the Israelites fashion the golden calf, God decides to wipe them out, but Moses intervenes and God rescinds the decision (Exod 32:7-14). According to Judges 2:17-19, when the people of Israel abandoned God, their enemies would vanquish them. But when God heard their groaning, he would relent (Judg 2:18: *nḥm, niphal*), raising up judges to rescue them. In 1 and 2 Samuel, God's change of heart alters the course of Israelite history when he "regrets" (*nḥm, niphal*) having anointed Saul king of Israel (1 Sam 15:11, 35). The divine change of heart ushers in David's reign. In 2 Samuel 24:16 God's change of heart rescues David and his kingdom as the destroying angel desists and heads toward the threshing floor of Araunah the Jebusite. For the first time since David conquered Jerusalem, we learn that the original Jebusite inhabitants (5:6-10) had remained in the city under Davidic rule.

David again confesses his sin and pleads with God to have mercy on the innocent people of Jerusalem, acting as an intercessor before God on behalf of the people as did Moses (though David is not innocent like Moses), who interceded on behalf of the people (Exod 34:9; Num 11:1-2; 14:19; and 21:7). David's prayer for forgiveness anticipates the completion of the Temple when Solomon will spread his hands toward heaven (1 Kgs 8:22) and implore God so that the people of Israel might always find forgiveness when they pray toward the Temple (1 Kgs 8:30, 34, 36,

---

[45] The destroying angel appears in 2 Kings 19:35.

39, 50). For the first time David refers to the people he governs as a flock of sheep, a metaphor that reaches back to the day he was anointed king. When Samuel, with God's help, found none of the sons of Jesse suitable as Saul's successor, he inquired as to any remaining sons. "There remains yet the youngest, but he is keeping the sheep," Jesse responded (1 Sam 16:11). Immediately, David was summoned from the flocks to be anointed king.[46] Now at the end of his life, in his final public act, David implores God for his new flock, the people of Israel.

5.7.4 David Is Obedient to the Word of the Lord (24:18-25)

David, who executed his own word to obtain the census, now submits to the word of the Lord. The prophet Samuel had built an altar in Ramah (1 Sam 7:17) and Saul built an altar (14:31-35) in Aijalon. Now David builds an altar in Jerusalem. Following Gad's order, he travels to Araunah, the Jebusite, who prostrates himself, calls himself David's servant, and acknowledges the king's authority to expropriate his land. David explains to Araunah that he must build an altar on property that he has purchased in order to stop the plague. But Araunah objects. His liege can have all he wants—his threshing floor for the altar, his livestock for the sacrifice, and his farm implements for the fire. David insists that he will not expropriate Araunah's property. David is not just building an altar to end the plague; he is establishing the location for the future Temple. This may explain why the narrator ensures that we know that the altar was not built on expropriated land; a contract of sale guaranteed the transfer of the property. This altar, the first one built in Jerusalem, wins David the forgiveness he seeks. The divine response foreshadows the words of David's son at the dedication of the Temple:

> If there is famine in the land, if there is plague, blight, mildew, locust, or caterpillar; if their enemy besieges them in any of their cities; whatever plague, whatever sickness there is; whatever prayer, whatever plea there is from any individual or from all your people Israel, all knowing the afflictions of their own hearts so that they stretch out their hands toward this house; then hear in heaven your dwelling place, forgive, act, and render

---

[46] David, in his first discourse before Saul, speaks about his days as a shepherd and how he risked his life to save his sheep (1 Sam 17:34-35). When God establishes a covenant with David in 2 Samuel 7, he reminds David that he took him from the sheep: "I took you from the pasture, from following the sheep to be prince over my people Israel" (7:8).

to all whose hearts you know—according to all their ways, for only you
know what is in every human heart—so that they may fear you all the days
that they live in the land that you gave to our ancestors. (1 Kgs 8:37-40)

David demonstrates the altar's efficaciousness when God hears his supplication and the plague abates. As the curtain drops on David's public
life, we are assured that Israel's future prayers for forgiveness will be
received by God from this altar, around which the future temple will be
built. This is David's final act.

5.8 Conclusion

These four chapters contribute to the conclusion of the narrator's
portrait of David in four ways: (1) they tell the story of David's decline
and departure from the public stage; (2) they reprise events from his
life; (3) they look forward to his legacy; and (4) they report David's final
public actions—the proper deposition of Saul's remains and the establishment of the first altar in Jerusalem. Now, too weak to keep warm,
David takes to his bed.

EPILOGUE

Let us not take it for granted that life exists more fully in
what is commonly thought big than in what is commonly
thought small.

Virginia Woolf, *The Common Reader*

David's hour upon the stage has been too brief. As I began this commentary I championed the narrator's art that had successfully turned
"the accomplishment of many years / into an hour-glass" (*King Henry
V*, Prologue). Now, as I conclude, I lament that there is not more sand in
that hour-glass. The narrator has brought me into David's inner world
and I would like to remain there for a while longer. Did the king garner
new victories, endure more family strife, and relish other passions? Was
Bathsheba the last woman he desired or did he take other women to his
bed before the lovely Abishag was brought in to keep him warm? Did
he quietly mourn Jonathan's death each year on its anniversary? Did he
confess that he had failed his daughter Tamar and then rescue her from
her desolation in Absalom's house?

With so many details left unsaid, we might complain that the narrator wasted precious narrative time on trivial matters. Did we really
need to watch Tamar kneading dough as she prepared the delectables
for her rapist? Did we have to listen to David's treble observations on
the approaching messengers who would announce Absalom's death?
Was it necessary to watch the flummoxed court officials as a penitent
David pleaded with God for the life of his newborn son? Yes, it was.
These seemingly insignificant brush strokes in the portrait of David
were essential because, as Virginia Woolf mused, life does not necessarily exist more fully in what we think of as "big" (the international
affairs of David's court), than in what is commonly thought "small" (an
edgy David awaiting the messengers). The art of our ancient narrator
celebrates Woolf's modernist insight.

The small moments pull me into David's private universe. I am not
a king, but I can stand with David as he mourns his beloved Jonathan,

spies Bathsheba, or orchestrates Uriah's murder. Even the national threat of usurpation is turned into a study of a father's misguided affection for his son. When David cries out for his dead son, wishing that he, David, were dead instead, we can feel just how much he has been transformed by this personal tragedy. Then we gaze into David's secret life and the flame of his innermost mystery burns in our own eyes. The narrator lures us to pluck out that mystery while at the same time thwarting our attempts to do so. David, like Hamlet, will not be played like a pipe. Facile labels such as saint/sinner, savior/villain, or beneficent/tyrannical become vapid before his complex moral ambiguity.

Of course, the David Narrative raises some "big" questions in Israel's epic history, such as the role of the monarchy in ancient Israel. But in this mingling of public and private affairs, the private overwhelms the public. We expect the king to function as the chief mourner at the funerals of Saul and Jonathan, but our hearts stop when David voices his love for the deceased Jonathan, his intimate confidant. We are less focused on the battle that will defeat a rebel than on the tableau of a worried father sitting at the gate of Mahanaim. In such private moments, when the narrative turns inward to expose our hero's vulnerabilities, the distance between David and myself collapses and Woolf's insight surfaces: life exists more fully in the small things. The David Narrative cannot be reduced to the big things.

These hints into David's inner life advance the evolution of the depiction of the human person by the written word. The crippling limitation of language is bemoaned by Addie Bundren in Faulkner's *As I Lay Dying*: "That was when I learned that words are no good; that words don't ever fit even what they are trying to say at." Our narrator, struggling to overcome the boundaries of language, has begotten a literary triumph: a nearly tragic hero, whose own personal flaws result in the deaths of the warrior Uriah and David's own son Absalom, while he escapes ruin only by divine intervention. David, a credible, dynamic character, emerges as the literary forerunner of Lear, Falstaff, Elizabeth Bennet, Dorothea Brooke, John Dowell, Stephen Dedalus, and many, many others.

The small moments of David's life, where his life does indeed exist more fully, bid me to undertake my own journey of self-discovery. When I want to upbraid him for being so blind to the patently obvious interpretation of Nathan's parable, he looks out at me from the biblical page and questions me about my own prevarications. What have I successfully hidden from myself that even the most accusatory parable will not bring to consciousness? In his half-truths, self-duplicities, and foolish, muddled thinking, I discover my own.

The story of David strutting and fretting his hour upon the stage of history has been far too brief.

FOR FURTHER READING

Biblical Commentaries and Articles

Alter, Robert. *The David Story: A Translation with Commentary of 1 and 2 Samuel*. New York: Norton, 1999.

Anderson, Arnold A. *2 Samuel*. WBC 11. Waco, TX: Word Books, 1989.

Auld, A. Graeme. *I and II Samuel: A Commentary*. Louisville, KY: Westminster John Knox Press, 2011.

Brueggemann, Walter. "2 Samuel 21–24: An Appendix of Deconstruction." *CBQ* 50 (1988): 383–97.

———. *First and Second Samuel*. Interpretation. Louisville, KY: John Knox, 1990.

Campbell, Antony. *2 Samuel*. The Forms of the Old Testament Literature 8. Grand Rapids, MI: Eerdmans, 2005.

Caquot, André, and Philippe de Robert. *Les Livres de Samuel*. Commentaire de l'Ancien Testament 6. Genève: Labor et Fides, 1994.

Conroy, Charles. *Absalom Absalom! Narrative and Language in 2 Sam 13–20*. Analecta Biblica 81. Rome: Biblical Institute Press, 1978.

Halpern, Baruch. *David's Secret Demons: Messiah, Murderer, Traitor, King*. Grand Rapids, MI: Eerdmans, 2001.

Hertzberg, Hans Wilhelm. *I and II Samuel*. Translated by J. S. Bowden. The Old Testament Library. Philadelphia: Westminster Press, 1960.

McCarter, P. Kyle. *I Samuel*. Anchor Bible 8. Garden City, NY: Doubleday, 1980.

———. *II Samuel*. Anchor Bible 9. Garden City, NY: Doubleday, 1984.

McKenzie, Steven L. *King David: A Biography*. New York: Oxford University Press, 2000.

Miscall, Peter D. *1 Samuel: A Literary Reading*. Bloomington: Indiana University Press, 1986.

Smith, Henry P. *A Critical and Exegetical Commentary on the Books of Samuel.* The International Critical Commentary. Edinburgh: T & T Clark, 1899.

Steussy, Marti J. *David: Biblical Portraits of Power.* Columbia: University of South Carolina Press, 1999.

VanderKam, James C. "Davidic Complicity in the Deaths of Abner and Eshbaal: A Historical and Redactional Study." *JBL* 99 (1980): 521–39.

Van Seters, John. *The Biblical Saga of King David.* Winona Lake, IN: Eisenbrauns, 2009.

van Wijk-Bos, Johanna W. H. *Reading Samuel: A Literary and Theological Commentary.* Macon, GA: Smyth & Helwys, 2011.

Literary Approaches

Alter, Robert. *The Art of Biblical Narrative.* New York: Basic Books, 1981.

Auerbach, Erich. *Mimesis: The Representation of Reality in Western Literature.* Translated by Willard R. Trask. Princeton, NJ: Princeton University Press, 1974.

Bar-Efrat, Shimon. *Narrative Art in the Bible.* Sheffield: Almond, 1989.

Berlin, Adele. *Poetics and Interpretation of Biblical Narrative.* Winona Lake, IN: Eisenbrauns, 1988.

Booth, Wayne C. *The Rhetoric of Fiction.* Chicago: The University of Chicago Press, 1983.

Gunn, David M. *The Story of King David: Genre and Interpretation.* JSOTSup 6. Sheffield: Sheffield Academic Press, 1978.

Noll, K. L. *The Faces of David.* JSOTSup 242. Sheffield: Sheffield Academic Press, 1997.

Polzin, Robert. *David and the Deuteronomist: 2 Samuel.* Part 3 of *A Literary Study of the Deuteronomic History.* Bloomington: Indiana University Press, 1993.

Walsh, Jerome T. *Style and Structure in Biblical Hebrew Narrative.* Collegeville, MN: Liturgical Press, 2001.

INDEX OF AUTHORS CITED

**Jewish and Christian Authors and
other Ancient Authorities**

Rabbinic Literature

Artists

INDEX OF BIBLICAL CITATIONS

The verses are cited according to the NRSV.